TAKING ON CHINA:
How I Freed My Husband from Jail
A Memoir

TAKING ON CHINA: How I Freed My Husband from Jail
A Memoir

Karen Patterson:
seekingtruthfromfiction.com

Cover design and artwork, cover photo, map creation and interior photo and graphics:
Jason Sweet of Jason Sweet Ad | Design | Photo
jasonsweet.com

Co-writer, editor, interior book designer
Our Family Lines
ourfamilylines.ca

Print ISBN: 978-0-9917075-5-3

"The artist Wu Yuren found out that China has little tolerance for dissent – and no justice in its courts. Many before and after have made similar, painful discoveries. Not all these cases make it into the public realm; many acts of defiance are known only to those who suffer, and their families. That's why it's important the stories of people like Wu Yuren are told. The world must know about the courage shown by the few who dare stand up to China's repressive government, and the sacrifices made by their family and friends who seek to free them. Karen Patterson's book about her attempts to get her husband's release is not just about the pain experienced by one family, but a window onto a country where freedom is no one's right."

Michael Bristow, Asia-Pacific editor, BBC World-Service

"Karen Patterson's story is one of bravery and resistance, a one-woman struggle against the repressive and Orwellian Chinese state. Anyone who met Karen was inspired by her battle to keep her family together, and to keep her husband Wu Yuren's case in the public eye after he disappeared into the regime's prisons. Taking On China is an important first-person account of Karen's ultimately successful fight."

Mark MacKinnon, senior international correspondent, *The Globe and Mail*

"One of the best things about doing consular work, which means helping Canadians in distress, is the opportunity to learn from how people react in the face of enormous challenges. Karen Patterson is an exceptional teacher. Her courage, unwavering loyalty, fierce intelligence, and fearless determination—which shine through the pages of her book—offered me an example I will never forget. May we all be so lucky as to have a friend like her."

David Mulroney, Ambassador of Canada to the
People's Republic of China, 2009-2012

"What terror strikes a wife and mother when her husband and father of her infant is thrown in jail without trial for nothing more than protesting the closure of his art studio?

Such dread, fear and confusion - the stuff of dystopian nightmares from Orwell's pen – we could only imagine until now.

Canadian Karen Patterson's book Taking on China reveals not only her frantic search of local police stations to find out where husband and Chinese artist Wu Yuren was being detained but also her emotional struggle and long bitter fight with a ruthless authoritarian state apparatus to set him free.

Her book shines a light on the plight of thousands of Chinese who take on the authorities in the name of justice and human rights to free loved ones wrongly detained. Few succeed and fewer still have the luck of a different nationality to tell the world."

Peter Simpson, freelance editor/journalist

"This story is more than inspiring. It's a heartfelt call to action, proof that even in China one person's relentless pursuit of justice can make a difference. To follow Karen step by step as she fights to free her unjustly accused artist husband from prison is to discover just how cruel and random the Chinese justice system can be to its own people. And how necessary it is to stand up for them, as Karen did, whenever we can."

Gillian Steward, columnist, *Toronto Star*

"Where, after all, do universal human rights begin?
In small places, close to home -- so close and so small that they
cannot be seen on any maps of the world. [...] Unless these rights
have meaning there, they have little meaning anywhere. Without
concerted citizen action to uphold them close to home,
we shall look in vain for progress in the larger world."
Eleanor Roosevelt

"I am a free man, and I am going out the front door."
Gerard Patrick Conlon, *Proved Innocent* (1993)

DEDICATION

Researching for this book, I came across what felt like reams of others in China who are, and have, experienced ordeals similar to Dawu's struggle. There are so many stories of injustices, assaults, illegal detentions and, in some cases, deaths. It's horrible. The lucky ones like Dawu get attention and eventually, justice. However, many others aren't so fortunate and are dead, missing or still behind bars. I'm dedicating my book to these people.

Dawu's story makes up a thread or two in a larger tapestry created from all the stories of human rights abuses. It's my human responsibility to tell his story, not for fame and prosperity, but for the hope that some-day, these stories will cease to exist.

This book is also dedicated to:
Miss Hannah Wu so she may know the story of her parents
and
my mother, Elizabeth Patterson, who worried about me for years and supported me through thick and very thin.

LIST OF CHINESE NAMES IN PINYIN:

Ai Weiwei - well-known Chinese artist, architect, activist, helps Karen get in the face of journalists, etc.

Bai Meili - Honghong's wife
Bai Dawei / Mr. Bai - director of The White Box in spring 2010

Cao Lin - Chinese artist friend of Karen's
Cao Tielong / Mr. Cao - cell mate of Dawu's
Chao Hongling - artist, good friend of Dawu's, has studio close to 798 Art District
Chao Hongmei - Dawu's first lawyer, sister of Chao Hongling
Chen Jun - 008 International Art Community resident, Dawu's friend/colleague, badly injured by thugs on the morning of Feb. 22, 2010

Dou Xiaojun - student of Dawu's who was beaten and detained by cops

Fan Xiuying - Chinese marriage counsellor who has worked in China, Japan and Canada
Flame - Chinese interpreter friend of Ray Chen's
Fu Zhenghua - Director of the Beijing Municipal Public Security Bureau (PSB)

Gao Brothers - Zhen and Qiang, artists, studio located near 798 Art District
Gong Jin - second lawyer for Dawu
Gu Duanfan - artist, Dawu's friend, has a studio in the 798 Art District
Guo Jian - artist friend of both Karen and Dawu's, works in Beijing and Australia

Hong Fengjian - student of Dawu's, artist, member of one of Dawu's art groups
Huang Rui - artist and business owner in the 798 Art District, founding member of the Stars Group of Artists

Jinzi - carpenter, contractor extraordinaire, amazing problem solver much in demand in the Beijing art community

Lan Lijun - Ambassador of the People's Republic of China to Canada, based in Ottawa, Canada

Lao Guanyuan / Officer Lao - friendly police man who speaks to Karen during Dawu's first detention in Mar. 2010

Li Guanyuan / Officer Li / Mr. Li - cop at the Chaoyang District #1 Detention Center who Karen speaks with the most over the course of Dawu's incarceration

Li Fangping - third lawyer for Dawu

Lian Qilei - Li Fangping's second chair during the Nov. 17 trial

Liu Liao - fourth lawyer, replaced Li Fangping when he wasn't available

Liu Xiaobo - Chinese writer, government critic, drafter of Charter 08

Liu Xiaoyan - first lawyer recommended by Ai Weiwei

Liu Yong - Karen's DJ musician friend

Lu Dan - Karen's friend who is involved in the music industry

Lu Ayi / Lu Jie - Hannah's third ayi

Ma Ling - contemporary/avant-garde artist who lived in 008 International Art Community, then moved into the Wuhuan Art Compound and was Karen's studio neighbour, ca. 2009-2011

Mao Xiangji - Dawu's photography friend who lives in Jiangsu province

Ming Yuan - interpreter

Ouyang Shi - fixer for Manke artist compound, tries to rip off Karen and Dawu

Peng Kailin - Karen Patterson's Chinese name

Qi Mei / Qi Ayi / Qi Jie - Hannah's first ayi

Qian Yuelian - Air China employee in detention for a misdemeanour

Qiu Ayi / Qiu Jie - Hannah's fourth ayi

Qiu Zaofan - Dawu's dad's girlfriend

Ren Qiu - cameraman for Ai Weiwei, and then for Karen

Song Ke - cameraman for Ai Weiwei, and then for Karen

Song Xiansheng / Mr. Song - mystery man who delivered art works from Dawu in jail to Karen on the outside

Tan Ayi / Tan Jie - Hannah's second ayi

Tang Funai - the *Troublemaker*, detained at the same time as Dawu but released after 10 days

Tingting - Liu Yong's fiancée

Wang Fang - Victoria Bodlington's husband

Wen Tao - administrative assistant to Ai Weiwei and then Karen

Wu Jinhong (Honghong) - Dawu's famous musician friend, knows Ai Weiwei

Wu Suling - Dawu's sister

Wu Xiangshou - Dawu's father, Karen's Ba

Wu Yuren - Dawu, also referred to as Ping, Karen's husband

Xing Kui - Karen and Dawu's neighbour, successful Beijing businessman, married to Lena Meier

Xiu Dawen - duty officer at the Jiuxianqiao Police Station the night Dawu was beaten, one of the cops who beat Dawu

Xu Pinglun - art critic and art curator

Xu Wanyan - works at the China Art Archive and Warehouse gallery

Yan Jianguo and Yan Rouhu - two high profile human rights lawyers who were consulted

Yan Zi - professional musician friend of Liu Yong's, lives in Tongzhou area of Beijing

Yang Jiechi - Chinese foreign minister, high ranking government official

Yang Yue - one of the cops who was involved in beating Dawu on May 31, 2010, at the Jiuxianqiao Police Station

Ye Mingming - well-known petitioner, petitions on Dawu's behalf

Yu Xing and Tao Lili - Chinese artist couple living in Europe; Lili was also illegally incarcerated in 2008

Zhan Yishu - The White Box Gallery curator

Zhang Wei - a common Chinese name in the local art scene, Karen mixes up the artists

Zhang Xiaodong - Dawu's studio assistant

Zhang Xindong - cop who shows up unannounced with camera on lapel of uniform coat

Zhao Aining - conceptual / avant-garde performance artist friend of Karen's since 2000

GLOSSARY OF CHINESE TERMS IN PINYIN

Ayi - nanny, housekeeper, child minder

Ba - term used by wife of husband to refer to husband's father
Baba - term used by Chinese child to refer to his/her father

Chai - to demolish something, the character for demolish is commonly painted on buildings soon to be knocked down

Danwei - work unit, the job that one is tied to and where each person's dossier is located
Ducha - complaint bureau

Fen - the smallest measurement of Chinese money, equivalent to a cent. There are 100 fen in 1 yuan
Feng shui - traditional Chinese aesthetic, positioning of buildings and graves etc. in relation to *wind and water*

Gonganju - Public Security Bureau / PSB
Gongbao jiding - a popular spicy chicken dish with peanuts
Guanxi - relationships based on connections, one with a lot of personal, familial, business connections will have the upper hand, easier to obtain powers, status, wealth, etc.
Guasha - a special treatment using a flat piece of polished cow horn to scrape the body to release bad energy
Guoan - secret police
Gugu - aunty, on the father's side

Heishihui - triad, Chinese mafia
Hexie - river crabs, character form has similar pronounciation as *harmony*
Hongbao - red envelop full of cash that is given to kids / youth during Chinese New Year in lieu of gifts
Houmen / Houmen'r - backdoor, channel for bribery; pronounced as houmer in northern and Beijing dialects Mandarin Chinese
Hukou / Hukou Ben - Chinese household registration system, book detailing a person's hometown/village, parents, location of work, etc.
Hutong - alley between traditional courtyard homes

Jianyu - prison, jail
Jiejie - older sister, commonly used when naming an older ayi, aunty, etc. such as Qi Jie

Kanshousuo - detention center

Lao - old, used before surnames as a form of respect
Lingdao - leader

Mafan - a lot of trouble (to do something), too much of a bother, an inconvenience
Meimen / Meimen'r - no door, no way to do something, no
Meiyou - no, do not have, nothing
Mianzi - face. To lose face in China is more than embarrassing, it can lead to severe feelings of shame, loss of status etc.

Pinyin / Hanyu Pinyin - the romanization (use of alphabet instead of characters) of Mandarin Chinese used in mainland China since 1950s

Renmenbi/RMB - the money of the People's Republic of China

Shenfenzheng - ID card

Tiegemen / Tiegemen'r - men who have a very tight friendship/relationship, solid as iron

Waidiren - outsider, someone from another city, province or territory in China
Wei - hey or hello in Chinese, used on the phone
Weishenme - why

Xingzheng juliu - civil or administrative detention
Xingshi - criminal detention

Yeye - paternal grandfather
Yuan - the official term for the currency in the People's Republic of China, 1 yuan has 10 jiao, or 100 fen. The symbol is ¥

Yuan - righting wrongs

Yuanxiao / Yuanfen - traditional Chinese New Year sweet dumplings served in a sweet broth. Represent the circle and reunification of family at Spring Festival time

Yum cha – another word for dim sum, popular meal in Southern China and Hong Kong

Zanzhuzheng - a temporary residence permit to live inside a particular city

Zuoyezi - the first 30 days of bed rest for a mother who has just given birth. An ancient practice that was designed to keep mom and baby safe, dry and warm post-partum. Still practiced today.

Legend

1. Tiananmen Square
2. Forbidden City
3. Wangfujing Shopping Street
4. Protest March on East Chang'an Avenue on Feb. 22, 2010
5. Jianguomen Police Station
6. Chaoyang District Public Security Bureau
7. Huayang Jiayuan Residential Complex
8. Sanlitun Shopping / Entertainment District
9. Canadian Embassy
10. Chaoyang Park
11. Chaoyang District Detention Center
12. Jiuxianqiao Police Station
13. Holiday Inn Lido Hotel / Shopping Plaza
14. Cappuccino Residential Complex
15. 798 Art District
16. Karen's Studio Space / Beijing Color Studio
17. Ai Weiwei's FAKE Studio / Residence
18. 008 International Art and Zhengyang Art Communities
19. Wenyuhe Courthouse
20. Suburban Residential / Gated Communities of Shunyi
21. Beijing International Airport
22. Huairou City Roundabout

TABLE OF CONTENTS

DISCLAIMER

Although a work of non-fiction, many names, dates and locations have been changed to protect the identity and privacy of those mentioned in the story.

Some dialogue has been recreated.

PROLOGUE

When I first arrived in China in 1994, I arrived as an English teacher. However, this book is not another book about the experiences as an English teacher in a foreign country. Instead, it is a story about a country I love, a country that is twisted by government and politics and a brutal regime that punishes its own beautiful people. This includes my then-husband, Beijing artist Wu Yuren, who remains a dear friend even though we're no longer married.

Dawu, Wu Yuren's Chinese nickname, was beaten by police and detained without charge in 2010. His legal rights were violated and he had no recourse. He was released from detention in 2011 after many months and many people working together to free him. I spent almost a year putting his life before mine to get him out. It almost killed me in many ways. The situation left us both reeling and in shock. You might think that his story can't be connected to yours, that what happened halfway around the world can't happen in your backyard. Nevertheless, we are all linked.

Dawu and I are no longer husband and wife, but we are friends and share a daughter, Hannah. Hannah and I live in Calgary, Alberta, Canada. The last time I saw Dawu was in 2015. It was through a coincidence that we met again.

While surfing the net in Calgary in the spring of 2015, I spotted an online ad for an art exhibition in New York City. Dawu was mentioned as one of the artists exhibiting at the show. When I clicked on the link, I discovered my ex-husband, who still lived in China then, was presenting a solo exhibition of his work at the esteemed Klein Sun Gallery (known now as the Eli Klein Gallery) in Chelsea, Manhattan's art district. The gallery was well-known around the world for featuring Chinese contemporary art and it was an honour to exhibit in the space.

I always knew that Dawu was a talented artist but I didn't realize that he had made it to New York. The Big Apple is one of the best places for artists to exhibit their works. A solo show meant Dawu had caught international attention. Dawu's exhibit date was less than six weeks away. I messaged him to confirm the news and he said his show *WU YUREN: ON PAROLE* was being featured from May 7 to June 27 and he would be there for the opening.

If Hannah and I went to New York City (NYC) in May, it meant she could see her dad again without having to fly halfway around the world. It was also an excellent opportunity for my daughter and me to go to New York for the first time.

I had always wanted to see the city and I was over the moon that Dawu was finally being recognized. It meant, too, that the time I had dedicated to getting him out of detention had paid off. I had done the right thing by standing by him. I felt like I was the one who had made his NYC dream happen. It had not been an easy road and even five years later, I was dealing with the fallout from the struggle to free him from China's authoritarian grip. My experiences in that country haunted me during my days and nights in Canada. The art show would be a way to put some of those bad feelings to rest.

I didn't have much time to prepare for the trip to NYC. I was working as a real estate agent and in the middle of a home sale, representing my first-ever condominium apartment purchase for a client. However, I sorted things out. I had no problem taking Hannah out of school. I've always thought that missing classes for something memorable is fine, especially since it was to see her dad in New York at his first solo art exhibition in America. As well, Hannah was a good student and could quickly catch up.

I was thrilled about the NYC visit. Not only was I going to a new city but I was going to be surrounded by artists again. As well, Facebook friends in China and across the U.S. posted that they were going to attend Dawu's show. I hadn't seen many of these people since I left Beijing in 2011, four years earlier.

On Tuesday, May 5, Hannah and I started our trip. We boarded a plane in Calgary bound for NYC. During the almost five-hour flight, I was bombarded with thoughts of the past.

I remembered how Dawu and I met. I remembered our days as new parents. I remembered him disappearing, only to reappear in detention. I remembered days and nights wondering how I was going to get him out of jail. I remembered how terrified I was that Hannah was going to lose her father. I remembered China's disregard for the "rule of law" and how it stripped its people of their basic rights. I remembered how the state justified its actions against Dawu with lies and how the deceit was perpetuated by every level of government and governmental body.

It was early evening when the flight from Calgary landed at John F. Kennedy International Airport. Hannah and I got our luggage and took a cab into Manhattan. Hannah and I were booked at a hotel near the Empire State Building. I mean, why stay far away from the action when you can be on top of everything?

Here I was, in the Big Apple, and it looked and moved just like it appeared in television and films. There were rows of brownstone buildings, traffic was always on the go and every second vehicle was a yellow taxi.

I recognized street names like Wall Street and Madison Avenue. We drove past Times Square and Tiffany & Co. It was like I was a character in a show. NYC is really the epicentre of Western culture.

I was looking forward to seeing Dawu and hearing about his life. He had re-married and had a son. I was also looking forward to speaking Mandarin again. Hannah is bilingual in Mandarin and English while Dawu speaks Mandarin and a few words of English. I used to speak reasonable Mandarin but it had been a few years and I was a little rusty. Nevertheless, with Hannah's interpretive assistance, the three of us would be fine.

While many thoughts were flying around in my head like paper kites, Hannah and I explored the city. We visited the Empire State Building and then went to the financial district and checked out the National September 11 Memorial & Museum. It took us five-plus hours to go through it and buckets of tears. It was the first time I had cried so hard in many years.

I had been a student at the Beijing Language and Culture University in the fall of 2001. Even though I was thousands of kilometres away from Manhattan, no words could describe the horror of how I felt about 9/11. This was the day I learned that things that happen halfway around the globe connect us all.

Hannah and I left the 9/11 Museum to meet with Dawu. We walked down East 22nd Street in Chelsea, Manhattan's art district. It was a warm day with the sun shining. Hannah, an expert in NYC navigation already, was excited to be guiding me through the bustling city. We walked towards the gallery where Dawu was giving his show some tweaks before the opening the next evening. It would be good to catch up with him in person.

When we were almost at the gallery, a man appeared on its metal stoop. For a moment, I thought it was the musician Bruno Mars dressed in a floral shirt, nice jeans, leather boots, a wide-brimmed hat and a happy smile. I looked again and saw it was Dawu.

When Hannah noticed him, she ran from me and jumped into his arms. He caught her and swung her around, their energy crackling. The bond of father and daughter was very much alive and something I was grateful to see. Sometimes, that connection could be fragile and thin. Not today.

I stood to the side, enjoying the late afternoon sun as I watched their reunion. Seeing my ex-husband embrace our daughter was touching. Then Dawu turned to me and smiled. We all hugged and I took several photos of Dawu in his Bruno Mars get-up while holding his daughter. (Interestingly, a shop nearby was playing *Uptown Funk*, a Bruno Mars tune.)

We walked towards 9ᵗʰ Avenue and found a restaurant. Dawu and I remarked that it reminded us of places in Beijing. It was in a nice older brick building and there were lights set over an outdoor courtyard that held a few tables. We were comfortable and able to chat.

Dawu was treating us to our dinner. Hannah took her father's hat and wore it the entire time. She also insisted on sitting next to him, further melting my heart. The food was good, as was the bottle of wine that Dawu splurged on. At the end of the evening, we hugged and told each other that we were so happy to be there, all three of us, in NYC. We went home to our respective hotels and I had a restful sleep in a never restful city.

The next morning, Dawu met up with us and we all went to Liberty Island, home of the Statue of Liberty. Lady Liberty was amazing, gorgeous in her light green-coloured robe, impressive size and what she stands for: freedom. The irony of seeing the Statue of Liberty was not lost on Dawu or me. It was a miracle he was even standing on Liberty Island. However, it was something we rarely spoke about. Dragging up the details and rehashing our experiences in China didn't belong in a day of sightseeing and happiness in New York. Hannah loved every minute of playing tourist with her father. They had been separated for too long and they were laughing, joking around, chatting and taking hundreds of photos together.

At the end of our tour, we went back to Chelsea. Dawu's show was opening that evening and Hannah and I had to get ready. There was no doubt that Dawu's art opening was going to a memorable time.

We took the subway to the Klein Sun Gallery. Near the gallery, we could see a crowd gathered outside it from several blocks away. Dawu was going to be a hit.

This was Dawu's first solo show in NYC and his first show outside of China since 2010. At the Klein Sun Gallery exhibit, I knew people liked what they were seeing since they were asking me many questions about Dawu, his art and the story of how he got to this New York gallery. I also recognized some friends and other faces from my days on the Beijing art scene, including the other artist who was on solo display, Cui Xiuwen. I had met the renowned Chinese artist in Beijing in the fall of 2000 during an art exhibition opening. We then ran into each other on and off for the next 10 years. Cui was clearly in her element here. She smiled at me and came over for a hug and a friendly catch up. I saw other friends from China at the Klein Sun Gallery as well and the event felt like a mini-reunion of sorts. It was an awesome opening in so many ways.

Dawu couldn't have been happier about the show. Me too. I was floating that night. I had really missed my years in Beijing and my connection to its art world. I once calculated that I had gone, on average, to an art show every weekend for eleven years. Sometimes I went to five or six in one afternoon.

At the end of the event in Chelsea, the stragglers gathered at the Grand Sichuan Chinese Restaurant. The place had red lanterns, round tables and classic Chinese paintings and embroideries on the walls. Oh, and the essential fish tank by the door (for *feng shui*). It was the perfect way to end the evening.

I was asked to sit with Dawu and some key collectors. The couple across from me, an older pair, were intrigued by Dawu and his art. After a few bites of food, the woman leaned over to me and asked if I would tell Dawu that the piece they were interested in was his neon-lit work titled *FREEDOM*.

"We'll put it next to the Picasso in the living room of our apartment overlooking the Hudson River," she said.

When I translated the woman's words to Dawu, his face lit up. I was grateful to be there for him at that moment because there was once a time when I didn't know if I would ever see him again. The conversation at the table turned back to English and the woman leaned my way again.

"So, what is his story?" she asked, pointing at Dawu. "What happened to him?"

The following is a lot more and a little less of what I told her.

"*Kailin, wo bei dale.*"

Dawu says this to me in Mandarin Chinese. In English, it means "Karen, I've been beaten."

He says these words through an open window at the police station on Tuesday, June 1, 2010. I'm standing on the sidewalk looking in. He's standing in a room, seemingly alone, holding his left arm with his right hand. Is he hurt? He definitely looks scared.

My usually stylish artist husband is dishevelled. The clothing that he takes great care in choosing is wrinkled and unkempt. His face is swollen as if he has been beaten and there are dark circles around his eyes. The arm he holds, he holds at a peculiar angle. It's his voice, though, that tells me something is very wrong. His voice, usually steady and deep, is wavering with fear.

He needs my help.

PART ONE

**"Whether foreigners are considered royalty or devils,
they are never just regular people."**
Lu Xun, Chinese literary essayist, poet and critic, 1881-1936.
As quoted in *The Courage to Stand Alone* (1996, p. 120)

"Everything is art. Everything is politics."
Ai Weiwei

**"If you do not change direction,
you may end up where you are heading."**
Lao Tzu, ancient Chinese philosopher and writer, founder of Taosim

G rowing up in Calgary, Canada, I never thought that my life would take me to China. My mother had told me to eat all my vegetables because there were children starving in China but otherwise, the country wasn't on my radar.

As a kid in the late 1970s, I did a lot of travelling with my mother, Elizabeth, and my sister Diane. In the fall of 1977, we flew to New Zealand, stopping in many small island countries such as Samoa, Tonga and Fiji, along the way. We bought pineapples, picnicked on beaches and wore *mu'umu'u* dresses.

Mom had good friends in Auckland, New Zealand so we stayed with them for a few weeks and visited some of their relatives on sheep farms. Mom, Diane and I mostly hitchhiked around the country or took buses. The hitchhiking was my mom's idea. I hated it. I thought we were thumbing rides because we were poor. It was embarrassing to be picked up by people who actually owned vehicles. Why couldn't we be like other families and just rent a car? However, back then, hitchhiking was an easy and safe way to get around — and fun, too. (At least for my mom and sister.)

We landed in Sydney, Australia just before Christmas 1977 and stayed with mom's cousin for about four weeks. At last, mom bought a car and the three of us spent the next two years touring Oz while on a "working holiday." Mom, a physiotherapist, worked and Diane and I attended elementary school in Sydney, Adelaide and Perth. In 1979, the three of us returned home to Calgary.

Despite the hitchhiking, my family's grand adventure instilled a love of exploring and living overseas in me. It taught me that the world was a big place and there was much more to see than just Canada. For an 11 year old, I was relatively well-travelled and hoped my future would hold more trips.

After high school, I took a year off before going to university. I returned to Australia, where I worked as a training teller at a Westpac Banking Corporation center in a trendy area of Sydney called Bondi Beach. I did that job for six months before meeting up with a Calgary friend in Bali, Indonesia.

Bali was cheap and I loved the atmosphere: the sights, sounds, smells and culture. My friend and I stayed in small hostels, which were quaint and had nice staff. Indonesian food was amazing and the people were friendly.

I felt a kinship with the Indonesians I was meeting and picked up a bit of the national language, Bahasa Indonesian. Being in Bali sparked my love affair with Asia. Unbeknownst to me then, I would end up spending 15 years in the largest country in Asia, China.

After I returned to Calgary from Australia, I entered the University of Calgary (U of C) to study cultural anthropology. I started a four-year program in the fall of 1988. Four years stretched into five because I added a minor in art photography to my studies.

During my last term at U of C, I took part in a summer field school in cultural anthropology in Tlaxcala, Mexico. I toured many housing structures to collect notes for my final honours thesis on the gender uses of space in Mexican households. It was awesome.

I took classes, toured ruins and learned Spanish while living with a local family. As a temporary local, I enjoyed figuring out how to take the bus, go to the markets and share in the daily routines of my most gracious hosts. It was a good way to get extra university credits and have fun and it gave me a strong interest and yearning to live abroad again.

I graduated from U of C in June 1993 with my honours Bachelor of Arts degree in cultural anthropology, minor in photography. I found a job at Robinson's Camera, a Calgary photography store, while I figured out how to get overseas again.

In the early 90s, an obvious path abroad for many new grads was to be an English teacher. In some Asian countries, there was a huge emphasis on speaking English. For many private schools in China, South Korea and Japan, employing native English speakers as teachers was great marketing, too. Teachers didn't even need to have TESL qualifications (Teaching English as a Second Language certificate) or have studied English literature to get a job in a foreign classroom. The institutions were just happy if you had a degree from a university. That was me!

I decided to try my hand at teaching English in China on the advice of an anthropology classmate of mine, Lorne Holyoak. Lorne had been in Shenyang, in northeast China, for a year with his wife, Lisa Hansen. They returned with glowing reports of an exciting experience with great food, interesting history and the fun of learning Mandarin Chinese.

My friends also said travel was easy, as was meeting other people, both expatriates (also known as expats: people who are temporarily or permanently residing in another country) and locals. It all sounded great so I decided to apply to teach English in Shenyang.

I put my application in with World Exchanges, the same company that hired Lorne and Lisa. Other companies sent teachers to Japan, South Korea and Taiwan but World Exchanges focused on China. It wasn't common for Westerners to go to China because the pay was low; however, the country was considered the *most interesting cultural experience.*

I didn't know what I was getting into as an English teacher. I had never taught before, let alone spoke publicly in front of more than about five people. I was best behind my camera and speaking to people one-on-one. As well, I didn't have any concept about living and working in China.

As a child, I didn't like Chinese food. As an adult, I had taken some Asian studies courses and picked up snippets of what China might be like from one of my anthropology professors, who was originally from Hong Kong. But heck, I felt I had the tools of the international trade with my anthropology degree. How could this not be fascinating?

With my young adult confidence, I felt I was good to go. I was keen and interested in picking up Mandarin. From what I read and tried to learn before leaving Calgary, it was completely different from the French and Spanish that I was used to learning. Mandarin has absolutely no roots in English, Spanish or French and I felt like it was going to take me a lifetime to pick up but I was trying. The tones and inflections of Mandarin were the most challenging and confusing. What was I about to get myself into?

My first stop on my way to Shenyang was Beijing, the capital of China. My flight arrived at the city's airport in late August 1994 and waiting for me and a few other new instructors was an expat English teacher in his 60s. The man had been in China for about a decade but could speak zero Chinese. The teacher was either not good at languages or Chinese was just THAT hard to learn.

The teacher led us through the crowded airport and into a vehicle. I was staying in Beijing for a couple of days before boarding a train for Shenyang, in Liaoning Province. My first glimpses of Beijing were through a dirty glass windowpane during a brief tour.

What I saw was fascinating and scary all at once. I wasn't unsettled though: I was excited. At this age and stage of my life, I was about adventure and being out there doing something different. This wasn't the first time I had been to a country where I didn't speak the language but for some reason, this felt entirely new. The sights, the sounds, the smells hit me in a different, unfamiliar but curious way.

Even though it was August and the air was warm, there was hardly any sunlight. It was blocked out by the fog of pollution. The air smelled too, like coal that has been heated. I wasn't used to the odour.

In Beijing, I felt like I had stepped back in time. The buses were ancient and there were so many bicycles on the streets. Not mountain bikes like in Calgary but old-fashioned types that looked like they belonged on the set of a 1950s film. The people seemed to be wearing the same type of clothing. Many were dressed in a kind of perma-press polyester pants suit. Everything looked tired and worn down.

It was surreal to visit Tiananmen Square (the name means *gate of heavenly peace*). I had seen it on the news in 1989 and here I was, standing in it. There were armed guards all over the place. Their faces were set in stern frowns and they didn't look at us, which wasn't the case with everyone else.

Cyclists passing by almost crashed because they were staring so hard at me and my soon-to-be colleaguesus. We were novelties! The rubber-necking did become annoying and I'd have to learn how to ignore the stares and tune out the words thrown at me. I wondered if this was how celebrities felt walking down a street in the U.S.

As I saw more of the city, I realized I couldn't read any of the signs. Nor was I going to be able to talk to the locals. I didn't want to be like that teacher who couldn't speak the language here, but was learning Chinese going to be impossible?

No, it wasn't. I worked hard at learning it. I lasted several years teaching in Shenyang and Shanghai, China, taking a break from 1996 to 1998 when I returned to Canada to obtain my TESL accreditation, among other things. I moved back to China and took a teaching position at a private school in Guangdong, a southern province of China close to Hong Kong.

I taught English and eventually, art history and photography for two years at the school. Being so close to Hong Kong, colleagues and I often spent weekends across the border enjoying reliable banks, a public transport system that was efficient and clean, movies in English and pubs with real beer. It was a nice break from China.

After living in China for at least four years, my Mandarin had gone as far as it could go on my self-study program. Having taught English for many years, it was my turn to take learning a language seriously and become a student. I needed to actually study the language if I was going to get much more out of what I was experiencing. I chose to attend the Beijing Language and Culture University (BLCU). It had a sound reputation in Beijing and the city was known for its language and culture programs. I moved north to Beijing to begin studies in August 2000.

I hadn't spent a lot of time in Beijing, only a few weekend trips. It was the culture and art capital of China, though, and I was keen to not only get my head in the books studying Chinese but to explore the art scene. I was loving China, the language and feeling at home with the culture and friends around me. I was open to experiencing more.

***

At that time in my life, in my mid-twenties, I had no idea what my future would hold, but I was feeling like China was a pretty good place to be for a few years. Although I was naïve about the politics of the country, I felt I had a rudimentary knowledge of the human rights situation there from what I had heard on and read in the news. I knew the government didn't like it when its citizens didn't toe the party line but that didn't pertain to me.

The average expat didn't get into trouble. If they did, they usually got deported. I had heard about expats being sent home but that was as far as my experience with the Chinese police went. I was more interested in staying in the country to study and meet cool people.

I met Dawu through an artist in the fall of 2001. It was Oct. 20, and I was invited by Zhao Aining, a Chinese conceptual/avant-garde artist, to photograph him at an underground performance and art exhibition. Zhao and I had been spending a lot of time together. While I was studying full time at BLCU, I also had a part-time job at the WanFung Art Gallery, a few blocks from the Forbidden City, the historical palace complex in Beijing. That was where I met Zhao and we started hanging out.

Zhao Aining was beautiful with stunning facial features. He had long black hair and was tall and slim. A lot of his work bordered on cross-gender but he wasn't openly part of the LGBTQ (lesbian, gay, bisexual, transgender) community. I wasn't his girlfriend but I had a crush on him. When he asked me to take photographs of him and other artists at the upcoming performance and art exhibition *0°C/ZERO DEGREES CELCIUS*, I said I'd do it.

Many artists had interesting artworks or ideas but didn't have the means to buy a good camera. They needed quality images to send to curators or to represent their art. I had a Swedish Hasselblad camera that took excellent photos and I was starting to be in demand as a photographer.

I did have a genuine interest in conceptual art like Zhao Aining's work. As a foreigner, I'd also be able to meet other Chinese artists and add credence to the show. At that time in China, having expats at your event was a kind of status symbol.

From a Chinese artist's point of view, having artsy foreigners at a show could lead to international invitations. I was often asked to go to shows with my camera despite not being active in the art scene when I lived in Canada. I went to many of the exhibits and events of my Chinese artist friends. I was drawn to shows partly because they were interesting but also I was bored studying Chinese in my dorm room. What better way to improve my language skills then to get out and talk with people who spoke Mandarin.

My good Canadian friend, Jon Campbell, would come with me to Zhao Aining's Saturday underground show. Jon was a Chinese language and culture student and we had met a few weeks earlier at BLCU. Jon thought the exhibit sounded fun and as a musician himself, wanted to hear the musical performance by Beautiful Pharmacy, a punky-alternative band.

On the Saturday afternoon, Jon and I caught a rickety bus from the subway station and headed 30 minutes north of the city. I had no idea where we were going but I had a rough address. The event was being held on some factory's grounds. This is where I first saw Dawu.

"Who is that guy?" I thought to myself, glancing at him during a group photoshoot. "He must be one of the new artists."

I was immediately attracted to Dawu. His long black hair was tied back in a long ponytail. He was very handsome. He was well built, not too muscular nor too skinny. He was average height, had a clear face and a friendly smile. He noticed me also.

He asked about my camera and we chatted in Mandarin about my Hasselblad equipment for a bit. I had seen his art and found it interesting, although I didn't completely understand it. It was well-executed in terms of placement and lighting but I didn't get what it meant. I did get our chemistry. It flickered between us as we talked.

He seemed to be interested not only in my camera equipment, but me. Another thing I noticed about him was that he spoke as if he was from out of town. It was hard for Chinese who grew up outside of Beijing to blend in with city folk. Non-locals were easily identified by how they spoke Mandarin. Dawu was no different. He didn't have the Beijing accent that placed a heavy "r" sound in speech.

Out-of-towners usually didn't want to be known as out-of-towners. They were looked down upon by Beijingers. However, every day hundreds of people moved to Beijing from other parts of China, eager to be creators. These people tried to distance themselves from their home communities, hoping to be accepted into the urban art community and, eventually, make their mark in the city. It seemed as if Dawu was not trying to hide his background. He was comfortable being Dawu. He made no effort to cover up the fact that he was not from Beijing. I liked that and kept talking to him.

My Chinese language skills weren't very good but they were good enough to chat with the handsome artist. Dawu told me that he lived in the Haidian District and was teaching at a new private school, not far from BLCU.

"I live in that district, too," I said in Mandarin. "I'm studying Chinese."

We talked some more about our lives and he asked for my phone number. I was over the moon but at the same time, a little wary. I had dated other Chinese guys before and I didn't want to be known as just another foreign girl dating a Chinese artist. If I dated a Chinese person this time, I wanted to be taken seriously. I also wanted to be able to talk to someone with ease and not have to worry about misunderstandings. Things had been lost in translation with my other relationships in China and that was why they had fizzled out. Could Dawu be different?

Maybe. For instance, he said he had dated a foreign woman before. As well, he liked cheese and red wine. I know this sounds weird, but many Chinese people don't like those two Western staples. Dawu impressed me with his taste buds. (Not to mention again, he was incredibly good looking.)

"We should meet up sometime," Dawu said.

There was one side of me who jumped for joy while the other side folded her arms and said, "No way." So, nothing came out of our meeting.

Two months later, I was asked by several artists such as Cao Lin, a very well-known Chinese artist, to photograph an exhibition at the Xidan Book Emporium, on Beijing's west side. I said I'd take the photos.

Cao Lin knew Dawu and I heard he was going to be there with his installation at the *KNOWLEDGE IS POWER: CONTEMPORARY ART EXHIBIT*. I went with my friend, Gord Hoffman, who was also interested in the show. Gord and I studied Chinese at BLCU and were in the same class.

I took the photos of Cao Lin's work, a bike with photos on it, and some photos of Ma Ling's works. I also snapped some photos of Dawu's work … just because. (I had actually forgotten what he looked like but I remembered the heat from our conversation in the fall.) Most of the artists never paid me for my work and assumed I'd give them the images for free. Dawu was different. He was the first to offer to pay for the film by taking me out for something to eat.

He called around Christmas time to invite me to dinner and after that date, Dawu and I started to hang out more and more. I was shy at first but opened up as we spent time together. I liked Dawu. He was funny, smart, handsome and talented. He didn't speak any English and it was forcing me to improve my Mandarin ... quickly. He was interested in me, my culture, my past and my future. He was also supportive of my photography and encouraged me to take photographs and travel to shows and exhibits with him.

I started a photography project called *BEIJING STATION*. I took portraits of expats living in Beijing with something speical they owned. I arranged to photograph my subjects on my balcony using natural light and black and white film in my Hasselblad camera. My subjects came to my place during the day. It was fun.

Dawu was my key to being more involved in the art scene and having a purpose for being there. I wasn't just a groupie, an outsider: I was married to the mob, so to speak (or at least dating the mob). Also, for someone with a cultural anthropology background who was always looking for that more profound Chinese experience, Dawu was it. He was like my gatekeeper, an interpreter of the culture and world around me. I could see myself staying in China with him.

Dawu and I lived only a few kilometres away from each other in the Haidian University District. He visited me often while I was living in the BLCU student housing complex that I shared with an Italian woman and her boyfriend from Mauritius. I visited Dawu, too, at his work. He was teaching art to young students in Beijing.

During our time together, he would tell me about his art works. One in particular stood out, a conceptual photography piece called *IMPERIAL CRIMINALS*. It was headshots of people with their *crimes* stamped on their foreheads. He had included a headshot of himself proclaiming himself as a *POLITICAL CRIMINAL*. It was a cool piece.

Despite our attraction and compatibility, I was a bit unsure about our relationship. I thought maybe we were moving too fast. We had only just met and now we were spending so much time together. As well, language was a struggle. I hadn't seriously dated someone who didn't speak English, at least at a basic level, and my Mandarin was not fluent. How well did we really know each other?

We continued to see each other. Dawu was patient with me and helpful with my art projects. He arranged for me to participate in a photography show, the *PINGYAO INTERNATIONAL PHOTOGRAPHY EXHIBITION*, in Pingyao City, Shaanxi Province, in the summer of 2002. He also helped get me published in the fall 2002 edition of *Contemporary Artist Art Condition*, a local art magazine.

When Dawu introduced me to other photographers, he introduced me as "an artist from Canada." That was new to me. I had never considered myself an artist ever, let alone in China. I considered photography a hobby although I felt I had an eye for it. I was an English teacher and learner of Chinese: Dawu was the artist. He lived and breathed art, like many of his colleagues. Dawu never struggled with calling himself an artist and some of that came from being so talented in drawing and creating. He was also knowledgeable about art and art history, not to mention Western philosophy. He was a huge repository of both Chinese and Western art for me. We compared notes and had discussions and debates about art and artists and the creative process. We were simpatico in many ways, despite the language barrier that was quickly being dismantled.

We enjoyed conversations about China, her history, the West and his childhood. Despite having a good relationship with his father, it hadn't always been so. He told me stories about how he was a latchkey kid, as most children were then, and said that his father punished him for minor offences, forcing him to kneel on a washboard for hours at a time. It was brutal and Dawu sort of hated his father for this. However, the adult Dawu could see that the abusive nature was a common byproduct of the Cultural Revolution.

Our relationship zoomed ahead in March 2002, only a few months after we started dating. We moved into a two-bedroom apartment together in Dongwangzhuang, a student ghetto north of the BLCU campus. It was a big move relationship-wise, too, but we both felt it was a good way to spend more time together. The direction towards marriage was one we were both heading towards. When Dawu and I talked about the future, he mentioned that he had a house in his hometown that he would happily sell to buy us something in Beijing, if and when it came to that. I liked that idea.

Living together meant I paid most of the bills, from rent to groceries, while Dawu was busy with his art. I was juggling a couple of jobs as an English teacher and International English Language Testing System (IELTS) examiner (non-English speakers who want to study in English overseas). I was also taking any part-time work I could find. It was tough but I never brought it up to Dawu. I had heard from other expat women dating Chinese artstis that this was "par for the course."

According to Dawu, real art was conceptual: it didn't have dollar signs attached to it. He often dissed other artists in his community who were making large amounts of cash from the sale of their works.

Some of the artists then were becoming Chinese millionaires after selling their works to foreigners. Dawu was against this and fine just floating along in a river of creativity and avoiding the swift river of consumerism.

One evening, Dawu brought home a video for us to watch. He put *In the Name of the Father* into our wonky DVD player and pushed play. The 1993 movie was based on a true story about the Guildford Four. The Guildford Four, three men and one woman, were charged in 1975 after an Irish Republican Army (IRA) attack on the Guildford Pub in Surrey, U.K. The defendants said they were innocent, although the police made them claim responsibility. The movie was about the Four's fight to clear their names after spending 15 years in prison wrongfully accused.

Dawu was impassioned by the Four's story. He related to it and told me it represented him, his family and how many injustices were occurring in China on a daily basis. In the movie, one of the main character's father's dies before the Guildford Four are released. To Dawu, that was not only sad but completely avoidable.

In the summer of 2002, Dawu and I wanted to find a place to live that was closer to Beijing's inner city, the trendy Sanlitun area and the budding 798 Art District. We thought it would be better to be around the art action and closer to my work commitments. I wasn't a student any longer; nevertheless, my Mandarin was rapidly improving, as Dawu didn't speak a word of English. I was working as an English teacher as well as working part-time at a college, Raffles Beijing (a school with campuses all over Asia-Pacific), where I was teaching photography and creativity. I was also subbing at the Western Academy of Beijing, an international school in the Shunyi District, an expensive gated community where many of the big multinational company employees lived.

With the help of a rental reator, we settled on a two-bedroom apartment on the top floor of a six-floor walk-up in the Tuanjiehu area. It was perfect! From the lovely park nearby to the proximity of KFC (in case I needed a needed a spicey chicken burger), it suited both our needs. Buses were aplenty and there were great fresh food markets. The pace and scene were high for a young couple who wanted to have fun and excitement in the city.

We moved into our little apartment on the corner of Yaojiayuan and Tuanjiehu Roads. It was home sweet home after Dawu painted the walls and we hung up his art and some of my photos. We were going to be happy here.

One of our favourite restaurants, Meizhou Dongpo, was around the corner. It prepared the most delicious *Gongbao jiding* dish. Made with spicy diced chicken, red peppers and peanuts, it was a treat to be able to walk to get it.

Dawu and I not only shared a common interest in art, but also in music. We'd often attend music concerts and listened to Chinese bands. Dawu introduced me to his rock and punk friend Wu Jinhong, affectionately known as Honghong. Dawu and Honghong had been friends since their youth in Changzhou. They were *tiegemen'r* — "iron friends" — friends who, despite upheaval, are solid and hard to break apart.

Honghong was one of the first punk musicians in mainland China. He was a character and always wore a leather hat. I liked it when he visited Dawu and me. Honghong was interesting and we could talk for hours about Western music, something that Dawu and I couldn't do yet. Honghong had a killer CD collection, too.

I had met many of Dawu's friends and it was time to introduce him to my friends and family. In November 2002, my boyfriend and I took our first trip overseas together. We went to my hometown, Calgary, for Christmas. It was an important trip because Dawu and I were planning on getting married.

Dawu was planning on asking my dad, Gordon Patterson, for my hand. It was an interesting situation when Dawu met my father. Dawu didn't speak English well and my dad spoke no Mandarin. I had to interpret and convey the message from Dawu to my father.

Dad gave his blessing. I was happy and my family could see that. They didn't think Dawu would be a stable provider but they did know he loved me.

Despite not being able to speak English, Dawu made my family laugh. He was engaging and fun — a good addition to our group. Dawu also got along well with my sister Diane's husband, Peter Abramovicz. Peter was from communist Poland and had that political landscape in common with Dawu. Peter's parents were Jewish and his mom escaped the Nazi concentration camps in the Second World War. She had been given a train ticket to the Soviet Union, where she ended up picking cotton in Azerbaijan for several years. She was lucky. Peter's father was not so lucky and was sent to the Auschwitz concentration camp in occupied Poland.

Peter and Dawu had many discussions about communism and politics and different ideas. I had to interpret for Dawu the entire trip and it was much more tiring than I had expected. It was hard having a conversation and translating it for someone else at the same time.

Prior to arriving in Calgary, I had organized two art talks for Dawu, one at the Alberta College of Art and Design (ACAD, now called Alberta University of the Arts) and the other at the University of Calgary (U of C) in the anthropology department. I thought it would be a good experience for him, the community and us. Dawu could introduce Calgarians to Chinese artists and gain some experience talking to an international audience. I would be the interpreter for both presentations.

The talk at ACAD was on Chinese contemporary and avant-garde art and artists over the past decade. The U of C anthropology department presentation focused on Chinese women artists in China. Dawu carefully selected several women to talk about, such as his friends Ma Ling and Chao Hongling. He had chosen works that could be considered offensive (nudity, etc.) instead of more common and traditional ink and wash paintings.

Some politics crept into the discussions during the talk at the U of C when a student from the China mainland started asking me questions in both

Mandarin and English. The student considered herself an expert on the mainland and all things Chinese but she didn't know about the Chinese art scene. She caused me some embarrassment in front of the audience.

The tone of the student's questions and remarks was accusatory. She manipulated the situation to make it appear like Dawu and I didn't know what was going on in China's avant-garde art scene. She asked my opinion on the attitude of Chinese avant-garde artists who were anti-government. She said that some of the artists were causing problems by lobbying against the People's Republic of China (PRC).

"No," I said, "that's not exactly true. Most artists in China carry a death sentence if they actively and directly speak out against the government."

The student's views were outdated and highly reactive. I was surprised but it gave me pause: she could have been sent by the Chinese consulate in downtown Calgary. The long arm of the Chinese propaganda machine reached far and wide. The authorities thought all artists were anti-government and out to cause trouble. Was this woman a Chinese government plant?

Dawu wasn't quiet during the exchange. He was taken aback by the student's questioning and responded to her. They squabbled in Chinese a bit but Dawu was trying to be a polite guest and refrained from arguing further.

After the exchange, there was an awkward silence in the room. The event ended on a bad note. We weren't even thanked for our time. The quarrelsome student had left Dawu with some questions as well. He, too, was concerned that she was watching him for the Chinese government.

Dawu made some good artistic connections through his presentations. He met U of C professor and artist Paul Woodrow, visual artist Chris Cran and multidisciplinary artist Adrian Stimson. Adrian is an Indigenous artist from the Siksika Nation. He invited us to visit him in his community and it was an eye-opening day for Dawu. He delved into a new culture and perspective. The artists laughed about the so-called "land bridge" that connected Asia and North America thousands of years ago and joked about who crossed it first.

My six-week trip home to Alberta was wonderful and Dawu liked Canada, but not enough to move there just yet. We headed back to Beijing in the new year. We had lots to do, such as plan two weddings.

Our first wedding was going to be in February 2003. We had to go to Dawu's home province of Jiangsu to be legally married in his hometown. It was required by law. In China, the official signing of marriage papers didn't happen at the same time as the party and family gathering. It was sometimes a year apart. Our second wedding was going to be the big family event and it was scheduled for May 2003.

There was a list of things Dawu and I had to do before we got married. We had to go to the hospital for blood tests and sit through a lecture and video on "How to be married and how to make love." The video was out of date and hilarious. All this was done to ensure folks were healthy and knew how to have sex before they conceived their first and only child. Some couples didn't know anything about the birds and the bees.

The One-Child Policy was in effect. This meant Chinese parents were allowed to have one child only. Dawu and I were the sole mixed-race couple in a class with about eight Chinese couples. When it came to time to talk to Dawu and me about birth control and the population control program, the nurse looked at me and said, "Oh, I guess you don't need that lecture."

For Chinese couples who were married and wanting a baby, they had to apply for a license or permit to conceive. They couldn't just get pregnant. The consequence of a baby that was due to arrive prior to obtaining a pregnancy or marriage permit may be a forced abortion. There were often lineups at abortion clinics around the country as abortion was seen as THE form of birth control, although pills and condoms were readily available. I wouldn't need the birth control talk because I wasn't Chinese and therefore, wasn't subjected to the policy.

A few days after Valentine's Day, Dawu and I were married. On a cold Monday, Feb. 17, 2003, we were declared husband and wife in a nondescript office in Changzhou. We could only get married here as it was the city deemed acceptable by my husband's residence permit book, his *hukou*. These hukou books are part of a China-wide system of household registration and state not only when you were born but in which city and to which address, etc. The system provided demographic information about residents in each region. However, it also actively limited where a person was allowed to live, especially those born in the countryside. The government wanted to control the population and demographics so everyone didn't move to big cities like Beijing, Shanghai or Guangzhou. (Dawu could live in Beijing because he had a temporary residence permit called a *zanzhuzheng*.)

Overall, our official wedding wasn't much fun. It was procedural and formal. We were the only ones present besides the officials. We did have dinner with some friends and Dawu's father, Wu Xiangshou, and sister, Wu Suling, afterwards. (Dawu's mother had died several years before from stomach cancer.)

After we were legally married, I had to say goodbye to my late nights hanging out with Dawu, chatting about anything and everything. I had a new job. I had to get up early each morning and bike to the Canadian Embassy for 8:30 a.m. I was a file clerk in the immigration department and guaranteed 40 hours a week. The work paid more than well for an expat living in China. My new position could lead to more lucrative positions.

The job ended almost before it started. SARS, severe acute respiratory syndrome, a viral respiratory disease, broke out in the country and was heading around the world. The Chinese authorities seriously dropped the ball with SARS because they waited close to five months before releasing the news to the public that they had a viral outbreak on their hands - one that didn't have a cure or vaccine. It was a disaster on a mega scale that cost many lives. Trust had been severely broken between the people and the authorities in their handling of the situation. As bodies started to pile up in hospitals in the country, the thought of this turning into a pandemic was causing nervous jitters among foreign and local communities.

In Beijing and other large cities, embassies, consulates and large companies employing expats began mobilizing quickly to repatriate employees and their families home. As part of the Canadian Embassy's risk management plan, all non-essential locally engaged staff were being laid off. That included me.

Alan Donaldson, a diplomat in the immigration section of the embassy, told me that he felt horrible but I'd have to leave. He said perhaps when the SARS issue had been dealt with, I would be rehired.

"Don't count on it though," he said "we just don't know what is going to happen."

I left and within a week later that April 2003, I was working full-time for the Australian Embassy, also in the immigration department. This time, I was an immigration officer. It was an even better-paying job and I had a flexible schedule. That suited me perfectly as I could use any extra time to organize my photoshoot work and finish planning my second wedding. I was getting worried that it wasn't going to happen.

Our big family wedding was only a couple of weeks away and SARS was still very much a part of life in China. My friends and family were coming from Canada for the festivities that Dawu's family was hosting in Changzhou. His father, sister, her husband, plus aunts and uncles and other family members were planning the event for Saturday, May 3. For Dawu's family, our wedding was a huge deal in many ways. He was the first son to get married out of his family and it was a huge deal that he was marrying me, a girl from Canada.

Not only was Dawu's family excited that their "Number One" son was finally getting married, but he was also marrying someone who could help him realize his dreams of travelling overseas for his career and a better life.

Dawu's friends, other artists and curators also proclaimed that he had it made, not to mention that he had legally bypassed the hukou registration system and lived in Beijing. They thought that by marrying a Canadian, his life would be easy. Canada was seen by many Chinese people as a socialist country where its people had access to "free" benefits and government support programs. It was ironic, given China was supposed to be a socialist-communist country.

SARS took the air out of our wedding party plans. In attempts to quash the outbreak in China, the government banned everyone in the country from taking trains, taking flights or driving from one city to another. Dawu and I simply could not leave Beijing, nor could his family visit us. We were stuck.

Amid SARS and a week before the wedding, my parents flew to Beijing from Canada. They arrived in the nick of time, as the officials shut down airports and prevented trains from entering or leaving Beijing on April 30. Sadly, my sister and many friends had to cancel their flights.

The Chinese authorities insisted everyone stay indoors. Wearing masks outside was the new normal. The streets of Beijing were deserted, not a soul in sight. It was eerie and scary. Nothing was moving in the once crazy-busy city and it was as if Beijing had been gutted of life.

Dawu was so disappointed we couldn't leave the city for the wedding but there wasn't much that we could do. He was sad that not one of his family members would be at the celebration. The big wedding they had planned just for us was cancelled.

Dawu and I ended up getting married but in Beijing, not in Changzhou. Friends in the city who were brave enough to go outdoors attended, along with my parents. Honghong was one such friend who made it to our "SARS wedding."

The wedding ended up being a hike up the Fragrant Mountains, where mid-point, Dawu and I exchanged vows in both English and Chinese, took photos and ate some wedding cake that we had brought up the hill. Honghong made sure my mother was taken care of and walked with her. She enjoyed his company and he was a gentleman.

Later, we all had dinner at the HanCun Restaurant on Qinghai Lake in the middle of an older part of Beijing. The celebration was lovely and worked out despite changing plans two days before our actual wedding day.

Even with SARS looming over that day, I was happy. Dawu and I were a strong couple. We were both working on our careers and supported each other and we had the backing of family and friends. Despite differences in culture and language, I loved him and China more and more. Marrying Dawu had made me a part of the country. I truly belonged in China.

***

I had wanted to wait a while after the wedding before getting pregnant but I was getting older by the day. I was 35 and there was no time like the present. I found out I was going to be a mother-to-be around December 2003. The baby's due date was predicted to be the end of August 2004. We had a few months to find a new place where I didn't have to walk up six flights of stairs.

Christmas was spent packing up our old apartment. We moved to a new place in January 2004. I wasn't really in tune with my growing belly. I was one of those pregnant moms who didn't take to it in the first few months. It wasn't until I was about five or six months pregnant that I got into it and started thinking, "Wow and yikes, I'm going to be a mom."

I felt cared for during my pregnancy because Dawu was attentive. My husband asked me to practice *zuoyezi* when the baby arrived. Zuoyezi is a traditional Chinese postpartum practice where once the baby is born, the woman has to stay in bed for 30 days and can't eat or drink certain foods. (Pigeon soup, though, is on the menu.) There are a few other restrictions and I think in earlier times, zuoyezi was followed because there wasn't any heating in the homes or running water and it lessened the risk of the mother and baby dying from eating bad food or going out and catching a virus.

When Dawu and I were together, we were our own culture, a mix. We were neither fully Chinese nor Canadian. Dawu loved cheese and wine, which weren't common foods for Chinese to enjoy. He liked Bob Dylan and Tom Waits (even though he couldn't understand what they were singing). I liked many Chinese dishes, musicians and the language. We traded our cultures, juggling them around to create our own. However, it was rather lopsided as we lived in China. I said I'd think about zuoyezi.

During my pregnancy, my husband and I got along well. We were newlyweds, happy and in love, and having fun preparing for the baby. Some people in China wanted only sons. Girls were considered a scourge. In the countryside in 2004, female infanticide was alive and well. Thankfully, Dawu didn't care what we had as long as the baby was healthy. We were going to raise the child together and be the best parents we could be.

I felt like I was living a good life. Dawu was my rock. Nevertheless, there were two ways he could improve to make things slightly better for me: cut down on his smoking and start earning a wage. Dawu smoked like a chimney, which we all know is unhealthy for anyone — but second-hand smoke is especially harmful to a growing baby. As well, we didn't have a lot of money.

I had my job at the embassy but Dawu didn't seem to be interested in making money through selling his art. I thought he'd eventually sort out everything and he'd stop with the cigarettes and start selling his work.

In May of 2004, Dawu was invited to be a guest lecturer at the University of Saskatchewan in Saskatoon, Saskatchewan, Canada. Lorne Holyoak asked him to teach for the spring session. Lorne was a full-time cultural anthropology professor at the university and the friend who had recommended I go to China. We were still good friends and he had met Dawu during a trip to Beijing and thought his experiences were a good fit for a contemporary Chinese art course.

Dawu couldn't speak English, so the school arranged an interpreter for the six week session. The guest instructor gig started in June and we thought it was a great chance for both of us to get to Canada before our baby was due.

Dawu flew solo from Beijing to Saskatoon and started teaching. He was a good instructor in the practical application of art, painting and art theory. I was super-proud of him.

I flew to Canada a couple of weeks later. While in Calgary, my sister Diane took me shopping for baby things that I couldn't get in China like cloth diapers and a breast pump. I was excited about all these new things and had a good feeling that Dawu's career was going to take off now that he was getting some overseas exposure, albeit teaching art to summer students in a Canadian university on the Prairies.

Dawu joined me in Calgary after his teaching job and my family threw us a lovely wedding-slash-baby-is-coming party. There was a barbecue with lots of food and gifts for Dawu and me and our bundle of joy. By this time, I was six months pregnant and showing.

My heart was full and I was happy to be heading home to Beijing. I was a little anxious about having a baby though. I hadn't spent a lot of time around them and I wouldn't have my own family to help me. However, Dawu told me that his dad, Wu Xiangshou, and the older man's girlfriend, Qiu Zaofan, would be moving in with us to help. It was a common practice in China. I wasn't in a position to complain since we were going to need the extra hands. I was going to be fine.

In the summer of 2004, I was preparing for the birth of my baby. I didn't know if I was having a girl or boy. Most, if not all, couples in China during the one-child policy years (1979 – 2015) weren't allowed to know the gender. It was prohibited by law to ask the sex of the infant prior to delivery. There was a myriad of reasons why but the most common and obvious one was that the culture favoured boys.

The government made the process of sexing the child in womb illegal. However, as Dawu and I were a mixed couple, we were an exception. During one of our regular visits to the gynecologist, we were asked if we wanted to know what we were having. We didn't care but said, "sure." Nevertheless, the doctor wasn't allowed to tell us directly what to expect.

"Your baby has sandwich lines," she said, "not a hot dog."

Ah! We were having a girl.

I went to a few pre-birth classes at the Beijing United Hospital, THE private American hospital in the city. I went to the classes alone, as Dawu was working. Beijing United was the preferred place for all moms to have their babies but it was not cheap: about $20,000 U.S.

I had thought about giving birth at home in Canada but since I was the sole breadwinner, it would have been impossible for me to take a year off from the Australian Embassy. As an expat but hired in China, I was employed under Chinese labour laws, which gave new moms four months of paid maternity leave. So on top of preparing for the baby, I had to prepare for returning to work quickly.

As the due date in August crept closer, I was beginning to realize how much I missed my family in Canada and wished they were going to be with me. I should have gone home to deliver my baby as some other expats had. Too late now.

Dawu and his family was excited about their new addition. Having a baby in China was a big deal. Much of Chinese culture is based on ancestors and the family. If you don't have a child, then you don't have anyone to look after you when you're old, nor do you have people to worship you as an ancestor after you die. Babies are good symbols for all generations.

On a late August 2004 morning, after an emergency C-section, Hannah arrived on the scene. She met her *baba* (father) first and then she was cleaned up and brought to me. Here was the game-changer. She was adorable. She was beautiful. She was our Hannah.

Hannah, me and her baba stayed in the hospital for the next five days as a C-section was considered major surgery. Dawu slept on the foldout couch in my private room. Hannah had a little crib on wheels, which the nurses moved out when I napped. When my baby was hungry, they'd wheel her back to me so I could breastfeed her. However, Hannah was having some problems with feeding and I wasn't allowed to leave the hospital until she latched. That was taking some time.

Overall, my recovery wasn't too hard. One day, I was treated to a full manicure and pedicure. Dawu and I were also served a four-course steak dinner while Hannah was wheeled away and looked after by the nurses.

It was an awesome experience. Guests came daily to see us at the hospital. Dawu's father and girlfriend, Wu Xiangshou and Qiu Zaofan, were there a lot of the time, usually with food. They didn't have to worry that I wasn't getting enough to eat. I was well-fed at Beijing United.

I phoned Diane and gave her the birth announcement. Of course, my family and friends in Calgary were happy for me and Dawu. They asked how the hospital was and I said I couldn't complain. My most important training was breastfeeding, which Hannah and I had to work at together.

Hannah was not latching on to my breasts to fed. Dawu was frustrated with me over it and I felt like he was implying that if he had breasts, Hannah would have latched right away.

"Yeah, whatever," I thought to myself. "Sure, go ahead with your obtuse fantasy and I will continue to work with the breasts that I actually have."

I ignored Dawu's silly comments and chalked it up to him being a new father. I did think he was probably a bit jealous. My attention had shifted abruptly from him to Hannah. He now had competition for my affections. This was a new experience for both Dawu and I and we would work through it. I did compromise over the zuoyezi requirements and ate the pigeon soup. (It was tasty.) In the end, Dawu and I were excited with our new reality.

We brought Hannah home from the hospital in a cab. Wu Xiangshou and Qiu Zaofan were waiting for us. The brand new grandfather was proud of Hannah. He was helpful and watched his granddaughter when Dawu and I needed to go out. We were moving homes again and had to pick out toilets for our new place that we had just bought and were renovating.

Dawu was eager to provide his little family with a real home. He helped me put a down payment on a brand new condominium unit on the 22nd floor of a highrise in the middle of Beijing. His contribution came through selling the house that he owned in Jiangsu province. I was looking forward to living in the Huayang Jiayuan Complex in Tuanjiehu with my husband and our daughter.

I leaned into my role as a mom with the diligent help and assistance of Zaofan. She had a wealth of experience as a mother and grandmother. I trusted her and she acted like we were a family. I appreciated that, since my parents and sister were far, far away.

***

I was on four months' paid leave from the Australian embassy and received my salary while I stayed home being a mom. Throughout my mat leave, Hannah and I walked around the community and into the Sanlitun area of Beijing. This was where there were great cafés and restaurants. We'd meet my friends on outdoor patios and chat. Some local folks were a bit freaked out that I was taking Hannah out so young. Even on warm summer days, Chinese neighbours and shop owners would lay into me about why it wasn't a good idea to bring Hannah outside. They thought it was too cold for a baby. These older Chinese women provided their comments unsolicited. I complained about it to Qiu Zaofan one day.

"I understand," she said. "It happens to everyone, not just you. Pretend you don't understand Chinese. That's what I'd do."

It was great advice and I used it. I simply walked away as a silly foreigner who couldn't understand a word the judgmental person was saying. Hey, it's China. In my experience there, everyone had an opinion and wasn't ashamed to tell you about it. Some of these same Nosy-Nellies never hesitated to tell me that I was lucky to have a half-Chinese child. There was a weird stereotype that half-Chinese kids were somehow far superior to fully Chinese children and were smarter and better looking. I cross-referenced this thinking with other expat moms who had half-Chinese kids. We all had heard the same story. Genetically, it was nonsense.

Hannah did have full Chinese citizenship. When she was born, she was automatically given Chinese citizenship, thanks to her dad. Her hukou registration would be in Jiangsu, like Dawu. However, I wanted Hannah proclaimed as a Canadian as soon as possible. Within her first month, I contacted the Canadian Embassy and applied for her citizenship. That process was going to take eight to 10 months.

Meanwhile, I did have to go back to work. We weren't poor but we weren't swimming in yuan. I loved my work at the embassy and thought Dawu would be able to sell his art at some point to add to the family coffers; he just needed more time. He had been busy getting our new place renovated and live-in ready. It didn't help that Qiu Zaofan and Dawu's dad had returned home when Hannah was around three months old. Everything besides looking after Hannah fell to Dawu.

The new father had been pushed to the limit in the last few weeks and we hadn't had a lot of family time. While I was caring for our new baby, Dawu was busy with the contractors who were renovating our new condo. Over four months, he lost about 15 pounds by working 14-hour days. He didn't have extra weight to lose in the first place. Dawu had to wrangle the builders, get materials, design the space, assist the workers and then help me at home. He wanted us to be in the new place before I went back to work at the beginning of December.

I was worried about who I was going to get to take care of Hannah while I was at my embassy job. In early December 2004, three days before I rejoined the workforce, we found a capable *ayi*, a nanny. Qi Mei came to us from an introduction from another ayi. At least we had one thing sorted.

Qi Mei had been a singing and dancing nursery school teacher for much of her career. She was now in her late 50s and as close as I could get to a mom for me and a grandma for Hannah. I had complete faith in Qi Mei.

The next couple of days were chaos. We were moving into our new place, looking after a newborn and I was about to go back to work. We got through it and began tuning in to a new rhythm.

Although I was spending time away from my tiny baby, the embassy made it as easy as possible for me to do what I needed to do for Hannah. The staff was so supportive. Dawu and I had gone through a major shift yet everything was falling into place. He was a good husband. We had a lovely new apartment in a choice part of the city, which was nicely finished thanks to him. Plus, we shared a beautiful baby. What could be better? I was satisfied with my lot in life. I loved China and all my dreams were coming true.

I was happy with my life in 2005. I was a new mom and I had a great job at the Australian Embassy. I had good support from both Dawu and our full-time ayi. She did most of the cleaning, grocery shopping and some food prep. Dawu and I both liked to cook so we traded turns making meals.

Dawu and I were homeowners. That was a first for me. My new place was not just any old dusty apartment but a gorgeously renovated brand new unit. When the sky was clear of the stinky smog, I could see the Fragrant Mountains on the west side of Beijing.

Our condo had a lovely outdoor terrace attached to it and we turned it into a garden oasis. It was a wonderful escape from citylife and Dawu was able to smoke outside. We hosted back-to-back barbecues on the terrace for what seemed to be two months straight. Dawu loved to grill and we invited different groups to join us for meals. Co-workers from the embassy, artists and expat friends had drinks with us while traffic honked far below. This was when Dawu and I became close with our neighbours, Lena Meier and Xing Kui and their children. It was nice to be friends with a couple who were almost like us.

Lena was Swiss and her husband Xing Kui was a local Beijing businessman. They had two children: Lilly, about three years old, and Hugo, about seven years old. The family lived down the hall from us and the kids gave Dawu and I a traditional housewarming gift of a loaf of bread and a small dish of salt when we first moved in.

Work was a quick 20-minute cycle away from our new home. I enjoyed pedalling down the wide boulevards where most of the embassies were based. If I didn't want to bike, I had other options like the bus or a cheap cab. I could also walk the route in 45 minutes.

I had a great life with Dawu and we didn't seem to have any problems. Of course, there was some marital discord over little things like what to eat for supper but those tiffs were over in a sigh. Our future was in sync and we both believed that Dawu's art would get recognized soon and he would be able to contribute to the household through it.

I paid for a trip to Thailand for Dawu, Hannah and I in early spring 2005. We could afford a vacation and I wanted to visit a friend, Gisele Lewis.

Gisele and I met in Beijing when I was looking for expats to photograph for my *BEIJING STATION* project. She was now living in southern Thailand and working as a college drama teacher.

I had been to Thailand in 1999 but Dawu had never been anywhere in Asia. Hannah was six months old and it was her first big trip. She went on her Chinese passport since she didn't have her Canadian one yet.

We introduced Hannah to the ocean and she wasn't a natural beach baby. She howled! The waves were too loud and scary for her.

We saw our friend, visited museums and saw interesting sites. Then, in a blink of an eye, our vacation was over. Our little family returned home, energized and happy. It had been a great trip.

Back in Beijing, Dawu and I talked about having another baby but not too seriously. Dawu was keeping late hours and I was working full time in an office and full time once I arrived home. We were content the way things were and made time to go out as a couple to events, parties and movies.

I worked at the Australian Embassy full time, Monday to Friday. My job had me interviewing people who had applied to immigrate to Australia from China. I spoke Chinese well by this point but my writing had declined. I mainly had to listen to people, not take notes.

I had moved up the ranks since starting in the immigration department in April 2003. I went from junior officer to a program manager and worked in the fraud squad. It was part of the compliance department and I conducted site visits on Chinese immigration applicants all over the country. I travelled to where the applicant was based, regardless of where it was in China, and ALWAYS unannounced.

Applicants, like any applicant anywhere in the world applying for a visa to another country, had to prove to me that what they were claiming on their application was genuine. It was a bit like doing detective work. I had to check out many things, such as documentation and relationships, to ensure people applying to go to Australia were legitimate. My success at ferreting out those who were trying to scam the system hinged on the surprise of my visit. It was fun, super-interesting and well-paid.

***

Around the time Hannah turned one, I took her on her second trip overseas to meet her other family and friends in Canada. Dawu stayed behind because we didn't have enough money for all of us to travel. Besides, he had art stuff to work on.

I wanted to show wee Hannah her other roots. I hadn't been home since my pregnancy in 2004 and it was time. At the end of August 2005,

Hannah and I first travelled to Japan to visit my friends Jackie, Rick and their three kids.

Hannah and I arrived at the Tokyo airport late at night and took the train to Jackie and Rick's house in the Shibuya District. When we got off the train at midnight, it was dark, raining and there was no one around. Here I was alone with a stroller, large suitcases and a sleeping baby in my arms. It was scary. I was an easy mark to be robbed if anyone had wanted to make some fast cash. I found a taxi parked just in front of the train station doors and gave the driver my friends' address in some form of English pronunciation of Japanese. The cabbie knew exactly where to go.

Arriving at Jackie and Rick's house 10 minutes later, I found the yard full of bikes and toys and the door to their house unlocked. I waltzed in with Hannah as my friends had instructed me to do. I left my stroller outside as I had been told it would be safe there. I would have been worried about it if we were in China.

Older Chinese people in Beijing liked to reminisce about the seventies and earlier eras when stealing was rare. That was not the case anymore. Many apartment buildings had multiple layers of security and units had double-locking metal screen doors. Bike theft was huge and many expats, like me, deliberately rode crappy bikes to deter thieves.

I found that China was very much a country of opportunity: if you think you could get away with something (theft, drugs, murder, corruption, etc.), then you did it. I think it was because many people weren't educated and they had been socialized in the Chinese version of the "rule of law." Laws in China could be twisted and bent and shaped depending on who you were and what you had to give. Japan was a much different place.

I found Japan to be so clean, orderly and aesthetically pleasing. Even the baggage handlers wore white gloves. It was such a contrast to China, where mostly everything was dirty.

In China, I found dust on every surface. Forget about using public washrooms there. I won't go into detail but they were a disaster. Big cities in China, like Beijing, were among the most polluted in the world. It was terrible, especially in the winter, when coal dust, vehicle and factory emissions and sandstorms blew in. I never wore white or hung my laundry out to dry because the clothes would get filthy. After riding my bike to work or home, I'd have grime all over my face. Everyone out and about on the streets habitually put their fingers in the corners of their eyes to get rid of the grey gunk gathering there. I felt like I was riding or walking through an exhaust pipe. Yuck. I tried not to think about my poor lungs.

It was nice to be out in the air in Japan without having to worry about getting a film of guck on my skin.

Our Tokyo trip zoomed by and in no time we were off to Canada, stopping in British Columbia (B.C.) to see my dad and stepmom and friends in White Rock. Three days later, we left for Calgary for a few weeks of visiting.

My daughter and I returned to China with our Chinese *green card* visas firmly in place inside our Canadian passports. Despite the fact that I was married to a local Chinese, I needed a visa to stay in China, which had to be renewed every year.

After my few weeks of travelling, I started thinking about how I could bring in a second income to put towards more trips as well as household items. Although I was happy at my embassy job, I had been mulling over a new venture with an American friend, Patti. We had met at a photography club and she was one of my first close friends in Beijing.

Patti Rizzo Wang came to China to teach English in the late 1990s. She married a Chinese-American man and they had twin boys. The family lived just a few blocks down the street from the Australian Embassy. I often used my lunch break to walk to her place for short visits.

Patti and I were having lunch one day in the warm autumn air when we came up with an idea to start a shop selling "gently-used" baby items. We'd buy gear from expats living in the Beijing suburbs and resell them to people who couldn't afford the overpriced new stuff in the city. The idea came from the second-hand and consignment stores we had shopped at in North America.

Dawu loved our idea but thought it was going to take a lot of work. Many Chinese liked to buy brand-new things only. Thrift stores weren't popular in China because people didn't want second-hand items. They wanted to show they could afford something new and, by extension, had money and weren't poor. Nevertheless, some "new" Chinese brands and products were inferior to Western "used" brands. A second-hand BABYBJÖRN brand baby carrier, one of the best in the world, was better than a new Chinese brand baby carrier.

That fall of 2005, Patti and I started Beijing's first second-hand store: the NU2YU Baby Shop. We reached out to expats and online chat groups to find folks who would sell their used goods to us. We collected the items and put them in a warehouse. We then set up our wares at local bazaars around international schools, embassy compounds or gated community clubs.

In the early spring of 2006, Patti and I decided to display our items in a room in my condo so my home turned into a store. We moved everything out of the warehouse and into my apartment and kept business hours. Who-ever wasn't working took the NU2YU shifts. Earlier in the year, I had made the decision to quit my job at the embassy. It was tough to step away from a decent-paying job but I thought that if I put all my energy into my new business, it would be more than profitable. As well, I had reached the limit of how far I could go up the corporate ladder at the embassy. In order to get a promotion, I'd have to become an Australian citizen.

One benefit of being an entrepreneur was that I had more time to spend with Hannah. I was also banking on Dawu contributing more dollars to our household. It was soon apparent that my future dreams would always be il-lusions. While I was busting my butt working and being a mother and wife, Dawu hadn't been doing much of anything, except for maybe sleeping.

Dawu wasn't working as hard on his art as I had thought. I had never paid attention to what he did during the day at home while I was at the embas-sy all those years. After I quit and was in the condo almost full time, I realized that my husband slept until 2 p.m. almost daily. Meanwhile, I was working in my store and looking after Hannah.

I was angry. However, I pushed that anger deep down inside me. Art versus art-making money was a sensitive topic for both of us. Dawu didn't believe in selling art for profit but he did tell me that he needed more time and support from me in order to create pieces. I told him that, of course, I'd support him but we needed to make money to afford our nice apartment and feed not just ourselves but our baby.

A bright moment did shine in our lives when my former University of Calgary (U of C) photography instructor, Arthur Nishimura, reached out to me. He wanted to bring Dawu to U of C as an artist in residence. It was an-other great overseas opportunity for my husband and his art.

Dawu left for a month in Calgary in mid-March 2006 and I stayed in Beijing to work on my business. In Canada, Dawu was warmly received by my family and Arthur. Dawu's residency wasn't a money-making venture but it was his first artistic stint outside of China, albeit on a small scale. I hoped it would provide some kind of inspiration and show him that his skills and knowledge were valuable assets.

While at U of C, Dawu taught, collaborated on projects and provided insight into the Chinese contemporary and avant-garde scene. At the end of his residency, he had a small exhibit at the U of C's art department's Little Gallery. Dawu was happy about the experience and I felt the euphoria of his artist residency, too.

Dawu's experience was cool and one that would further connect him to Calgary and the art scene. Although we both knew that he wasn't interested in moving to Canada, it was good to be seen outside of China. I was very grateful for Arthur's help in this way.

Dawu and I seemed to be living life on a rollercoaster – up and down and down and up – one minute a struggle, the next flying high. When Dawu returned home, he didn't go on to produce art and had nothing to sell. He had nothing to add to pay the bills or to feed Hannah or to keep the roof over our heads. He wasn't making an income and wasn't interested in making money. I had to pay for everything. I had had a glimpse of this when we were first going out but I thought he would change. Love is blind.

I thought I had left my photography behind when I had a baby and a business, but in 2006 I found myself behind the camera again. Dawu encouraged my artistic side. He saw potential in my art and was introducing me to people and ideas.

Dawu and I went to the 798 Art District on a regular basis to see friends, eat at good restaurants or attend one of the many, many exhibitions. The district, also known as Dashanzi, is made up of former Bauhaus-style ammunitions factories that were converted into artist spaces. The collective artist village was a place to gather and exchange ideas, share works and ideas with artists, curators, collectors and the public. It was an important place, pre-social media in China, for face-to-face meetings.

I ended up doing a major photo shoot at 798 in the studio of Chao Hongling and Gu Duanfan, two of Dawu's artist friends who were a married couple. Their space was huge and it had great lighting and backdrops. My shoot was called The *BI-RACIAL DOLL PROJECT* and featured children of mixed ethnicities who lived in Beijing. The work came from my personal experiences of having a child who wasn't fully Chinese. Some Chinese had told me that since Hannah was half-Chinese, she would be richer, happier and more successful because of her mixed parentage. I wanted to educate Beijingers about the generalizations and stereotypes about children like Hannah.

I took photos of about 20 children but only used images of 16 for the final piece. I didn't pay the models but each contributing family received a print. The result was 16 small squares with an image of a mixed-ethnicity child in each one.

I also asked the mothers to write a 500-word essay on what it was like to be pregnant in China with a half-Chinese baby. It was amazing to hear what the moms said because it was the same experience as mine. They wrote about people believing a mixed ethnicity baby was better than a Chinese baby. Kids with blond hair were treated with reverence and respect. (It wasn't a given that a half-Chinese baby had black hair. Hannah's hair was a dark brown.)

I never got the chance to exhibit *THE BI-RACIAL DOLL PROJECT*. I was so busy with other things and my photography was sidelined. I was the sole breadwinner in my family and needed to make money. Not art.

Toward the end of 2006, an art collector I met through a "wives only" book club, the Beijing TaiTais Book Club, asked if I wanted to come for tea and chat about a business idea. Joanna Danois, an expat from Belgium, wanted to open an art gallery, mainly as a means to get close to the artists so she could buy their works. Joanna knew I was married to an artist and so approached me about the gallery. My role would be to connect with the artists and their art and her role would be to find the buyers for the art. Thus, the Front Line Contemporary Gallery was born.

We decided that we didn't need a brick-and-mortar space because we could showcase items online. It was an interesting venture and I was eager to introduce Chinese contemporary artists to Joanna and her art collector friends. I didn't think Dawu was right for the gallery. He didn't create many "for sale" pieces as he preferred performance or large-scale installation works. Those were hard to sell to individuals. Museums or collectors tended to buy his stuff.

Meanwhile, I started Job #3 around the same time Joanna and I launched the gallery. Just before I left the Australian Embassy, my friend Patti introduced me to Shelley Warner, who ran Asia Pacific Access (APA). The company offered destination service consulting and resources for expats living and working in China. It helped people find adequate housing and good schools for their children. Patti had been working with Asia Pacific Access for a while and thought I would be a good fit as a destination service consultant. It would also give me a stable income. She was right.

The year turned into 2007 and it was a hot time in the art worlds of Beijing and Shanghai. Prices were climbing up and up. Young Chinese artists, who had just graduated from good art schools, were making as much money selling their works as reputable *masters* in Canada or the U.S., artists who had been honing their craft for years and had built up solid reputations. There was a joke in the industry that a Chinese artist could shit on a canvas and sell it for heaps of money. The point was that prices were overinflated.

It was crazy and insane. Expats were buying up Chinese art at astonishing rates. Dawu might have been able to cash in on the art fever but he wasn't interested in making art for the sake of making money. Many artists in 2007 went from eating cheap noodles one day to being able to buy a brand new car the next. The "new" art world of sales took many artists out of poverty.

Dawu and I weren't destitute but like anyone, more money would have been nice. That way, I could step away from one or two or three of my jobs! I suggested Dawu paint under the pseudonym just for selling art. He wasn't interested. He told me art had to have meaning. He couldn't be a sellout.

Dawu believed we should both be artists who did art all day and weren't worried about the bills. Sure, we could do that before we had a baby and bought our home. We had more freedom in the past. Now we had responsibilities. We argued over selling his pieces but we only ended up going in circles.

I ended up renting space in our building to house items for the NU2YU Baby Shop and then ended up running the business by myself. Patti decided to leave the store in the spring. The first year we hadn't made much money and she didn't want to put any more energy into the venture. She sold me her share of the company and moved on to other pursuits. We remained good friends.

The second-hand store, the gallery and APA consulting consumed most of my time. The time I was not working, I was spending with Hannah. Dawu was beginning to resent the businesses, as they were moving me away from my creative and artistic endeavours. When he been single, Dawu lived on a shoestring budget. He had jobs teaching at art schools and made his money stretch. But he was no longer alone.

6

Working three jobs was not sustainable and so I had quit my consulting role with Asia Pacific Access. I was sorry to let go of the gig in the fall of 2007 as I had found it interesting and cushy. I never had to drive – I had a driver. I didn't have to worry about scheduling – I was usually given an itinerary. I never had to worry about finding new clients – people kept moving to Beijing. But it was time to focus on my businesses like the gallery and the NU2YU Baby Shop.

I was also worried about the state of my marriage. All couples fight. It's a part of resolving issues and airing out the relationship. Dawu and I had one giant argument and instead of resolving anything, it fractured our foundation. Dawu had offered to help me with renovations for the second-hand baby item store.

I had rented an empty apartment several floors below ours and was turning it into a shop. I wanted to remove the crappy, falling-apart laminate flooring in the "new" place and Dawu said he could replace it with shellacked concrete. We had the same type of floor poured in our home. Dawu had been the one who organized and watched the process during our renos in 2004 and I trusted that he knew what he was doing now.

When the floor was finished, Dawu came upstairs and told me it was a lot rougher than what we had in our place. I examined the new floor and it looked fine. I never gave much more thought to it until I was moving things into the shop a week later. That was when the floor started crumbling.

I was upset. My nice, new, high-end second-hand shop was opening in a few days and now the floor was falling apart. When I asked my husband about what was happening with the concrete, he whipped a mug off the counter with a whack of his hand. The cup, full of tea, splashed and shattered against the wall. He then started ranting and raving while walking around the apartment. He stalked into our bedroom bathroom and I cringed as I heard a ceramic dish hit the wall. I was a little frightened.

I tried talking to him but he was freaking out. He was out of control. He kept saying he was angry at me because my focus was all about these stupid businesses and not on art. He said we had lost focus as a family. I said, sure, the focus had changed but it was about paying the bills. They had to be paid or else we'd be out on the street.

Nope. He wasn't having any of it. I didn't want to stay in our house with things flying through the air so I scooped up Hannah and went to see a friend. Dawu needed to calm down. Clearly, we had some issues and they had erupted like a volcano. You can't put hot lava back inside the mountain.

From this point on, there was tension between Dawu and I. There weren't daily flare-ups but the heat was always there, bubbling under the surface. Dawu moved closer to his art and I focused on paying the bills. We both loved Hannah, of course, but there had been a shift in our relationship.

***

Dawu went to Germany in June 2007 as part of a large exhibition by the renowned Chinese artist Ai Weiwei. The show was called *DOCUMENTA* and it was held in Kassel. It was a prestigious event since this particular exhibition only took place every 10 years or so. Ai Weiwei was invited to participate and instead of sending over an installation piece as most artists did, he decided to send one thousand and one Chinese people to Germany as his work. His piece was titled *FAIRYTALE* and Dawu was one of the people chosen to fly to Europe.

Not everyone picked to travel abroad for the art piece went to Germany at once. Ai's point was about migration and global access for Chinese people. Many Chinese never got the chance to leave their country because travel was expensive, people weren't paid well and government red tape was a hindrance. While Dawu didn't know Ai Weiwei personally, my husband already had a passport and could go to Germany. He wasn't allowed to leave Kassel but he could wander around the city and take in the sights for the week he was there.

Dawu had a great time in Germany. His own works travelled, too. He had submitted them to two major exhibitions, one in Barcelona, Spain and the other in Houston, Texas, U.S. He also had two big exhibitions in Beijing, one in the TangRen Art Gallery, a major gallery in 798. His work for that show was called *STRIKING BACK TO THE ORIGINAL - GOLD* and it was an installation piece that simulated a large rock with remnants of gold in it. Instead of breaking the rock open to get the gold, his rock protected the gold in it.

He was happy to be part of TangRen Gallery and I was happy he was being recognized. I was proud of him. I really felt that we were part of the art community and that Dawu's career was slowly growing.

Meanwhile, one of my favourite people, Hannah's nanny Qi Mei, resigned because her daughter was having a baby. Tan Jie then joined our family. (*Jie*, meaning older sister or aunty, is commonly used for an older ayi.)

Tan Jie was in her early 60s and had been born and raised in Beijing. She cycled to and from our home and did a lot with Hannah, but we all missed Qi Mei.

Attending art exhibits with Dawu was my main social activity. Art exhibitions were hubs where artists could connect. An artist who wanted to meet the right people had to attend shows. Often, there were exhibits after exhibits all on one day. We'd hear of others once we hit the first opening and off we'd go to the next.

Dawu and I attended as many art exhibitions as we could. My husband was most interested in the more conceptual works that were not necessarily easy to sell. His favourite art galleries were more of the European type in the 798 Art District.

The 798 Art District wasn't just buildings with art slapped on the walls. No, there were well-known galleries established there such as The Galleria Continua, an international contemporary gallery owned by Italians. The Tan-gRen Gallery was financed by Hong Kong owners and included many contemporary pieces from artists everywhere. All these galleries kept a stable of Chinese artists but also included many internationally known artists. The 798 galleries ran the gamut from extremely pricey works, like canvases by Pablo Picasso, to cheap prints of green bamboo shoots.

The district was busy when several big shows and/or well-known artists were exhibiting. The lesser-known galleries would benefit from this as everyone went from place to place, trying to get to every exhibition. It was a fun thing to do on a weekend evening. Sometimes at the events, there was wine and cheese and other free booze and food. If you were lucky, the gallery owner or an artist would invite everyone out to dinner and after that, things would let loose at a karaoke bar. It was a great atmosphere and it wasn't just about art or an artist, it was a time to network and connect before Twitter and Facebook.

Some of the art cliques were led by certain artists who were in charge. These artists at the top invited those "under" him or her to certain art exhibitions. The artistic hierarchy was strong when I was in China and Ai Weiwei was one of the leaders. He had international exposure and influence in not only the Chinese world of artistry but also the globe. Ai wielded a lot of power in the artistic community and some of it was handed down to him by his father, the acclaimed Chinese poet Ai Qing.

Ai Qing has a complicated history with his country. He was considered a radical and traitor, according to the Chinese government in the thirties. He joined Mao Zedong (Marxist theorist, revolutionary and the founding father of the PRC) in 1941 and the Communist Party in 1945. Ai Qing was also considered essential to the building of the PRC in 1949.

Ai Qing wrote widely acclaimed poems praising China's revolution, as well as short stories describing the suffering of peasants, beggars and victims of war. His words earned him official party praise but when Mao Zedong began purging intellectuals in 1957, Ai Qing was chucked out of favour. He ended up living and working in the harshest, most northern parts of China toiling under manual labour. In 1975, he could come back to Beijing. The country was then under Deng Xiaoping (the Chinese communist leader who did away with many orthodox communist doctrines) and he restored Ai Qing's party membership and reputation.

Ai Weiwei's relationship with China was as complex as his father's. Despite being a thorn in the side of China's government, Ai Weiwei wasn't entirely hated by the authorities. He annoyed the government with his criticisms but he was able to do much of what he did as an artist, creator and dissident because he was somewhat protected by his father's legacy. Not only did Ai Weiwei have strong family ties to the upper echelon of Chinese society, but he had also lived and worked in the heart of the art scene in New York City in the 1990s. That also gave him standing in the Beijing art world.

Ai Weiwei was at the top of the artistic hierarchy in China and abroad and wielded real power. Compared to him, Dawu was closer to the bottom of the pile. While Dawu was talented, had connections and was friendly, he didn't have international appeal. Dawu's name was starting to make the rounds in a certain clique that included his friends Gu Duanfan and Chao Hongling. The married artists were exhibiting in important conceptual exhibitions in Beijing at galleries like the TangRen Gallery that held global cache. Nevertheless, Dawu hadn't been thrust into the spotlight for his art just yet.

One of the first artist friends I made during my early days in China, Zhao Aining, was doing well selling his art in 2007. He was known for his photo-based and performance-based conceptual artwork. Through my role at the Front Line Contemporary Gallery, I got the chance to sell his art. My hours at the gallery were not many but the income was good for the amount of work I did. My business partner Joanna and I split the proceeds 50/50.

I was grateful to have the nanny and Dawu's support while I was busy or away scouting art or products for NU2YU. Nevertheless, as I got more into my businesses, I spent less time with Dawu. I didn't like that I couldn't spend more hours with him but our mortgage hung like a weight around my neck. I loved our home and I didn't want to lose it, but I was struggling.

I tried to get Dawu to come to couples counselling with me in 2007. I even found a Chinese counsellor who had also worked in Canada, spoke English as well as Dawu's dialect of Chinese. Fan Xiuying focused on marriage and relationships and could give us some insight into fixing our marital problems. What more could we ask for? It had taken me a long time to find Mrs. Fan and she was lovely. Dawu and I set up an appointment for our initial meeting with the counsellor. We arranged to talk at a Starbucks since Dawu didn't want to go to an office.

The meeting was on Monday at 11 a.m. I was happy that we would be getting the help we needed. Then, two hours before the appointment, Dawu and I had a huge fight (over something little) and he told me he wasn't going to see Mrs. Fan. He was not keen on going anyway and the fight gave him an excuse. He had told me that Chinese people don't go to counselling, they worked things out through family and friends. What was I doing contacting a stranger about our problems anyway?

I phoned Mrs. Fan and she said she would talk to Dawu over the phone. She also offered to see us for free because she felt we needed the help that badly. I was frustrated and sad. Things were blowing up.

A few days later, I was doing NU2YU deliveries with one of my drivers when the phone rang. It was Mrs. Fan. I was excited to hear her voice as I thought she was calling to tell me Dawu was eager to sort things out.

"How did it go with Dawu?" I asked after we exchanged pleasantries.

"I wish I had better news for you," said Mrs. Fan. "I am not sure I can help you two. Dawu isn't interested in speaking to me. I am very sorry."

She added something about abuse and the Cultural Revolution but I wasn't listening at that point.

"I wish you luck," she said.

I was gutted. Dawu didn't want our marriage to work. That was what he was saying by not talking to Mrs. Fan. Tears ran down my cheeks. I was standing in the middle of the road, somewhere out in the northeastern suburbs of Beijing, and my world was falling apart. A million questions spun in my mind.

Would Dawu and I stay together?

Would I have to leave China?

What was going to happen to our awesome home?

What about the life that I had built up over the years?

Who was this man who couldn't manage a 20-minute phone call to save years invested in a marriage?

This was a new side of Dawu, one that was many shades darker than I had realized. The answers to those questions could wait. I needed to go back to the shop and carry on with the work of the day. I cleaned up my tears, drank some water from my bottle and asked the driver to take me home.

If Dawu didn't want strangers meddling in our relationship, I would try it his way. I would approach one of his friends, quietly on the side, and get help. I thought about who and it was obvious that Honghong and his wife Meili would be best suited to talk to Dawu. I contacted Meili and asked to meet with her and her husband. I didn't tell my husband what I was doing.

Honghong, Meili and I met in their garden courtyard. We had tea and ate some nuts and talked. I told them about how Dawu had refused counselling and that I was frustrated about the inequality of the income and paying bills. They shared my frustration but also let me know that Dawu was really trying to be a good family man.

Honghong said he knew living with an artist wasn't easy but I had to believe in Dawu and be patient. Honghong also suggested that he'd talk to Dawu about painting and paying the bills with the sales. I trusted Honghong would speak to Dawu. I left the meeting with a positive focus and would wait and have faith in the process.

Dawu and I were cooking in the kitchen a few weeks later when he told me that he had spoken to Honghong. Dawu then asked me if he could sell his work at the Front Line Gallery under the name Aaron Wu ... if it didn't harm his career. I told him that that was an amazing idea.

Dawu was talented in painting and drawing but didn't think it was challenging enough. This is why he was focused on building his conceptual art career with works that were either multimedia, big installations or video. He didn't want to be known as a painter. He had been creating art with an artist collective called the 008 Collective. Together, they pushed the boundaries of traditional art. Some of their works were experiences and resembled, in many ways, performance art. For example, the group travelled to Changbai Mountains, a range of mountains in Liaoning province on the border of North Korea.

The artists went in winter and created rock and ice installations and then returned in spring to video the thaw. The project was titled *LOOKING FOR MONSTERS IN CHANGBAI MOUNTAINS* and was based on a myth that there was an oversized human monster roaming the peaks. It was interesting and thought-provoking but it wasn't art that could be sold. It did satisfy Dawu's and his peers' artistic curiosity by concentrating on ideology that removed conventional artistic thinking. Dawu loved it.

While he was thinking outside the box with 008, he was also doing his own paintings for money. However, for some reason, his commercial works weren't selling in my gallery. I was frustrated. He was frustrated. Furthermore, Dawu needed more space, physical and otherwise. He was trying to paint at home but he needed so much room for his large canvases. As well, in the summer, our place was hot. He had moved to the basement of our building but there were no windows and the air quality was poor down there. He had to have better working conditions. In mid-2008, we agreed he needed an external studio.

A good solution was the 008 International Art Community. Some of the artists from the 008 Collective had signed 20-year leases with the Beijing Jinyu 008 Trading Company Ltd., a property management company. The artists formed the 008 International Art Community that was housed in a warehouse built around a courtyard. There was studio space available for Dawu in the compound so he inked a deal with the management company.

He was going to have a living space there too, as it would make things easier on our relationship. Dawu and I weren't engaged in full-on daily fights but there were a million little bitches, tits and tats, spits and spats and a few roaring arguments that signalled that we needed some time apart. His move would be a break of sorts as we both took a breather from our marriage. This way, I could carry on in our lovely apartment in downtown Beijing with Hannah. Dawu could visit us easily and was excited about the changes, especially his new studio.

Some of the 008 artists spent a lot of money fixing up their spaces to not only work and showcase their art but to house their families. Dawu didn't have a huge budget and this was a point of contention between us. He didn't have the money to do everything he wanted because I wasn't about to pay for it all. I did contribute a bit and with his own funds, he finished his studio so that he had a kitchenette, two bedrooms, a full bathroom and a huge living room and eating area. The space had large 6 metre (20 foot) windows and the natural light that streamed in from them was amazing. Perfect for making art!

Dawu, Hannah and I were still a family and I considered Dawu to be my partner even though we lived apart. We were going through a rough patch but neither of us considered divorce as an option. He was trying to bring in money by selling his pieces and I knew he was working hard.

Dawu was a serious artist and with his new studio, he could focus on creating instead of having to share space with me. It really did reduce the tension between us. I thought it was a huge step forward in our relationship and we might be able to live under the same roof again at some point. I was happier and so was he.

Dawu and the 008 International Art Community were busy creating a style of art that freed the artist from the conventional drawing, painting, sculpting arena. To put it plainly, they were allowing themselves to get weird and allow for creation. Probably one of the biggest pieces, as well as the most complicated and costly, was when the entire group (including wives and kids) went to Manila, Philippines, for a site-specific art exhibition called *7 DAYS*.

In the early spring of 2008, 10 artists from 008 Collective participated in the unique show. The massive project was sponsored by Osage Gallery in Hong Kong. Part of the *7 DAYS* project saw the artists taking up residence for a week at the University of Santo Tomas. The show was something the 008 artists wouldn't have been able to do easily in China. However, abroad and away from the always-watching government, the collective could do what it wanted. Dawu's piece was called *CAPTIVITY* and was part performance and part installation. He took the role of a prison guard and "watched" a makeshift cell for six days and nights straight. There were no actual prisoners, the project was more a statement about imprisoning the ego. The ego being a kind of prisoner to the human it dwells inside.

Dawu dressed the part of a prison guard and remained behind "bars." He had borrowed a security guard uniform from somewhere in Manila and stayed in the residence room for the whole week. Chao Hongling was also exhibiting there along with Gu Duanfan and seven others. All of the artists had similar lengths of stays and were happy to exit the university after the seven days were up.

The artists received a lot of local attention in Manila and word of their show spread to Hong Kong. China was not interested, though. Chinese artists who go overseas weren't in the spotlight unless they did something that the government deigned positive and brought great trade to the country. Most contemporary and avant-garde artists didn't do that in the eyes of the Chinese authorities.

While Dawu was ensconced in his art piece, I explored Manila with Hannah. Although the trip was for the art collective, it was nice for Hannah and me to relax and get to know another country.

Before and after Dawu went into his "prison," he stayed with us in a nice four-star hotel. There wasn't much intimacy between Dawu and me as Hannah was a handful and we were busy with the 008 group. It had been a long time since Dawu and I had been on a romantic date. By this point in our relationship, passion wasn't in our vocabulary. It seemed easier to let it go rather than try and bring it back into our lives.

I was proud that Dawu was part of the exhibit in Manila. The 008 Collective seemed to be really pushing the envelope, albeit not making money. It was an exciting time for Dawu and the group of artists. The exhibit was a good break for me, too. I was starting to fray from the pressure of work and life. I wondered if my relationship troubles with Dawu were common. I didn't talk about it with my girlfriends as it was too personal. Also, I felt a level of shame about the situation, especially with my friends who seemed to NOT have any problems with their spouses.

Dawu, Hannah and I returned to Beijing. There was no backlash over Dawu's prison guard show and he continued working on expressing his ideas in different ways. While he wasn't making money, Chao Hongling and Gu Duanfan were building strong careers. They were exhibiting internationally and doing very well. I thought Dawu would join their ranks soon.

In the spring of 2008, I brought a business partner, Nina, on board a new company. I had met Nina De Jong through a "momtrepreneur" group that I had been a part of for about three years. Nina, from the Netherlands, was trying to set up a furniture and accessory company in China. We met and realized that her idea worked well with one that I had been thinking about starting: a boutique selling new baby items, not second-hand. This included an interesting chair.

Lucien Bronginart was a friend of mine who worked for SAS, (the Scandinavian Airline Service) as a flight attendant. We met years ago when he answered one of my ads when I was looking for expats to photograph. I took Lucien's portrait and we became friends.

Lucien was based in Sweden and flew to Beijing almost every month and visited me often. On one trip, Lucien brought Dawu and I a Tripp Trapp highchair from Stokke, a Norwegian baby products company. The chair was in what looked to me like a million pieces but Lucien put it together quickly in front of my eyes. The high-end highchair grows with your child and I wondered how the chair would sell in my shop.

When the Tripp Trapp went up for sale in NU2YU, the response was overwhelming. It seemed everyone wanted to buy the chair. That was how Lucien became my supplier. He'd buy the highchairs off the Swedish version of eBay or Kijiji.ca and bring them to me as his carry-on luggage. Then, I'd buy them from him. I started to get so many requests for the chairs that I was months behind on orders. What to do?

How about finding out if I can get the Tripp Trapp chairs directly from the distributors?

I contacted a Stokke sales team and two Norwegian men were sent out to meet me. Alas, they weren't exactly sold on my second-hand store. They said I needed to re-arrange my idea.

"If you agree to open a boutique full of new baby and child products, we will supply you directly as the only store in Beijing selling Stokke."

While the offer sounded fantastic, I had to talk to Dawu. He liked the idea and we were both excited about the shop opportunity. (Not so much excited about writing the business plan though.) The Counting Sheep Boutique was born with Nina as a partner.

I now had two shops, the Counting Sheep Boutique and the NU2YU Baby Shop, in two units of my apartment building. While I was living on the 22nd floor, the NU2YU Baby Shop was in the basement and Counting Sheep was on the first floor in a two-bedroom apartment. The location for both places was ideal because it was close to the Sanlitun area, which had a high population of expats and wealthy Chinese people. I was in business.

8

I loved going to Saturday afternoon art openings. It was a big component of my life with Dawu. Being part of the art scene was exciting and different from how I would have spent my weekends had I lived in Canada. If I were home, I'd probably be hiking or biking or skiing down a mountain. Not in China. Life here was less active but no less dynamic.

Many of Dawu's activities were based on his artistic lifestyle. He would argue art theory and discourse and politics until the wee hours with his circle of artist friends. Their preferred time to meet and discuss topics of a wide range while drinking tea and smoking mountains of cigarettes was any time after 11 p.m. They'd be up into the wee hours and my husband often returned home just before the sun rose.

I never believed Dawu was fooling around on me, it was simply part of the art culture. Just like his hours. He almost never woke up before noon. He didn't temper his lifestyle after Hannah came along. This was partially why I stepped back from my own creative projects. The other reason was work. I was either at my businesses or with Hannah.

My daughter was a strong Mandarin Chinese speaker but her English was only OK. Her English grammar was basically Chinese translated into English – cute but not correct. She had many friends, loved her teachers and school and enjoyed activities such as swimming and gymnastics. She knew she was loved by both her mother and father and we would do everything in our power to protect her.

When Dawu moved into his studio at the 008 International Art Community, I thought we were pushing the reset button. He would spend some time on his own and then come back to me. However, moving to 008 only drove us further apart.

My husband had always been politically minded and when we first got together, he was focused more on shaking his head over some of the Chinese government's decisions. Dawu rarely got directly involved with issues. Over the years, though, he was getting increasingly agitated by the state of affairs in China. I remember taking buses with him through older Beijing neighbourhoods and he was so upset that the traditional buildings were being torn down to make way for shopping malls or skyscraper. He couldn't contain his disappointment that the PRC was choosing "new China" over "traditional China."

Dawu was not materialistic at all and he hated the swooning over making money. He was a proud Chinese who loved the history and culture, specifically old traditional Chinese culture, and he saw it being removed and erased because the authorities were giving in to making a quick buck. That sort of materialism embodied new China and new China was often out of reach for many Chinese people.

My husband also spoke out for those who didn't have a voice. When an Italian girl was brutally murdered nearby our home in the summer of 2006, Dawu thought the police weren't doing enough to find the perpetrator. He stayed out on the street where she was killed and organized a candlelight vigil for her. Dawu had a big heart and wore it on his sleeve.

When Liu Xiaobo, a writer, scholar and critic in China, created Charter 08, Dawu discovered something he could wholeheartedly support. Charter 08 was a petition calling for immediate government reforms in China. Even though the charter was published on Wednesday, Dec. 10, 2008 (the 60th anniversary of the Universal Declaration of Human Rights), it had started to float around the country and online earlier in the fall.

The charter was a suggestion to the government to adjust its power and the way it governed. It was not a call to overthrow the regime. Over 300 people, including Chinese lawyers, government officials and dissidents, risked their freedom by signing the charter. Dawu also put his signature on the document.

By signing the charter, Dawu was risking arrest and jail. Nevertheless, he did it. He put his family and livelihood on the line because he believed he could make a difference and slow down new China. Dawu has always been somewhat different and unlike many who were addicted to the new money coming into the country, he wanted no part of it.

Other signatories to the charter included prominent Chinese citizens inside and outside the government: Bao Tong, a former senior Communist Party official, Chinese-Tibetan poet and essayist Woeser, — and of course, Ai Weiwei. Charter 08 was looking for adjustments in areas such as law. It called for 19 changes, including an independent legal system, freedom of association and the elimination of one-party rule. Liu Xiaobo and the others involved in writing, drafting and editing the petition weren't preaching revolution. However, the authorities took the manifesto as harsh criticism. The people in charge were not open to any sort of change or opinion on how they should rule. The People's Republic did not serve the public.

The charter was a hefty document and brought up many points that most people from Western countries take for granted, such as freedom of the press. It was stunning to read the manifesto and know that the liberties that exist in many places in the world, didn't exist in China. As a Canadian in Beijing, my life hadn't yet been affected by the Chinese government but I would soon know what it was like not to have access to an independent judicial system.

The Chinese government didn't want attention drawn to its broken and one-sided systems and so said little publicly about the charter. Instead of listening and responding, the authorities arrested Liu Xiaobo on Dec. 8, 2008. The dozen or so police who swarmed his home around 9 p.m. carried a warrant for his arrest on "suspicion of inciting subversion of state power." They took him away to a secret location outside of Beijing. The oligarchy was demonstrating that it had no reason to change. There was absolutely no room for dissension.

Ai Weiwei's name was on the 08 Charter. Many people around the world looked up to the famous artist. He easily accessed English social media platforms, namely Twitter, as he spoke English well. He was impressive in almost every sense of the word. Galleries wanted him, journalists needed him (for his perspective and ability to express himself without a translator-interpreter) and the community regarded him well.

Ai created installation artworks as well as videos about people who had been wronged by the government, and, because he could push the envelope further than other Chinese critics, got away with it. I've always felt that had he been a regular Chinese artist or dissident from a nobody background, he would have been *accidentally suicided*. Accidently suicided was a term used to describe an accidental death that was probably more like a setup. For example, if there was a dissident that the government didn't want to deal with anymore, he or she may "fall" out a window. The death will look like he or she leaned too far out when actually, the person was pushed. It was a common way of getting rid of people during the Cultural Revolution. However, the government didn't want common citizens to learn from Ai Weiwei. The regime wanted Ai to be disliked and treated with suspicion. In the Chinese media, the authorities made him out to be an evil man and not to be trusted.

Dawu was supportive of Ai Weiwei and liked what he was doing for the underdog in China. For me, Ai was one of those Chinese artists who had totally made it not only in China but everywhere. He was talented and many of the big curators and galleries internationally wanted a piece of Ai

Weiwei. He was big in stature and big in personality and reputation – he was in demand. I had seen him at art shows but he didn't know who I was. To me, he seemed untouchable and unapproachable. However, I was basing my knowledge of Ai on myth, rumour and hype swirling in the art community.

I stumbled back into the art community in January 2009 with the Beijing Color Studio. It started as a sort of accident. The business began on a whim one winter's Saturday afternoon after a friend asked if Dawu would be open to spending a few hours painting with her kids. She'd pay him for the materials, time and expertise.

The day with the children went well and Dawu and I thought about holding regular workshops for kids in his 008 studio. It wasn't long afterwards that we started the Beijing Color Studio with mostly expats as clients. I was the chief organizer, as Dawu didn't speak English. At first, we held one-on-one classes. The daylong sessions included Dawu working with the kids so that by the end, they'd have produced a painting. My husband was patient with the little ones and brought out talents from children aged 12 months to 12 years.

I felt that the painting workshops were great for Dawu and I. We spent more time together developing the idea and then running the workshops. However, Dawu felt that the classes prevented him from spending time on his real art. He was becoming more and more involved in the governance of the 008 community, too. He was a real leader, a risk-taker, and the artists there appreciated those skills.

I could tell that Dawu was becoming quickly frustrated with the workshops. He wanted to be out doing his own thing and not hanging out with expat English-speaking families. Anyone who met us together would think we had a great relationship but we started fighting when clients weren't around.

It was spring 2009 when I closed NU2YU. It had about three or so good years but it was a lot of work at the end of the day. As well, the niche market for gently-used Western baby items was waning. More and more products were making their way into Beijing. A massive charity shop, Roundabout, opened by a woman from the U.K. in 2008, was diverting business from my business. Roundabout's prices were lower, too, because items were donated to the thrift store and not sold on consignment like NU2YU. I couldn't compete and decided to close my doors.

I remained at the Counting Sheep Boutique with Nina. There was more money and prestige associated with this shop because it sold new merchandise. Also, the boutique held classes and was a community hub.

Dawu and I were both stressed about money. I was working a lot to pay for our nice home and Dawu was frustrated that his career was slow. He had some good exhibitions and works but he wasn't seeing much in the way of overseas invitations or sales. (Mind you, he wasn't looking for sales, necessarily.) Our condo was also dragging us down. It was hard to keep up with the mortgage payments.

I was giving everything I had to my businesses, daughter and relationships. Except it was piecemeal. I felt like I was a part-time entrepreneur, part-time mother, part-time wife and part-time friend. I was little bits of things and my life was being frittered away.

Dawu looked after Hannah from time to time. Co-parenting with him was fine but not perfect. I was still the primary caregiver and at least he made the effort to be around. Hannah was young and went with the flow. She was her happy little self most days.

For all intents and purposes, Dawu and I were still married. I did miss having him around the house. The common threads that bound us tightly together were our daughter and the art scene. As long as we had those, we couldn't be torn apart.

9

The same problems that were in our marriage kept cropping up in our separation. The major one was money. I felt wholly responsible for the mortgage on our condo and the household bills. Dawu had hardly contributed to our family funds in the past and now that he was out on his own, I rarely saw any money from him. I worked so much and worked so hard and I still was living paycheque to paycheque.

Our condo was becoming a burden but I loved it so much. So did Dawu. It was a dream home: nice airy rooms, large outdoor spaces and the building was in a great location. It was the first piece of real estate that I had ever owned. I didn't want to sell it. Nevertheless, it was a home meant for a family and only Hannah and I lived in it. Our neighbours, Lena and Xing Kui, had sold their place for a nice little profit about eight months earlier. Dawu and I thought we should do the same in May 2009 while the condo market was hot.

I told myself that I had to sell the condo if I wanted to be debt-free. In the spring, Dawu and I listed our place. It didn't take long to sell, about 30 days. I felt gutted while we were in the negotiation room with the buyers. I loved my home and didn't want to let it go. However, Dawu and I did very well on the investment and tripled our money in about five years. That was the one upside.

The physical move was heartbreaking and overwhelming. Hannah stayed with friends while all of our stuff — all my stuff — was boxed up, loaded into a truck and hauled away. I had hired a moving company to pack everything. I had no interest or energy or emotional strength to move us.

My entire household was taken to Dawu's 008 studio. I cried all the way there and cried while the movers unloaded my things into Dawu's space. I didn't have a new place to put anything yet and the 008 studio was large enough to act as temporary storage. I was now officially homeless.

I had tried to get another place a few weeks earlier. In a brief spell of optimism, Dawu and I had thought that we would take the earnings from the sale of our condo and invest in a live/work space for both of us. We had driven by a place close to 798 called Manke Space. Dawu asked around about it and found a contact person, Ouyang Shi.

We had lunch with Ouyang Shi and he told us we could rent one or two units on a long-term contract. Dawu and I could renovate the space to be more like a home, not just a studio. We actually put down a deposit and were excited about the prospect of our new uber-cool home and the possibility of being a whole family again. I had even thought about revisiting my photography work. However, while Dawu and I were at a party with some artists, we overheard some people talking about how the Manke Space was going to be demolished … soon.

How could this be? Dawu was FUMING. The next day, he confronted Mr. Ouyang, who was caught with his pants down. He sheepishly admitted to the deception and gave us our money back, not a *fen* missing. Dawu was pissed off and it was another blow to our possibility of starting over. Our decision of staying together or breaking up changed on a daily basis but without having a home we picked out as a couple, the choice was made for us.

I knew that I did not want to live with Dawu in his 008 studio. It was his space. Not mine. I'd feel like I had to tiptoe around him. Fortunately, Emma Porter let Hannah and I stay with her and her daughter Jenny for a week or so before we left for Canada for the summer. Emma was Canadian, too, and we met in Beijing a few years prior. Jenny was around the same age as Hannah and they were best friends.

June was a mixed bag of emotions for me. I was mostly sad and when the month was over, I went to Canada. I flew home to get away from Dawu and China. I was tired of him and tired of China. The children's painting party workshops that Dawu was doing with me were successful but he wasn't into it as much as I was. Understandably, though, as he wanted to get on with making conceptual art. I didn't want to push him about expanding the Beijing Color Studio business because I could see that he was frustrated with me. The feelings were the same on my side. He was frustrating to me.

We were fighting and annoyed with each other. I wanted to have some time on my own and take Hannah to show her more of Canada. She had been there twice but had been so young. She was now close to five years old and I wanted to give her more memories with her gran, aunt and uncle and cousins.

Perhaps when I returned to China, Dawu and I could sort things out. Or was this the end? I constantly swung from wanting a divorce, to not wanting a divorce. I didn't want to be a single mom nor did I want to leave China. It had been my home for a long time and I felt more at ease there than in Canada. All my friends, my community, many of my coming-of-age memories were in China. I was scared of moving back to Canada with no job and starting from scratch with a child. However, I would have the support of my family. That was one attraction of calling Canada home again.

I returned to Calgary with Hannah for a five-week trip in the summer. We went camping with my family, visited friends and hung out with my mom. Then, Hannah and I flew to B.C. and saw my dad and stepmom and other friends. At the end of August, it was time to go home.

Home. I didn't have one. I felt displaced. Perhaps I should just turn around and stay in Canada. I had been doing some job searching while I was in Calgary and connected with some galleries but I didn't know what I wanted. I think the people there could tell my heart wasn't in it. I was wishy-washy when speaking to anyone about employment and didn't have any concrete start dates. I was coming from embassy work and being an entrepreneur for several years and was at loose ends.

My family and friends in the city were supportive of me coming home. They'd love more time with Hannah and of course, would help me with my transition. I still had the Counting Sheep Boutique and maybe Nina would let me be an owner based in Calgary. Maybe she'd buy me out? I had many hours to think during the flight from Canada to Beijing and I made up my mind. I was going back to my roots.

My biggest worry was telling Dawu that I was taking his daughter thousands of kilometres away. He was waiting for us at the airport when we arrived in Beijing. He had made an effort to pick us up, organizing a friend with a car to drive him to the terminal. Dawu was happy to see both Hannah and me. I decided I should tell him right then and there about Canada.

We were at the airport Starbucks when I told him Hannah and I would be moving back to Canada. I had half-expected he'd make a scene but he didn't. He simply asked me to explain why. When I told him it was time that I returned home, he agreed it might be for the best. His shoulders slumped and I knew he was clearly disappointed with my decision. What other choice did I have? Our relationship was on hold and we didn't have the tools to move forward. He wouldn't go to counselling and he wouldn't work on us. I couldn't sit around waiting for him. I had to get on with life. Without him.

Dawu reluctantly dropped us off at Emma's and then went home to his studio. It was good to be back in Beijing with a plan. I was making the best decisions for Hannah and me and I couldn't wait to tell my friends that I was going home. Dawu would survive. He would still see his daughter, just not regularly. Maybe he would come and see us in Canada.

Before I had left for Canada, I bought a car from an expat who was soon to be leaving China. The vehicle was a Honda Fit and I paid with it with some of the money from the condo sale. I studied and passed (with flying colours - 95 per cent) the English version of the Chinese driver's test. There was no road exam, only a computer test of about 100 questions. Some of the questions were hilarious, such as "It is OK to drive with flip flops on?"

No.

My new-to-me vehicle was supposed to be a great convenience for whatever direction my life was going. That was before I had decided to head to Canada. Now the car was a nuisance. I can't drive it to Calgary. Maybe I could ship it to the Canadian West Coast and then drive it home? At any rate, it was nice to have a vehicle now so I could get out of Emma's hair from time to time and run errands.

In August 2009, Dawu and I hosted an adult-only painting and wine party as part of our Beijing Color Studio. It went well but I was too focused on leaving China to think about it as a business model. I had started my re-location plan and was getting my ducks in a row. Dawu and I weren't on the best of terms. We always seemed to be fighting. Over the same thing for the millionth time. Money.

Dawu had finished a well-paid commission a couple of weeks after I got back from Canada. I would have liked it if he garnered some more of these projects. This one had come to him easily. In May, he had been asked by an expat family to paint their portrait. They were about to leave China and return to the U.S. They asked Dawu, who was an exceptional portrait artist, to paint them with their four children.

It was a simple request and Dawu had ample time to complete the piece. This was his first commission in a long time and it was a great oppor-tunity to get his name out in the expat community as a commission artist. At the end, the family was pleased with Dawu's work and I was pleased they liked it. I hoped it would give Dawu a chance to do more of this type of work. Nope. After he finished the piece, he said he didn't want to be known as a commission artist, he wanted to develop his practice as a conceptual artist. I had to throw my hands up in the air.

I think Dawu needed me but was too proud to tell me. Instead of attracting me to him by being kind, he was mean and always put me down. He criticized me and that made it hard for me to want to spend time with him, even as a friend. I didn't feel he was spending quality time with Hannah, either. This further fuelled my interest in returning home to Canada.

Dawu was stressed as well but he took it out in a different way than me.

I might have a drink or two but Dawu found something — someone — else. I found this out by accident.

I was planning Hannah's fifth birthday party. We were holding it at Dawu's studio and I had a car full of helium balloons to drop off there. I didn't tell Dawu I was coming and arrived at his studio early in the evening. There was a light on in his room but when I went to open the door, it was locked. That was weird. It was usually open.

I knocked and Dawu answered the door in his underwear. That part wasn't so weird. I'd seen him in less. Then, a body, a female's body, darted across the room behind him.

"Who was that?" I asked.

He wouldn't answer.

I loosely tied the balloons to a bannister and walked quickly to the back room where a woman was hiding behind the door.

"Who are you?" I asked her.

She didn't have to tell me. I knew at that moment.

She was a prostitute.

I walked back to Dawu and told him in no uncertain terms that the woman must be gone by the morning. Then, I got into my car, slammed the door and drove away crying. Dawu texted a couple of minutes later, saying he told the woman to leave immediately. Like it mattered.

I was angry, hurt and upset all at once. Even though Dawu and I were separated, I felt betrayed. I had a horrible sleep and in the morning, I returned to the studio with Hannah as if nothing had happened. Then, because the universe wanted to laugh at me some more, I discovered the balloons had worked themselves loose and risen to the top of the 12-metre high ceiling. Crap.

Dawu and I made our way through the party and Hannah was none the wiser. The next day, Dawu and I agreed to meet for lunch to talk about *Her.* We sat in the afternoon sun and had lunch at the Art Café in 798. Then he told me the story.

Dawu said his summer had sucked ever since I had left. He was alone and he was overwhelmed by the renovation work he was doing on his 008 studio. He had gone along with friends to a bathhouse. Many folks in China, mostly men, still bathed and showered at public bathhouses. It was a traditional thing to do. However, bathhouses sometimes could involve other, less desirable activities, depending on what you were into. This is how Dawu met the woman. He said she was a student who was doing this to make money to help send her brother to school in Beijing.

I knew that Dawu didn't stray outside our wedding vows while we were living together. His story made sense. I listened and told him I was disappointed. He apologized profusely.

We remained separated.

August 2009 was a rocky period. There were many ups and downs and I was emotionally drained. I didn't want to live with Dawu in his studio, but I couldn't keep living off the kindness of friends. It was clear that I would need to find my own space. However, how could I sign a yearly lease when I was going to move around the world sooner than later?

Then, Dawu and I were both essentially homeless. Dawu and the people at the 008 artist village were being evicted. They were given until October 2009 to pack up and leave. The explanation was that the land was going to be converted to higher density buildings. Reading between the lines: luxury-style condos were going to be developed on 008 land.

Dawu was angry, as it had taken him so long to find a suitable place to live and work. What would he do now? How would he get his money back? Where would he go? It also spelled the end of our Beijing Color Studio.

In China, it wasn't easy to challenge an eviction notice, or any sort of notice, from the authorities. It was a top-down society. The power usually stayed at the top. People lower down did not have much of a say in anything. Well, the 008 group was going to try to say something.

It started organizing a protest about the unfair treatment and to ask for money back. Dawu was leading the charge for compensation. The eviction was, in many ways, the beginning of the end of Dawu's freedom in China. He set off a domino effect that eventually led to his illegal detention.

PART TWO

"Injustice anywhere is a threat to justice everywhere."
Dr. Martin Luther King Jr.

"To criticize is not to overthrow the state."
Tan Zuoren, human rights activist, Aug. 2009

"China's Communist Party should 'retire with grace'...
in any country, the real change must come to people,
to individual creativity,...
Under the totalitarian system, without freedom,
that opportunity to utilize individual creativity stops...
elections are an important symbol of democracy since that gives
people some sort of power to control to change, and that also gives
them some kind of responsibility and involvement."
Dalai Lama, in talks with Barak Obama, White House, Feb. 2010

I was getting everything sorted out so I could move on and away from China. I hadn't raised the possibility of selling the Counting Sheep Boutique with my partner Nina yet, but it was on my mind. If I returned to Canada, I could use the money from the sale of the business plus the sale of my condo to buy a home back home.

The company had garnered an award nomination for me. A boutique customer liked my business ethos and put my name forward for *Entrepreneur of the Year*, a category in the Women in Business Awards. It was my first time being nominated for anything and I was excited my company had been recognized.

The winners were announced at a gala in June, before I left for Canada. I had gone to the event but hadn't bothered writing an acceptance speech. There were many women doing great work and I was happy to be in a category with them. I knew I probably wouldn't win. I went to the evening event for the food, to network and to sit with my fellow female entrepreneurs. The Entrepreneur of the Year went to a woman who had created a charity and was doing good work for impoverished people in China.

Nina and I sat together at the gala and met other businesswomen and shared trade secrets about doing business in China. I was introduced to Stephanie Miller at the event. Stephanie, an American, and I hit it off. She was an anchor in the art scene and we knew many of the same people. She loved Dawu's work and felt he was a strong artist. We promised to keep in touch.

Another one of my businesses was also winding down. The days of painting parties were ending at the 008 Beijing Color Studio since Dawu was being evicted. I organized a few more workshops in September 2009 but that was it. I wasn't too upset, as it was just a matter of time before construction started on the 008 land.

Moving home was my focus and I was set on going to Canada. I even hosted a large going-away party for myself and 40 guests on Saturday, Sept. 19. The event was held at the Orchard Restaurant, a nice place with a lovely garden in the Shunyi District. I had hired a band and paid for the food and was looking forward to seeing my friends. I wanted to go out of China with a bang!

On the way to the restaurant, Dawu and I had a huge blowout fight in my car. In front of Hannah. Dawu was angry and mean to me. He told me that he was glad I was leaving China. He said I sucked as an expat and never gave Beijing a chance. He said I wouldn't succeed in Canada either because I was a horrible businessperson. His words surprised and hurt me.

I had no idea he felt that way about me. I had imagined he would be celebrating my return to Canada alongside me. We had worked hard to stay friends and support each other. But he obviously couldn't wait to get rid of me. Starting right then and there.

"Let me out of the car," he said. "I'm not going to your party."

I stopped the vehicle at the side of the road and he got out. Nothing I said was going to change his mind. He refused to get back in the Honda.

I couldn't shield Hannah from the argument. She knew her parents were both terribly upset. I was a bit embarrassed showing up at the restaurant without Dawu. I told people he wasn't feeling well. Everyone seemed to accept that. I couldn't accept the way Dawu had berated me. I was sad and confused but it cemented my reasons for leaving. I was sick of him being angry and yelling at me. It used to be over things like money and time — big things in a relationship; however, now he was turning things personal and attacking me.

I took a mental step back in the restaurant and slowed my breathing. I was going to enjoy my party. This was a treat for me, Hannah and our friends. The turnout was great and everyone signed a guest book and gave me gifts. Everyone who was invited showed up except for Dawu.

In the days leading up to my bon voyage party, he had told me he was fine with me leaving. Nevertheless, he was now angry and upset. His actions did not match his words.

The next day, Hannah and I, along with Emma and Jenny, went hiking along the Great Wall in the Huairou District. That was when I had an epiphany.

I was hurting Dawu by taking his daughter to Canada.

He didn't want her to leave. He didn't want me to leave.

Instead of asking me to stay, he was pushing me away.

Maybe I could stay in Beijing if I separated my life from his.

By the time I got back to the car, I had changed my plans.

I was remaining in China.

China had been my home for the past 13 years. I had friends, businesses and a community here. As well, I couldn't take Hannah away from her father. However, it wasn't just that. A small part of my reason to stay was intuition. I sensed that I couldn't go. I felt I needed to be in Beijing and no matter how much I argued with myself, that nagging feeling would not go away.

My friends in China and Canada were shocked that I had decided to stick around Beijing. Dawu was happy but of course, not overly demonstrative about the change in plans. He asked how I could be so indecisive.

There was no question that Dawu and I loved each other. Nevertheless, we had cultural, personality and economic barriers to overcome and it was obvious that these had formed into thick and high walls. Dawu, as always, had managed to break some cracks in mine.

While he was living at 008, he was spending some time with Hannah. At the same time, he was getting more and more wrapped up in the battle for compensation. Dawu and the other artists from 008 were being forced from their properties and taking on the government in the fall of 2009. Usually, people never thought about asking the authorities for money in exchange for losing their homes. It was a losing battle since the regime swatted away the nuisances. Not this time. This time, the challengers were well-educated and well-connected.

The residents of 008 knew what they had signed up for because they had understood the contracts and their agreements with the government. Dawu and his artist colleagues had, in essence, signed long-term lease agreements and paid to live and work in buildings on state-owned land. It was there in black and white: access to studio space for 20 years. By forcing the artists off the property, the government was proving it held no regard for its citizens. The contracts had been a waste of paper.

I had found that contracts in China were generally not worth the paper they were written on. The words weren't binding and it was a huge issue surrounding Chinese and Western business deals. Agreements were often ignored by the Chinese government and foreigners couldn't do much to enforce obligations. Furthermore, a contract seemed to be only a starting point, and negotiations could carry on past the signing date. This caused a lot of confusion, anger and complicated business dealings between Chinese and foreigners. If the Chinese authorities didn't care about the formality of contracts with outsiders, it definitely didn't care about its people.

Dawu needed his space for his livelihood. His studio gave him the breadth to expand and build ideas. A creative space is essential to any artist and for Dawu; it couldn't be at home where his role was as father and husband, among many others. Even though we hadn't invested much into 008, we were out-of-pocket ¥50,000 RMB (CAD 8,500). It wasn't a huge loss but it was a loss. The money was worth fighting for in the end (or so we thought then). Meanwhile, other artists were in a much worse position than us.

They were losing their homes as well as studios, galleries and workspaces. Some said they weren't going to move from 008 and were going to hold onto their properties no matter what the government said. There was no way they were going to let the development company take over the land without a fight. Leading the battle was Dawu.

Even though Dawu had left 008 by November, the artists there had made him their *lingdao* (leader). I found that out when I saw a chart on a 008 studio wall listing all the members and who was in charge of what. Dawu's name was at the top — right at the top. I wasn't too happy about his new position and thought he was using the protest as a way to avoid work.

Dawu walked right into the role of commanding his beleaguered colleagues. He was angry that they were getting evicted, presumably by a development company that wanted to *chai* (knock down) the artist compound to make way for luxury condos. He was more ticked off when artists in a neighbouring creative village, the Zhengyang Art Community, were also given eviction notices. There was a major fight brewing between the collectives and the government.

The land grab by greedy developers and the government officials was nothing new. It had been a thorn in the side of many peasants and homeowners across China for decades. It was an unfortunate result of mad-paced development that had started in the country in the 1990s. The government and companies were ruthless and grabbed property. There was rarely market value compensation handed out.

Dawu, the 008 collective and Zhengyang collective did reach out to the government with a diplomatic approach at first. The artists began with petitions, organizing meetings with authorities, etc., to try to stop both artist villages from being destroyed. In the summer of 2009, they held rallies and demonstrations near the 008 and Zhengyang to no avail. No one who counted was listening. The artists were going to lose their money and their homes at the whim of a development company that had the backing of local authorities. The artists were screwed and losing their patience for polite discourse.

The plight of the 008 and Zhengyang artists wasn't getting the traction it needed to change the government's mind about paying the artists what they deserved. No one inside or outside of China was broadcasting the horrendous stories of the state getting away with forced evictions coupled with lousy financial compensation. The lack of interest in the issue was frustrating for Dawu and the rest of the artists and the eviction deadline was looming. They had until the end of October to move on.

For me, the end of October was filled with travel and a new prospect. I was fortunate to attend my father's 80th birthday in B.C. Dad paid for my ticket and I left Hannah with Dawu while I travelled to Canada. I used the visit as a working holiday and also flew to Calgary to do a bit of legwork for a project I had been thinking about for a long time.

Since 2000, I'd been approaching Calgary galleries to see if any of them were interested in being part of a Chinese contemporary art exhibition. I felt strongly about it because I thought the city could benefit from the introduction of Chinese contemporary art. It was interesting and collectors in Vancouver and Toronto were already buying and investing in the art. I was determined to have a show in Calgary someday.

In the summer of 2008, I had a bite. A Canadian art curator, John Franklin, liked my idea of bringing Chinese artists to Canadian cities where they'd create art. Finally, someone was finally listening to me and seeing the value in what I had to offer and could appreciate Chinese contemporary art. I was excited. This had been a sort of dream of mine for many years.

John and I promised to keep in touch. He had unanswered questions, such as who would fund the project. I said I would do some work on my end. I returned to Beijing happy I had found a home for my artistic vision.

Meanwhile, since it was the end of October, Dawu and the 008 and Zhengyang artists were supposed to be out of the compounds. They had been told to move by the end of the month. But there was no way they were going to listen. On Saturday, Oct. 31, Dawu and some other property owners dug in their heels and refused to leave. They were staying.

The local authorities retaliated by ordering the electricity and water be cut off, making living conditions at the compounds untenable in the cold weather. Dawu and his group of activists tried pushing back. There was a scuffle when his group protested against the workers who came to turn off the utilities. Dawu called me and asked me to witness the protest. He thought the police wouldn't do anything too rash if an expat was present.

I arrived towards the end of the struggle. I was slow getting there because although I wanted to support Dawu, I also didn't want to get into trouble. Right after I showed up, a young artist, Dou Xiaojun, was hauled off to jail. He was one of Dawu's former students and as his teacher, Dawu was horrified. He felt responsible for Dou.

Everyone was worried about the young man and I drove Dawu to the police station as quickly as possible. Gu Duanfan and others followed us there. Dou was eventually released after a few hours but not before Dawu and his crew had spouted off to police about what had happened.

Dawu was fired up after the event, as was Gu and several of the others. It fuelled verbal abuse and anger towards the officers at the detachment. Dawu and his group yelled and swore at the police. The artists were pissed that the authorities had the audacity to shut off the utilities, let alone evict them. This was going to be a long winter.

That day was Ground Zero for Dawu and the artists he led. That was the first time someone from the 008 and Zhengyang art communities had been detained. Even though Dou hadn't even spent a full day in jail, the authorities had shown their might vis-à-vis Dou's short detention. It was a warning: the next time, the police might not be so lenient. Despite the caution from the cops, Dawu realized he had to do something bigger to catch the attention of the world. Otherwise, the artists would just be beaten until they went away.

With colder temperatures coming and the heat off, it was impossible for Dawu to stay in 008. He decided to leave. He could afford to do this. Others couldn't and stayed behind. Leaving didn't mean Dawu was done in the fight for justice. It meant he had to figure out another way to protest the evictions.

Now that Hannah and I were staying in Beijing, I had to find a new home for us. We couldn't keep staying with friends. Sophie Baker, another friend who let us stay in her place when she was away, and Emma, had both been so kind. However, my daughter and I needed our own space. That was how we ended up at the Cappuccino residential complex. The rent was reasonable and the condo was a good size -- three bedrooms.

I was working since the Counting Sheep Boutique was still in business. However, Nina and I closed our second shop in the Shunyi District. It wasn't profitable and the amount of effort to get it out of the red wasn't worth our while. My partnership with Nina was also under some stress. She wanted out of the company, along with her investment. I wasn't sure what was happening with the books and who owed who what amount so I hired an accountant to reconcile the paperwork. Nevertheless, I kept busy delivering online orders, attending various bazaars around the expat communities and networking.

Attending my Beijing TaiTais Book Club meetings kept me sane. Reading was always something I made time for and I loved getting together once a month with the group. We were good about discussing the book we were reading but we also kept things social with dinner and drinks.

I felt like I had a good life balance after I decided to stay in China. I had friends, both Chinese and expat, I could meet for coffee or a meal or just hang out with our kids. I was straddling both communities and didn't feel out of place in either. Despite the unravelling of Dawu and me, life was rich and I was eager to see what was around the corner.

A large part of keeping grounded was my sessions with a counsellor from the U.S., Dana Lee. Since 2007, Dana had been helping me sort out myself and come to terms with my relationship with Dawu. She made me understand that no matter what happened to Dawu and me as husband and wife, we still needed to be dad and mom to Hannah. Lessons like these were important and I wanted Dawu to benefit from talking to Dana as well. But counselling was off the table for him. He wasn't open to it. Period.

Another thing that cleared up some scars on my heart was joining an Adult Children of Alcoholics group. Dana had suggested that I go and explore my childhood growing up with an alcoholic. My mother was an intelligent woman and I loved her with all my heart. Nevertheless, she struggled all her life with addiction, primarily alcohol and low self-esteem.

I had never dealt with that in a meaningful way before attending the group and I learned a lot about mom, my family and me. I also wanted to make sure that I knew who I was and that I wasn't passing along any damaging thoughts and actions to Hannah.

In November 2009, I saw John Franklin again. The Canadian curator was in Beijing and I hosted him for a day. I introduced him to the 798 Art District and some galleries. We met Dawu, who had been keen on the Canadian site-specific project, as well as other artists who were also interested in going to Canada to work. The exhibition would be a chance to create fresh new pieces while in different cities instead of dragging old work to Canada from China.

I felt good about this professional artistic opportunity. It was right up my alley and I had some great connections in China. It would be a good start to an art career in Calgary if I ever did return to my home city. I was glad John visited when he did because it was during the annual 798 art exhibition that showcased performance and contemporary art. There were many interesting artists at work and openings happening. It was easy for me to show John around when there was such a flurry of activity. We parted with promises to keep in touch. There were still many things to consider and work out.

Around the same time, Dawu found a new studio in the back of 798 at 2 Jiuxianqiao Road. He had been desperate to find another place before 008 was flattened by bulldozers. When he moved into 798, he brought along a large dead snake that he had acquired that year. It was a sculpture reference (a model) for a piece of personal artwork that he had made -- a larger-than-life-sized plaster replica of the snake.

China was such a place where all sorts of materials were readily available for whatever you wanted to do, from snakes to body parts. You just needed to have a concept and some money or connections or both. One of the most famous avant-garde artworks coming out of China in the past 20 years or so involved a performance by a quirky artist by the name of Zhu Yu.

Zhu Yu did a piece of performance artwork during the Third Shanghai Biennale in Shanghai in 2000. He ate parts of a human baby. The work, *EATING PEOPLE*, involved the artist boiling and consuming some of a fetus he said he stole from a medical school. Despite the incredible and obvious shock value, he was pushing the envelope and raising issues about morality. He was later prosecuted for the work.

Dawu didn't eat the snake he bought. He didn't know what kind of serpent it was but its scales were a mixture of grey, blue and brown. The snake, which measured 1.5 metres (5 ft.) long and 12.7 centimetres (5 in.) in diameter, was alive when it came into Dawu's possession but it met a terrible end. He put the reptile into a big clear jar of alcohol and it thrashed around until it drowned.

I thought the serpent muse was creepy but Dawu didn't. He was an artist and the snake was simply another piece of material to use for an art project. The jar with the dead reptile travelled with Dawu from 008 to 798, where it sat in a quiet corner and watched him and anyone else who came into the studio.

Dawu's new space worked out well in terms of location. He lived closer to the Cappuccino apartment so we worked out a more regulated parenting schedule. Nevertheless, Dawu was spending less and less time with his daughter.

Dawu was becoming consumed by the 008 and Zhengyang fight for compensation. He was the leader of the movement and it suited him. Dawu was a natural boss. He was charismatic, well-spoken, smart and fair. (Unlike many of China's political leaders in this period.) As well, Dawu wasn't willing to cut his losses on the soon-to-be-razed studio/home/workspace. He was upset that others were going to lose out to a government that did not care. It took whatever it wanted, whenever.

Dawu believed that if the artists worked together, they'd get their money back. He was willing to be their leader because he had the time, the vision — and most importantly, the fire.

Sometimes, I wished Dawu had put as much energy into rebuilding our relationship or creating art that made money or at least, art that could be collected. That time was over.

As friends, Dawu and I continued to go to art exhibitions and other events together. I still cared for him even though we were always bickering.

Despite Dawu being a bit of a rogue, he found a space for me to resurrect the Beijing Color Studio. We went to see it in early December 2009. It was a large studio next to our friend and avant-garde artist, Ma Ling. Several years earlier, Ma Ling had encouraged me to date Dawu and she was the one who had told Dawu about this place.

While at the space, Dawu and I fought over little things and big things, such as the amount of money I was going to spend on making the studio my own. Urgh. Why did we fight over stupid things all the time? Why was he so controlling? Why couldn't he just let me have the lights that I wanted?

I think it was because he was so involved with 008 and Zhengyang that he had a hard time switching hats from "leader" to "friend."

I was looking forward to having a space all to myself. It would be all mine, too. Dawu and I were talking about divorcing. It was sad but inevitable. We were living separate lives. All we had in common was our daughter and a love of art.

In mid-December, Dawu and I met at Starbucks at the Lido Hotel, not far from 798, to plan our eventual parting. I told my soon-to-be-ex-husband I was unhappy staying in our marriage but I needed him for my visa. Despite having been married to a Chinese national and having spent 13 years in China, I still required a visa, obtained through Dawu, to live in the country. I was dependent on him for that one thing.

Dawu and I also talked about our lifestyle changes and directions. We had drifted apart. The only thing left to do for Dawu and I as a couple was get a divorce. Official separation wasn't a thing in China. You were either married or not. I told him he needed to still be in Hannah's life as her father — not an occasional babysitter. His daughter needed him.

"If you don't make time for her," I said, "you'll lose her."

He agreed but said it was hard for him to find the time since he was constantly occupied with 008. Which I already knew. However, I said he had to create space for her.

We used napkins to hash out the details of our next stage in life. Dawu was resigned to the fact that I'd have full custody of our daughter. I had a steadier income and more reasonable working hours. He would provide visas for Hannah and me as well as help me set up my studio. We'd wait until the new year to make everything official. That was when my visa would expire, too. There was nothing else to talk about. We hugged, shook hands and for a brief moment, the future didn't seem all that bad.

Christmas 2009 was upon us. I wasn't sure what the holiday would look like since Dawu and I were about to be divorced. It was our first Christmas apart in seven years and I was afraid this one would be lonely. Nevertheless, we spent it together as a family.

Dawu picked us up for Christmas Eve dinner and pretended to be Santa Claus, to the delight of Hannah. Santa gave her a pair of inline skates. Then the three of us went for dinner together. There were some uncomfortable moments, such as when Dawu took a few runs at me for not having any direction in my life as well as for spending too much on Christmas presents. Still, the holiday was about making sure Hannah knew she was our number one priority. We were there for her through the good and bad times. She had such a great time with both of us present. We saw the joy on our little girl's face and that was our biggest gift.

Dawu was a busy man. He had been managing the 008 and Zhengyang artists much like a business office. He organized a contingent of people and they had meetings, discussions and designed strategic plans – everything a regular company did. As well, he had fallen back into his night owl ways. He went to bed around 3 a.m. and got up any time after noon. At this point, there wasn't much room for Hannah in his life with those hours. That was why having him around at Christmas was important to all of us.

On the same day, Friday, Dec. 25, 2009, the creator of Charter 08, Liu Xiaobo, was sentenced to 11 years in prison by the Chinese government. The regime had found the writer, scholar and critic guilty of subversion. Ai Weiwei had been in the courtroom and tweeted about the decision.

"This does not mean a meteor has fallen. This is the discovery of a star. Although this is a sentence on Liu Xiaobo alone, it is also a slap on the face for everyone in China."

There was outrage from around the world and international civil society groups called for Liu Xiaobo's release. In China, he was hailed as "China's Mandela" – referring to Nelson Mandela, the South African leader who spent 27 years in prison for protesting against apartheid.

The move by the government to put Liu Xiaobo behind bars was a huge blow to Dawu and his friends who supported the charter. However, they didn't do or say anything publicly to denounce the sentence. It was too large of a risk for their necks.

A few days before the new year, I went to the new gallery space Dawu had found for me. I wanted to see what kind of potential it had. Dawu and our contractor, Jinzi, met me there and we talked about renovation plans. Jinzi was a construction genius and could create almost anything. I agreed to hire him in early January.

I was happy getting the ball moving on my very own space. The new and improved Beijing Color Studio would be up and running in 2010 and it was an exciting prospect. I'd be back in business as well as back into my photography. Meanwhile, Nina and I were still looking for buyers for the Counting Sheep Boutique.

I was also applying for jobs in Beijing. I was looking at working as an English teacher or else picking up an administrative position at an international school. I was getting some interviews but they never went anywhere.

Being employed in China would mean I didn't have to rely on Dawu to stay in the country. However, since we remained legally married, I'd use him one last time as my ticket to continue living in Beijing. On Thursday, Dec. 31, I went to the Canadian Embassy and picked up my new passport so Dawu could help me apply for my 2010 visa. I was, once again, committed to life in China.

Ringing in 2010 also meant ringing in a fresh start. I had turned the page on my relationship as well as a life in Canada. I was now focused on what was important to me such as my daughter.

Hannah was happy and enjoyed her activities, such as gymnastics and swimming, and she had many friends. Dawu and I were separated but we were co-parenting well. We didn't have to see eye-to-eye on many household or personal issues anymore. Beijing held other opportunities for me, too. I just needed to be patient and continue to work hard while waiting for the right moment.

The plans for the Beijing Color Studio were coming along. Dawu designed an awesome glass and metal door for the entrance. However, that was it for him. He had no more time to help me. All his hours were going to the 008 and Zhengyang art communities' compensation movement. In fact, he told me that he was annoyed that I wasn't beside him while he was fighting the government. However, whenever I had asked Dawu about the artist villages, he never gave me the straight goods. He got impatient and said I had no clue about what was going on. He'd tell me I didn't care, nor was I reliable enough to be involved. So why would I spend so much time and energy on HIS thing now?

My thing at the moment was my studio business. I bought backdrops, lighting and equipment to continue as a portrait photographer. I started planning classes and workshops that would pay the rent. I also had to look for instructors to replace Dawu.

Dawu's reputation as an activist was growing. His reputation as an artist was not.

Over the years, starting around 2001 when we first met, Dawu had anywhere from about three to 12 art exhibitions per year. In 2007, he worked with an artist group from the 008 community and that gave his creations some exposure but he wasn't a top household name in the art world, globally or locally.

The reputation of his home province, the Jiangsu area of China, helped him capitalize on his artist-as-activist image. The region had been known for producing art, music and science scholars over the past century or so. I remember when we were dating in 2002, Dawu and I visited one of the older universities in Beijing. We went into the main hall and looked at the famous names of scientists on the wall. Most of them were from Dawu's region. He was proud of that.

The Jiangsu area was part of the southern culture of China, which was sometimes seen (especially by those from the south) to be somewhat academically and intellectually superior to the northern part of the country. In a way, this meant Dawu was respected by many just because of where he was from.

Another reason for Dawu's burgeoning influence was that he wasn't scared to call out the government over the illegal demolition, a human rights abuse. Some of his bravado was because he hadn't been in any real trouble yet. What he was afraid of was not being heard by the international community. He was stressed about not getting the attention the compensation cause deserved.

In between working on his human rights case, Dawu was creating a new artistic piece connected to the compensation movement. Dawu was incorporating the 008 and Zhengyang struggle into a show called the *RESOLUTION PERFORMANCE ART EXHIBITION* to highlight the injustices at the compounds, as well as show how some Chinese artists like Ma Ling, Huang Rui and The Gao Brothers face discrimination and harassment in China. The show was scheduled for the new year and it would hopefully draw international attention to the plight of the 008 and Zhengyang artists.

I felt like I was coming back into my own at the start of the new year. I wasn't tied to anyone and I could do whatever I liked. I was hanging out with old and new friends in interesting places like FUBAR, a secret watering hole hidden behind a hot dog stand. When you pushed a button on the wall, it quietly opened to the bar. I loved this place. It was fun and had good cocktails. I went there often with my friends Emma and Badr Benjelloun. Badr was an expat from Morocco working in Beijing in the IT industry.

While at FUBAR, I met a guy with the wildest hair I had ever seen. I promised him a beer if he let me photograph his hair. He agreed and gave me his contact details. It got me thinking about a possible new photo project: portraits of the weirdly wonderful people living in Beijing. It was something I could do with the Beijing Color Studio!

Having my own studio to set up was fun. I installed a water machine (no one, absolutely no one, drinks water from the tap in China) and had Jinzi, my contractor, install some long ceiling-to-floor white cotton curtains. I had a cool space and I was excited about getting into photography again.

I was in my studio on Tuesday, Jan. 12 when my phone rang. It was Dawu wondering if I could take some photos of the art exhibition that he and the 008 and Zhengyang groups had organized. The show *RESOLUTION PERFORMANCE ART EXHIBITION* was highlighting the injustices at the compounds. I wasn't planning on going anywhere that day. There were driving restrictions on certain roads for any license plates ending in 2, like mine. I couldn't drive without paying a fine. It was freezing out, too, and that meant freezing fingers since I used my bare hands to focus my mostly-metal camera.

I'd rather be in my warm studio putting the finishing touches on my work but Dawu was insistent. He was almost begging me to document the show. He knew I would capture quality artsy images, not just snap one-dimensional digital images from a digital camera. I hesitated but finally agreed to go. I packed up my Hasselblad, tripod and several rolls of film. Thankfully, the route to the art show at the 008 headquarters took my car on unrestricted roads. I wouldn't be fined.

I arrived on scene to find it buzzing. There was a huge crowd gathered across the road from the 008 compound. The media was there, along with recognizable faces like Huang Rui, a prominent artist who formed part of the Stars Group. The Stars Art Group was an ensemble of contemporary and avant-garde artists who banded together in China in 1979. They were miles ahead of their time. Through their works, they were part of the social and cultural criticisms leading up to the 1989 Tiananmen Square protests.

The Stars Art Group hosted its first exhibition in Beijing in 1979, *STAR ART EXHIBITION*, in Beihai Park, near the China Art Gallery. However, that show was shut down by officials. The artists then held a protest calling for cultural openness and they were successful. The show carried on. Nevertheless, shutting down exhibitions became a common practice by Chinese officials. As the art industry grew, so did the number of shut-downs and cancellations. Probably one of the most famous was the *CHINA AVANT-GARDE ART EXHIBITION* held in early February of 1989. One of the artists, Xiao Lu, created an installation/performance work, *DIALOGUE*, which involved her shooting a gun into a phone booth as part of her act. Her pellet gun went off within the first two hours of the show, causing it to be immediately shut down by authorities. Exactly four months later, the Tiananmen Square massacre took place. Xiao's gunshots were often called *the first shots of Tiananmen.*

Huang Rui was at Dawu's *RESOLUTION* art exhibition because the older man believed in helping the artists spread the word about what was happening to their collectives. Huang Rui was dressed in half white, half black and carried an umbrella with the YinYang symbol on it. Having a famous artist like Huang Rui at the event lent credibility to the cause. China was a very hierarchical society and it was especially prevalent in the art community.

I started shooting photos of graffiti painted on the abandoned 008 buildings. The artists spray-painted slogans that were catchy and to the point such as *Fight for human rights* and *expel bad business interests!* One graffiti image was a pig's head and a knife. It was kind of a violent cartoon but these artists were angry. They had been working for compensation for almost six months and not received anything other than heartbreak. They had had enough and were using spray paint to lash out against management, developers and local authorities. If they happened to drive by, they would see it. The local police would have seen the graffiti, too.

Besides the spray painting, there were performances and Ma Ling was involved in one while dressed in a white gown. Dawu was part of a group piece. He felt that it would be more powerful to work together rather than alone. As well, he didn't want to be seen as benefitting from the show.

Dawu's performance-based concept had people lined up, shoulder to shoulder, holding a brick, a symbol of construction. They stood in front of the 008 headquarters for about half an hour and that was where I found him.

Dawu was wearing my *serape*, a Mexican shawl-type blanket that I had bought in the early 1990s when I was a field student in Mexico. Dawu really liked the traditional garmet. He looked handsome in the shawl and stood tall and proud. Xu Pinglun, a well-known art curator, was standing next to him. The curator's presence made it clear that not only artists were joining forces against the government.

People were enjoying the exhibition. No one was shouting anti-government slogans or protesting the PRC. The show was a peaceful and artistic way to bring attention to the issue of forced evictions. The artists were defending their rights creatively.

Dawu was happy to see me and hoped I wasn't too cold. The exhibit coincided with the coldest day recorded in Beijing since 1951 and I had no doubt about that. Many of the show attendees were wrapped in comforters and heavy blankets. It definitely proved their commitment to standing up for what they believed in.

Dawu asked me to keep taking photos so the show would be recorded. The peaceful movement needed to be documented and it could be a breakthrough for his cause. I snapped images from the press conference that Dawu had helped organize, as well as pictures of Dawu meeting with media. Of course, the police were there. The artists weren't naïve to think that the cops wouldn't show up. Both uniformed and plainclothes officers had been watching the 008 compound for months. They had probably been watching Dawu for a long time, too. He stood out as the leader.

The show made some ripples throughout the Beijing media and even a representative from the German Embassy showed up in his black Mercedes. Many renowned Chinese artists had good relations with the embassies in Beijing. Some of the European embassies were keen on Chinese contemporary art as well, and had solid Chinese art communities in their own countries. It translated to foreign clout for artists in China. When embassy representatives showed up, there would be accountability from the cops. Police were less likely to act badly in front of foreign guests.

The exhibit was marred by some hooligans. Some unknowns from the local community invited a handful of thugs to break up the event. They arrived at the show and began hassling some of the artists. The police got involved Dawu exchanged some words with one of the officers. They had a yelling match over the right to hold the exhibition. Other than being told to shut up, Dawu was left alone. One artist was taken away by police and held for about three hours, then released.

I had left before the cops arrived and shut down the show. Before I collected Hannah at the ayi's, I dropped off the film at my favourite photo processing place inside 798. I was excited about the pictures. I not only wanted to make copies for Dawu and some of the other participating artists, but I wanted to post some images on Facebook. It would be my tiny role in getting the word out about what was happening to the 008 and Zhengyang residents.

On Jan. 18, I posted 15 photos to a Facebook album called *Anti-Demolition, Anti-Gov Chinese Art Performance Event at 008*. The pictures received many likes and comments of support. I felt proud of my assistance towards Dawu's cause.

Later in the month, I went to another one of Dawu's art shows at the Linda Gallery in 798. Things were falling into place in many ways personally for Dawu and me. We were friends (most of the time) and I was able to go out without worrying about either him or Hannah, who was with her capable nanny when not with me. I had hired a woman named Qu to look after my daughter. The ayi had three kids herself and lived not far from the Cappuccino apartment complex. She was well-versed in taking care of children so I felt fine leaving Hannah in her care and going out. I hung out with friends and attended some concerts. I saw the Japanese atmospheric instrumental musician DJ Krush, as well as a show by the Canadian singer-songwriter Patrick Watson.

Patrick Watson played at the Yugong Yishan bar in the older part of Beijing, not far from the Forbidden City. The singer was promoting a new album, *Wooden Arms*, and one of the songs, *Beijing*, is, well, about Beijing. The venue was small and so there weren't many people between the singer and me. It was an intimate concert and the performer played most of the instruments and even came down on to the floor. It was cool and one of the moments when I just loved being in Beijing.

Chinese New Year was marked in February in 2010 and school was out for four weeks, so I decided to take Hannah on vacation to Australia. I had family there and friends from when I used to work for the Australian Embassy. There would be many children for Hannah to play with and the beach was calling my name. The closest beach to Beijing is Nandaihe Golden Beach and it's not very big. Besides, it was winter in China and even though Beijing wasn't as frosty as Canada, it still didn't have any warm sand and blue seas.

Dawu grew up with much colder weather than the Chinese capital. The winters were brutally cold in Jiangsu province, about a 10-hour train ride southeast of Beijing. When Dawu first took me to his family's home, several years before, I swore I would never return. (Alas, I did go back a few times.) The wintery days in Changzhou were sunny but there was no heat streaming from the sky nor from any heat source inside Dawu's sister's traditional stone house or their dad's concrete apartment a few blocks away. There was no central heating and even indoors, everyone wore several layers of clothing. Despite it being the middle of winter, the windows were kept wide open to capture any ray of sun.

In Dawu's father's place, the bathroom had some hot water to wash with, but it was scheduled by the local building management to save money and resources. Dawu and I bought a space heater at the local department store but we could only turn on the heat when I was in the bathroom. We didn't want to consume too much electricity. I felt like I was camping inside for the week. The experience did make me appreciate my lifestyle in the city and it gave me greater insight into the life that Dawu and many Chinese people face.

Because of Jiangsu's harsh conditions in winter, Dawu's father moved to Beijing for three months. He had lived with us every year since Dawu and I had been together. It was great for Hannah to have her *yeye*, grandfather, so close. He spent hours doting on her. It was funny to watch the pair as Hannah spoke Mandarin and Yeye spoke his local dialect. (I sometimes felt that my Mandarin was better than his! Needless to say, I had spent years and years studying Mandarin and then wound up marrying someone whose family spoke a local dialect far different from what my textbooks had taught me.) Mandarin and the local dialect shared some similarities but not many. However, Hannah understood her grandfather even though she always replied to him in Mandarin.

Yeye was with the three of us when we went for an early Chinese New Year dinner on Monday, Feb. 1, 2010. Hannah and I would be away in Australia during the actual Chinese New Year celebrations, which fell on Valentine's Day, Sunday, Feb. 14. As much as Dawu and I were living in separate households, we still did things together as a family, especially Chinese New Year, the most important time of the year in China.

Chinese New Year, or the Spring Festival, was the equivalent to Christmas. Families gathered around a round table for Chinese New Year dinner to celebrate the end of one year and the beginning of the next. The date of Chinese New Year was determined by the lunar calendar and so the date was not fixed as it might be in the Gregorian, or Western, calendar.

During the Chinese holiday, older people gave younger people red envelopes, known as *hongbao*, filled with money as well as other small gifts.

Families spent time together watching parades, setting off some firecrackers and eating a fine meal filled with traditional New Year foods. One of the dishes was *yuanxiao* or *yuanfen* (depending on the dialect). It was small balls of dough made out of rice flour and filled with a sweet paste. They were then soaked in a sweet broth and served on the fifteenth day of the lunar celebration. The balls represented the roundness and unity of the family and of the year.

Dawu, Yeye, Hannah and I ate our pre-New Year's supper at a local hot pot restaurant down the road from the main gate of the 798 Art District. Dawu was grouchy and cranky with all of us but I tolerated him for Hannah. She wouldn't see her father for three weeks. Dawu didn't want us to leave and almost begged me to stay and help him with his compensation work. He suggested that I go to Australia another time because it wasn't a good time for him. He had a lot to do and since I was a foreigner, I could connect him to the expat community and the world.

It was strange he was asking me to be involved now because whenever I had asked previously, he snapped at me and said I was too unreliable to help. Whatever that meant. Nevertheless, I told him I was going to relax on vacation and I would only be a phone or Skype call away if he needed anything.

He said it should be him relaxing as he hadn't had a break in months and he wasn't going to get one until his work was done. I knew that "his work" meant the struggle for justice for the 008 and Zhengyang collectives, not his art. At that point, I was concerned that he had almost abandoned his art practice. He had been absorbed by 008 and Zhengyang and determined to win against a government that never lost a fight.

Dawu was ready for a fight and I was ready for a vacation. On Wednesday, Feb. 3, 2010, Hannah and I left for a three-week trip to Australia. Dawu was not happy and didn't understand that I wasn't leaving because I didn't support him. We had been through a lot in the past few years and I needed a break.

Hannah and I busied ourselves in the sun. We went to zoos, museums, beaches and enjoyed our time away from the drama in China. I didn't give a second thought to what was going on back in Beijing. I hadn't heard a peep from Dawu since a confirmation text that he sent right after I let him know that Hannah and I had landed safely Down Under. Meanwhile, Dawu was mobilizing the artists and their supporters.

On Sunday, Feb. 14, Dawu and his groups held a party and press conference at the main building of 008. Dawu, as the leader, was vocal during this event and talked about the injustices the tenants had faced. Local authorities and the secret police showed up but there was no violence. Of course, Dawu had exchanged words with officials but he wasn't hauled away in handcuffs. He told me some of what had happened when he called Hannah and me in Sydney. We talked over Skype on the evening of Thursday, Feb. 18.

My daughter and I were sitting at my friend Brooke Poole's kitchen counter talking to Dawu. His face, encased by a scruffy beard and moustache, was the same familiar face I had fallen in love with. But something was different. Perhaps it was the deep furrow in his brow or the way he clenched his teeth. We were chatting when he mentioned that he and some others were organizing something, something that would make the government sit up and listen. I should have listened, too, but I didn't press for details. I was relaxing and had just shared a bottle of red wine with Brooke. I chose to look past the underlying anger and frustration in his voice. I was on vacation. That didn't mean that I wasn't worried about Dawu. I was. Nevertheless, I thought some of the problem was Dawu and his idea of losing face. Face, known as *mianzi* in Chinese, was an important part of life for many people in China. There was no true equivalent in so-called Western culture. Sure, we get embarrassed but we generally move past it. In China, you must prevent this kind of embarrassment at all costs. Otherwise, you'll have loss of face: the loss of honour, respect and status. In public, a child would never argue with his father because that would shame the father and he would lose face.

Wars are fought in China over face. Marriages end because of face. Businesses lose money because of face. Employees are demoted, promoted or fired because of face. Children commit suicide because of face.

For Dawu, loss of face meant being part of a group that had been working for over half a year to prevent their studios from being knocked out from underneath them … yet they hadn't accomplished much of anything. There was pride, hurt, anger, face and financial loss hanging on this project. Dawu was keenly aware of how strong he had to be in order to keep the group motivated. Some of the artists had already left, bored or done with trying to battle the authorities. Others, who hadn't invested too much, just packed up and moved on.

Dawu wasn't giving up. He felt passionate about the issues the artists were dealing with. If they fought for whatever they could get, be it financial compensation, it was better than walking away and letting the government win. Dawu was a leader who was trying to build inroads so his fellow peasants, who were constantly being booted off "government" land, wouldn't end up with nothing or worse: in detention or dead.

There was an edge of anger and frustration to his voice that night. It had been there for a while and I had heard it through the years of arguing and fighting with him, but it was sharper now. The politics of the artists were consuming his time and energy, moving him away from creating art and towards potential trouble. But I was in the throes of a holiday. What could I do anyway? I was in Australia, soon to be seeing friends in Canberra. Dawu would have to deal with whatever he was doing on his own.

Still, on the train to Australia's capital the next day, I couldn't stop wondering what Dawu was planning. Whatever it was, I hoped it was going to help his cause.

"Hi Karen," started the text from Emma on Monday, Feb. 22, 2010. "You might want to get yourself to a TV and watch the news. Dawu has just marched on Chang'an Avenue."

I was sitting in a hip bar in downtown Canberra, Australia, with my friend Dave Johns. It was just the two of us, old friends, catching up. Dave and I had known each other for over a decade since my days in Shanghai in the mid-1990s.

I usually left my phone at home but I had decided to bring it with me that night. I didn't understand the words on the screen in front of me. Marching on Chang'an Avenue was illegal. Dawu wasn't stupid. He wouldn't take his protest to Chang'an Avenue. Would he?

I hopped onto Twitter to read the latest posts coming out of Beijing. Some tweets were talking about an artist-led demonstration on Chang'an Avenue. It began to sink in that Dawu had done something. Something terribly bad — dangerous, in fact. That was what he had been talking about over Skype.

I tried to call him from the bar but he wasn't answering his phone. It was frustrating being in Australia when everything was blowing up in Beijing. I told Dave what was happening and he was concerned. He pointed out that I would be leaving in a few days. Things might look better in Beijing.

I tweeted at Honghong and Ai Weiwei and asked if they knew where Dawu was and to tell me what was going on. They each told me not to worry, that everyone was safe and Dawu was OK. Phew. He hadn't been hauled off to jail. Perhaps the protest wasn't a big deal.

Despite the gentle messages from Honghong and Ai Weiwei, I couldn't help worrying and wondering about how Dawu's stunt was going to impact Hannah and me. Would the authorities let us back in the country? I hadn't ever gone through anything like this before. What were the consequences of Dawu's actions on his family? I didn't know.

After a rough night's sleep, Hannah and I left Canberra the next day on a train for Sydney. We went to the airport a day later to catch our flight home. I hadn't told my daughter that I was worried about what her father had done, but I was sure she noticed I was on edge.

The entire five-hour plane ride, I agonized over Dawu's actions. I wondered what possibly could have prompted him to organize a march in such a politically sensitive area of the city. For some demolished studio money and pride? What pushed him to go so far?

Returning to Beijing proved to be smooth sailing. I had been worried that there would be some sort of warrant out for my arrest in connection with Dawu but I was relieved when I made it home without police involvement.

I was certain that Dawu, at some point, would be in trouble for his march. Protests of any kind in China were illegal. Nevertheless, he was very much safe and sound at his 798 studio when I saw him after my trip. Dawu was excited about what had happened and felt that the protestors had finally made their point.

"We had to march," he said. "It was the only thing that would get anyone to hear us."

Dawu explained that he and the 008 and Zhengyang artist groups had been working 24/7 on trying to win compensation for their evictions. They tried to talk to the various levels of government and the developers. The collectives tried negotiating. They tried meetings, petitions and holding the *RESOLUTION* performance art exhibition. Sure, they attracted the attention of some ambassadors, international media, local artists and supporters but nothing really came of the show. Dawu's group was starting to feel that their struggle was all in vain. There was, of course, face involved: How could they still be struggling after many months of planning and organizing and not have moved an inch toward the finish line?

The artists were frustrated. There was pride, hurt, anger and financial loss all balled into the one cause. Dawu needed to kick into high gear to keep the group motivated. Some people had already left, bored with trying to battle the authorities in China. The small group, about 11 or so people who remained, was at its wit's end.

Dawu claimed it wasn't only money the protestors were after. They wanted to pave the way for their fellow citizens, those who were constantly being booted off state-owned, "government" land, sans compensation and left to fend for themselves. It was against human decency and human rights. Dawu and many in his group had travelled outside of the country and had seen democracy in action. That empowered the artists and they looked to better the future for the Chinese people. What does that sound like? Tiananmen Square.

I told Dawu that he was brave. His group was the first since 1989 to march in protest on Chang'an Avenue. Nevertheless, it was a stupid thing to do. Dawu shot back, asking what choice did he and the others have?

The compensation movement had turned physical the day before and the government was now not only getting away with taking land, it was also getting away with beating people.

During the early morning hours of Monday, Feb. 22, Dawu and the group had just finished a meeting to find another direction and create yet another strategy. That was when they received a desperate call from one of the Zhengyang artists who had been squatting in the village. He was scared by a mass of about 80 thugs who busted into the Zhengyang compound.

There were about 20 residents still living at Zhengyang despite having no heat, water or electricity. The squatters who had stayed behind had built a makeshift yurt in the middle of the compound. It was their home complete with bunk beds, a stove for cooking and sitting areas. It was 2 a.m. when the thugs, wearing balaclavas and armed with pipes, arrived and began their destructive mission to frighten the Zhengyang squatters into submission.

The goons were on a rampage, bashing cars, smashing windows and beating anybody who crossed their path. Dawu immediately called the local police responsible for the 008 and Zhengyang areas and asked for the cops' assistance. It should have taken police five minutes to get to the Zhengyang compound. It took them over 30 minutes to arrive on scene. By the time they got there, the mob had wreaked havoc on the village by damaging property, vehicles and injuring more than a half a dozen residents.

Dawu and five of his friends arrived at the compound within minutes of receiving the desperate call. The thugs then started to attack Dawu and his group. Dawu and Gu Duanfan were beaten with metal pipes and Chen Jun, a good friend and artist colleague of Dawu's, was bashed over the head. After police finally gained control of the situation, the 008 and Zhengyang protestors were left battered and bleeding. Many, like Chen Jun, had to go to the hospital and receive treatment for deep cuts and large purple bruises.

Dawu and those who hadn't been as badly injured headed back to 008. Talking amongst themselves, they realized that the developer had probably sent the mob to Zhengyang. The hooligans knew exactly how to get into the compound, through the back gate, and where to find the artists in the middle of the complex. As well, the cops were a five-minute drive from Zhengyang yet it took them well over half an hour to get there. It had been a setup.

To Dawu and his group, it was proof that their compensation mission was not going to be heard. This called for revenge. It was proving too difficult to deal with an already corrupt system that brutalized its people. Enough was enough.

Dawu had an idea. The collectives were going to take their issues to the streets. That same day. The plan was to march on Chang'an Avenue, a route running through the centre of Beijing, intersecting the infamous Tiananmen Square. This would catch the world's attention.

Tiananmen is where over three thousand people were massacred in 1989 by Chinese government forces. Students and others had been peacefully calling for government reforms for several months that spring. The oligarchy tolerated the protests for a couple of months until June 3, when Chinese troops went into the square and started firing on the demonstrators. Since then, it has been illegal to march anywhere in China without a permit (which, of course, no one would ever apply for, nor would they ever get one). Dawu and his friends were not thinking about paperwork. They were focused on how to bring attention to their plight. So … they decided to march on Chang'an Avenue on the morning of Monday, Feb. 22, 2010.

The group thought this would certainly bring their housing issues and unfair treatment by the government to the forefront of the world. They invited Ai Weiwei to join their cause. Through his wide social media network, he was able to invite many foreign journalists to the march. Where was I at this time? Still in Australia with Hannah. I had no idea what was happening.

The artists would march on Chang'an Avenue in protest of the lack of human rights. Dawu organized a team to create banners so they had something to show passersby that they were, in fact, an organized cause and not just hooligans out on the streets. The group was able to set up a basic route and get the word out to friends, supporters and the international media in a matter of hours. Plans for the illegal march were underway.

About 15 people started walking east on Chang'an Avenue, heading for Tiananmen Square. Chen Jun, who had been injured in the early morning brawl with the masked goons, was using a wheelchair that was pushed by Dawu. All of the protestors carried banners on bamboo poles calling the demolition of the artist compounds illegal and asking the government for compensation.

The group walked right on the road, interfering with traffic. Ai Weiwei stood on the sidewalk, a witness to the protest but not a participant, and took photos and tweeted about the situation. The protestors were also photographed and interviewed by foreign media, including *New York Times* reporter Andrew Jacobs. Broadcasters from the BBC, the British Broadcasting Corporation, and AP, the Associated Press news agency, were also present.

The march didn't last long. Dawu and his team walked for about 15 minutes and then the cops showed up, ordering them to stop. The police were polite but Dawu and the demonstrators exchanged a few words with them.

Despite some pushing and shoving, no one was detained, hit, beaten or arrested. Dawu and his group broke up quietly and peacefully and returned to the 008 headquarters without any drama.

The protest, though, was a big deal. It was all over the international news (not local news as Chinese state TV didn't, nor wouldn't, cover the march). Both expat and Chinese friends were calling and texting me, asking me what had happened. I had no clue what was going on.

A couple of days later, on Wednesday, Feb. 24, Dawu was debriefed by police at a Chaoyang District hotel. Officials said despite the violence that the 008 and Zhengyang collectives had experienced recently, their march was unauthorized and violated the relevant law. Nevertheless, authorities would try to step up security at the compounds and continue to work towards a resolution in the compensation dispute.

Dawu had hoped that this meant the beginning of the end for the people fighting the evictions. Indeed, the development company was ordered to pay the artists in exchange for their properties. Like Dawu had shrewdly surmised, the attention the demonstration had garnered from the foreign media had put pressure on the authorities to deal with the artists' issue. The politicians didn't want China to be shown in a bad light in the Western media.

Dawu was being hailed either a hero or an idiot depending on whom he, or I, talked to. A few people thought his plan of action was incredibly courageous. Others thought he took too much of a risk and would pay for it down the road. There were some Chinese artists who felt that the march had made Dawu into a target for the authorities.

Dawu stayed in Beijing. There weren't any obvious ramifications from the march. Life went on and Hannah still spent one-on-one time with her baba.

A few nights after arriving home from Australia, Dawu invited me to attend the 008's end of Chinese New Year party. It was being held at the 008 compound headquarters. I decided to go. I have to admit, I did feel slightly guilty about not having been there for Dawu and his cause. The demonstration wasn't to shirk work. The group had a valid reason for protesting and had attracted the interest of the media after the march.

The grand event was held on another cold February evening. I drove there solo and when I walked into the party, a few hours later than expected, people went out of their way to introduce me as Karen, Wu Yuren's wife. My English name was not commonly used by Chinese people. By using Karen and not Peng Kailin, my Chinese name, and even introducing me at all, it signified that Dawu was rising in the ranks of importance. The march had catapulted him to a higher status within the art community of China.

People seemed to be impressed by his ability to motivate the masses. He was making a name for himself — albeit in politics, not necessarily in art. Despite all that had transpired between Dawu and me over the years, I genuinely felt proud of him that evening. I told him so and he nodded in thanks. He was proud of what his group had accomplished: getting the government to listen.

For the party, the remaining residents of 008 had cleaned up the space, hung art on the walls and created a festive atmosphere out of the abandoned art studio. There was a mound of Chinese New Year snacks such as White Rabbit candies, a creamy candy that had an edible rice paper wrapper, as well as sunflower seeds, cookies and crackers. There were also oranges and other fruit, alcohol, tea and light refreshments. Artists, their supporters, neighbours as well as some local and foreign media attended. Everyone had a great time laughing, drinking and eating. Well ... almost everyone.

Some plainclothes police, *guoan* (China's secret police), showed up. They were parked outside the compound, watching people coming and going from the party. Dawu and a couple of the other hosts invited the police in for some snacks but they refused. They remained a few metres away from 008, sitting inside their unmarked police car.

The appearance of the authorities didn't dampen the spirit of the party. The police hadn't arrested anyone at the march and Dawu knew there would be a chance he would be under surveillance. During the 008 party, I was texting Emma about the police presence and what was happening. She had a coveted overseas VPN and took my comments and posted them to Twitter.

The Chinese government had a firewall, an information barrier, that censored online content, especially Western social media platforms. There were ways to get around the firewall, such as by using a proxy server (VPN) to hide your IP address. However, most VPNs had to be purchased outside of China. Thanks to Emma's VPN, we got the news out about the cops showing up to the 008 event. If anything did go south, there would be a record of it.

When the firecrackers jumped into the air around midnight, it was an amazing sight and sound. Everyone except for the guoan joined in to set off rockets and sparklers. There were hoots of joy and clapping as the pyrotechnics buzzed and burst in the sky. The new year had a double meaning for Dawu and his friends and they were free to enjoy the night and the future.

Dawu was on a high and propelling himself forward on his wave of activist success. He loved his country and now that the issue of compensation had been dealt with, he could focus on his art. He was looking forward to sharing his talents with his people. However, his friends at the party thought he should leave China.

"Take Dawu to Canada," Chao Hongling told me.

"Dawu needs to get out of China," Gu Duanfan said.

It wasn't a bad idea — but it wasn't a good one either. Dawu and I weren't a couple so I couldn't tell him what to do. As well, what would he do in Canada? What would I do? In China, he was a rising star in terms of being a person of influence. He had stood up to the government and won.

I was trying to let go of the feeling that something big was going to happen. I had lived in China long enough to know that the government wasn't above retaliation. It hadn't done anything to Dawu … yet. If he continued to push the authorities, at some point, they would push back.

Having the secret police at the event made me realize that Dawu might be in more hot water than he thought. Would that hot water be splashed onto Hannah and me? I shuddered to think of how I would explain to our five-year-old daughter that her father was behind bars.

During the party, I asked Dawu about moving to Canada with me. He told me he wasn't scared of being arrested over his advocacy work.

"I feel like I will be like Nelson Mandela if I go to jail," he said. "No problem."

Dawu felt a kinship with Mandela. As well, Dawu was inspired by Liu Xiaobo, who had been called "China's Mandela" when he was imprisoned in 2009. Both Liu Xiaobo and Mandela stood up for what they believed in and Dawu believed he was like them. If it meant he had to go to jail for sticking up for the 008 and Zhengyang artists, so be it.

Dawu and his mates had clearly broken the law. They illegally marched on Chang'an Avenue, a road that was heavily connected to issues that had been domestically and internationally sensitive for the Chinese government for years. Dawu and his followers had exposed a common, but horrible, human rights situation to the world. The Chinese authorities did not like this and had been humiliated. They had lost face and would have to settle the score.

At the party, Dawu was surrounded by people who thought he couldn't do any wrong. They were his people, his supporters and his reason for doing all of this. He was bathing in glory, a type of glory that he hadn't reached with his art practice. He was a celebrity in this crowd.

14

The presence of the guoan at the 008 party made me feel like I had to walk on eggshells. I knew the Chinese government worked in ways that were considered illegal in other countries like Canada. The authorities in China didn't seem to need warrants to get information on Dawu. Police could barge into my home at any time and take what they wanted. Dawu's friends certainly thought something like that was going to happen and that was why they told me to get him out. They knew how the winds of China blew better than I did. Canada was looking more and more like a potential haven for Dawu.

I started researching the process of getting him to Canada as soon as possible. I wondered if we could just leave everything behind, hop on a plane with Hannah and deal with the consequences on the other end. A more official route would be to ask for advice, so I called the Canadian Embassy. I talked to a woman there about my plan and why I was thinking of such an escape. She was sympathetic and offered support to me but was unable to help Dawu. He had to apply for a visa to go to Canada.

"He's not a Canadian citizen," she said.

My idea of dashing away with Dawu was dashed. I didn't want to get into trouble with both China and Canada. The embassy woman said Dawu could immigrate but it would take months of paperwork.

I was relieved Canada remained an option for Hannah and me. When I had my baby shops, expat customers married to Chinese partners often asked my advice on which citizenship their children should hold. I would always tell them that the mother should always hold the same nationality as the child. I used the tsunami that hit southern Thailand in 2004 as an example. It was a massive emergency and there were people from all over the world in that region. A Canadian mother would be eligible for Canadian consular support, but if her child was a Chinese citizen, she would not be able to obtain Canadian Embassy help. Hannah was Canadian.

A couple of weeks later, I was feeling better about the whole illegal protest/guoan situation. Spring was coming to Beijing. It was now early March 2010 and it was a good time to be in the city. The air was warm and the pollution was pushed to the side by the winds.

The nice weather meant I wasn't a sweaty, snotty mess when I arrived at my Beijing Color Studio. I looked around my space and I was proud of what I had accomplished. The nervousness over the police and Dawu and I being under scrutiny had worn off since nothing had happened. I was less interested in getting my ex out of China, since I had work to do on my business.

I was about to open my computer on Thursday, Mar. 4, when I got a call from Ma Ling, my studio neighbour. She was crying, asking if I knew what was happening to Dawu. She explained that his studio assistant, Zhang Xiaodong, had called her asking if she had seen Dawu. Zhang lived with Dawu and knew he hadn't come home the night before. Wu Xiangshou, Dawu's father, was also staying with them and worried.

Ma Ling didn't know where Dawu was and this upset her. I went next door to her place to calm her down. Talking to her, I realized part of her anxiousness was wrapped up in the 008 and Zhengyang protests. Ma Ling had been a part of the original 008 artist compound eviction. She was in full support of asking for compensation from the development company. Although she didn't march on Chang'an, she did attend many of the protest meetings as well as participated in the *RESOLUTION* art event in January 2010.

I told her that I didn't think there was any cause for worry. I joked that maybe Dawu was staying with a new girlfriend. However, Ma Ling didn't find the humour in my insinuation. Zhang showed up and joined us for a cup of tea. Dawu had been out of contact with him for about 15 hours. That was unusual. Zhang was Dawu's human calendar as well as his boss' driver. The studio assistant knew when and where Dawu needed to be, who he'd be meeting with and get him there. Nothing was left to chance, especially since Dawu was impatient with public transit. Zhang chauffeured Dawu all over Beijing.

Zhang and Ma Ling told me to check the Jianguomen District police station, a large centre near Chang'an Avenue, to see if Dawu was there. The police would have to answer my questions; legally, I was Dawu's wife. I didn't think he was at the detachment. Nothing had happened to him since the march, so why would the authorities go after him now? Sure, there were secret police lurking around but that was to be expected. Right?

Zhang then told me something that changed my mind. He said that Dawu and several of the other marchers were collected by police yesterday afternoon and taken to a medical clinic called the Chaoyang Injury Appraisal Center. Dawu never came out.

The activists had been lured to the clinic under the pretense that the government was concerned about their health. Since the melee with the armed thugs at 008 was intensely physical, the authorities brought Dawu and several others from his group to the centre to be assessed by physicians. Dawu thought the authorities were being considerate and looking after its people.

Zhang was waiting in his Jeep outside the clinic for Dawu, ready to drive him home after the doctor's appointment. He watched as five of Dawu's group left the centre in the back of a van. Surely Dawu would be next. Zhang waited and waited and then walked into the centre and asked what was going on. What he said next frightened me.

"There's a rumour that Dawu and three other protestors were taken to the Jianguomen police station," Zhang told me. "One of the clinic staff said Dawu might be there."

That was all I needed to hear before I drove off to the station. Zhang followed in his Jeep. At the detachment's front desk, I asked for Wu Yuren.

He was there.

Thirty minutes after arriving, Zhang and I were introduced to Officer Lao. I was anxious, beads of sweat popping out on my forehead, and I wanted to demand answers. Showing attitude, though, wasn't going to get me anywhere in this situation. I let the officer do most of the talking. At first, I didn't believe anything he said.

I had read a few things describing how people were treated in detention in China — horribly. I had expected the police at the Jianguomen station to be no better. Nevertheless, Mr. Lao told us that Dawu was being treated well – fed and watered in his own room. I suspected the officer was lying or hiding what had been done to my husband.

"Dawu is on his best behaviour," said Officer Lao.

As the officer continued to talk to me, filling me in on what was happening to Dawu, my walls started falling down. Mr. Lao seemed open and honest, even friendly. He told me Dawu was at the station because he hadn't obtained a permit to march on Chang'an Avenue.

"Who would ever be given a permit?" I asked.

"That's not really the issue," said Officer Lao.

According to him, Dawu had broken a strict law and could get up to three years in prison. Bile snaked up my throat. What have you done Dawu?

Officer Lao allayed my fears. He was patient with me and told me that since Dawu was cooperating, his sentence could be reduced. Talking to the cop calmed me down. I was confident that Dawu had not been abused and perhaps a prison term would be waived. I asked if the three other protestors were being treated as fairly and I was assured that they were.

"We are being lenient since this is Dawu's first offence," said Officer Lao. "We might not be so in the future, if this were to happen again."

The officer took me to see Dawu, who was handcuffed and sitting in a chair next to a cop. I could see Dawu wasn't upset at all and it looked like he was enjoying himself. He was talking to police officers about their work and they were asking him about his art practice. He was not being tortured.

Officer Lao told me and Zhang that we would have to wait a few hours before Dawu could be released. Meanwhile, it was almost time to pick up Hannah from school. I texted my friend Debbie Mason with a weird request. Debbie, a good friend from the U.K., was a journalist who had a radio show and spoke both Chinese and English. Our kids often played together. Debbie was the perfect person to take my spot while I went and retrieved Hannah and got myself something to eat. Debbie wouldn't be uncomfortable or upset by the situation.

I rushed off to get Hannah home while Debbie waited at the station in my place. When I returned about an hour later, my friend told me that she could do a story about Dawu if need be. I appreciated Debbie's support but it looked like everything was going to be fine.

At about 6:30 p.m. exactly, a stairwell door opened and out walked Chen Jun, the artist who had been hit on the head with a metal pipe at 008. He had a concussion on march day and used a wheelchair to take part in the protest. He was walking now and passed Zhang and me in the waiting room. He shook his head at us, signalling that we were not to approach him.

I went to the window and watched as he crossed the busy road in front of the station and hailed a taxi. I wasn't sure where he was going, or if he even had enough money to pay for a cab, but I was happy that he was a free man. Meanwhile, Zhang drove to Dawu's studio. He was preparing a fake computer in case we had to hand one over to the authorities.

Over the next half an hour, two more protestors walked through the door, free. They spotted me but didn't say anything. I was sitting on the edge of my seat, hoping Dawu was going to burst into the reception room next. At 7 p.m., a cop told me to get into my car and follow the police station wagon. The cops were driving Dawu home.

It was dark and rush hour traffic was still buzzing around me when I got into my vehicle. I saw Dawu emerge from the detachment, flanked by several officers. They put him in the car and got in with him. Then, the driver indicated for me to follow them. I did, hoping I wouldn't lose them amongst the busy streets. I wondered if the officers would speed away, taking Dawu with them to some unknown torture dungeon. Ugh. I had watched too many crime shows and a few nefarious storylines played in my head.

Thankfully, the officers delivered Dawu to his studio and his upset father. Tears poured down Wu Xiangshou's face as he grappled with the realization that Dawu was in hot water. It was a father's worst fear. Dawu was one of Wu Xiangshou's two children but the only son. Boys were considered the most precious to many Chinese families so the fact that Dawu was in trouble with the law made Wu Xiangshou afraid for his son's future.

The officers had given Dawu back his phone in the car but now asked for his laptop. The computer had important and possibly inflammatory material on it like photos and contacts. Thankfully, Zhang gave the police the second laptop he had filled with junk. Dawu's real laptop had been hidden away.

The police then instructed Dawu to keep a low profile. That was that. They left. It was all over.

I gave Dawu a big hug. He was home. Zhang and several artists were waiting for Dawu, too. He sat down after serving all of us a cup of Chinese tea. Then, he slowly recounted the details of the past 36 hours.

Dawu said he noticed a police car parked at the gate of his 798 artist compound studio, not long after we had all thought the dust had settled. Plainclothes police officers got out and took Dawu and several others who had also been at the march to the Chaoyang Injury Appraisal Center. They were told they were being summoned to the nearby medical clinic for a check-up.

The check-up had been a trap. Oh, the protestors had been thoroughly examined at the centre. They were weighed, had their pulse taken and were poked and prodded by medical staff. Once that was done, Dawu's group was told to shut off their phones. Then, they were escorted down stairs, through a door and outside, where they were put straight into a waiting police van. By the time Dawu and the other artists realized what was going on, it was too late.

Dawu and his crew were taken to the Jianguomen police station. The cops processing the men there were agreeable. The officers were polite, almost friendly, and didn't use violence to control Dawu or extract information. Dawu said he was treated properly and treated to a nice meal. He even talked about art with one of the officers. The cop had never met an artist before and was amazed by Dawu's talents and knowledge.

Of course, Dawu had built a rapport with some of the officers. He was always making friends and didn't care what your rank was in society. He was most interested in the depth of humanity in a person. However, he wasn't an idiot and knew he had to protect himself.

He was friendly with the cops but didn't give them any information beyond what they asked for during questioning.

The authorities had made a record of who had been marching on Chang'an Avenue. Ai Weiwei had been on the sidewalk and not considered part of the protest. He was safe. Dawu wasn't.

Dawu's brief stint in jail turned him into even more of a celebrity. Everyone was fascinated by his courage. Dawu himself wasn't fazed by his arrest. In fact, it emboldened him and made his desire to stand up for the Chinese people stronger. Andy Warhol, the famous American artist, once said, "Everyone will be famous for 15 minutes."

I couldn't help but think that this march business was Dawu's 15 minutes. The cops had warned him to keep his nose clean but I knew it was probably just a matter of time before he got into trouble again. But I had to keep going with my life.

15

My business at the Beijing Color Studio was moving forward. Since Dawu was clearly out of the picture as an instructor, I needed a new art teacher as I was not highly qualified in painting or drawing. My friend and former neighbour Lena highly recommended Jane Smart.

I phoned Jane and we talked. She had an arts degree from a recognized university in the U.K. and was the perfect person for the job: young, talented, keen and available. She took the instructor position to my delight.

Shortly after my conversation with Jane, I got a distressed phone call from the nanny who had been with us for a few months, Lu ayi. She was at home looking after Hannah. The ayi was crying and sounded scared.

"The police are here," she said, her voice trembling. "I don't know how to answer their questions."

I gripped the phone tighter and swallowed hard.

"Is Hannah OK?" I asked.

Lu ayi said Hannah was fine and I breathed a sigh of relief. The police weren't going to take my daughter but they weren't leaving my apartment. They had told the ayi that they were confirming my household registration. However, deep down, I knew it was about Dawu's cruise along Chang'an Avenue.

"I'm coming home," I told the ayi.

I immediately got in my car and drove to the Cappuccino Complex. On the way, I called Dawu and told him to get to my place. Now!

We both showed up to find two officers sitting comfortably in my living room. The nanny and my daughter were hiding in a bedroom. It was a scary situation for my family and certainly for Lu ayi. Most Chinese believed that impromptu visits from the cops were a sign that something wasn't right.

I was polite to the officers while Dawu was boisterous and cocky. He never swore at the police but he was giving them the gears about harassing his wife and child.

"Why are you here?" he asked the cops. "To annoy me?"

The officers took the questions in stride and said they were only there to get some general information on the building. Dawu and I knew better.

It had all been a test.

The police now knew who made up Dawu's immediate family, who he employed as his daughter's nanny and that he was protective of all of us. If the cops needed to find Dawu quickly, they knew exactly how to do it. All they had to do was show up at my home. On the other hand, the cops' appearance confirmed to me and Dawu that our movements were monitored. I did not like this at all. Could I be "accidentally suicided" when the vehicle I was driving was cut off, sending it into a pole? I was scared. Canada was back on the table.

Maybe there was another, less official, way to Canada?

I contacted my well-known artist friend in Calgary. Chris Cran and Dawu had met in 2002 when Dawu lectured on Chinese contemporary art at the Alberta College of Art and Design (ACAD). I was hoping Chris could help me arrange some sort of passage for Dawu via ACAD. There might be an art program Dawu could teach or a lecture he could give. I was worried and trying not to seem desperate, but I was looking for anything at all that would get Dawu an official invitation to Canada. Chris said he'd see what he could do but couldn't guarantee anything.

16

Dawu incorporated the land grab for 008 and Zhengyang into an installation piece he was doing. This one was for a show at the White Box Art Gallery in the 798 Art District. The opening was scheduled for Monday, Mar. 15, 2010. At first, Dawu had told Zhan Yishu, the White Box Art Gallery curator, that he was going to exhibit another work. However, at the last minute, Dawu made a switch. The curator was not happy with the new piece: a work that critiqued the government's lack of interest in supporting the artists who had their land stripped from them by developers.

The night before the opening, Hannah and I showed up to help Dawu with his installation. His art piece was in a jumble on the ground, waiting for him to put it together. Lying about were building materials, chains, cheap sleeping bags that migrant workers commonly used, and many other items. One part of the installation was lit up by a white neon bar. To power the light, Dawu had bought a standard-sized gas generator. Once the installation was completed, it resembled a makeshift construction site. It was a reference to the non-stop demolition and building plaguing modern China and Dawu's conceptual interpretation of 008 and Zhengyang's struggle for compensation and justice.

Hannah was excited to see her dad and was running around and playing with parts of his installation piece. I was relieved that Dawu was back into his art, even if it was a clearly political, very political, art piece.

The White Box Art Gallery was packed opening night. Dawu's work was well-received and praised by peers, other curators and visitors. Many important people in the art world were there as well as the guoan. The secret police always attended 798 exhibitions in attempts to suss out any sort of dissension. Galleries had to submit a list of participating artists prior to an opening and Dawu had assumed, correctly, that the police would know he was at the White Box. They definitely saw his unfavourable political piece.

Despite Dawu's civic commentary, the show was allowed to continue. However, relations between Dawu, Zhan Yishu and the White Box gallery owner, Mr. Bai, were very much strained. The curator and owner were pissed off.

Zhan Yishu and Mr. Bai hadn't expected such a glaring anti-government installation. They were livid. Dawu was pushing the boundaries again. He wanted to draw more attention to the 008 and Zhengyang eviction situation and he had done it. He had also made it look like Zhan Yishu and Mr. Bai condoned artists speaking out against the reigme.

That evening, many of Dawu's Chinese artist friends approached once more and pleaded with me to get Dawu out of China. I didn't bother to explain that I had been trying to do just that and things weren't promising. Chris Cran was unable to do anything for Dawu and I was back to square one.

A few days after Dawu's exhibit opened at White Box, the police shut down the entire show because of his work. Although Dawu knew he had been pushing his luck, the move surprised him. In the past, a couple of his pieces had been yanked, but for reasons other than censorship. In 2005, his installation and performance piece titled *MONKEY KING WREAKS HAVOC ON THE CRYSTAL PALACE* was halted by the authorities and Dawu was almost arrested. That was because he had loaded a homemade "missile" onto a flatbed trailer that was drawn by horses into a swanky luxury condo complex known as Jianwai Soho, on Jianguomen Road in the middle of east Beijing. Police thought Dawu had a live projectile and was going to blow something to smithereens.

Dawu had to make some amends after the White Box show. Although he felt his human rights work was more important than anything else at that time, he didn't want Zhan Yishu and Mr. Bai to look bad, only the government. Dawu wrote a letter of proof for Zhan Yishu and Mr. Bai saying they were not connected to the 008 and Zhengyang project. Personally, the damage had already been done. There was a falling out between Dawu and Zhan. Zhan Yishu was angry with Dawu's exhibit and Dawu was annoyed that Zhan sided with the government.

Having Dawu's latest project pulled by authorities did draw attention, albeit negative attention, to Dawu. I took the exhibition being closed as another sign telling us to leave. I downloaded a package of forms from the Canadian Embassy website and gave it to Dawu's assistant Zhang. I urged him to make Dawu fill out the Chinese portion of the application while I dealt with the English side. I would get him to Canada on a basic tourist visa. As well, I looked for jobs for Dawu all over Canada, not just in Calgary. I wondered if the authorities would think we were dodging them if Dawu, Hannah and I left China. How would that affect us in the future?

I had been bugged and followed in the past couple of weeks. One afternoon, I had texted Emma from my car and told her that I would be at her place soon. Directly after I sent the message, a marked cop car began following me. The blue and white station wagon with numbers tailed me until I parked at my friend's home. Then, the police vehicle parked a few vehicles behind mine. I watched the officers watch me as I got out of my car and entered Emma's building. I then watched the cops from her window. The police waited for me for about half an hour before they left.

Emma and I laughed at the incident at first.

"They could have at least used a ghost car!" we chuckled.

Later in the evening, while I was home with Hannah, I started to get the creeps. The police didn't have to use an unmarked car. They didn't care if I knew they were following me. The thought propelled me into my daughter's room to check on her. She was fine but was Dawu putting her in danger with his antics?

We were going to be under surveillance from now on. It made even driving to the grocery store menacing, knowing the cops were watching my every move. I stopped driving through dark areas at night and didn't answer my door unless I knew who would be there. All of this could have been avoided if we just got out of China. Nevertheless, Dawu was reluctant to leave. He told me he hadn't done anything wrong. Therefore, he was not going to run away to Canada.

Dawu was right. He hadn't committed a crime so why did we have to hide? The more I played with the idea of leaving, the more I realized that I, too, didn't want to flee China at the drop of a hat. I had spent the past 14 years here and I was tied to the community in several ways: by family, friends, my businesses and my studio. It wasn't all about me. What about Hannah and her grandfather, friends and activities? My 42nd birthday was coming up in a few weeks. I'd celebrate it in Beijing, not Calgary.

Dawu also had something to celebrate. On Wednesday, Mar. 17, after months of battling the government and developers, the 008 and Zhengyang artists were being paid what they were owed. Dawu was one of the people who received the money and doled it out. It was a great day but a dark cloud remained. Some of the artists still feared retribution by the owners of the development company. It had been the developers that had sent in the thugs to rough up people in the first place. Now the company had to pay up and it could turn on the artists again. It was a vicious cycle.

At the end of the month, Dawu called me with terrible news: his dad had a stroke and had been admitted to the local Jiuxianqiao hospital. I was shocked as the 70 year old always seemed healthy.

I was concerned and although Dawu wasn't falling apart on the phone, I could sense he needed me at the hospital. Oh dear, not Hannah's yeye. Wu Xiangshou was a loving and generous grandfather as well as a father-in-law. I called him *ba*, for father. He and I tried to have conversations but his Mandarin wasn't good and I didn't speak his dialect. Nevertheless, we could get some jokes across to each other as well as sit in comfortable silence. Ba was my ally when I fought with Dawu.

Wu Xiangshou stayed with us every winter and I looked forward to his visit. He went with us to parties and art exhibitions and sometimes looked after Hannah. He adored his granddaughter.

Wu Xiangshou was a special man.

Hannah and I drove to the hospital where many of Dawu's art friends, including Chao Hongling (also Hannah's godmother), Zhang, Hong and Gu Duanfan and others, were already waiting with him. Being admitted to a hospital in China costs money. If you needed emergency or special services, you usually needed to pay someone to get your name moved to the top of the list. Welcome to a communist state. Health care was not free and your access to services was based on cash.

Someone in Dawu's group had already greased the wheels so Ba could have better care. I didn't know who had stepped up with the money but the bribe worked. Wu Xiangshou had been treated promptly and was resting on a gurney in the hospital corridor.

Hannah's yeye was alive but his skin was green. Dawu told me that he had been out when Zhang and Hong went by his studio and found Wu Xiangshou slumped over a bowl of rice, his head resting on a wooden antique coffee table. They called Dawu and he rushed home.

Wu Xiangshou had been stressed earlier that day. An artist and resident from the former 008 art compound, Zhang Wei, had been stirring up trouble. He wasn't happy with his share of the compensation money and accused Dawu of ripping everyone off. Angry, Zhang Wei had burst into Dawu's studio and started shouting at him.

Zhang Wei said that Dawu had kept most of the money for himself.

There was also some pushing and shoving and Ba tried to stop it. All while this was happening, another disgruntled former resident was filming the whole encounter. It was a stressful ordeal and perhaps too much for Dawu's father to handle emotionally and intellectually. He collapsed a few hours later over his meal.

I was concerned for Ba and distressed for Dawu. How could Zhang Wei have done this to him? They were friends, or at least acquaintances on relatively good terms. However, it looked like times had changed.

I turned my attention to Wu Xiangshou, who was lying on the gurney in the crowded hallway of the local no-frills hospital. He was trying to maintain his last thread of dignity while dressed in a thick hospital gown. I looked at Dawu. He had dark circles under his eyes. He was tired and wasn't going to get much sleep that night.

Wu Xiangshou stayed in the hospital for a few nights. I visited often and several times, found myself sitting by his side, along with a couple of Dawu's friends. They reiterated that I needed to leave China with Dawu and Hannah. That was the only way to keep Dawu safe and lessen the worry for his father. I was back to considering going home again. Later that week, I carefully composed a letter to Diane, asking my sister to invite Dawu to Canada.

I had panicked about getting Dawu to Canada. As the weeks went by, the threat of arrests and more guoan visits faded. Wu Xiangshou was back in Jiangsu province by the beginning of spring 2010. The stroke hadn't left any lasting damage and Dawu's father seemed fine, health-wise. I suspected, though, that he was constantly stressed about his son. Nevertheless, things were looking rosy for Dawu.

The TangRen Gallery had an opportunity for Dawu coming up in the late spring. It offered him a solo exhibition in Hong Kong. The third edition of *ArtHK 2010 (ART HONG KONG)* was taking place in May at the Hong Kong Convention and Exhibition Center. *ArtHK* was an Asian contemporary art fair that displayed the region's best contemporary art. Dawu was invited to be part of TangRen Gallery's stable of exhibitors.

I was excited for him. It was Dawu's inaugural solo exhibition anywhere and he had the backing of a major Beijing gallery. ArtHK meant international exposure. Dawu asked if I'd go as his translator. Of course, I'd go! Besides, Hannah and I were due a trip to Hong Kong Disneyland.

Before going to Hong Kong, Dawu was stopping in Bangkok, Thailand, on his own. He had heard about the major anti-government protests happening there. The National United Front of Democracy Against Dictatorship (UDD, also known as Red Shirts) was calling for political and socio-economic reforms in Thailand. Dawu was going to join the Red Shirts.

"Can't you just go and watch from the side, if at all?" I asked, worried he'd put himself in a precarious position in a foreign country.

"No," said Dawu. "It's my duty to stand with pro-democracy supporters protesting against dictatorships."

A couple of weeks before the trip to Hong Kong, I threw myself a combined birthday-slash-grand-opening-of-my-studio party in April. The event was to launch my business and me into my 42nd year.

It took me several days to organize everything. I brought in enormous arrangements of pink cherry blossoms from the Laitai Flower Market and used the flowers to decorate the Beijing Color Studio. I arranged to feed everyone with food from a Uighur restaurant. (Uighurs are a Muslim ethnic minority group from China's Xinjiang region.)

My new assistant Jane introduced me to a cool band called Girls Are Waiting to Meet You. It was formed by expats and the band was hired to play at the party, as was my DJ friend, Liu Yong. Liu Yong was a professional DJ and was going to spin some music for me. Dawu and I were separated and living separate lives but I knew he was struggling with my friendship with Liu Yong. My ex-husband thought I was dating the DJ. That wasn't true. Liu Yong had been with his girlfriend, Tingting, for about three years.

Before the party, Dawu dropped off two huge bags of fruit for the buffet table. He said he would be back later that evening with some friends. That made me look forward to the event even more. Hannah was going to be at the soirée and the three of us would be together for my birthday.

Dawu arrived at the party when it was in full swing. However, he hadn't brought anyone with him. He told me that his friends weren't able to make it, citing that they had other commitments.

"That's too bad," I said and went to have fun with my guests.

Overall, the party was a highlight of my past several years in China. All my friends, business associates and acquaintances attended. Other residents around the Beijing Color Studio compound joined me, including Ma Ling. She was someone who I had known since I first arrived in Beijing in 2000.

It felt like the night was mine. Everyone seemed to enjoy themselves drinking, eating and dancing. Jane gifted me two "topless" waiters who were body painted to look like they were wearing clothes. It was very cool, risqué. I wasn't thinking of anything other than how I would spend my days with my business, my community and my family around me in China.

After my birthday and the studio launch, it was time to celebrate Dawu's upcoming art breakthrough. It was a major accomplishment for him to be chosen for Hong Kong by the TangRen Gallery. To represent a larger gallery in Beijing was a significant step up. It meant Dawu's work was being noticed by the right people and that he was gaining ground in a very competitive industry. Even Dawu was excited about his upward progress in the art world.

To mark the milestone, I asked Dawu to join Hannah and me for supper. It would be my treat, as I was happy to toast his success. It would also give us a chance to work out the logistics of travelling to Hong Kong together.

I chose to have dinner at a new Malaysian restaurant in Beijing, close to the Lido Plaza and hotel area. The restaurant had been highly recommended by several friends over the past several weeks. Nevertheless, Dawu balked at the thought of eating somewhere "foreign." He also thought it was too splashy and expensive.

"Don't worry about the price," I said. "I'm paying for it."

I thought he was being ridiculous. I didn't understand why he was making a fuss over the restaurant. As well, I was somewhat offended because we typically eat at Chinese restaurants. This was something new and fun. However, he was giving me all sorts of excuses and trying to back out of going out with me and his daughter. I picked him up anyway.

Dawu was in a funk the second he got into my vehicle. At the restaurant, the server brought us menus and that was when Dawu brought out his anger. He started to rant, saying that he couldn't see anything on the list that resembled a meal. Why were we here in the first place? He went on and on and when his food arrived, his words got sharper and more pointed at me.

He told Hannah that I wasn't a good mother and that I didn't care about anyone other than myself. I wasn't sure where any of this was coming from and it hurt my feelings. All I had wanted to do was celebrate his success. He wouldn't stop insulting me and I started to cry. I had to leave the restaurant and sob outside while Dawu and Hannah remained at the table, laughing and talking about me. He kept telling our daughter how bad of a mother I was. That was the last straw.

It was one thing to direct barbs at me but via our daughter, who was way too young to figure things out for herself? No way! I was furious by the time they both came outside after their meal was over. I told Dawu right then and there that I was NOT going to Hong Kong.

I still had to drop him off at his studio. I cried the whole drive there. Before he got out of the car, I reiterated that I wouldn't be going anywhere with him. I guess he didn't believe me because he called the next day.

"Hey," said Dawu, "so are you going to come to Hong Kong with me? You need to prepare your passport and other documents now. Zhang will drop by today and pick them up."

"Um," I said, "I told you last night that I wasn't going with you."

"Ah, are you sure? Are you sure that this is what you want to do? Is this your final decision?"

"Yes," I said. "You need to find someone else."

Dawu hung up. We didn't talk to each other for several days. However, he had the balls to call and yell at me for not knowing where his credit card was and to ask some travel-related questions. He wasn't asking either: he was demanding and simply hung up on me if I didn't know the answer. I ended up putting an alarm on my phone so every time he rang, I knew it was him. Then, I could mentally prepare for what was coming down the pipe.

By now, our marriage was over, over, over but we were slow to officially dissolve our legal union. We hadn't contacted a lawyer to sign any papers. Nevertheless, I began to see who else was out there for me. I went online and signed up on some dating sites such as Plenty of Fish (POF). I advertised myself as *a foreigner looking for friendship in China*. That was how I met Mike Kuo. We started messaging each other through POF.

One day, Hannah and I popped into our local Jenny Lou's, a small grocery store chain that sold imported expat foods that I couldn't get at a Chinese store, like Kraft Dinner and Corn Flakes. I was in the shop picking up some things when I noticed a tall Chinese man staring at me from across the store. He kept changing the angle of his head to measure me up better. I wondered if I knew this guy. Maybe I had worked with him at the Australian Embassy.

He walked over to me and in excellent English asked, "Are you on Plenty of Fish?"

It was Mike.

It was an awkward way to meet for the first time, especially since I had my daughter with me and the store was filled with shoppers. I gave him my business card and he said he would call me. We quickly said goodbye and I thought that was it. Later that night, he texted me and said he was very happy to have met me in person and asked if I would I like to go out on the weekend.

"Yes," I replied.

A few days after my first face-to-face encounter with Mike Kuo, he called while I was making pasta. I was boiling the spaghetti when the phone rang. I answered and we shouted over the sounds of the overhead fan and bubbling water and managed to arrange to meet that evening for a beer. It would be an innocent drink and we'd go from there. I was excited about the prospect of a date — although nervous, too. I hadn't been on a date since I had met Dawu almost nine years earlier.

I drove to Jenny Lou's grocery store and parked. Before I got out of my car, I spotted Mike waiting for me on a corner of the street. He wore a black and white T-shirt, jeans and had a big smile on his face. He waved at me while I crossed the street. I was trying to be cool so I pretended to be extremely interested in the pavement and looked down.

I didn't have much experience in playing the field. After Dawu and I met, we almost immediately moved into together. Maybe if we had spent more time actually getting to know each other, we wouldn't be getting divorced. Or had even got married.

Mike and I shook hands and had a drink on the patio at the Eldora, a nice pub. We started talking and getting to know one another. Mike had worked as a private driver during the 2008 Olympics. He had chauffeured athletes and officials to and from events. Mike was a rarity in Beijing as not many locals had driver's licences. He had found his great gig through a Spanish friend. That's when I began to wonder if Mike wanted to go out with me because he thought I might be able to help him score jobs. Hmm. On my end, I did think that having a friend who could drive a car in the city might come in handy one day.

We finished our drinks and moved on to another place for pulled noodles and nan bread. After eating, Mike came right out and asked if I wanted to go to my studio and hang out. I was shocked that he even knew I had a studio. He must have done some online sleuthing. However, it didn't put me off, as I didn't feel threatened by Mike. He gave me good vibes so I was fine talking with him some more.

We did have more conversation and beers at the Beijing Color Studio but that was it. I dropped Mike off at his compound close to 12:30 a.m. We said good night and see you later.

A Memoir

We saw each other a few more times in the following weeks. We fell into a routine of going for a meal, drinks and then heading to the studio. There were some romantic undertones mixed in with friendship. I told him about Hannah but was not prepared to have them meet just yet. Besides, I didn't think Mike was long-term material. The whole time I was hanging out with him, Dawu was in my thoughts more than I liked.

Mike was six years younger than me and wanted kids of his own. At the age of 42, I was done with having babies. The big red flag, though, was that he did NOT like Beijing's art scene. He thought artists were hooligans (his words), perverts and lowlifes. I mean, how do you get through to someone with his mindset about the genius of Zhang Dali, Wang Qingsong, the Gao Brothers or even Ai Weiwei? Mike didn't appreciate these fine artists and thought they were a waste of space. For me, it demonstrated how deep Chinese government propaganda penetrated. Mike believed that contemporary and avant-garde artists were users and takers and shouldn't be respected.

Besides being squired around by Mike, I attended my beloved book club, went to music festivals with Emma, Badr and other friends and hung out at 2 Kolegas (pronounced Dos Kolegas, which means "two colleagues" in Spanish), one of the coolest bars in Beijing. It was a busy time and I was relaxed and feeling chill knowing that Hannah was well taken care of by her ayi. I had Qiu ayi pretty much at my beck and call for about CAD 1.50 an hour.

Dawu and I had Hannah's education taken care of, too. The Daystar Academy, an international bilingual school, was the only one of its kind in Beijing in 2010. In May, Dawu and I registered our daughter at Daystar for the upcoming academic year starting at the end of summer. The school had an excellent reputation but it was expensive compared to local Chinese schools. Tuition at Daystar was $6,000 U.S. (CAD 8,260) a year while other schools were in the hundreds of dollars. Dawu and I were splitting the costs. He was going to chip in by selling some of his art.

I put a hefty deposit of ¥15,000 RMB (CAD 2,500) to hold Hannah's spot at the school. It was worth it. Hannah was going to have the opportunity to learn in both Chinese and English. Dawu was keen to see his daughter go too. The Beijing Color Studio business was making some money and I could contribute my portion of the tuition.

During this time, I was still working on getting out of the Counting Sheep Boutique. As well, a friend had put my name in to be considered for a Women in Business award. I hadn't won anything at the previous year's event but it wasn't about winning -- it was about networking and being a part of the Beijing business community.

I thought I had a good shot at the *Entrepreneur of the Year*. The winners were announced at a gala in Beijing on Thursday, May 27 — the same day as Dawu's Hong Kong art opening.

While Dawu was at his show, I was at the Women in Business gala at the Marriott Hotel. I was sitting at a table facing the announcer and when she started telling a story about the winner, I knew she was talking about me. I had butterflies while I listened to her share how the Beijing Color Studio grew from an idea to a grand art studio that attracted all sorts of talents and people. Then, she said my name.

"Karen Patterson."

All of a sudden, the room got quiet and all eyes were on me. Then, my table erupted into applause. I was astonished and couldn't believe that I had won. I was glued to my seat. Fortunately, I quickly found my feet, walked to the front and accepted the glass trophy. I gave a short speech and thanked the supporters of my studio, my customers and clients and the Women in Business organization. It was a true Hollywood moment for me because I was then blasted by the flashes of cameras going off around me. Several television reporters interviewed me, too.

I texted Dawu about my honour and he immediately responded. He said he was happy for me and his art show with TangRen was also going well. The exhibit was well-attended and there was a lot of interest in his work. I couldn't help but think that we were truly at a new point in our lives: friends and respected peers.

It was pouring rain when I left the Marriott to get a taxi after the gala. My skin was cold to touch but I was warm inside. I was elated by my win and felt like I was moving onto bigger and better things. I was proud of my studio, my accomplishments and felt that all of my previous business dealings had worked together to garner this honour. At that moment, I was on top of the world. Almost nothing could make the evening better. Except, of course, congratulations from my daughter.

I woke Hannah when I got home and showed her my award. She beamed like a light although I wasn't sure she understood why I had received it. We read a book, cuddled and fell asleep moments apart from each other that night. At last, my life in China was bearing fruit.

19

I picked Mike up at his compound near to the Lido Holiday Inn Hotel the day after winning my award. We were going to buy ceiling fans and koi fish for my studio aquarium. I showed him the award and he had no idea what to say other than congratulations. I could tell he was confused as to how my business could garner such an achievement and how I could be so boastful about it. Many Chinese are modest and might downplay an award. I have found that it's a somewhat Confucian value to be humble and not express pride in your talents and abilities. To Mike, I was being cocky and arrogant.

Despite my cultural misstep, Mike and I went out. He negotiated a good deal on a fan for me and had some good insight into the fish, too. As a child, Mike raised lots of fish and turtles in his family's apartment.

At the store, there were so many fish! There were many colour choose from: gold, silver, black, yellow, white, speckled. Sizes too: big, um and little. I settled on several smallish koi, some goldfish and a r fighting fish for Hannah, which would live on our dining room tal the studio. From a fengshui perspective, the fish would bring a se peace and, ultimately, business to the studio (or so I was told by fish shop owner). I was happy to hear that, because I had a r my business. The award last night was just the beginning.

On Saturday, I took Hannah to her baba's studio. D his good run in Hong Kong and spilling over with p turned with some gifts for his daughter. She loved I and pencils and was excited to spend the weekend v to hear about Dawu's trips.

He told me that participating in the Th side the Red Shirts made him feel like he was Around the world, people in other countrie their governments. As for Hong Kong, D play his art and many people were talkir He criticized me a bit for not accompai tions were asked in English and he coul

"I'm happy you won your award," in Hong Kong."

OK! On that note, I told Dawu I'd be back the next afternoon to pick up Hannah. I also reminded him of Hannah's performance for International Children's Day. The important Chinese holiday was just around the corner. Hannah had been preparing a dance routine with her classmates and they'd be performing it on Tuesday, June 1. Dawu assured me he'd be there.

That evening without Hannah, I had time to reflect on my life going forward in China. I had made the right decision to stay. I had a great family, friends and the Beijing Color Studio was evolving into a bonafide enterprise. I was lucky Ma Ling thought of me when the place became available. It was perfect.

My studio was probably safe from the talons of luxury developers. The small space was stuck squarely between the busy and noisy fifth ring road artery and active railway tracks. No one in his or her right mind would want this tiny, clamouring, awkwardly shaped piece of real estate.

Another dream was coming to reality, too. John Franklin had been in touch with me again. My Chinese art exhibition in Canada was a go. My job was selecting and coordinating the artists. Dawu would be assisting me and it was great that we could work on the project as artistic partners.

By the middle of Sunday, I had enough of alone time and was ready pick up my daughter. I drove into Dawu's 798 compound around 5 p.m. spotted him and Hannah playing with a soccer ball. Dawu was distract- kicking the ball back to her only after she shouted at him. It didn't match igh-spirited Dawu I had seen the other day. The Dawu here was in a ent space.

Ah, those artists. I never knew what mood Dawu was going to be in he moment to the next. I parked on the side of the alley and watched and her father continue their game – half-heartedly on Dawu's part, e-heartedly on Hannah's end.

u held his phone in one hand and moments later, it rang just as ked the ball to him. He was instantly absorbed in the call and ways to miss the ball. The move made Hannah giggle and she ball, retrieving it for more fun with her dad. However, Dawu his hand that he was taking time out.

d in to play and I could overhear some of Dawu's conver- led like the person on the other end was asking to use his erator. Dawu said the caller could borrow the equipment. e piece of equipment to use in his exhibition at the White

Box gallery in March. That was the show that upset the curator, Zhan Yishu. The generator had been sitting idle in Dawu's studio since the show was shut down by the government.

As enthralling as the one-sided conversation was, I had to go. I told Hannah to get her things and she ran to grab her stuff from Dawu's studio and say goodbye to Mike, Dawu's fat black and white cat (named Michael Jackson because of his song Black or White. The overweight feline had followed Dawu home one day.) I told Dawu we were going and reminded him about the Children's Day event. He mumbled something unintelligible. Hannah hugged and kissed her father and we drove off in a cloud of dust. Hannah was waving out the back window until she couldn't see her father anymore.

PART THREE

"Governments are obliged to ensure the right of free expression -
even if the speaker advocates a different social system."
Thorbjorn Jagland, selection committee for Nobel Peace Prize 2010

'Perhaps in the future, we will live in a world
where people's actions are guided by
principles of the rule of law, and not by face...
To live in China now is a big risk...
I have no confidence in the [legal] system."
Karen Patterson, spoken just after Wu Yuren's first trial, November 2010

"The further a society drifts from truth
the more it will hate those who speak it."
George Orwell

T here was only one day left before International Children's Day. I was busy on Monday, May 31, organizing my own Children's Day event for Beijing Color Studio. Since the date fell on a weekday and most schools and families would be having their own celebrations, I decided to host the studio painting party on Sunday, June 6. I talked to Jane, my instructor, about buying materials, managing the kids and parents, payments and other such aspects.

I had found an excellent niche for my business in the city. Most programs and camps in Beijing were academic (such as math improvement) or language-based (learning English) but I was offering a chance for kids to be creative and work and play with art. I was getting a great response from parents, too, as they were signing up their children to take part in my studio's workshops.

That Monday afternoon, I sent a lengthy email to my family and friends detailing Hannah's school and extracurricular activities, my Women in Business honour and Dawu's solo exhibition in Hong Kong. I added some notes on Dawu's leadership role in securing compensation for the 008 and Zhengyang artists, as well as his march on Chang'an Avenue. I said I was proud of him for sticking up for others, despite the fact that he could have been risking his future. The government wasn't fond of people who called for reform. However, Dawu seemed to have escaped the full wrath of the communist authorities. I ended the letter by saying that so far this year, without a doubt, things had not only been challenging but also very exciting.

I sent my note off into cyberspace and then left to meet my friend Sophie Baker. We had a great time catching up. It was a lovely afternoon, the perfect temperature, and our conversation flowed easily. Around 4:30 p.m. I was confident that Hannah would be OK because, according to my co-parenting schedule with Dawu, it was his responsibility to pick her up from school. I would fetch her from Dawu's studio after my dinner. This was a common arrangement: Dawu picked Hannah up and would hang out with her until I arrived to get her later in the evening, usually around 8 p.m.

Sophie and I kept chatting and the topic turned to Dawu and how horrible he had been to me prior to going to Hong Kong, especially during the Malaysian dinner back in early May. I told my friend that I'd like to divorce him but it was expensive. Dawu and I had met with a lawyer, who wanted to charge us an exorbitant fee of over CAD 9,000 to sign papers.

Another thing was, for some reason, I couldn't quite get around to signing the forms to dissolve my marriage with Dawu. Nevertheless, I told Sophie that I was excited for Dawu and his success at his recent exhibition and I felt he was moving in the right direction in terms of his art. Sophie agreed.

One of the things I liked about Sophie was her capacity to appreciate someone like Dawu, despite his many shortcomings and my biased words. She had compassion for him as well as me. Neither Dawu nor I were evil people. We just didn't seem to work as romantic partners anymore.

I usually don't check the time when I'm out with company because I think it's rude, but a strange compulsion came over me to look at my phone. I certainly wasn't concerned the evening was running over or that I had to be home by a certain hour. Hannah was safe with Dawu at his studio and I was having a nice evening. The time said 7:30 p.m.

Around 8 p.m., it was time to get my daughter. Hannah came out to meet my car at Dawu's studio. She told me Zhang had picked her up and been watching her. Dawu hadn't been around the studio at all. That wasn't unusual. When Dawu was busy, Zhang acted like Hannah's babysitter. Dawu was an artist and a grown man and he didn't have to tell me what he was doing or where he was. He only needed to be there for Hannah's International Children's Day dance tomorrow.

Back at the Cappuccino Complex, I made a last-minute call to Jinzi, my contractor, regarding installing the ceiling fans in time for Sunday's kids' party. With all that in order, I gave Hannah a cuddle before tucking her into bed and saying goodnight. I was surprised my five-year-old daughter went to sleep so quickly since she was so excited about the next day's performance.

International Children's Day is a national holiday and a big deal in China. Chinese culture focuses much of its energy and resources on children. In 1949, along with the founding of the People's Republic of China, came International Children's Day. Traditionally, the day was filled with games, activities, food and shows. Most schools organize morning performances so families have the afternoon to spend together.

In the morning, Hannah and I had to take a taxi to her school due to the mandatory licence plate restriction. My number was up that Tuesday --

no driving for me. We arrived at the Caihong Road Kindergarten and I sent Hannah to her class before finding Emma in the crowded courtyard. Her daughter Jenny was dancing as well. I hadn't heard from Dawu and assumed he had slept in, which wasn't uncommon. If he said he would be here, then he'd be here.

Just not on time.

Since Hannah started attending the kindergarten in 2008, Dawu and I had been there every June 1 to watch her dance. Dawu was expected to arrive on time for the 9 a.m. celebration and watch his daughter perform in the school's courtyard.

Squeezed shoulder-to-shoulder while awaiting Hannah's dance number, I texted her father's cellphone. When I didn't get a reply, I called him. No answer. I was angry he wasn't here and my heart drooped for Hannah. Her father had probably slept in after staying up late and chatting and visiting with other artists. He was making my blood boil.

The doors to the courtyard opened and for an instant, I thought all was saved. Dawu was here! But no, it was Jenny's father instead. Hayden Koh, Emma's Singaporean husband, got there in time to film the girls dancing with around 40 other kindergarten students.

Each child knew the routine by heart. Who knows how long the teacher made them practice but the performance was cute and the kids were happy. Emma and I couldn't get over how adorable our girls were. It wasn't little kids wobbling about but a well-organized show. All the children were dressed in the same red-and-blue outfits, singing a classic Chinese song while doing movements to it. At the end, some kids did the splits, not something Hannah or Jenny were capable of yet.

After the performance, Hannah asked where her dad was. I told her he had slept in. I was sad for Hannah that Dawu missed her show. I was going to have a word with him about disappointing his daughter. First, we were invited to Emma's house for lunch.

Emma and Jenny lived a stone's throw away from the kindergarten. Emma called a chain eatery popular with expats, Annie's Italian Restaurant, and gave our meal order. Then, my phone rang and I reached for it thinking it was Dawu. I was going to give him a piece of my mind. But when I answered, it was Zhang, Dawu's studio assistant, on the line.

"Dawu didn't come home last night," he said.

"Well, is he dating anyone?" I asked. It was not as if he told me of his every move but he especially wouldn't have told me anything if he had plans with a girlfriend.

"No," Zhang said. "I haven't been able to reach him on his phone since around 4 p.m. or so yesterday afternoon."

The last communication Zhang had with Dawu was when Dawu asked his studio assistant to pick up Hannah from school. Dawu had mentioned then that he was on his way to the police station but didn't say why. Zhang didn't ask why either. Hello! It seemed to be an obvious question.

When Zhang woke up alone at the back of 798 art compound and there was no sign of Dawu, he knew he should be concerned. Me, not so much. Dawu had spoken out against the Chinese authoritarian government a few times already and nothing much had happened. What made Zhang believe Dawu was in trouble now?

"We need to figure out what's going on," Zhang said. "We need to find him. Meet me at the Art Café at 1 p.m."

Instead of feeling worried, I felt inconvenienced. I had a perfect afternoon set up, starting with dropping Hannah off with her former ayi, Qi Jie, who loved Hannah dearly and wanted to spend a part of Children's Day with her. I was going to have some downtime for me and go for a beer with Mike. Now that had turned into Dawu-time.

I cancelled my date with Mike, dropped Hannah off at Qi Mei's and continued to the café, near Dawu's studio at 798, to meet with Zhang. Searching for Dawu was not my top priority and I let Dawu's assistant know this when I saw him at the Art Café, artist Huang Rui's restaurant. Zhang was pale and worried.

"I think we need to start checking police stations," said Zhang.

"Why on Earth would we do that?"

"I told you, he was heading to one when I last heard from him."

"That doesn't mean anything. Why would the police hold Dawu?"

Zhang shifted in his chair.

"Dawu got into some trouble the other night," said Zhang. "It wasn't his fault."

"What did he do this time?"

Zhang told me that Dawu had been asked for a favour by Tang Funai, a known troublemaker and the owner of the Sugar Jar, a CD shop inside 798. The story was that Dawu had been helping Tang arrange an extension on his lease with the 798 property management company. The management did not want to renew with the artist and so it cut his utilities. Without electricity, the store couldn't function. Tang then borrowed Dawu's generator. However, the generator disappeared from the Sugar Jar.

Tang and Dawu realized the 798 management took it and that fired them up. The two drove a scooter to the police station onsite at 798. They were going to complain to the cops about the property management company. Yep, this was just like Dawu. He could be stubborn and he hated when things were unfair. He always looked out for the underdog.

Zhang bowed his head to keep from looking at me but I could already see the concern in his eyes. My brain downplayed the situation. The management of the 798 artist compound was administered by a private company. If Dawu had management problems, he might go straight to the local detachment to voice them. It made sense Dawu would try the legal and easiest option first. As per China, though, the cops wouldn't have intervened and that would have pissed Dawu off. I thought he was letting off steam somewhere.

I sighed. The more I thought about it, the more I suspected that Dawu was with a lady friend, winding down after another interaction with brutish Chinese administrators.

Dawu wasn't missing, he was laying low. But what if he wasn't?

Dawu and I had only just reached a sort of point in our lives where we were both successful. What had he done to bring us both down? I had managed to glide into a state of oblivion over the last month. It was easy to do when things had been going so well. Here was my wake-up call.

"I guess we should check out the police station, then," I said.

I paid the bill and Zhang and I left. I wasn't convinced that Dawu was in hot water, not boiling hot anyway. I was still annoyed that he was inconveniencing me yet again. Nevertheless, if our good friend thought Dawu was in trouble, I needed to help.

Zhang's Jeep didn't have any driving restrictions and we took off in it, heading for the Jiangtai Road Police Station, close to where I lived. Zhang parked in the designated visitor parking lot and we walked to the detachment.

When we went into the station, I noticed the building had cold granite tile floors, floors that were common in almost every "new" building in China in the early 1990s. I found the police stations eerie with their nondescript white walls, steel metal bars gleaming like teeth, too many doors leading seemingly to nowhere and men and woman who all look identical. They wore the same blue uniforms and never smile.

The only sign I could read was in English, reminding "Foreign Aliens" to remember to renew their visas.

Do not overstay or you will be fined.

There was no line-up when Zhang and I went up to the lone officer sitting behind a thick pane of glass. Through the partition, I briefly introduced myself and asked, in Chinese, if the woman had any evidence of Wu Yuren in the police records or knew his whereabouts. She looked at me blankly. While I wasn't bilingual, my Mandarin pronunciation and grammar were fully correct.

"*Meiyou*," she finally answered.

Meiyou was a common way of getting rid of someone who you didn't want to talk to. It basically meant *I don't know, nor do I care.*

I certainly cared and I repeated my questions, adding that perhaps she might want to look in her records or ask another officer. After an annoyed look at me, she got up and walked away. I hoped she wasn't getting someone to throw me out.

She returned, accompanied by a male officer, who didn't lunge for me. I was not getting turfed out. However, I wasn't sure why it took two officers to give me one piece of news.

"We don't have jurisdiction over the 798 Art Zone," said the policewoman, "these two stations do."

She wrote down the addresses and handed me the slip of paper. I thanked her and Zhang and I left.

In my previous exchanges with the police, they were polite and helpful despite rarely smiling. I had no issue with the way I had been treated in the past. Today was different.

Not far down the road, Zhang's Jeep broke down. The vehicle conveniently sputtered out near a mechanic shop. Zhang said he'd get the Jeep fixed and meet me at the next detachment, Jiuxianqiao Police Station. I walked to my apartment and reluctantly got into my Honda Fit. There was a licence restriction for me and I was wary about driving. Police were standing on every corner and I'd get an expensive fine if they spotted my number.

I drove to the station. The detachment was an older two-storey brick building on a tree-lined street. The parking was right out front, actually on the sidewalk. Drivers were forced to park around trees and pedestrians. Just as I got out of the car, I spied Dawu in a window.

His face relaxed with relief when he saw me. I was startled when I saw him. He was dusty, dishevelled and unkempt. His face was swollen and he was holding his right arm. I had never seen him like this, even after some rough encounters with authorities in the past. The look on his face and the tone of his voice made me realize that this was serious. Much more serious than I had imagined.

"Kailin, wo bei dale," he said.

21

Dawu needs my help. I take a step towards him but before I can say anything, someone slams the window shut. The glass is covered in Mactac vinyl and a white curtain. I can't see a thing.

I stop dead in my tracks. What just happened? What's going on? There must be some kind of misunderstanding. Seeing Dawu in pain and frightened frightens me. Surely though, there's an explanation. He can't be hurt. He can't be hurt because he didn't do anything.

I rush into the station. If I thought the first place was eerie, this place is downright terrifying. It's like a centuries' old fort with decaying cement and a drawbridge for a counter. That drawbridge is the way to Dawu.

The drawbridge comes down with a slam when an officer sees me. I'm halted at the counter by a woman who tells me to go sit down. I am not about to sit like an obedient dog while Dawu is being held in that torture chamber.

I approach the counter and give my name and then Dawu's full name, Wu Yuren.

"I just saw him a couple of minutes ago," I say to the policewoman.

She nods and points to an empty row of seats in the waiting room. Before I go sit, I write my name and phone number in Chinese characters and hand it to her. She accepts it and says someone will be with me soon.

Soon isn't soon. The minutes are adding up but the police behaviour isn't. There's no one in front of us so I know they must be stalling. As well, the officers I dealt with in the past were sympathetic. There must be a good reason they're making me wait now. There must be a good explanation of why Dawu is hurt. Right?

Zhang arrives at the station and we make small talk. We look at the photos of the police officers on the wall. Did one of them hurt Dawu? Which one of them will bring him back to us?

After about an hour, the policewoman at the drawbridge is joined by a tall man. I had noticed his picture on the wall. He appears ... nice? Maybe he has some answers. I walk up to him and ask about Dawu. Both officers stare at me like I've asked them to cut off their hands. Finally, the man speaks.

"He is not here."

"Yes, he is," I say, taking a deep breath in to maintain my composure. "I saw him. He talked to me."

"He's not here," says the man, avoiding eye contact.

My temper is wrestling with my self-control.

To date, my experiences in China have been that you won't get far if you lose your cool. For Dawu's sake, I need to be chill and calm.

I sit back down, my mind chucking Chinese and English insults at the clowns controlling the drawbridge. Zhang and I wait a further two hours and only then do we get some answers. Not the ones we want to hear.

The tall policeman says Dawu has been transferred to the Chaoyang District Detention Center, a high-security facility. I've never heard of the place but it doesn't sound like a cozy spa. My mouth goes dry thinking Dawu must be in some real trouble. I realize the whole time Zhang and I have been sitting on our butts, the police were working on sending Dawu to jail. They must have taken him out the back door, away from us.

"Why is he at a detention centre?" I ask.

The officer smiles at me and says, "Your husband has been very bad. He has done something illegal and beat a cop. This is our policy to move him."

"What do you mean, he has beaten up a cop?" I ask. "Dawu would never do that! There must be some misunderstanding, why would he do that? Are you sure it was him? He must have been provoked."

What in hell's name is going on? The officer tells me that Dawu had come to the police station on his own accord after spray painting rude and disrespectful things all over the main gate and walls of 798.

WTF? Dawu sprayed graffiti all over the 798 buildings? Why would he have vandalized his art gallery district? I do have to admit, Dawu sometimes has a temper. Nevertheless, I don't think he would damage property he cares about, especially buildings owned by friends. Could it be possible that Tang did the spray painting and Dawu just stood beside him? Could Dawu have egged Tang on? It is something Dawu would have done? Maybe.

I'm getting angry at Dawu again. He put himself at risk by associating with a stupid person. Not only that, Dawu has disappointed his daughter by putting a stranger before her and missing her big performance this morning. When is he going to grow up? Maybe he hasn't been beaten at all. Maybe he fell while running with Tang. Maybe Dawu deserves his little trip to detention then. Still, I should see if he's all right.

"Would you give me the address of the detention centre?" I ask.

The other officer writes it down for me.

"Don't go there now," she says. "It's closed for the day. Go tomorrow."

I thank the officers and Zhang and I leave the station. We walk past the room where Dawu had been hours before. The window is open again but the room is empty.

I drop Zhang off at Dawu's studio and decide to take a drive to 798. There is a part of me that doesn't believe the police. Why would Dawu spray graffiti all over the beautiful red brick walls of 798?

I need to check out the graffiti for myself. Driving through the east gate of 798, I pass the Bauhaus buildings, part of a former ammunition factory built by Germans in the 1930s. Here is when I start to see the stark black writing on the walls. Right in front of my eyes, are slogans in Chinese. The words are nasty, targeting the 798 management.

798 management is shameless!
798 is robbing the people!
798 robbery, shameless!

I hate to admit it but it sounds like Dawu. The language is terrible and the graffiti is unsightly. I am angry — angry at Dawu for being so stupid and making a mockery and embarrassing 798 and the artist community. How am I going to answer questions about this? I didn't know Dawu had it in him to do this to himself, his reputation and his family. After marching on Chang'an Avenue, he knew he needed to play it straight. Needless to say, if he did beat a cop over the generator, it would certainly warrant being thrown into a major detention centre. Hot flames of shame and embarrassment rise in my chest.

My husband, soon to be ex-husband, is clearly out of control. I must have had something to do with it, too. Maybe I should have done more to keep him in check. Maybe I'm too soft or forgiving.

I guess Dawu hadn't learned anything from his first short stint in detention in March. The police let him off lightly then. What will they do to him this time?

The flames in my chest burst into an angry inferno. I'm a crying, raging crazy wife yelling at Dawu. Tears are pouring down my face. Dawu deserves to be in detention.

"Fuck off," I scream at him. "I hope you rot in jail! I am done with you. Try to find someone to help you now! You have pushed away everyone."

When my furor turns to cold ash, I wipe away the tears. Tomorrow morning, I'll rise with the sun and then head to the detention center. I'll find Dawu and rip him to shreds. Yes, that's my plan. He's going to know how much he hurt his family. However, what I don't know is that tomorrow, June 2, will be the start of eleven months of hell.

Karen and Dawu wearing traditional Chinese coats. Spring 2002, Beijing.

Karen and Dawu's marriage license
booklet photo. Mar. 2003, Beijing.

Dawu carries Karen part way up the
Fragrant Mountain on their wedding day.
May 2003, Beijing.

Karen and her Hasselblad
camera photographing migrant
workers for her photo project
BACKGROUND. Summer 2005,
Beijing.

A portion of *BACKGROUND*,
by Karen Patterson,
digital photo, 2005.

Dawu and Canadian
artist Chris Cran.
Nov. 2002, Calgary, Canada.

All photos by Karen Patterson unless otherwise noted.

Graffiti written on the walls and buildings of the 008 Art Community,
"FIGHT FOR HUMAN RIGHTS, EXPEL BAD BUSINESS PRACTICES". Fall 2009, Beijing.

Performance art by Huang Rui during the *RESOLUTION
Art Festival* at the 008 International Art Community. The
characters in black on white are pronounced like the word
"China" in English but mean demolish in Chinese.
Jan. 2010, Beijing.

Dawu's controversial performance and installation art
piece at the Soho Luxury condo complex, *MONKEY
WREAKS HAVOC AT THE CRYSTAL PALACE*. May 2005,
Beijing.

Hannah and Dawu in his 008 studio. This photo was published extensively in the media alongside articles reporting on Wu's case, 2010 to 2011. Summer 2008, Beijing.

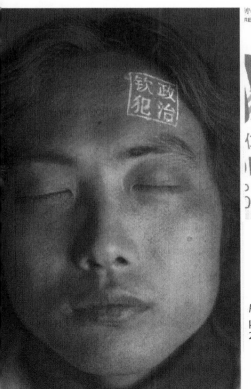

Karen and Dawu at the opening of THOSE YEARS exhibition in the 798 Art District. The exhibition was shut down a few days after this photo was taken. Mar. 2010, Beijing.

POLITICAL CRIMINAL, from Dawu's photo series titled IMPERIAL CRIMINALS. Spring 2001, Changzhou, China.

I'm burning with frustration and anger when I wake up on Wednesday, June 2. I have to spend my time digging Dawu out of a mess at the fucking detention centre. I'm so angry I could wring his scrawny neck. The police officers can be witnesses. At least I don't have to reorganize Hannah's schedule. She's still with her former ayi, Qi Mei, and will remain with her until Dawu's situation is straightened out.

Which will be soon.

I get dressed quickly and then clear my calendar for the day. I've been arranging classes, photo shoots and networking to keep building the Beijing Color Studio. I'm busy, too. Then I storm out of my apartment, slamming doors on my way, though not intentionally. Hopefully, this will all blow over by the afternoon, as it had in the spring. The authorities then had released him after 36 hours. I'm sure they'll do the same today. First stop, I have to pick up Zhang on the way to the Chaoyang District Detention Center. He is at the 798 studio waiting for me.

Loud music fills my Honda Fit as I take off down the street. If I have to wait all day for Dawu, I'll be pissed. Last time he was in "jail," he had takeout delivered right to him. A junior clerk fetched food from a local restaurant so Dawu could have something to eat. Detention can't be too bad.

This all must be a big misunderstanding anyway. The police couldn't be serious that Dawu has beaten a cop. Dawu does get angry but he wouldn't have crossed the line and hit an officer. He knows the limits.

Dawu has never physically hurt me but he's scary when he's upset. When we were first dating in 2002, Dawu was painting a series that he hoped to sell. He was frustrated with the way the work was turning out and he put a screwdriver through the canvas. He sometimes yelled at me and once threw my mug full of tea across the apartment. It smashed into the wall and left a stain. But he never touched me. That's how I know that no matter how much he was raging against the authorities, he wouldn't have been that stupid to attack, verbally or physically, a police officer. He knows what he can get away with. Or not.

I pull up in front of Dawu's studio where Zhang is waiting. It looks like he hasn't had any sleep. The bags under his eyes say he's still worried. I turn the music down so we can chat.

"It's going to be fine," I say.

"Maybe," he says, "but whatever you do, when you talk to the police, just ask for the facts."

I agree with him. I'm not one to fly off the handle in most situations. I'm perturbed at Dawu right now but I'm not going to go after the authorities and get into trouble, too.

The Chaoyang District Detention Center is near the outskirts of east Beijing. The drive there isn't too long and we arrive around 10 a.m. and park on the road. The four-storey building looks like a small factory. We're visiting the detention cellblocks, which are at the back of the area. To get there, we have to go through a heavily fortified door at the side of the building. There's a line of people slowly marching past a guard to show him their ID.

"Uh oh," I think to myself. "Do I have the right papers?"

Zhang is waved through when he presents his *shenfenzheng*, his Chinese ID card. I don't have one, as I'm Canadian, so I show the guard my Chinese driver's licence. It gets me in the door but I'm told to bring my passport next time.

There won't be a next time.

We walk into some sort of processing lobby. It's a room with a long counter at one end. Officers in their blue suits and hats sit on the other side, serving a long queue of people. These people all have family members inside. Some folks are crying, some have frowns of worry and some are expressionless. They ask about loved ones and hand over money and clothing for the detained. Some of those being held could be in there for anything from murder, stealing, forgery or being "caught" for something that the government doesn't like, such as simply attending a church service or writing about the PRC in a negative way.

Zhang finds us the right line where we can inquire about Dawu. I had thought we'd see him in here. Then, we'd sign him out and take him home.

Where is he?

We get to the officer behind the counter and ask him if he knows Wu Yuren.

"He came in last night," I add.

"That man is in trouble," says the officer with *Mr. Li* written on his police nametag. "He's going to end up with a criminal record. He hit a cop and is going nowhere."

The room starts to close in on me and I feel very hot.

Mr. Li turns his hand into the shape of a gun and points it at his head. "Pow, pow," he says.

Is my husband going to be executed?

I try to keep a blank look on my face, despite feeling like barfing up my breakfast. I need to be composed.

"Well, can we at least see him?" I ask Mr. Li.

"No," he says, laughing again. "No, you won't be seeing Mr. Wu for quite some time."

23

Dawu is not coming home with me. He's staying at the detention centre. My body has been on high alert since discovering how much trouble Dawu is in and I fight to keep the tears off my face. Before leaving, Zhang and I find out that Dawu will stay in jail for at least one month in a room with at least 10 other men. He'll be fed three meals a day but have no contact with family or friends during that time. Not even phone calls. I'm allowed to drop off bundles of clean clothes to him during the week between 8:30 a.m. and 11:30 a.m., but that's it.

I drive Zhang to the 798 studio and I go home. This morning was overwhelming and I feel the urge to write my sister in Canada, not only to tell her what's happening, but to process my thoughts. By writing this all down, it'll somehow become real. So much has happened and so much has not happened. I email Diane and let her know the little I know.

My studio is empty since Hannah is with her ayi. All I want to do is hug my daughter. I wonder how I protect a five-year-old from all of this? Do I keep the bad news from her? Do I give her the bad news? If yes, when?

I don't tell Qi Mei what's happening when I phone her and ask that Hannah stay a couple more days. I say that Dawu is travelling home to Jiangsu province. It's about 12 hours by overnight train from Beijing, not far from Shanghai. I say he went to deal with a sick family member. I'm not a liar by nature but this should buy me some time while I figure out what to do. There is no guidebook for dealing with a detained husband in China.

Qi Jie believes my story, no questions asked. It's a huge relief I don't have to stress out about Hannah. I can leave her as if nothing has changed. I tell Qi Mei that I'll pick up my daughter on Friday.

"That's fine," says the nanny. "Hannah is happy."

I'm grateful for Qi Mei and appreciate that she can take care of my daughter almost as well as I can. As part of my coping plan, I want to keep Hannah's routine normal. Even if that means I'm not part of her day.

Because I don't know what's going on, I dismiss thoughts of reaching out to the Canadian Embassy. I'm Canadian. Dawu is Chinese. What can Canada do for him? Actually, what can I do for him besides keep his laundry clean?

Thoughts of divorce float around in my head. Dawu and I hadn't started official proceedings but we had talked about it. We remained separated but hadn't dissolved our marriage.

I wonder if being Dawu's wife is going to cause problems. He could be a liability to me, to Hannah. Nevertheless, I'm not going to let Dawu face this alone. Neither is Zhang.

As much as Dawu is Zhang's "boss," they are also friends. For now, Zhang assures me he'll deal with all matters that don't have to do with "next of kin" and will keep the studio running and answer all calls and inquiries from friends and colleagues. News travels fast. Already close to a dozen artists have called me to ask Dawu's whereabouts. I start forwarding the calls to Zhang. He tells anyone who is not a close friend of Dawu's that he went home to tend an ill relative.

I need to vent so I ask my friend Mike to meet me. He's a good listener. Mike says it's no problem to see me and we meet at a restaurant. As his English is very good, we don't bother speaking Chinese. It's a relief that I can freely talk and let go without having to think about each word in Mandarin.

I spill the beans to Mike over a beer. He's not an artist and so not connected to that scene. I feel like my secret is safe with him.

"Dawu is a hooligan," says Mike after hearing my story. "He must have done something to deserve being beaten."

I shake my head. I can't believe what he's saying. He goes on to tell me about his friend, who was picked up a decade ago for trafficking drugs and was given 10 years in prison. I'm aghast that Mike is putting horrible ideas into my head. I don't want Dawu to spend any time in prison, let alone a decade. The more we talk about the police and Dawu, the more I'm learning that Mike doesn't think there's anything wrong with the way the police acted.

"Artists aren't trustworthy, Karen."

Mike is not the sympathetic ear I thought he was going to be. Instead, he makes me feel worse about Dawu. Then again, I knew Mike bought into the brainwashing and propaganda that the government feeds the masses about artists being disrespectful citizens. I won't be sharing anything else about Dawu with this supposed friend. I finish my beer and leave.

On the drive home, I start thinking that maybe the only way to get Dawu out of this mess is by bribing someone like a police officer. Paying off officials is illegal in most countries and China is no different. However, it happens all the time here. If you're caught, there are severe consequences like ... death. If you're not caught, you can escape your charges and get on with your life.

Crap. Bribing won't work. I need someone on the inside and neither Dawu nor I have any police connections. Artists and cops don't really move in the same circles. Besides, I have no clue as to how that backdoor system actually works.

My body feels like it weighs a ton as I get out of my car. A lot of worry, stress and pain have been packed on my shoulders in the course of this one day. It's time for bed. If I can sleep.

As I get ready for bed, I think about pulling Hannah out of the Daystar Academy, the prestigious school she's supposed to be attending in a couple of months. We might not be able to pay for it now. Dawu and I were looking forward to our daughter attending this special school. However, Dawu was splitting the costs with me and his portion was coming from the art he sold. Now buyers aren't going to want to purchase a tainted artist's canvas. His overseas career doesn't stand a chance either. He can't get a visa to travel if he has a conviction. My anger towards Dawu flares up again. Great. There goes my sleep.

I roll over and look at the clock. It's 7 a.m. I slept a bit but fitfully. I'll need 400 more hours before I'll feel rested. I've got to get going, though. The calls and emails are rolling in. The other artists from the Chang'an Avenue march are freaking out and telling me I must get Dawu out of detention before the end of this month — the end of June 2010. Otherwise, it will be too late. He'll continue down the road to court and a trial and, ultimately, be convicted and kept in prison for who knows how long.

Some Chinese friends insist I should find a backdoor, a *houmen'r*, channel to get Dawu out. This is, after all, China and the backdoor is usually more open than the front door. Honghong is ready to hand me more than ¥100,000 RMB (CAD 16,700) to use for bribe money. I'm not going to take it. Not yet, anyway.

My once-beloved adopted country is changing into something I don't like. Dealing with police and politics is beyond my comfort zone. It's scary. I'm not sure what's happening and feel like I have a blindfold on. I don't know where to step next.

I take the cues from my Chinese friends. I hear the fear and concern in their voices, just as much as I'm sure they can hear it in mine. They are worried for me and feel a duty to help the foreigner help her Chinese husband.

I switch between fear and anger. Getting angry is my brain's way of dealing with the frustration of the situation. I think about Dawu and think about what I'd yell at him if he was standing in front of me.

"Ah, fuck!" I'd say. "Your careless and reckless behaviour has caused me to be embarrassed. You're stupid and selfish. You pick up the pieces of your wreckage. You explain this mess to Hannah."

Hannah is still with Qi Jie so I have time to think. I reflect on what has happened so far. I can't believe that Dawu was given no rights and no representation and yanked straight to jail. He didn't even get a chance to make one call to me. Why can't the authorities at least let me see him? I am his wife.

It's all strange and scary and it's not over. But I don't know where to start to end it all. Maybe the end is the official end of our marriage. I should get that ball rolling with the divorce lawyer again. It feels a bit like I'm abandoning him, but he got himself into all of this. It calls for some tough love.

I need to talk to Dana, my counsellor. I had left my last session with her on high note a few months earlier. This appointment will be much, much different.

In the afternoon, I drive to her practice at the Yingyang Center, a yoga and reading centre, in Shunyi. Her offices are nicely furnished with a few tasteful Chinese antiques. Dana knows Dawu was questioned back in March but she's heard nothing of what's going on now. I tell her about the current situation and say that I'm scared and not sure what to do.

"There is a part of me that doesn't want to help him," I say to Dana.

I'm already burned out and tired of Dawu being short with me. He hasn't been pulling his weight as a co-parent and not spending time with his daughter. I'm busy with my own life. I have a business to care for, and the income from it goes to feeding our child.

"Let him rot," I say to Dana.

"If you don't help him and something goes wrong, do you think you might regret not doing anything?" she asks.

Dana says she understands my frustration but suggests I shouldn't ignore my husband if I have the power to do something for him. She tells me I should work towards getting him released, for Hannah's sake if nothing else.

Dana also strongly suggests that I make sure that I surround myself with close friends, friends who are supportive and can help with such things as childcare. Dana's advice makes sense but I leave after my hour with anger burning within me. I'm embarrassed about what I just said to her. I wish Dawu would just go away.

I start driving home but then decide to use a piece of Dana's wisdom. I'm going to see a close friend who lives in the area. I point my vehicle in the direction of Lena's home. Lena is an amazing woman who embodies great strength and sense. She doesn't know what's happening with Dawu but I'm sure I can confide in her.

When I pull up to Lena's place in Shunyi, tears are threatening to jump out of my eyes. I knock on her door and she opens it.

"What's wrong?" she asks.

The tears start falling.

"Come on in, hon," she says, hugging my shoulders.

She makes some tea while I tell her what happened. Her husband, Xing Kui, comes home and joins us. They are concerned and can't believe what has been happening. Xing Kui listens intently and then says that he has a police friend who works in a station near to where Dawu was picked up.

Xing Kui tells me that he'll make some calls and get back to me. After some more sniffles (me) and comforting words (Lena and Xing Kui) I thank them for their time and leave after one more hug.

The act of talking about Dawu to people who are able to support me, has helped me. That night, I sponge off some of my sadness and put on a more joyful mood. I'm attending a networking event, *Entrepreneurs Only*, with a new friend, Lu Dan (who we call Dandan). I met Dandan through Debbie Mason, my journalist friend who sat in for me at the police station when Dawu was arrested and released in March.

Dandan was born in China and is very entrepreneurial. She's the founder of a company that manages and catalogues various musicians' work from all over China, from classical to rock. For example, if a movie producer is looking for a particular score for a scene, he or she will contact Dandan.

I am attending this event to hopefully attract more clients to the Beijing Color Studio.

I enjoy all aspects of my job, including networking. Tonight's event is taking place at a Xiushui Street restaurant. It should be a good time to connect with new customers. Dandan and I meet at the venue at 7 p.m. I'm not telling her what's going on with Dawu. I don't know how she'll respond. She could be like Mike and tell me that Dawu deserves to be in prison forever. No, tonight is for me. Folks want to talk business and learn about what I'm doing in China.

Although I'm trying to focus on my own stuff, Dawu is distracting me. His problems hover over me like a giant balloon. Wow, this is not a good time to be chatting with other entrepreneurs about what I'm doing in this country. It's so bizarre and I've had enough of acting "normal" for the evening. I head home and hit the hay. I am tired, exhausted. Tomorrow is June 4. It could spell freedom for Dawu.

For the first seconds, after my eyelids flutter open, everything is right with the world. Then, there's that sinking feeling when I realize it's not. My usual morning routine has been thrown off. I don't have to get Hannah out of bed. I don't have to rush to get her to school and get me to the studio. I don't have to make breakfasts or lunches or suppers. I don't even have housework or errands. I have to get my husband out of jail.

Today is Friday, June 4. June 4 is an important date for modern China: it's the anniversary of the Tiananmen Square massacre. Commonly known as the June Fourth Incident in China, the massacre has made a huge impact on the country.

Dawu was in his late teens when the Tiananmen Square protests began in the spring of 1989. The peaceful movement calling for change had spread to cities and towns around China and Dawu marched in his hometown of Changzhou alongside other young and idealistic youth. Meanwhile, in Beijing, things were escalating. Protestors were gathering in Tiananmen Square. Then, on Saturday, June 3, the People's Liberation Army (PLA) started clearing the demonstrators from the square. They were crushed by violence.

The PLA killed thousands of civilians: students, workers and anyone else in its way. On Sunday, June 4, "order" was restored in Beijing. The government had control once again over its people and the protests ended. An official death toll was never released but the actions of the government plainly showed that it was not interested in listening to the people of China.

Now, on either side of the June 4 anniversary, the government checks mail, monitors the internet more closely and generally crushes any public voicing of the historical event. It also blacks out overseas newscasts, including from Hong Kong, that talk about the 1989 tragedy. Many who survived Tiananmen Square and sinologists (those who study China) hope that someday the truth is told and there is accountability from within China.

Those who do speak out about the protests are usually quickly and severely squashed. For now, the massacre is remembered in silence. The regime NEVER acknowledges or mentions the Tiananmen incident / massacre in the state media — TV, radio, newspaper, online — or anywhere else in mainland China. To the authorities, it never happened.

Sometimes, the government likes to show how justly it is and sometimes, releases people from jail around this time. Dawu's friends think that'll be the case with him. I hope they're correct.

Zhang Xiaodong, Hong Fengjian, Gu Duanfan and Chao Hongling, among others, are hoping for some leniency to come Dawu's way today. Following their lead, I also have my fingers crossed in the hopes that the government wants to show how fair it is. It could at least grant Dawu some communication time with me or a lawyer.

If Dawu was being held in Canada, he would get at least one call. I would have seen him by now. I would have access to information on how to help him. Here in China, there's nothing. I wonder if I should reach out to the Canadian Embassy.

I have not heard from the Jiuxianqiao police station. The officers there had said they'd contact me if they knew anything. They knew perfectly well where he went and never bothered to call me. I guess that's my answer.

Last year around this time, Dawu and I had done an event together for International Children's Day. We held a painting party at Dawu's 008 studio space and had about 50 kids come through the doors to try their hand at being artists. It was a busy day and the children enjoyed it and Dawu revelled in his interactions with them. What a difference a year makes.

I've planned the same sort of event for this year at my own studio in two days. I talk to my assistant, Jane, about the painting party. She'll be a second pair of hands for the Sunday, June 6 occasion. I tell Jane a little bit about what's happening with Dawu and then we spend the morning getting the loot bags made up for the 25 children we're expecting.

I thought work would be good for keeping Dawu out of my mind. It's not. The question "How can Canada help?" keeps circling in my head all day. It goes round and round like a ferris wheel and it's beginning to make sense. Some Chinese friends have encouraged me to call the Canadian Embassy to see if officials can do anything for Dawu. He's not Canadian but he is married to one. At least the embassy could give me some information. Right?

It's 5 p.m. and the embassy office is still open. I'm connected to Jack Oliver, who has been working in the Canadian Embassy consular section for about 20 years and has seen this type of thing a lot during his career, in and out of China. However, Jack tells me that because Dawu isn't a Canadian citizen, the Canadian government can't help him. It's pretty much that straightforward.

Despite the fact that Dawu and I are legally married in Canada and China, the Canadian Embassy has no legal jurisdiction or authority to ask the Chinese government about Dawu's case. He's a subject of the Chinese government, not of the Canadian government.

Jack says Dawu has a good chance of getting out of detention before the first month is up. The embassy employee adds if he doesn't, I should find the "right person" to help release Dawu.

"Wow," I think to myself. "Did I just hear a suggestion about a backdoor?"

Dawu's studio assistant has some news for me on that front. He tells me over the phone that Honghong, Dawu's rock star friend, might be able to "pull some strings" with a high-ranking contact.

"Please tell Honghong not to give them a lot of money," I say to Zhang. "Dawu needs to be able to repay the debt when he's out."

I don't have a clue how much a bribe would cost but I'm trying to balance the stark reality of the financial consequence Dawu will face when he's freed. We don't share a bank account so I have no idea how much money he has. Frankly, I don't have the money to pay someone off.

What is the cost of getting someone out of jail anyway?

Worst-case scenario, it could be around ¥800,000 RMB (CAD 160,700). I come up with this sum after friends tell me that foreigners are often charged ludicrous amounts of money because of the stereotype that we have a ton of it. I can only scrape together half that amount. I better not be on the hook for any of the cash. This seems like a petty thought, but I have to think of all the angles. I still need money for basic living expenses for Hannah and I, regardless of where Dawu is currently.

When I speak to Honghong, he says he or others will take care of the payment. It doesn't even need to be money. It could be a piece of art or a favour.

"The most important thing is getting Dawu out of jail," he says.

The musician repeats it'll be a friend who pays the contact, neither Dawu nor me.

"Don't worry," he says. "This is China."

Ah, yes, this IS China.

I have never crossed anyone's palm with silver anywhere. Bribing does happen in Canada but in China, it's a kind of modus operandi. This is the place where everyone is indebted to someone for something. Bribery isn't seen as a crime, it's common and in many ways, part of the system, so to speak.

If you want to get your kid into a certain school, you can pay an official to open the door. If you are pulled over for a major traffic infraction, pay a bribe and get the ticket to go away. Dawu's friends will sniff out that one pliable person who can be given cash in trade for talk.

While I've been talking to Dawu's studio assistant, he tells me we should meet Ai Weiwei. Zhang and Hong Fengjian, a young former student of Dawu's, think Ai could open a door for Dawu or offer some help in some way. Zhang suggests we visit the artist tonight and sets about organizing a visit, not an easy task. Ai is a busy man and doesn't agree to see just anybody. Zhang will need to explain how we are somebody. I leave it to him to figure out.

It's late in the evening when I head to Ai Weiwei's compound with Zhang and Hong Fengjian. I'm apprehensive about going to Ai for advice since I'm not comfortable asking anyone for help. I'm used to relying on myself. That's not how they do things in China, though. Hong Fengjian is an example of that.

Hong was a student of Dawu's when he taught in Changzhou in the 1990s. When Hong moved to Beijing, Dawu was obligated to help him out as Dawu had been his teacher. Hong and other past students have crashed at our place on the foldout sofa in the living room. This is part of the culture in China and its Confucian value of filial piety. The relationship between teacher and student is an important connection, just like the relationships of parents and children or husbands and wives. As Hong has spent time at Dawu's home, he now feels indebted to his teacher.

I have no idea if Ai will want to help but I'm open to hearing anything that might shine a light on a path out of this darkness. I don't know Ai personally and Dawu didn't know him well, either. Ai is sometimes affectionately called *Lao Ai* (Old Ai) by many Chinese fans, colleagues and artists. Adding *lao* to someone's surname in China is a common way to refer to someone who is highly respected and older than those around him.

Born in 1957, Ai Weiwei is part of an older generation of Chinese contemporary artists who started out around 1979, after Mao Zedong died and the country started releasing the shackles of the Cultural Revolution. After Mao's death, some aspects of Chinese society were opening up and that included art. Artists didn't have to adhere to the strict "revolutionary romanticism" of Mao's era and could express themselves in other ways. Ai was part of this first wave of artists, which included others such as Huang Rui. Ai was a big part of creating 798 and smaller artistic communities associated with it.

Ai lives and works in a walled compound in the village community of Caochangdi, about a five to ten-minute drive north of 798. He returned to Beijing in 2003 after living in the U.S. and is a big influence in the Chinese contemporary art scene. He was included in the designing of the Bird's Nest, the showcase stadium for the Beijing 2008 Summer Olympics.

Ai Weiwei is very much in demand. I'm wondering how he's going to react to this meeting with me. I'm about to find out.

The artist's studio, called FAKE Design (the word *fake* in Chinese sounds like the "F" word in English), is accessed through an aqua blue gate. Besides the compound name and a civic number, there isn't any indication that it's the home of the famous Ai Weiwei. Well, almost no indication.

Outside of the walls, there are surveillance cameras, pointing down at the gate. Ai's watching those watching him. Sometimes, the guoan park on the street, diligently seeing who is visiting the property. The Chinese authorities want to know who is going through those gates. When you go to see Ai, you know you're being filmed. Like us.

It's a particularly hot and muggy night, putting all of us on edge. Zhang and Hong are nervous about talking to Ai Weiwei. They don't want to put him in an awkward position. I'm sweating and rivers run down my back as we walk through the compound gate.

It isn't lost on any of us that today is the 21st year since the Tiananmen Square Massacre. Just another of many ironies of the day.

Thanks to Zhang's efforts, we have an appointment to speak to the artist. Yet when the three of us show up at Ai's door, he ignores us for the first hour. Ai is tall with a salt and pepper beard. Despite his height, he is rotund. His big belly is like a large drum from which a big voice booms out of. We sit in a room while his other guests pass us by. He always has a variety of projects on the go and is currently the subject of a documentary.

(Ai often speaks out against the Chinese authorities. In 2009, Ai, along with a group of citizen investigators and lawyers, tries to bring justice to schoolchildren and their families after the devastating earthquake in Sichuan. It causes a huge stir in China and the government retaliates. Police confiscate belongings and people are arrested. However, since Ai's father was connected to the Communist Party of China, the artist is protected like an angel wearing a halo.)

At last, Ai acknowledges us. He converses in Chinese with Zhang and Hong while I'm lost in a haze of sweat and brain fog. I can't follow them at all. I do know Zhang is reminding the great artist that he knows Dawu through the February march on Chang'an Avenue. Ai had attended but deliberately did not step on the actual road. Thus, he was not a part of the protest.

Ai Weiwei says he'll use his social media, especially his Twitter account, to try and get the word out about Dawu. Ai tells me I should be posting stuff, too. He says we should never lie about where Dawu is because if we make stuff up, then there will be too many conflicting stories and no one will know fact from fiction.

"Be honest but vague."

The artist-activist seems to think that a lawyer should be able to see Dawu before the end of the month. Again, it's suggested we pay off someone to make that happen.

Again, my question is: who?

Who is this magical person I can hand money to and have the door of Dawu's cell spring open? Does a list of houmen'r gatekeepers exist? It definitely isn't going to be anyone I've met at the detention centre. That would be too direct and open. I had heard stories about bribery in China but never thought I'd be involved in my own tale.

Ai offers the name of a lawyer, Liu Xiaoyan, who might be able to represent Dawu and get me information. The famous artist makes a call to the man, who says he's out of the country and way too busy. With that, our meeting is over.

It's been about an hour and Ai Weiwei is unable to offer much in terms of concrete solutions to Dawu's problems. Maybe I am asking too much of the older man. However, if Ai Weiwei, a mover and shaker in China, isn't able to do anything for my husband, what chance do I have? I'm at once underwhelmed and overwhelmed. We thank Ai for his time and he walks us to the main gate. He shakes our hands and says that he will keep in touch.

"Don't worry," says Ai. "Dawu will be OK but we need to start now to work on getting him out. We can't wait."

I want to believe him but I fear I've hit a dead end. We're stalled and nothing is moving forward. As we walk away from the compound, Ai closes the heavy gate behind us. The thud of the steel door sounds ominous. I'm not one to be superstitious but in this country, I feel it's a signal that things are going to get worse for Dawu. As well, it's close to midnight, almost the end of June 4, and there's no indication that Dawu is going to be released.

26

Yesterday was not Dawu's "get out of jail free" card. He remains cut off from the world, from me, from Hannah. This isn't a problem many expats experience in China and I continue to plow ahead into unknown territory.

The one thing I must do is find the right person who will talk to me about what Dawu needs me to do. That wasn't Ai Weiwei. Then again, maybe Dawu will come home today or tomorrow. Maybe the authorities wanted to keep him over the Tiananmen anniversary in case he stirred up trouble. The police wouldn't want to appear weak by letting a newly-released artist start protesting again. Some optimism seeps into my mind.

Lena's husband Xing Kui phones me to say that his police friend is accusing Dawu of hitting an officer. It's a serious offence and there's nothing the friend or Xing can do for my husband. I thank Xing for his time but I'm disappointed and think he could have done more. Xing is from Beijing and that brings prestige and respect in this city. He has strong connections through his family and the business community. Too bad that Dawu doesn't have such connections in Bejing. He's from the countryside and considered a *waidiren*, an outsider, in the city.

It still sounds odd that Dawu knowingly hit an officer. The story doesn't make sense. Something else is going on. Nevertheless, I can't get to the bottom of it without seeing my husband. I need to keep pushing for information. I have a few strands of truth tangled in a web of lies.

I hope they're lies.

I'd like to rant and rave at Dawu. I'd like to shake my fist at the Chinese government but for now, I'll bundle up my anger and bury it in a dark place in my mind. I have to be calm and cool and keep asking for information … and help. Even though I don't like wasting other people's time or patience.

I wonder if I'm going about this the right way. I've been talking to people, phoning officials and running around trying to find clarity. Maybe I should sit back and let Dawu deal with the repercussions.

Urgh, I don't know. I just don't know. My emotions swing one way and then the other. I want Dawu freed but I also want to slam the door in his face. I want him here for Hannah but I also want a divorce.

Why can't my life be simple? Regular? Normal?

I have my kids' painting party tomorrow and I have things to do — fun things — to get ready. Life goes on in some ways. I go out and buy snacks and beverages and make sure I have enough paints. I make sure my helpers are coming in. Five people are going to be at my studio. Jane, Mike, two other assistants and a cleaner who will tidy up after the event.

The assistants are Belinda and Kai, a couple from Europe. Kai is an artist and has already taught some art classes for me. I'll need the extra pairs of hands as I am expecting about 25 or so kids. There will be no political talk tomorrow and hopefully lots of giggles and smiles.

I'll need to be on my best game tomorrow to face the parents – ex-pat and Chinese. They won't know about Dawu and are apt to ask about him and wonder why he isn't teaching the kids. I'll simply tell them that Dawu can't make it this year. That isn't a lie.

I'd like to bring in some money with the party. At least break even. It's a marketing ploy as much as anything. It's a good introduction to my studio and might bring students back for classes or camps over the summer.

After I run some errands, I pick up my daughter from Qi Jie's home. We're off to her gymnastics class at the Canadian International School on Liangma Qiao Road in Chaoyang District. The school isn't far from where we live.

I try to keep a low profile while I wait for Hannah. I make small talk with the other parents and keep the topics to the weather and what our children are doing. None of the parents know what's happened to our family.

After my daughter tumbles about for an hour in the gym, she goes to swimming lessons in the school's pool. Jenny, her friend, takes classes too and I sit with Emma. We start chatting, quietly, about my life.

As I'm talking to my friend, I start hearing my words. I sound so dramatic spewing about prison and bribes. I should be laughing. What I'm dealing with sounds more and more nonsensical with every sentence I speak. The whole situation is hilarious, actually.

"It's not at all that serious," I tell Emma. Then I repeat it to myself.

In fact, today feels almost like an ordinary day. For the past two years, Dawu and I have been separated and I've been ferrying Hannah to and from her activities solo all that time. Dawu has been out of the daily picture for a while and Hannah and I have our own routines. We're back in the swing of things, just the two of us.

Next up is soccer. Then that's the afternoon over. So far, I've done a good job of keeping Hannah's world as normal as possible. I've been giving her the impression that everything is OK. It probably will be soon. This time next week, Dawu and I will be arguing as if nothing happened.

Tonight, I'm off to a Bon Voyage party. It's for my American friends LeeAnn and Jeff Bissell. I say goodbye to Hannah and the babysitter and I head out. I met LeeAnn through the Beijing TaiTais Book Club. Jeff is her husband. They've lived in China for about 18 years, much longer than me, and raised their children through the international schools here. They're finally leaving the country and moving to San Francisco. They've been a great source of knowledge for me about stores and schools in Beijing but I don't want to tell them about Dawu. They probably have no clue what to do about a husband in jail.

The party is a nice distraction and many mutual friends are here. It seems that most people don't know about Dawu. I do talk to Lena and Xing although not in any depth. I don't want to ruin the party by bringing up Dawu to anyone. This is a party to mark an ending and celebrate a beginning for LeeAnn and Jeff. I'm not going to make the evening all about me.

Dawu's situation is also a bit embarrassing, a kind of shame. How many people like telling their friends their spouse is in jail? Not many. Also, since I don't know what's really happening, I don't want to make a scene. I'm also afraid that folks will judge Dawu, as Mike did. I need answers so I can defend Dawu if need be.

The party is being hosted at a private home and the gardens are lush and lovely. The weather is perfect, not too hot and not too humid, and the catered food is tasty. In all the recent turmoil, I haven't had much time to eat, so the hors d'oeuvres are especially appreciated.

In between the snacking, I've been chatting away to people and telling them about my painting party tomorrow. I'm careful not to mention Dawu. Most of my friends know we're separated and aren't about to bring him up anyway.

I chat with another separated friend, Chad McKinnon, and we somehow meander into the topic that has been consuming my life for the past few days. Chad has heard about Dawu's predicament and asks me about the situation. I tell him that Dawu supposedly hit a cop and I don't believe it's true. Chad, who is American, says he was once arrested in the U.S. for punching an officer of the law. It was a less-than-shining moment in his life and he had been drunk at the time. The American cops threw Chad in the back of a cruiser and... took him home. They did not take him to jail.

I repeat to Chad that I doubt that Dawu hit a cop. He knows it would be a stupid thing to do and would incite immediate retaliation. Though Dawu can get fairly wound up, he would never cross the line into physical violence.

There must be a misunderstanding or someone is lying about what my husband did.

Chad and I end our conversation talking about cops and how actions and words can be misinterpreted and corrupted, regardless of where one is in the world. People are arrested every day, everywhere. However, Chad isn't languishing in an American prison. He's at a lovely garden party in Beijing.

Chad's experience adds to my growing optimism. I bet it's only a matter of time before Dawu is let out. I feel good when I leave the party. Driving home, I think this will all be behind me sooner than I think.

27

The painting party marking International Children's Day is underway. I'm happy and excited about it. It's a way to retain some normalcy. Part of that is having Hannah beside me today. My Beijing Color Studio is filling with families arriving with smiling kids on Sunday, June 6. Twenty or so children are here to get into art. The studio looks amazing and I'm glad to have Jane and my helpers on hand. We're constantly in motion, running to get more paint or new brushes or saying, "That looks fantastic!"

Despite Mike not being supportive the other day, he's pitching in now. He's brought along his brother and his family to the painting party. My other assistants, Belinda and Kai, are proving to be great with the kids. I'll be employing the couple when I can throughout the summer.

At the end of the party, we send the burgeoning artists home with loot bags. The bags are cotton and have my studio's logo printed on the front. I'm proud of what I've built and today was successful business-wise. I wish it had been a success personally.

It's like there's a tiny piece of me missing or something sharp poking into my side. I'll laugh at a joke and then ask myself if I should be laughing. Should I be enjoying myself when I don't know what's happening with my husband? I'm not sure how seriously I should be taking his detention. How serious is it?

On Monday, the Canadian consular official, Jack Oliver, shines a tiny beam of light on the situation. He tells me that within the first 37.5 days of anyone being detained in China, he or she are not allowed much communication with the outside world, including family and lawyers. However, there is a chance, a slight chance, that Dawu will be let go once he has served 37.5 days. Under Chinese law, a prosecutor has 37 days to approve an arrest.

If the detainee is an expat in China, detained in a Chinese detention centre in the expat section, then the embassy can send a representative from the consular division to visit, hear the detainee's side of the story and confirm that the detainee is being treated well and not being tortured. Dawu is not an expat. He's Chinese, being detained by the Chinese authorities inside of a detention centre for Chinese. There's a huge difference in how these people are treated. Dawu has no right to visit with family or speak to a lawyer.

Dawu's human rights are being trampled. He has been forcibly disappeared and has no access to legal counsel. Is that all that has been done to him? I can't shake the idea that the authorities are trying to re-educate Dawu in a forceful and physical way – a brutal and torturous way. Then the logical part of me says, "No. They're probably interrogating him verbally."

Both sides of me admit I don't know.

I'm torn between many mixed emotions and blended thoughts. I also think that because Dawu is married to me, he thought he could get away with things that others couldn't. He felt that because I'm a foreigner, I'd have some sort of superhero-Canadian-power to help him out of any Chinese mess.

I email my jumbled speculations to Diane in Calgary. I've been in contact with my sister almost every day. I want to not only fill her in on the drama unfolding but to make sense of it myself. By writing everything down, it makes it real. Fact can be stranger than fiction and this is my daily reality.

I don't want Dawu to be crushed by the Chinese government machine. I know I have to help my husband but I don't have to do it as his spouse. I add in my message to Diane that I'm going to contact a lawyer — a divorce lawyer — soon. I want to move on after I get Dawu out. I want to unhook him from my life and Hannah's. It's about time.

28

I do not have superhero-Canadian-powers — and thus, can't bust Dawu out of detention. Nevertheless, Canada is the touchstone for the Chinese friends who drop by to see me. They tell me to contact the Canadian Embassy for help. I tell them that I did and Canada can't do anything for Dawu. The friends don't understand that the embassy can provide consular assistance only to Canadian citizens.

"But Dawu is married to you, a Canadian," the friends say.

"That doesn't make him a Canadian," I say.

I don't make the rules. The Canadian Embassy's role is to help those with Canadian citizenship, not spouses who are citizens of another country. At least Hannah is Canadian.

Despite my determination yesterday to get the divorce going, I realize there are more pressing matters. I will need a lawyer but not the type that can release me from marital bonds.

There is a chance Dawu will be released after he's served 37.5 days in detention. If he isn't out after that time, he'll need a lawyer. I should have someone lined up for him. Just in case.

I may not have superhero powers but I am super-resourceful. I know the right person to contact. It's Sherry Lok, a lawyer from Singapore who consults for a Beijing law firm. She's also a friend. I talk to her and she's concerned for Dawu and the fact that I haven't heard anything from or about him. She can't represent him as she's a foreigner and foreigners working as lawyers in China can't go to court or represent a Chinese person in China. Sherry says what she can do is make some calls for me.

She does and then tells me that as far as she can figure out, I definitely should not hire a lawyer just yet. She tells me that hiring a lawyer could be construed as disrespectful to the Chinese justice process. I should wait a couple of days and then bring Dawu's story to a foreign journalist. If the media picks up Dawu's thread, the coverage might exert some pressure on the government. However, under no circumstances should I criticize the government. Sherry says if I go on the offence, the authorities will consider that an attack and a reason to keep me in the dark even longer.

Sherry adds that Dawu must not admit to anything. Not one thing. How am I supposed to tell him that? I can't see or talk to him. I feel like I'm back at the start, albeit with some advice that I can work with now.

I contact some of the journalists who were helpful when Dawu was protesting the razing of the artist complexes and marched on Chang'an. My list includes Evan Osnos with *The New Yorker* and two U.K. reporters: Peter Foster with *The Daily Telegraph* and Tania Branigan with *The Guardian*.

I go to work at my studio while waiting for the reporters' responses and the Gao Brothers drop in. They're Dawu's friends and I know them, but not well. The Gao Brothers are two artist brothers, Zhen Gao and Qiang Gao. They're from Jinan City, not far from Qingdao City, in the province of Shandong, several hours by train southeast of Beijing. The Gao Brothers work in the mediums of performance art, photography, large installations and multi-media. Much of their works tends to be charged with political and social nuances and often include images of Mao Zedong.

According to the government, this is denigrating to Mao and threatening to China. It doesn't help that the Gaos' father was a teacher and considered a radical during the Cultural Revolution. He was taken by Chairman Mao Zedong's paramilitary group, the Red Guards, and was either beaten to death or committed suicide. The brothers' mother, Wu Jiayun, tried to find out what happened to her husband but no one (except for the authorities) knows the answer. It's one of many strikes against the Gaos and the regime refused to let the artists leave China until 2003.

The Gao Brothers live near my studio. They've heard about Dawu and are very concerned for him and me. I tell them I'm fine. I'm not really, but what can they do if I burst into tears? I ask them if they want some tea.

They sit down and remove their hats (they almost always have hats on) and we chat. It's a bit weird as I've never had a conversation alone with them. Usually, Dawu is with me. The other thing is, the brothers only speak Mandarin so I have to concentrate and focus intently on what they're saying and what I'm saying. Nevertheless, the Gao Brothers are great at putting me at ease. They say they know what I'm going through and hope Dawu is OK. They've known him for many years and respect him as a person and artist. Dawu is their friend and because of that relationship, I'm their friend. The brothers know of a lawyer in the far west of the city who could help me. They give him a call but he says he's too busy to take my case.

Oh well.

Before the brothers leave, they tell me that I can drop into their studio any time. I thank them and say I'll be in touch if I need anything. Of course, at this moment, I'm not sure what I'll need next. They give me hugs on their way out. After all, one of their most famous international performance pieces involves group hugs.

The brothers, Zhen and Qiang, along with Dawu, are part of the avant-garde conceptual art scene, which the government doesn't like. The 798 Art District was created as an attempt to allow the artists and galleries some freedoms, all while under the watchful eye of the authorities. It's not a coincidence that the local branch of the police has an office inside 798.

Most of the famous Chinese avant-garde and contemporary artworks are collected outside of China, either by museums or private collectors. Some avant-garde and contemporary artists in China are drawn to foreigners not just because they are "rich," but because of their connections outside of the country. The thought that Dawu might have been dating me because of my "Canadian-ness" had crossed my mind at the beginning of our relationship. I brought him overseas but Calgary isn't exactly a mecca for international art and artists. Most Chinese artists want to land in New York, Berlin, London or Paris – places I have no connections too. This is why I believed Dawu married me because I'm me.

During my previous conversation with Jack Oliver, the Canadian consular official, he asked me several times if Dawu had recently applied for a tourist or other style of visa to visit Canada or another country. If he had, then the Canadian Embassy could have fast-tracked him and got him out of China once the 37.5 days were up. Canada could use his application as evidence that he had been on his way there before being jailed. However, it's all moot. Dawu hadn't applied to go anywhere outside of China before being detained.

Dawu and I had talked about moving to Canada a few times over the years. However, it wasn't what we wanted. Although I didn't want to become Chinese and relinquish my Canadian passport, I liked living in Beijing. It was easy for me to get an annual permit to live in China. After Dawu's short stint in jail in March, I had filled out most of the paperwork for us to leave for my home country. But he never signed the documents and I didn't push him on it. I wasn't ready to leave Beijing either.

The number eight has a good numerical meaning in Chinese culture and today is Tuesday, June 8, 2010. Chinese numerology is an ancient system where certain numbers are believed to be auspicious, or inauspicious, based on which word they sound like. For instance, 6, 8 and 9 are auspicious; whereas 4 and 7 are inauspicious. Numerology is embedded in the history of China and has been around for thousands of years. The number eight has long been regarded as the luckiest number in Chinese culture. The pronunciation of eight in Mandarin sounds similar to the word "fa," which means "to prosper."

Eight also contains meanings of success and high social status. Many business people favour this number. I don't think it was a coincidence that the Olympics were in Beijing in 2008 and the Games started on Aug. 8.

"Let's see what happens on June 8," I say to myself.

It has been just over a week since Hannah and I last saw Dawu. Our daughter is home with me today. I had told her that her baba is visiting Yeye and now she wants to talk to them on the phone. I tell her that her dad didn't take his phone with him.

If all Dawu has to do is serve 37.5 days and then he's freed, Hannah won't need to know anything other than he was away. When he returns, it'll be our turn to leave. I'll go home to Canada.

I've been toying with the idea of pursuing a Master of Arts degree in intercultural communications from Royal Roads University in Victoria, B.C. Perhaps I can start online courses in China and return to Canada and finish the work in person. Regardless, I think that having a plan for me is a good idea. Plan A isn't working out the way I had imagined it.

Plan A had been to raise Hannah with Dawu and have a work/life balance where it was possible for me to do my own art, my photography. I had my studio, a great Hasselblad camera and newly-purchased lighting and backdrop equipment. I had come up with another project too, taking pictures of mixed-race couples. I would also interview the pairs and perhaps publish a book one day. I related to my idea because I'm part of a mixed-race couple. Plan A meant exploring this idea plus other projects and concepts.

Plan A is turning into Plan Fading Away. Plan B, leaving China, is at least tangible.

I write emails to past professors and employers and ask for letters of reference to send to the university. The afternoon is filled with promises of new ideas, a new place to live and a new direction for me. Then, I get ready to have the Beijing TaiTais Book Club over to my Beijing Color Studio this evening.

Supper is the host's responsibility. I'm too frazzled to focus on preparing a meal so I call Annie's Italian Restaurant and order some pizzas. In Chinese, I carefully give my address and directions to the studio. I'm 95 per cent sure the delivery person will make it to my space. My Mandarin tones aren't perfect and sometimes the delivery person isn't familiar with the area, as it can be a rabbit warren, but I'm sure the food will arrive. I think my guests will be able to find me too and dinner will be waiting for them.

This past month's book was a pick by me. I had given the ladies a collection of short stories by Li Yiyun to read. The book is called *A Thousand Years of Good Prayers* and about Chinese women. I haven't had time to actually read much these days although I'm on the same page as the other book club members.

I've come up with the idea to ask each club member to choose a story out of the collection and illustrate it. My own personal story won't be in the mix tonight. I've decided not to talk about Dawu because he could be out in three weeks. This could be a wee blip in time. Why confuse and confound everyone?

About nine women attend the book club and they love my studio. They each paint something from one of the stories. I'm not expecting masterpieces. It's more about reflection. Of course, there's also wine (along with the delivered pizza) to shake the artistic side loose in my friends.

Jane is on hand to direct the painting portion of the evening. Many of the women are shy at first but then they start to enjoy putting the paint on the canvas. There is chatter about kids and husbands. I talk about Hannah but not Dawu. I'm able to carry on, relax and have fun. This is important for me. These women are successful and chic. I don't want to air my dirty laundry. I want to enjoy the evening. So I do.

At the end of the event, I'm content. Was the 8th a lucky day? To sum it up, nothing else terrible has been added to my ordeal. I'm happy to have been in my studio and it was used in the manner that I had intended it to be: friends getting together, sipping wine, eating pizza and painting. Despite not telling the women about Dawu, I felt supported by them. The ladies of the Beijing TaiTais Book Club made me smile and laugh and I feel like I'm moving in the right direction.

T he one thing I'm allowed to do for Dawu is drop off clothing for him at the detention centre. I have no idea what he needs but I when I go by the jail to find out, I'm told by the folks at the front desk that underwear is a good choice.

I buy some underwear and head back to the detention centre. When Dawu's out in 37.5 days, he'll have a stockpile of briefs and be no worse for wear. Pun intended. What keeps me moving is the belief my husband will be out in 37.5 days. The number is my mantra. I repeat it in my head like that annoying *99 Bottles of Beer on the Wall* song. I don't think Dawu has done anything to be charged with, so he can serve his sentence for being a loudmouth and then get out.

At the centre's front desk, two uniformed men are stationed behind the low granite counter. They spot me standing in line behind at least 20 other people, also dropping off items. The guards look straight at me and begin to play punch each other – slow-motion blows to the cheeks and then to the jaws. What is this dramatic scene all about?

They're making fun of Dawu.

"Hey!" I say, "that's my husband you're mocking. Cut it out."

I can't get too cross at the men. I have to show the guards that Dawu and I aren't angry or violent people. We're reasonable. For the two men behind the counter though, it's all about face. They have the power. I have none.

I ask them to tell me what they know because they know who I am. They say it's not their responsibility to inform me about anything happening inside the centre. They tighten their lips. I'd like to tighten my hands around their necks. It's my turn to play act now.

I transform into a polite woman who nicely tells the guards that I haven't heard anything from the authorities or had any news about Dawu in over a week. Finally, one of the officers breaks and, at last, gives me something concrete to go on.

The guard looks at his computer and then me and then back to his computer. He begins reading off the screen, a screen I can't see.

"Wu Yuren," he says, "detained since June 1, 2010. Reason for detention is obstructing and attacking a police officer."

"Excuse me?" I ask.

I've been speaking Mandarin with the officers and I'm hoping my interpreting skills are on today. I'm fluent in areas of art, culture, shopping, raising a kid and immigration (from when I worked at the Australian embassy) but this is my first foray into the legal side of life in China. My detention and criminal Chinese language skills are very basic at best. Throw me a bone!

The man repeats the charge. Dawu is in detention for "obstructing and attacking a police officer."

It's a blow to the gut.

"Are you sure that's what it says?" I ask. "You're sure?"

The officer shapes his fingers into a gun and casually waves his hand in my face. He then says Dawu's crime is punishable by execution. I'm not sure that punching a police officer in China means Dawu should get the death sentence. The guard is probably yanking my chain, playing with the foreigner married to the "cop hitter."

I want to scream and cause a scene and make the officers as uncomfortable as I am. I can't believe what I am hearing. This has got to be a false accusation. I'm stuck to the floor. If I looked in the mirror, my face would be as pale as snow. No one reaches a hand to pat my shoulder or offer a kind word. People don't usually comfort strangers in China. To show strong emotions in public is to lose face.

"Would you please write down the charge for me?" I ask.

One of the guards quickly scribbles some characters on a piece of paper and hands it to me. I put the note in my pocket to decipher later. I guess I have to give the men here some credit. They're giving me information on the sly. They shouldn't be telling me anything since I haven't received an official statement or received any call about him.

Now, what do I do? I think everything just got worse. Fuck the face. I can't keep my composure. Tears run down my cheeks and the officer talks around me to the next person in line. The guard is done with me.

I don't believe Dawu hit a cop. I later confide everything to Patti Wang when we're having lunch at a restaurant. Patti is easy to talk to and knows Dawu. I feel I can talk to her without feeling embarrassed or judged.

Here it goes....

I tell her the whole story, from the beginning, to today.

She reacts with surprise and concern that I've been dealing with this on my own. She suggests that if Dawu gets out in the next few days, he needs to leave China and says he should attend a Catholic mass at the Italian Embassy.

Once inside the embassy, he should speak to a priest and ask for asylum. However, I fear that would ruin Dawu's chances of applying for permanent residency in Canada.

"He needs to leave China," says Patti again. "Right away."

She says she wishes there's more she could do to help. She has already done so much for me by giving me support and the chance to speak my truth. With lunch over and our ideas spent, she gives me a hug and we say our goodbyes.

I drive to pick up Mike. He needs my help, too. He hurt his ankle last night while playing soccer and I've agreed to take him to the hospital a few blocks away from the 798 Art District. The hospital is a little out of my way but the favour is more of a convenient distraction. Besides, Mike can translate that slip of paper the guard gave me. Mike's English is pretty good and I'd like to understand, fully, what charge Dawu is facing.

When Mike reads the paper, he tells me it says, *fang ai gong wu*. It has nothing to do with an official charge. Mike tells me it's like the four-character Chinese idiom *kill the rooster to scare the monkey*. Mike suspects the officer is hinting to me that Dawu is a rooster that's being used to teach "the monkey" a lesson. The monkey could be other artists. There's a myriad of reasons why detaining my husband could be used as a warning to other artists. It could scare them into not protesting or speaking out against the government. It could be a cover-up for corruption in the police ranks. It could be retaliation for Dawu's success in winning compensation for 008 and Zhengyang.

Mike doesn't think any of the above is true. He thinks Dawu must have hit the cop and must accept the consequences. Mike doesn't understand what I'm going through. I guess my situation is weird for him: I'm a separated Canadian woman whose Chinese husband is in jail. He says I should get out of Dodge, or in this case, Beijing, with Hannah and never look back.

Mike is kind of right. What's holding me back? Oh right, the artist who punched a police officer needs me. I remember when I briefly saw Dawu, broken and upset, inside the police station a week ago, he was so scared. He was afraid and that was what surprised me most. He never gets scared.

I'm stirring up thoughts and plans and decide that my work is to find out the minimum and maximum punishments for obstructing and attacking a police officer. Maybe I'm grasping at straws now if I think Dawu will be out after he serves 37.5 days. That could be a drop in the bucket. Thing is, I need more information before going back to the Canadian Embassy or hiring a high-powered lawyer.

Until I have more knowledge in my arsenal, I make a Counting Sheep boutique delivery. I've just received an online order for a maternity bra and a top. I pick up the items from the basement warehouse in Huayang Jiayuan and deliver the package to an American woman a few blocks away. She loves the clothing and is satisfied with her purchase. It feels good to talk to someone who has nothing to do with Dawu.

Facts are going to help me more than my assumptions about what's going on with Dawu's situation. I should know more before making any significant decisions. I don't want to screw anything up. Dawu might only have one chance to get out.

I've let a few people, like my counsellor Dana and a confidante, Patti, know what's happening to Dawu. They've been supportive. However, my wider circle of friends doesn't know anything yet. Even though it's 2010 and much of the planet is plugged into social media, the "great wall" of China blocks much of it. Dawu isn't making the rounds over Facebook, nor is he making headlines in the local newspapers. Illegal incarceration rarely does.

Censorship is the name of the game for the Chinese government. Since democracy doesn't live here, neither does freedom of the press. As interesting as Dawu's situation is to much of the rest of the world, it's a non-issue here. Dawu is one of thousands of cases per year. I don't mind that his name isn't being splashed all over the front page — when he gets out, no one will be the wiser and life will continue as normal.

Normal for Dawu and I is living life apart. I should get into contact with the divorce lawyer we met with last year. I'll have the papers ready for Dawu to sign when he's released. But is that something I should spring on him just as he's being sprung?

One second I convince myself this is the right thing to do. Then the next second I convince myself this might not be the right thing to do. Grrr. I wish someone would just tell me what the right thing to do is.

I'm going to see friends who can take my mind off the unravelling of my life. Liu Yong was at my 42nd birthday party. He's a young Chinese DJ and we originally met last year at a New Year's Eve party.

Liu Yong and I like to talk about music and he set up a sound system in my studio. We also share an interest in cars because we both drive cute little cars. He drives a Lada and I drive a Honda Fit. It sounds like a weird connection but not everyone has a car in Beijing. Liu Yong and I talk about finding the best parking spots, where to get the cheapest gas and our latest near misses on the city streets.

This afternoon, Liu Yong has invited me to meet some of his friends, including Yan Zi, a studio musician who plays bass. We're going to Yan Zi's home in Tongzhou, about a half an hour drive east from my apartment. At first, I don't want to go out. I have a lot on my mind and I don't feel like meeting new people. However, Yan Zi is going to introduce me to another photographer, Frank. Another selling point is that Yan Zi is keen to cook southern Chinese food for me. He knows I used to live in Guangdong province and that's where he's from. In China, sometimes you have to do stuff you don't want to do for the sake of the relationship. Obligatory dinners and events are part of the cultural deal. I give in and say I'll be there.

Liu Yong drives Frank and I to Yan Zi's. During the car ride, I discover Frank is an expat from Italy and he wants to know about my photography studio. He knows a lot more than I do about studio photography but since I'm the one with the space, he thinks perhaps we can collaborate somehow. Maybe I can learn more about studio lighting from him. I have the equipment but don't really know how to use it. Frank does.

We arrive in Tongzhou and it isn't a very interesting town. It's just row after row of apartment blocks. Yan Zi and his girlfriend live in a nice place but it is tight for five people. The good food outweighs the cramped environment.

Yan Zi is pleasant and a competent cook. He makes salted chicken in the Hakka style. (The Hakka are a minority group originally from the north of China.) Salted chicken is my favourite and it's made with, you guessed it, salty chicken. The dish has crispy skin and it's delicious. The conversation at the supper table is light and there is no mention of Dawu other than we are separated. I talk to my new friends about how I came to China as well as the music and art scenes. As a musician, Yan Zi has played with several bands around China. He has, of course, heard of Honghong, Dawu's rock star friend.

During the nice dinner, my phone rings. I answer it because it's Meili, Honghong's wife. I wonder what she's calling about?

"We can't get the money," Meili says. "The deal fell through."

She's talking about the bribe Honghong and I discussed a few days ago.

I excuse myself from the table and leave the room so I can concentrate on what she's saying.

"Honghong was hoping to get some money from the TangRen Gallery," Meili says. "It's not going to happen."

The TangRen Gallery had sponsored Dawu for an exhibit and appearance in Hong Kong in late May. Honghong had hoped the gallery would be able to "sponsor" Dawu again. It can't.

The gallery management feels they don't have the money or a strong enough connection to Dawu to support a bribe.

I'm in a small dark bedroom with the windows covered by heavy curtains. I open the drapes for a bit of light but everything feels like it has fallen into a pit of blackness. Honghong is Dawu's most connected friend and he can't do anything. Although I hadn't relied on the bribe angle as a serious option, it had at least been a possibility.

What the fuck am I doing? Here I am, out in Tongzhou at some place with some people I hardly know, having supper, drinks and chatting about music and art, when I really should be at home with Hannah working on a plan for Dawu. What is wrong with me?

The room is spinning and my heart is fluttering like bird wings. I'm feeling hot and nauseous and I steady myself with a hand on the cool wall.

I am in over my head.

Before hanging up, Meili insists I contact the Canadian Embassy again. She tells me to ask for Amber Long, the ambassador's secretary. She's heard Ms. Long might be able to help.

I'm upset and disappointed once again but I'm grateful that our long-time friends, Meili and Honghong, haven't given up on Dawu or me. I take a deep breath and head back to the soiree. I have to tell my friends that I need to go home.

Liu Yong drives Frank and me back to the city. It's late and Frank is falling asleep in the back seat. We are about 15 minutes out of the city limits when my phone goes off again. It's Chao Hongling, Hannah's godmother and another close friend. Chao Hongling and her husband, Gu Duanfan, are grounded people, total pillars in my books, and would do anything for Dawu.

Hongling is serious and direct as usual over the phone. She asks what has happened to Dawu. She's heard some rumours through the art grapevine and wants to hear, exactly, what's going on. I say I'll call her from home.

When I get through the door of my apartment, I dial Hongling. After I give her a brief rundown of Dawu's situation, she tells me something that rings alarm bells in my mind. Hongling says Dawu isn't being detained over one punch but over several things he has done in the past couple of years. She explains that she thinks he's being held because of his illegal march on Chang'an Avenue in February. She and Gu Duanfan hadn't participated in the protest but she feels it's directly connected to Dawu's troubles. She thinks that he is also being targeted because he signed Liu Xiaobo's petition in 2008 calling for immediate government reforms.

Dawu signed his name close to the top and right under Ai Weiwei's signature. Hongling thinks the government wants to take Dawu down a peg or two. Isolating him in jail is a start.

She ends our conversation telling me that she and Gu Duanfan want to help. I add her to my list of supporters and tell her I'll be in touch if I need anything.

It's late in the evening but I send another email to Peter Foster, a journalist. Peter writes for *The Daily Telegraph* and we met in March when he interviewed Dawu and me about Ai Weiwei and the art scene. Peter had been involved in a large project about the life and times of Ai Weiwei. I didn't realize then that several months later, I'd be asking for Peter's assistance to free my husband. I send the journalist what I know and what I have on Dawu's case.

This morning I didn't want anyone to know what's happening with Dawu but I've changed my mind. I'm hoping Peter can spread the word in the English papers and garner support for my husband. I know the communist state-run media isn't going to do this. It's known for its intense censorship and propaganda.

Before I climb into bed to end the day, I try to get in touch with how I feel about all of this.

I'm scared. That about sums it up.

Now that this most recent backdoor bribery "deal" has collapsed, it's a sign that getting Dawu out of detention isn't going to be as easy as once thought, nor is the situation as temporary as it first seemed. I'm also scared Dawu might die. He could be tortured, sent to a labour camp, or worse yet, executed.

How would I explain Dawu's death to Hannah? She's an innocent five-year-old who adores her father. Should I tell her what's happening? Where do I start? She can't even grasp what jail is.

Hannah has stuffed animals, we call them stuffies, that she plays with regularly. She has them all divided into little families, where every baby has a mom and most have dads. I sit up in bed. I can't divorce Hannah's father. No. It's not the right time. He needs us.

I still love Dawu despite everything. He's Hannah's father. As much as Dawu and I have had problems, he's human. I'll regret it if I abandon him.

I remember when Dawu and I first met in October of 2001. He had a southern accent when he spoke Mandarin. It was so strong that even I, the non-native speaker, heard it. I teased him mercilessly and it gave us hours of laughter.

He also couldn't figure out Hanyu Pinyin. (Pinyin is the official romanization system for standard Chinese in mainland China.) I had to teach him how to read and write Pinyin. We had fun together learning Chinese and exploring Beijing in those early years.

Those days are long gone. We're not together as a couple. Our marriage disappeared. It evaporated over time, drop by drop sucked into the air. I had noticed the love dissipating but was too tired and too busy to do anything about it. However, I'm not going to let Dawu disappear.

Chao Hongling is on the phone and she's not mincing words. She wants me to come to Dawu's studio to meet with Tang Funai, also known as Tang. I know him as the Troublemaker.

It was Tang who started the nasty business with the 798 management. He's the one who borrowed Dawu's generator and who roped him into spraying nasty slogans around the art district. Tang is not on my good side.

"I don't want anything to do with that man," I say to Hongling.

"He has information about Dawu."

My temper is raging as I pull up to Dawu's studio in the afternoon. Walking into the room, I see Chao Hongling, Zhang, Dawu's assistant, Hong, Dawu's former student, and the Troublemaker Tang. Needless to say, I'm not in the best mood when I come face-to-face with Tang. I start ripping into him until Chao Hongling tells me to calm down.

"He has news for you," she says.

One of Chao Hongling's assistants enters the room with a video camera. Tang agrees to go on the record and tells us what he knows. It's his version of the story but from what he tells me, Dawu did nothing to warrant being branded a cop hitter.

My ears are buzzing with anger but I start to tune into Tang's words. He says he and Dawu were at the Jiuxianqiao Police Station on May 31 to complain about the Sugar Jar being seized and threatened to be shut down. The 798 management had cut the electricity to Tang's shop, hence the need for Dawu's generator. Because Dawu owned the generator, Tang asked him to come along. That's not all, though. Before Tang and Dawu went to the station, they spray painted some of the buildings around the compound.

Tang was angry on a number of fronts. He was upset that Dawu's generator had been taken and he was fuming over being evicted. His fury also motivated Dawu to take action. Together, they vandalized 798 property in a purposeful act of defiance. Yet, here's Tang. Free.

Tang was with Dawu when they were both transferred to the Chaoyang Detention Center. That transfer occurred after I saw Dawu, hurt and bewildered, in the police detachment window. Once Dawu and Tang arrived at Chaoyang, Dawu was sent to the indictable offences (serious crime) side.

Tang was sent to the misdemeanour side.

"I never saw Dawu after that," says Tang.

Tang was released from the detention centre after a 10-day stay.

"How nice for you," I say, not in a kind way.

The Troublemaker got to go home. Meanwhile, Dawu is stuck behind bars while I run around, trying to figure out how to free him. It's all Tang's fault that my husband and Hannah's father is stuck in a cell. All my anger finally has a target.

I yell at Tang in Chinese, "*Weishenme* (why)? *Weishenme? Weishenme?*"

For me, Chinese is my fight language. Dawu and I argued in Mandarin all the time and I have a solid base in belligerent Chinese. Nevertheless, my words turn to tears and I break down. Tang follows.

I realize Tang is concerned about Dawu. Even though I want to punch and kick the Troublemaker, his tears show me that he does feel bad. Most importantly, he feels responsible.

He should.

My crying is the release valve I've needed. After 10 days of my sadness being shut down or bottled up (or whatever analogy), it's all out in the open. Some Chinese people aren't good about showing this kind of raw emotion but Tang is blubbering beside me. This doesn't mean I'm about to forgive him.

Tang should never have invited Dawu to go with him to the police station. He should have told Dawu to go home, knowing he was already on the wrong side of the law. Dawu should never have gone within 100 metres of any police station. Alas, too late now.

Tang is paying some sort of price. He tells me his business has been shuttered for good. The Sugar Jar CD store is no more. The music shop had been right across the alley road from the TangRen Gallery. It was a hole-in-the-wall kind of place and was long and narrow. It housed many different types of authentic and pirated CDs.

Most CD stores in China are selling pirated CDs, illegal copies of originals. No royalties are paid to the original producer or artist. The music is sold for dirt cheap and the cover art is sometimes photos quickly snapped of the original artwork. China basically missed the entire vinyl era of records and albums because, at its height in the 1960s and 1970s, China was going through the Cultural Revolution. The only music allowed, if at all, had to be sanctioned by the Chinese government. Record players would have been seen as bourgeois and removed or thrown out along with any vinyl from earlier decades. The pirated CD and cassette tape industry leapt over the vinyl era.

CDs and tapes are easier to copy over vinyl. You can get some interesting "arrangements" thanks to the editing of the Chinese totalitarian state. I bought a tape of Sinéad O'Connor's music and one of the songs was missing. *Black Boys on Mopeds* wasn't in the mix. That song compares Margaret Thatcher's policies to that of the Chinese government that caused the massacre on Tiananmen Square.

Tang is grovelling and tells me he'll help me in any way possible.

"Can you help me find the words to tell Hannah?" I ask him. "What should I tell her about her father who has disappeared?"

Tang's head droops. He stares at his shoes.

It's an emotional meeting and awkward, especially for Chao Hongling and Zhang. However uncomfortable, there's a part of me that isn't going to be restrained. I want them all to feel how deeply Dawu and I have been negatively impacted by Tang. Dawu is paying the price for someone else's silly problems with a management company.

After the meeting and still at Dawu's studio that afternoon, I call the Canadian Embassy once again. Maybe, just maybe, there's something that has been missed.

There isn't.

From what Jack Oliver, my Canadian consular contact, is telling me, Dawu is in serious trouble. Mr. Oliver is working from his experiences and what he has seen in China. He thinks that because Dawu hasn't been released yet, it's going to be bad news.

"Get a good lawyer to go in and meet with Dawu," Mr. Oliver says.

He can't recommend anyone directly but tells me to check the embassy's website for a list of names.

"This is the time to act," he adds.

I quietly thank Mr. Oliver and hang up the phone. I'm overwhelmed by how thick the figurative wall in front of me seems. I can't even make a hairline crack in it. This day has been horrible between the heated exchange with Tang, the unanswered questions and the unfounded assumptions. It's time to go home. I want to be alone. Today has been too much.

33

During our meeting a few days ago, Ai Weiwei had told me he was going to tweet about Dawu's false imprisonment. I've been checking Ai's social media to see if he has been putting anything out about my husband.

Yes!

There's a reference to Dawu's detention and the original march on Chang'an Avenue in February.

Ai has a growing following online, especially Twitter. The platform is capable of sharing an immense amount of uncensored information to everyone around the world. In China, most Twitter users have to be careful about what they say online but Ai has some leeway thanks to his family ties and an overseas VPN.

The artist and activist also has an audience outside of China. He's famous, speaks excellent English and can parlay that into followers. Ai is a champion for the people and regularly criticizes the Chinese government for denying its citizens basic human rights. Nevertheless, although Ai has power, he still has to be careful.

I've heard from journalist Peter Foster. It's great to be in touch with a reliable foreign correspondent. Hopefully, he has seen Ai Weiwei's tweets.

I take Hannah to her Saturday gymnastics class at the Canadian International School. She loves bouncing around with her friend Jenny. I watch my daughter and her best pal tumble on the floor. They have so much energy at this age. I'd like a fraction of it. It's taken all my strength to keep acting as if nothing is wrong. Hannah is only a child. She doesn't need adult problems.

Later that afternoon, I take my daughter with me to a meeting with Chao Hongling at the TangRen Gallery in 798. There's an exhibition I'm interested in seeing and the gallery is a convenient place to meet. We sit in an office space chatting. Hannah is playing quietly with one of her many stuffie toys. She always carries a couple with her when we leave the house.

My conversation with Chao Hongling turns to my pet project, the exhibition that I'm trying to organize in Canada. Chao Hongling and Gu Duanfan would like to be part of the endeavour and she has a list of other artists who are interested, too. Dawu will also be a participant. When he's out of jail.

Chao Hongling tells me there's nothing I can do right now about Dawu.

"Go home and be with Hannah," she says, looking at my daughter. "She needs you. She needs her mother."

"Do you think I should tell her what's really happening with her dad?" I ask.

Chao Hongling admits that perhaps it's best to keep going with the little lie that Dawu is away at his family's home. Having a father locked up might be too much for Hannah to handle emotionally. It's more than enough for me and I'm an adult.

"Try not to worry so much," says Chao Hongling. "The art community is here for you and it'll find a way to look after everything."

Hannah is getting hungry and tired. Nevertheless, since we're already at the TangRen Gallery, it's a shame not to catch a couple of other 798 exhibits. I convince her to go to one or two before heading home where she can play with her toys and have lunch.

We enter the main building in Section D of the 798 Art District. This houses the main Bauhaus-style gallery space. There is an exhibition worth seeing, one including some international artists, so Hannah and I begin walking around. There are several other artists with their spouses at the show. I know a few of them. I say a cursory hello but I feel their eyes linger on me. When I glance over, they quickly look away.

My secret is out.

A couple of people dare to approach me and ask questions, with Hannah standing right beside me.

"When is Dawu going to be released?" one artist asks.

I position myself between the questioner and Hannah and nod at my daughter, hoping this man will take the hint that I can't talk right now. I don't want my daughter to hear any of this. The man isn't getting it and asks again about Dawu.

Of course, I know that people aren't being malicious. Everyone is curious and wants to know what's going on and why and how they can help. Nevertheless, Hannah thinks her dad is in Jiangsu province visiting family. I have to walk away from this conversation.

Abruptly turning around and leaving people in mid-sentence is rude and no way to treat acquaintances. I don't care. I'm in protective mode. I need to look out for Hannah. She's my priority — not answering their queries. I hope that people understand that this isn't my usual demeanour. I'm usually happy to speak to artists at openings … but not today. Nope.

When the next person approaches me, I try to use body and facial expressions to tell the woman that I can't talk – I'm here with Hannah. So instead of leaving the conversation, I tell her what I've been telling Hannah.

"Dawu is sick and presently in Jiangsu Province," I blurt to her, loud enough for the whole room to hear.

The woman isn't buying it and neither is anyone else. I can hear the whispers rustling like leaves around me. I can feel my face turn red. It's the price I have to pay for keeping Hannah out of the ordeal. I don't want her to find out. We're going to have to leave the exhibit. Hannah is a clever and tuned-in kid and will definitely pick up on the changes, however nuanced, in the gallery. She's going to know something is going on if we stay here any longer.

We have to leave.

The whole situation sucks. It's super awkward and I hate awkward situations, especially in a second language and culture. But here I am. I look and feel like a freak: flushed face, wide eyes and pursed lips. I am rooted to the spot, looking for an exit. Then, Hannah gives me a break. She dashes away when she spots something interesting.

As quickly as I can, I tell a few artists around me about what's really happening with Dawu.

"He's been detained," I say. "I haven't heard from him in a week and a half. I have no idea what's going on."

They say they had heard he was locked up. That's the end of the conversation. Hannah is back, grabbing my hand and gripping it tightly.

"I've got to get Hannah some lunch," I say to the small group. "See you later,"

"Good luck," a few of them say to me as I head out. "We wish you well."

I know they sincerely mean it. They won't reach out to me though. Artists in the wider community are scared that the authorities will come after them, too. I understand this. It's a real fear and I don't want to put anyone in a bind. I also understand that the government could be watching me, who I'm talking with and where I'm going. I have to be careful as well.

The rustling of leaves gets louder as I stroll to the exit. I can't do anything to stop the muffled whispers and gossip. People will be discussing rumours and trading opinions about Dawu and what he supposedly did or did not do. There are always going to be those folks who chose to believe in fiction over fact.

There isn't a word for the emotion I'm experiencing: somewhere between embarrassment, shame and confusion. Crawling under the proverbial rock and hiding would be great right now. Instead, I hold my head high and walk out of the room with Hannah by my side.

If I had been alone, I might have stayed and tried to counter the rumour mill. However, the last thing I need is to hear lies or unsolicited advice. I have found in China (and it's everywhere in the world) that there are many do-gooders. Folks love telling you what you should and should not do ... even when you haven't asked for answers.

Most of the artists at the gallery today probably think Dawu is behind bars because of his political activities. He did sign Charter 08 and march on Chang'an Avenue — middle finger salutes to the authoritarian regime. The authorities are making sure he never uses that finger again.

34

I have been avoiding the detention centre. I'm not going to go to a place where I'm hassled and mocked. I can make myself feel like shit. I don't need prison guards doing it for me. Besides, Dawu doesn't need more underwear. What he needs is to get out of there. I've been clinging to the idea that when his initial detention is over in 25.5 days, he'll come back to me. Now, I doubt this idea more and more.

Since the word is out about Dawu, my friends are calling. Stephanie Miller, my entrepreneur friend, phones and says she's concerned about Dawu's situation. The whole ordeal is making her sick to her stomach because she has gone through something similar.

"Do you have time to meet for a chat?" she asks me.

I'm glad of the support and curious about what happened to Stephanie. I don't know her well but we've spent time together professionally. She's also familiar with Dawu's work and thinks he's a solid, creative artist.

I tell Stephanie that I'll meet her at Timezone 8 Café, a newly-renovated and artsy café in the 798 district. I spot her and we take seats close to the back of the restaurant. She's nervous and doesn't want anyone eavesdropping on our conversation. She tells me her story and I'm blown away. She has a Chinese ex-boyfriend who was detained like Dawu. It all sounds familiar.

The ex is also a contemporary and avant-garde artist who was detained in China a few years ago. It was all due to some sort of "misunderstanding" but the government had been keeping its eye on him for a while. The ex was outspoken about the Chinese authorities and never minced words.

Stephanie's ex was taken and held in solitary confinement for most of his six months in detention. He was kept in a cement room under high security. Once he served his "term," Stephanie took him to the U.S., where he is now.

Dawu's story resonates with Stephanie and this is why she's reaching out to me. I had no idea that she had gone through something so life-changing. However, it's not as if false imprisonments are broadcast on the evening news. Stephanie says she thinks what happened to her ex-boyfriend and what's happening to Dawu is the systematic targeting of artists.

There seem to be three demographics that the authorities have in their crosshairs: the poor, migrant workers and artists. Whenever something goes wrong in China, the government finds a scapegoat. Then, it punishes one group for the sins of another. The poor might have their access to jobs cut, migrant workers might not be able to travel for work and artists get exhibitions closed down ... or their studios demolished. All three groups can be thrown into jail without being charged with anything.

Stephanie has an uncensored view of the communist party's policies in China. She hates the government and knows it has the power to do anything it wants to anybody. She points out the crackdowns on the Gao Brothers, friends of hers. She says the art scene in Beijing is under intense scrutiny and alludes to spies infiltrating artist collectives and galleries. These spies report on anything the government can construe as being anti-government.

While some artists like Dawu and Ai Weiwei are voices for change, hoping to lift people out of poverty and misery, high-ranking communist party officials are laughing in their faces. The government takes and takes and takes, kicking people out of their homes and flattening them to put high rises in their place. Then, officials ensconce their mistresses in the newly-built luxury condos.

It's a farce.

Stephanie and I take a moment to pause and reflect on how politics has twisted the lives of everyday people in China. It makes it hard for me to see how Dawu is going to get out of detention soon. Nothing in China goes from A to B. The most infuriating thing for me is, I can't even talk to Dawu and get his side of the story.

"What do I do?" I ask Stephanie, hoping she holds the answer.

"Don't let him disappear inside," she says. "Don't give up."

I'm not about to let Hannah's father fade into the background of her life. However, I don't want to forget that I need to live, too. Tonight, Mike and I are going to an Usher concert. The American singer and performer is in Beijing and it's a chance to pretend I'm somewhere else. There are times when I need to lose myself in something other than Dawu's problems.

I'm hanging out with Patti. She invited me over for a dip in her pool and we are talking while sitting in the sun. I enjoy sun tanning but most Chinese don't like it. Having "dark" skin means you work outside and must be from peasant stock. Some people in Beijing believe the whiter your skin, the better off you are in life.

Patti and I chitchat about this and that, meandering around topics until we land on Dawu. We rehash his options, including the one she has already suggested: attending a church service at the Italian Embassy and then asking for asylum. That might work if he wasn't behind bars.

On my way home from Patti's, I deliver a Counting Sheep Boutique item. A woman had purchased a Grobag, a fancy sleeping bag for infants. I realize on the car ride home that it has been precisely two weeks since Dawu disappeared.

It feels like a lot longer. So much has happened. Dawu has taken over my work, my life. I'm appreciative that my trusted studio assistant, Jane, is covering for me at the Beijing Color Studio. I also have Kai and Belinda, other part-time staff, who can come in and work. I'd like to be able to get back to managing the studio full-time soon. Before Dawu was put in jail, I had been spending every day in the studio developing programs and working on marketing. That has all screeched to a halt.

The next day, Hannah and I are invited to visit Lena and Xing Kui at their country house for the weekend. The property is in the mountains of Huairou, just north of the city. It's about a 90-minute drive to the house and close to a section of the Great Wall of China. The area is popular with tourists and a lucky few expats, such as Lena and Xing Kui, who have managed to lease country homes from the locals. Some expats take the rural homes "as is" (pit toilets and rudimentary kitchens) while others renovate the houses to city living standards. My friends have put in toilet facilities, a modern kitchen and air conditioning.

Hannah and I have a good time with Lena and Xing Kui at the country house. We've been barbecuing with the family, going for walks and hanging out. The adults don't talk much about Dawu but Xing Kui does reiterate that he can't be of much assistance to him. What can I say to that?

A part of me wakes up every day, hoping and wishing that a magician will appear and zap Dawu out of jail. Then, zap him to a country where he'll be safe from the hocus-pocus of the Chinese authorities.

But this isn't Harry Potter. There are no magical spells. Only curses.

On a calm evening when the kids are all in bed, Lena asks me how Hannah is doing. I say that Hannah is fine but she's still in the dark about her father.

"You must tell her the truth," says Lena. "Tell her now."

Lena feels that Hannah will be emotionally harmed if I don't share what's going on with her. I respect Lena's opinion as she's a great mother, an amazing kindergarten teacher and a respected role model. Lena adds that I'm lying to my daughter. Instead of protecting her, I could be teaching her how to live in denial and distrust others.

"Won't Hannah be scared if she knows her father is in a terrible place and we can't do anything to help him?" I ask. "Isn't that worse?"

Hannah loves her dad and won't fully understand the situation. I mean, she's five years old. Nevertheless, the more I think about it, the more I know Lena is right. I need to be upfront and show my daughter the correct way of dealing with hard realities. I will tell her after I've had time to gather my thoughts.

Hannah and I stay at Lena and Xing Kui's second home for a couple of nights. Then it's back to the dirty, noisy city. After the quiet of the country, Beijing seems to be clattering around louder than usual. A place I once found enchanting, I now find downright annoying.

A good friend's mother is coming to visit me today. Maureen is my friend Colleen Lashuk's mom. I know Colleen through my university years in Canada. Several weeks ago, Colleen emailed me and asked if I'd meet Maureen and her male friend for a meal in Beijing. I happily agreed. However, this was before the ordeal with Dawu.

"No problem," I say to myself. "I'll be the coolest of cucumbers and treat Maureen and her friend as if it's a regular Beijing day and Dawu isn't behind bars."

It's weird and funny and ironic how, on some days, I want to tell the world what's going on while on other days, I want to keep mum about it. Somedays, I want to shut down and turn off. I don't want to have to deal with anything connected to Dawu. I'll get my chance with Maureen and her friend.

I welcome my overseas guests into my Beijing Color Studio. It's a good place to meet since it's near 798 and they're interested in art. Maureen is curious about Beijing and my life here. We chat about every topic BUT Dawu. The Canadians aren't stupid and so we do touch on the sensitive topic of the Chinese authorities and the government. They know some of what's been happening in the country in terms of its atrocious human rights record. I talk about some artists who are being detained but I don't let on that it's my own husband who is, as we speak, sitting behind bars. The irony of my life these days is painfully obvious, at least to me.

Maureen is a professor of international social work at the University of Calgary and has a lot of experience living abroad. She understands it's not easy living in different parts of the world under governments that don't believe in democracy. She might find Dawu's story fascinating but for me, I can't even begin to open up about it. I want to be normal for a few hours.

After a while of China-chatting, we move on to see 798. We look around the complex and drop in on some of the keynote exhibitions and galleries. Maureen and her friend are thoroughly impressed with the contemporary and avant-garde art. We eat at a restaurant inside 798 called #6, one of my favourite Chinese restaurants. It's owned by an artist couple, Cang Xin and his wife, Xiang Xiaoli. It's in an old building that was one of the original factories when the 798 district was an industrial area. The cuisine at #6 is Sichuan and delicious. After our meal, my guests tell me they've had a great time and we part company.

I feel I've done my job well if they have no idea about what I'm really going through. I've shown them the beautiful side of China, not to mention some of the best of Beijing. I'm not sure how Maureen and her friend would feel about the country as a whole if they truly knew the ugly side. I'm not going to be the one to ruin their view. I don't want to put a black mark on their stop in Beijing.

When I get home, I receive a message that further taints my hope that I'll see Dawu soon. Well-known Chinese avant-garde artist Yu Xiang has reached out to me via social media from the Netherlands. He tells me about an event that took place in 2008 when he was living in Beijing. His wife, Tao Lili, had gone to a local police station to sort out some papers and documents in regards to the couple moving into an apartment complex.

Lili was not getting answers to simple questions and the simple errand turned nasty. She was upset and started arguing with the cops. The dispute almost became violent and the police ended up carting Lili away to a mental institute. Yu Xiang spent the next few years working to get her released. Once she was out (with no apology from the authorities), the couple moved overseas. Yu Xiang says he is telling me all of this because he doesn't want me to give up. It could take days, months or years before Dawu is freed. But never, ever, give up.

It's a "regular" Saturday. This morning I'm working on my application for a master's degree at Royal Roads University. I had been thinking about going back to university and I have some time today to put to good use. Once Dawu is out of detention, I'll be free to leave China and attend school.

I daydream and escape to Canada for a few minutes. I'm imagining walking around the beautiful Royal Roads grounds. I had visited the campus last fall in 2009 when I went to Victoria, B.C., for my dad's 80th birthday. The grounds, complete with a stately castle, were inviting with leafy trees, lush gardens and fresh ocean air. I can see myself studying at the university and putting Beijing behind me. Alas, this is all in my head right now.

There is somewhere I can go today to "get away." The China Art Archive and Warehouse (CAAW) is genuinely a lovely gallery. It's just past the 798 Art District and was designed by Ai Weiwei for friends. The gallery has an elegant grey brick exterior and a grass courtyard. The interior of CAAW is just as nice. It's filled with works from many of the best Chinese artists, such as Chen Lingyang, Han Lei, Hong Hao and, of course, Ai Weiwei. Dawu would like to have his art in here, too, but he has never been invited to participate in any exhibits.

I wonder if Ai Weiwei will be at the gallery. Then I can ask him if he has had any response from his tweets. If he's not there, maybe his friends will have heard of Dawu's plight and know some way to open a door. Anything is worth a try.

I'm so glad to have my own wheels. The CAAW is an out-of-the-way gallery in the further reaches of northeast Beijing and sometimes difficult for taxis to find. I drive Hannah and me to the gallery and we stroll around looking at the artworks. However, I'm getting the feeling that people are looking at me.

Am I paranoid after the other day at the TangRen Gallery? No, people are definitely gawking. It's difficult standing here with my daughter knowing that people are staring at us. It makes me uncomfortable.

When I slowly move from piece to piece, there are eyes following me. I hope that's all that happens. I still haven't told Hannah about her father and I don't want these people to spill the beans. Thankfully, when some folks do approach us, they don't ask any questions about Dawu. They only express their concern for me.

Xu Wanyan, one of the CAAW managers, says he wishes he could help me. The Gao Brothers are here, too. The brothers know what it's like to be in my shoes – the awkward glances, the murmuring, the feeling of always being watched. The two men give me hugs before I flee the gallery with my daughter.

On the way home, I look at Hannah in the rear-view mirror. She looks so small sitting by herself in the backseat. I'm afraid of burdening her tiny soul with major adult problems. I'm not only scared to tell her about her baba but I feel lousy about it. It's terrible news to deliver to a kid. How do I even start? Should I just be direct? Should I come out and say, "Your dad has been beaten and is now being illegally detained for something he didn't do."

Hannah is not going to get it. She'll only get upset. Again, I put off blowing up her world. Weekends are for enjoying life.

Monday it's back to business. I visit the detention centre and ask the guards a round of questions.

"When can I see Dawu?"

"When is he going to be let out?"

"Why won't you let me see my husband?"

The staff only has one answer: "Your husband is here because he beat a cop. It's a serious offence."

The guards will not give me anything on Dawu. They won't budge from the story I've heard over and over again: Dawu hit a cop. Visiting the detention centre is demoralizing and it was hard to enough to get the motivation to go through the door. I don't want to return. Ever.

When I'm home, I check the Canadian Embassy website for its list of lawyers. I also ask around for names of other attorneys. I reach out to my community and contacts, namely Ray Chen, a well-known language translator in China, and Xing Kui. Lena's husband couldn't use his police connections for Dawu but he knows some lawyers and gives me a few names.

In between working for Dawu, I work on my studio business. I'm going ahead with the kids' camps that I've been planning for the summer. Jane and Kai are my instructors for the creative classes.

I email notices to parents, former clients, about the studio camps in hopes they'll sign their children up for a few sessions. I keep the message lighthearted and fun. The last thing I want is for the parents of these kids to know about Dawu.

Dawu's situation could influence prospective customers and they could decide against sending their kids to my camps. His detention is not good marketing material. Quite the opposite.

It has been my experience that most expats living in China have no idea how the Chinese government operates. The authorities rule by force, coercion and any other means possible. Many expats turn a blind eye to this. I was no better a few weeks ago. Now, though, I'm afraid my peers could judge me for what's happening with Dawu.

Some expats take the authorities in China at face value and don't consider that things might (and do!) run differently here. Dawu's case is complicated and since I don't know his actual cause for being thrown in jail, I feel like I don't have the words and framework to fully defend him.

I'm living a dual life: one as a woman whose husband is in prison; the other as a woman who has everything going well for her. I don't want my clients to meet the first woman. This is why I smile and pretend everything is fine and dandy. However, my plan cracked last week during a business meeting.

A facet to my "nothing is wrong" persona has been to court buyers for the Counting Sheep Boutique. My partner Nina and I have been talking to two women, Natalie Champan and Lily Lim, about taking over the business. They're both expats with Chinese heritage. Natalie is from Thailand and Lily is American.

Natalie has owned and operated a chain of massage centres in Beijing, the Nirvana Massage and Spas, and so she knows what she's doing in terms of clients, customers and running a business in China. Counting Sheep offers Natalie and Lily a new venture and a chance to collaborate. Plus, they both have young children and can use the products and pass on their reviews to customers. It's a perfect fit all around.

I'm meeting with Natalie and Lily again today, sans Nina, who is busy. I told the women a few days ago about Dawu. It was a day I couldn't keep the smile plastered on my face and Natalie was going through a terrorizing time, too. Her son had been kidnapped and was being held for ransom. It's any parent's worst nightmare: having a child taken and not being able to protect him or her. I couldn't imagine the pain Natalie was feeling so I shared my story with her.

Natalie says her son has been returned to her. She is married to a prominent businessman and the motive for the kidnapping was money. Natalie hopes Dawu has been returned to me. I tell her no, he remains in jail and then I move on to business.

Talking about my husband to expats makes me feel uncomfortable. I don't want pity or sympathy. I only want Dawu out alive and healthy.

The prospective business partners seem genuinely interested in my welfare and my company. I would like them to buy the boutique. It would be great to have two savvy women take it over. I would have one less thing to worry about if I decide to leave China for grad school. There's one more thing I need to deal with today: telling Hannah about her father.

After supper, I take a deep breath and tell my daughter that I need to talk to her. We sit on the couch and I begin giving her the real story of what is happening with her dad.

"Your baba is in jail," I say, "because the police didn't like something that he did."

"Is he going to be OK?" she asks as big fat tears roll down her face.

I put my arms around her.

"He's going to be fine. Nothing is going to happen to your dad and nothing is going to happen to us."

"Why can't he come home?" Hannah asks. "Is he going to die?"

I tell her that he's alive and that mom is working hard to get him out of detention. She has many more questions but I say she should keep them for when her baba comes home.

I feel 50 pounds lighter now that I've told Hannah the truth. I don't have to tiptoe around her and pretend all is well. I'm also glad I kept my promise to Lena. She was right. It wasn't fair to keep Hannah in the dark.

My daughter has one more question for me tonight.

"Can I see baba in jail?" she asks.

That brings up another complication. I'm not sure if I should take Hannah to the detention centre to see where her father "lives." It's a depressing place and I don't want to scare her into thinking her father is never getting out of there. Because he is coming home.

Isn't he?

Tuesday, June 22, is an unusual summer day for Beijing – clear and sunny. Mike and I are going to have a picnic while Hannah is at school. We're heading towards Huairou, around Lena's country home. I'm driving and I pull off at a nice shady spot, close to a creek, for lunch. The weather is comfortably warm and there's a slight breeze drifting from the nearby woods. The place reminds me a bit of my family cabin in Millarville, a town in the middle of rolling hills and horse farms about a 45-minute drive southwest of Calgary.

The Millarville property has been in my family for several generations. It's close to a creek and I have many happy memories associated with the area. We used to go there on holidays and weekends when I was a child. When I was in university, I'd throw parties at the cabin. Since I've been living in China, I never get the chance to visit Millarville. There are too many other things on the go when I'm home for a visit.

The creekside picnic with Mike in Huairou puts me at ease despite the low hum of anxiety that constantly vibrates my body and soul. There's only so much I can do for Dawu and I've done what I can for now. I'm also exploring the ideas that Chao Hongling put into my head the other day. She told me that the art community would come through for Dawu. That it'll help me, help him.

I wish I knew what would make Hannah feel a little better about what's happening to her father. When she comes home from school later in the afternoon, she launches a million questions at me.

"What is it like inside the jail?" she asks.

"What does dad eat in there?" she asks.

"When will he get out?" she asks.

She's worried about her baba and I can't do anything to lessen the stress.

Hannah has always loved playing with her stuffies. Tonight, she grabs Gruffalo (a terrifying character in a children's book) and sends it to "jail" by lobbing the plush toy across the room. Hannah has also learned a few new words in both English and Mandarin.

Jail / prison – *jiānyù*, and
Detention centre – *kānshuǒsuǒ*.

It isn't cute. It's breaking my heart.

At an appointment with Dana later in the week, I talk out what's happening to my child. My therapist explains that Hannah is processing her feelings through play. As Gruffalo was being tossed around, Hannah showed that she understood that jail is a bad place where bad people go. I'll need to reinforce that her father isn't bad. He didn't do anything wrong. (At least I hope he didn't.)

My own family and Western friends agree that I did the right thing by telling my daughter about what's happening to her father. I told Hannah because I'm her mother and we're both Canadians. Despite Hannah's tears and Gruffalo being sent to jail once or twice daily, I feel in my heart that telling her was the right decision.

My Chinese friends think I should never have told Hannah. They're horrified my child knows that her baba is behind bars. I've found that in Chinese culture, no one wants to be the bearer of bad news. That means a loss of face to both the receiver and deliverer. Instead of saying what's wrong, efforts are made to conceal information and beat around the bush. It's interesting that I'm still surprised by some cultural differences even after all the years I've spent in China. It can be hard to be stuck between two worlds.

I'm being encouraged by Chinese friends not to tell Dawu's family anything, so I haven't. Since his father and sister don't live in Beijing, it's easier to keep the news from them. I've been concocting elaborate stories and lies to explain Dawu's absence and silence. For instance, I've told Wu Suling, Dawu's sister, that her brother was on an art exhibition trip aboard and had to leave his phone at home. It's easier this way.

I stick out like the proverbial sore thumb at the detention centre. Not many expats have Chinese husbands behind bars. The guards tending the line know who I am. They know I'm the wife of the man who hit a cop. I'm the wife of the man who is anti-government and doesn't respect authority. My husband is among the lowest of the low. He has lost all face.

The guards have more face than Dawu and that translates into power over him… and me. During my time in China, I've seen that even if you have a wee bit of power, you use it. No matter what. I've had bank clerks or staff behind postal counters ignore me or else serve me in an almost hostile manner because they considered me below them. It's the same now. The guards know I want information about Dawu and they know they're my only option at the moment. They're not going to give anything to me. However, if I knew which one to bribe, maybe I could get what I wanted through the backdoor.

The backdoor can be opened for anyone and anything if you pay the price for the key. Don't have good grades but want to get into a good school? Find the backdoor. However, in Dawu's case, I can't even find the front door. Worse yet, my Chinese friends, like Honghong, have had the backdoor slammed shut in their faces. That's, as the Chinese say, *meimen'r*: no door.

The guards this morning can't be bothered to taunt me, nor are they giving me any information. I'm being stonewalled. I drop off some money, socks and another pair of underwear for Dawu. Other families are doing the same thing for their loved ones. We don't look at each other while standing in line. I leave the centre without a word to anyone other than the staff.

There is a bright light on the horizon. Chao Hongling has told me her sister is a lawyer and she might be able to help Dawu. For free! As one of Dawu's closest artist friends, Chao Hongling has been my confidante in the past few weeks. I'm sure her sister, Chao Hongmei, is someone I can trust wholeheartedly.

I'm meeting the attorney and Chao Hongling at the artist's studio in the 798 Art District this afternoon. I think it's a good idea to use her sister's services and I'm backed up by Dawu's studio assistant, Zhang, and Dawu's former student Hong. They both say that Chao Hongmei knows what's happening with Dawu and will have no problem taking on his complicated and delicate case.

There's also the bonus that she's agreeing to do the work pro gratis. I have no idea what another lawyer would charge me to take the case but I don't think it would be cheap. The rates are not printed in the *Lonely Planet Travel China Guide*.

There are a few people at the meeting this afternoon including me, Chao Hongmei, Chao Hongling, Gu Duanfan, Zhang, Hong and Tang Funai (the Troublemaker). There's also a random man whom I've never seen before. He's introduced as a couch surfer who has been staying at Dawu's studio. Why the couch surfer is here I don't know but perhaps he's able to help somehow.

Our discussion is being filmed by an artist in case he wants to develop some sort of creative piece out of the meeting. I don't care about what I look like for the camera. I already know I have black circles under my eyes, deep furrows in my brow and an ugly frown -- but I would like to be able to speak freely without having the annoying lens shoved in my face whenever I open my mouth. The other reason the group is recording everything has to do with accountability. What I say goes on the record.

That goes both ways.

The lawyer, Chao Hongmei, gives me the impression that she knows what she's doing and what to do in terms of Dawu's case. I've been told that only a lawyer can see him at this point as per the Chinese legal system. Family members aren't allowed access to Dawu until the 37.5-day period is up. Chao Hongmei tells the groups that she'll try to see Dawu today and find out what's going on and how he is feeling. I feel my face light up. It's not faked happiness but an honest-to-goodness smile. I'm feeling optimistic and relieved that Chao Hongmei will have a chance to talk to Dawu. I'd like to be the one to see him first but at this point, Chao Hongmei is a great alternative.

Perhaps the visit will be a turning point. Perhaps this is all the pressure needed to spring Dawu. Maybe he'll tell the lawyer that he's coming home in just over two weeks, when the 37.5 days are up. I envision Chao Hongmei's meeting going smoothly. With her expertise, I should be able to get the real answers to my big questions. Maybe, just maybe, I'll be able to see my husband.

Zhang drives Chao Hongmei, me and other members of our entourage to the detention centre in his Jeep. Parking isn't a problem outside the Chaoyang District Detention Center. We all go inside and I manage to shrug off the negative vibes reaching for me from the damp corners of the building. The guards are calm but there are no smiles while they check our IDs. I sign a form giving the lawyer permission and the authority to meet with Dawu.

Chao Hongmei has turned from a confident lawyer into a nervous Nelly. At the studio, she had been standing tall and talking with force. Now she's giggling at odd times, her actions are quick and her posture is slouched. I know that the detention centre can feel overwhelming with its uniformed staff, heavy steel doors and sad-looking families. It's OK to be on edge in this place. I usually am when I'm here. However, Chao Hongmei is now putting me even more on edge. She's been ignoring me, too. Any time I talk to her, she flicks her hand at me and won't answer my questions.

Huh?

I've asked her several times, in Chinese, about what she's going to do when she sees Dawu. I have a few questions that I'd like specific answers to, such as:

"What the hell happened?"

"Was Dawu beaten?"

"By whom?"

"What's going on now?"

"Did Dawu hit a cop?"

Nevertheless, Chao Hongmei turns away from me, dismissing me like I'm a child. She's acting like she's not in the least bit interested in knowing what I need to know. When I try to talk to her again, she walks away from me and joins in the chatter of the group.

Perhaps I've upset her with my questions? Maybe she thinks it means I don't have faith in her as a lawyer and I think she doesn't know what she's doing? That's not it. She's my only line, my only connection, to my husband right now. I've been waiting for almost three weeks for answers to questions that have kept me up at night and kept me constantly wondering about Dawu. This afternoon, she'll be able to quiet the thoughts in my head. She'll be able to make sense of this whole nonsensical situation that's dragged on for far too long.

Chao Hongmei is now being escorted out of the room for her meeting with Dawu. My support group sits and waits in silence with me. We shift in our chairs, watching the thin black minute hand of the clock spin around and around. People coming into the centre steal glances at me. I bet the rubbernecks are thinking, "What on Earth is a foreigner doing in here?"

A door swishes open after about half an hour. It's Chao Hongmei. We swarm her, eager to hear about Dawu. However, she's eager only to get out of the detention centre.

"Let's go," she says, avoiding my eyes and walking away from me.

I place my hand on her arm, hoping she'll pause.

"Is he OK?" I ask.

She keeps heading for the exit and doesn't say a word to me. My heart jumps into my mouth. Is Dawu that badly hurt that she can't tell me?

"Is he injured?" I call after her, barely getting the words out.

Chao Hongmei doesn't answer. She won't look at me. She goes outside with her sister. Zhang, Hong and the rest of the crew are trailing behind.

What the fuck is going on?

Chao Hongmei stops to talk to the group. I overhear her say she's tired and worn out. That's too bad, but I want to know how my husband is, the man who is actually behind bars having who knows what done to him. I bet he's tired and worn out.

"How is Dawu?" I ask.

Again, Chao Hongmei turns her back on me.

"Mother of Jesus," I scream to myself.

My eyes start filling with tears but I quickly wipe them away. No sense in letting everyone know I'm upset. It'll just make them back away from me, the emotional foreigner.

While I'm trying to figure what to do, Chao Hongling decides that Chao Hongmei needs lunch and I need to back off.

"Karen," says Hongling, "it's probably best if you go home."

With that, Chao Hongling whisks her sister away and puts her into a vehicle. Some others from our group, including Tang, get in with them. I'm left behind, my mouth hanging wide open, with Zhang and Mr. Couch Surfer. What just happened?

Zhang says he'll text Chao Hongling to find out which restaurant the Chao sisters are heading to and we'll follow. The three of us get into the Jeep and proceed to wait for the directions to the secret lunch place. Then, Mr. Couch Surfer jumps out and climbs into the car with Chao Hongling and Chao Hongmei before they all drive away. It's all so very odd.

I understand why Mr. Couch Surfer got out after Chao Hongling calls Zhang. He is being told to take me home. Under no circumstances am I to join them at the restaurant.

"What the fuck!" I spit in Chinese. If Chao Hongling hadn't already driven away, who knows what I would have done to her vehicle. I'm angry and hurt and upset. Even the Troublemaker gets to know what happened during Chao Hongmei's meeting.

Why don't they want me to hear the news about Dawu? Out of any-one, I have the right to know what my husband, and the father of my child, said in the meeting. I'm confused and feel betrayed by my friends.

Later in the evening, Zhang brings me some information. At lunch, Chao Hongmei had told the group that Dawu never hit a cop. Aha! I had known that in my gut the whole time. I feel the tightness in my chest release a little. I knew Dawu hadn't hit anyone. Knowing that fact only makes me want to fight harder for his release.

Why wouldn't Chao Hongmei tell me this to my face? Why wouldn't her sister, Chao Hongling, let me know the news? She knew I was struggling to find any shred of information about Dawu. She has listened to me pour my heart out. The sisters had intentionally blocked me from my husband. Zhang, bless him, is also angry. He's been left out, too. He's Dawu's most trusted assistant and is still in charge of his studio and bank account for Pete's sake! This is crazy. We both thought that Chao Hongling would have my back. She's one of Dawu's closest long-time friends.

After talking with Zhang, I think I've been used. Chao Hongling might be jealous of Dawu's recent claim to fame. Since he marched on Chang'an Avenue, he has shot up in prominence in the art world. He was getting a lot of attention and now that he's in jail, maybe she thinks he'll parlay it into something bigger? She used me to get to him to find out what he plans to do next.

Chao Hongling doesn't seem to give a shit about my feelings — only that I'm the key to getting Chao Hongmei access to Dawu. They needed me but were not really concerned about me. Here I was, thinking Dawu and I had such great friends who were willing to support us and give us their valu-able time and expertise when really, they only wanted us as part of a bizarre show.

The one snippet of news that I managed to glean today from Chao Hongmei's visit with Dawu was that he never hit a cop. If that is true, why is he being held in the criminal section of the detention centre? How it is that Tang the Troublemaker is out and Dawu remains behind bars? I start think-ing things over and come up with two versions of what could be happening.

Scenario #1: Chao Hongmei et al don't want me to know the real truth because it's painful. Scenario #2: Chao Hongling is jealous of Dawu and trying to control his image. She's exercising her power and showing that she is the only one with information on Dawu. She's scheming to have him stay in detention as long as possible. If he gets out soon, he'll be able to cash in on the "success" of the Chang'an Avenue march, thus, overshadowing Chao Hongling and her husband Gu Duanfan.

I'm only coming up with these ideas to try and figure out Chao Hongling and Chao Hongmei's weird behaviours. I can't talk to anyone in the art world about this. They'd all side with Chao Hongling — not Dawu's wife, the woman he hasn't lived with for over a year.

Fuck them. I'm going to get my own lawyer.

I call Ray Chen and ask about attorneys. I also ask him to be my interpreter. I'm going to need one. In most situations, I'm confident and capable with my Chinese language skills. However, I do find I'm holding back when it comes to talking to anyone in authority about Dawu. I chose not to ask a question or ask for clarification for fear of embarrassing or humiliating myself in another language. As well, I don't want to say anything that could get Dawu in hotter water. I need to know exactly what is going on. Period. As a highly sought-after translator, Ray is a busy man but he says he has time for me. He also says he'll send me the names of some good lawyers. Great!

While speaking to Ray, he drops a bomb. He says that Chao Hongmei is an international trade and economic lawyer, not a criminal lawyer and the type Dawu needs. What the heck? This is nuts. I'm going to have trouble trusting Chao Hongling again. It's this kind of asshole behaviour that ruins friendships. However, was I ever friends with Chao Hongling or was it just Dawu? My life sucks.

On top of all of this, my business world is falling apart. A child with hand and foot disease showed up at one of my day camps this morning. I'm in the midst of trying to find someone who can wash and disinfect EVERYTHING in the studio — from the floors, to the walls, to the furniture, to the art supplies. Everything in my life seems to be spiralling out of control. How soon until I totally lose it?

At the end of the day, it's my assistant Jane who slows my spin towards utter destruction. She has found a cleaner with a flexible schedule. The woman will start sterilizing my studio tonight.

I'm frustrated beyond all belief. Over the phone, Zhang confirms what Ray Chen told me yesterday. Chao Hongmei is an international trade and economic lawyer. Not a criminal lawyer. The news makes me want to rant and rave at the Chao sisters. Chao Hongmei had no idea what she was doing when she went into the detention center to speak to Dawu. No wonder she acted nervously.

Chao Hongmei wasted a huge chunk of my time. She was rude too! The woman is not at all experienced with sensitive criminal cases. I guess I got what I didn't pay for. The next lawyer I will pay and she or he will not be connected to the art scene. The lawyer will be independent and not connected to anyone other than me. I want someone who will answer only to me and not have obligations to any "middleman" from the 798 Art District.

Zhang asks if I can meet Chao Hongmei at Chao Honging and Gu Duanfan's place. I'm reluctant until he says the lawyer is finally going to debrief me about her meeting with Dawu. I have nothing to lose except more time so I might as well go.

When I arrive at the studio, there's a small group gathered. Zhang is here along with Tang Funai, Chao Honging, Gu Duanfan and Chao Hongmei. The lawyer seems sad. She isn't my favourite person right now but she isn't displaying the arrogance that I saw yesterday. Today, her shoulders and chin droop and she gives me a wan smile when I say hello.

Chao Hongling tells me that Chao Hongemi has bad news for me. My hands immediately tighten into balls and I take a deep breath, waiting to release my tension. What am I about to hear?

Chao Hongmei says she thinks the cops have set up Dawu. He's being framed. This is what she gleaned from him when they talked yesterday. He told her that on May 31, he went with Tang to the Jiuxianqiao Police Station to complain about the stolen generator. That's when the two were arrested and separated. They were put into two different rooms but not charged with anything.

After being questioned for several hours, five cops took Dawu to the detachment's empty cafeteria and beat him. They pulled his shirt up over his head until his arms stuck straight into the air. This particular style of punishment is called being "airplaned" and it was common during China's Cultural Revolution. (The technique was documented by Li Zhensheng in his book *Red-Color News Soldier.*) Dawu couldn't see what was coming next, an assault with punches and kicks.

A cop broke his finger while assaulting Dawu. The officers blamed the injury on Dawu, saying he did it. How that was possible when Dawu was upside down in a position akin to being in a straight-jacket is beyond me. The cops also taunted Dawu, antagonizing him into verbally hitting back. His jeers were captured on a voice recorder but the beatings weren't recorded.

After the assault, the police were terrified to learn that Dawu was married to a foreigner. When I arrived at Jiuxianqiao, he was immediately taken to the detention centre for further processing. While there, he felt that the beating had left him with internal injuries so he requested X-rays be done. One was taken but Dawu was never shown the results, nor has he received any medical treatment.

At the infamous lunch yesterday, Chao Hongmei and the group decided that all of this must mean that Dawu had been set up. Tang wasn't beaten by the police because he hadn't flouted the law and marched on Chang'an Avenue. Dawu is being punished for setting off an explosion of international press and social media attention centered on the 008 International and Zhengyang artist communities evictions. As well, and most importantly, the coverage of the February protest shone a negative spotlight on the developers that forced them to compensate the artists. Thus, the planners are going to be shelling out a lot of money and lose a huge amount of face, not only in China but around the globe. This is hitting a sensitive nerve within the Chinese government and the regime is humiliated and embarrassed. Someone has to be punished.

Dawu.

The authorities are turning him into an aggressive and dangerous activist who has no respect for anyone, especially the police. Hence, this is why Dawu is behind bars and Tang isn't.

Once Chao Hongmei delivers her news, she bolts out of the room. She doesn't want to lose face, either. I suppose I can forgive her for yesterday, even if it is only for cross-cultural "lost in translation" sort of reasons. I can now see that Chao Hongling is trying to help Dawu, she just picked the wrong way, and lawyer, to do it. By trying to shield me from the latest information, she wasted precious time. Dawu doesn't have time.

Troublemaker Tang is making more trouble for Dawu. Tang has applied for a formal review of the case. He wants the government to look into the treatment that he and Dawu received at the Jiuxianqiao Police Station. Chao Hongling and Gu Duanfan advise him against it. They think an inquiry will only jeopardize Dawu's case, as the cops aren't going to admit guilt. They'll only push harder to keep Dawu in detention.

The meeting lasts for close to four hours and I'm still frustrated at the end. We might have some insight into what's happening but we're no closer to springing Dawu. Sigh. Can't the authorities just pick up the phone and tell me what's going on? I already know the answer to that.

No.

Chao Hongling catches up to me before I leave. She says we should ensure Tang isn't going ahead with his plan to press the authorities. Nevertheless, Chao Hongling is worried about being spotted with me and Tang and being implicated in Dawu's case. She's also stressed that a secret police officer could hear me talking to Tang. She suggests I take my car and drop Tang off at the subway station. My vehicle is a safe place to chat, as no one will see us or be able to record our conversation.

Tang accepts a ride from me and before dropping him off safely at his stop, I ask him to withdraw his review application. He says he'll do anything I want and agrees to drop the matter. I hope he sticks to his word.

I do realize that many of the Chinese people who are helping me are risking something, whether it's their reputation or work, but I'm not getting anywhere. I had thought I needed on-the-ground, grassroots guides to take me through the complicated systems and processes that sometimes operate in the shadows in China. This is exactly why I listened to Dawu's friends and let Chao Hongmei talk to him. Yet that didn't work out the way I expected.

I've been in a holding pattern for weeks and don't know how to break out of it. My expat friends are great at supporting me emotionally but they don't know anything about how China operates on legal, governmental and judicial levels. I'm stuck between two worlds.

At least Chao Hongmei didn't charge me for her work. That's a relief. I'm worried about how much a criminal lawyer is going to cost. I'm arranging to talk to a person Ray Chen recommended. Gong Jin is supposed to be a great lawyer. Hopefully, he'll see me this weekend.

41

Tang better keep his word and not file for a formal review into Dawu's treatment by the officers at the Jiuxianqiao station. There's no way the cops will come clean about assaulting my husband. Almost no one in a position of authority in China's recent history has ever apologized to its citizens.

Whether it was the atrocities during Tiananmen or the Cultural Revolution, no level of government has accepted responsibility for what happened. It simply doesn't have to be accountable for the famines, injuries, persecutions or deaths it causes. It's the government. Dawu's case is no different. The police will go to the ends of the earth to avoid admitting they unlawfully beat him, let alone detained him illegally.

I go to my Friday morning appointment with Dana. I talk to my counsellor about Dawu and how the whole situation is affecting me. I tell her I believe helping him is still the best decision but it's hard to see the light at the end of the tunnel when there are so many walls in the way. As well, Dana and I talk about how Hannah is reacting to her father being in jail. She is continually asking how her baba is doing. I'm leery about taking her to the detention centre to show her where her father is being held. Dana suggests it's best Hannah stays away from the jail for now. My counsellor says I need to continue to seek support and comfort from good friends, listen to my favourite music and look after myself. Dana is awesome and I know that she is concerned for me.

After our 55-minute session, I deliver flyers for my business around the Shunyi District. I'm advertising my Beijing Color Studio summer camps for children. Many of the kids who come to my workshops can be found in this area full of expat families. It's a wonder I'm still running the studio while trying to free Dawu. I'm not sure how long I'll be able to keep going like this. Today, though, I have found the energy somewhere.

In the evening, Chao Hongling calls me and asks me to meet her, Gu Duanfan, Zhang and Hong behind the Cave Café at 798. It's dark by the time I arrive to find my friends waiting for me in Chao Hongling's vehicle. I climb into the SUV and take a seat. Chao Hongling tells us all to remove the batteries from our phones and leave everything in the vehicle.

We walk to a random café where we sit and chat a distance away from the other coffee drinkers. Is Chao Hongling going overboard with all this secrecy? Should I be this paranoid, too? I never thought the government would use my cell phone to spy on me. It's creeping me out but it's a good lesson – I can never be too careful.

Chao Hongling is direct and tells me that she and the other artists are removing themselves from helping me. It's too dangerous for them. She explains that the government might be using Dawu to trap other anti-government artists. Some of the artists who marched on Chang'an have already been added to the regime's blacklist and can't afford to aggravate the authorities.

As of now, Chao Hongling and her husband work relatively freely in China. However, if they get in trouble with the law, there's a real fear they'll face harassment. Their studio could be sacked or they could have a show shut down or face possible eviction from their studio at 798.

"Look at how the Gao Brothers were prevented from leaving China for so long," says Chao Hongling. "They were hassled for years and still can't live and work in peace."

She doesn't want to cross the line the government has drawn in the sand. As much as Chao Hongling and Gu Duanfan love Dawu, they can't risk their livelihoods.

Holy shit.

I feel like I've been slapped in the face. At the same time, how can I argue with her? She and the other artists are worried about their lives. Technically, I can leave China anytime I want. They can't. I have seen and heard how the government and authorities have treated artists over the years. Take Cao Lin, a well-known artist from western China: in 2006, he was doing a performance at an art exhibition on the outskirts of Shanghai when he was harassed by police. He was then detained, illegally, for three months and who knows what happened to him during that time. When he emerged from jail, he had a stutter.

Zhang and Hong say they won't abandon Dawu. Zhang is paid staff in Dawu's studio and so he feels a certain kind of responsibility towards his employer. Hong, as one of Dawu's former students, shares a strong bond with him. I'm glad I have them on my side. I'm Dawu's foreign wife who doesn't know much about the Chinese justice system. Nor have I had any experience with Chinese jails and the judicial system, and I'd be floundering a lot worse than I already am without Zhang and Hong.

Chao Hongling has some more choice tidbits to leave me mulling over.

She and Gu Duanfan are upset with me for celebrating my birthday and studio launch with a big party in April.

"That was really selfish of you," she says. "You should have known."

"Should have known what?" I ask.

"You should have known that the party would attract attention, attention that Dawu didn't need."

In early March, Dawu had been released from 24-hour detention. My party was in late April and I held it to mark my 42nd birthday as well as celebrate the opening of my business. I had invited more than 150 people, pretty much everyone I knew from friends, to artists, to business associates. What was wrong with that?

Chao Hongling says I shouldn't have asked anyone from the art community to attend. I had put her and Gu Duanfan on the guest list but they didn't show up. That was fine by me. At least Dawu came and I thought he had a good time. Chao Hongling says no and tells me that Dawu left halfway through because of the police.

"The police?" I ask.

According to her, several plainclothes officers attended my event and were scoping out the scene. I had no idea then because I didn't know everyone at my festivities. I had told my guests to bring friends so I wouldn't have been able to point out who was a plus-one and who was an informant. Chao Hongling says amidst the celebrations, Dawu had been "invited" by the cops to go outside for a chat. To drink tea, as it were. She adds that the cops had spoken to Dawu earlier that day and warned him to stop making trouble. They knew he was riling up artists and he couldn't make a move without the police knowing when, what, where, why and how. The officers also said he was being watched and they proved that when they harassed Dawu at my party. After the cops cautioned him a second time, he quietly returned to my event with nary a word mentioned to me about the incidents.

I hadn't noticed him missing. I was focused on making sure the party was running well. Even if I had seen him leave, I'd have thought he was going out for a smoke. Besides, we were separated. He didn't need my permission for anything.

From Chao Hongling's perspective, hosting a big party and inviting artists so soon after Dawu had been in detention was a stupid thing for me to do. Especially because of Dawu's anti-government pursuits. I had put him and other artists in danger. Chao Hongling and Gu Duanfan boycotted my event. They didn't want to be seen there by the police. The artist couple did not want to be connected to anyone or anything that could jeopardize their careers.

I had no idea. Call me naïve but it wasn't my intention to cause problems or add to anyone's difficulties. I was only throwing a party. If someone had been upfront with me then and told me that the event was a terrible idea, I might have postponed or cancelled it. Dawu hadn't said anything to me about the guoan before or after my soiree. Perhaps this shows me how much Dawu and I have drifted away from each other.

Lastly, Chao Hongling strongly suggests that I cancel tomorrow's appointment with the lawyer, Gong Jin. Chao Hongling doesn't want me to name her or her husband or her sister in conjunction with Dawu's name. They don't want to be exposed to the authorities as people working with Dawu. They're scared. I'm confused.

Chao Hongling says no lawyer will take Dawu's case after a quick visit from police. The cops will track down Gong Jin and demand he gives them Dawu's file with all the names and details inside. If the attorney refuses, the government will strip away his licence. Chao Hongling tells me that hiring a lawyer for Dawu will be like finding a unicorn. Impossible.

Everyone is scared and paranoid. I'm finding it hard to discern real fear from fear-mongering. It doesn't matter anyway. My Chinese support group has been mostly disbanded. It had been a warm summer's evening. Now I feel a chill coming over me. I'd better get home.

Hannah feels the same as me tonight, at odd ends. She's crying and demanding to see her baba. I'd like to see him, too. I'm not going to cancel my meeting with Gong Jin. He's all I have at the moment.

Finding out that close friends are frightened for their lives every time they talk to me isn't great for my emotional state. I feel like an abandoned boat, drifting away from the safety of the shore and out into the wide-open sea where anything can happen. Despite Chao Hongling and Gu Duanfan saying they can't be seen with me in public anymore, they did tell me they'd try to find a fixer who could get information for me. I haven't been completely unanchored from the Chinese art community.

An expat friend has invited me to *yum cha* (dim sum in Cantonese) at a lovely restaurant in the Chaoyang District. It's not far from my home at the Cappuccino Complex. Rebecca and her husband Brandon Charm are hosting the event. We're friends and have been in touch over the phone about Dawu. The couple isn't sure how to help but inviting Hannah and me to yum cha on a Saturday morning is one way.

I enjoy the meal and the company. It's a good start to the weekend. Emma and Jenny are also there and some other expat friends, too. They've heard about Dawu by now and gently inquire about him. I answer their questions to the best of my knowledge, which as you know, is next to nothing. After the meal, Rebecca and Brandon offer to take Hannah for the rest of the day so I can meet the lawyer without having to worry about my daughter. Everyone wishes me well as I leave the feast and head out to Gong Jin's office.

I'm not cancelling the afternoon meeting with the lawyer no matter what Chao Hongling said to me last night. I want to prove to her that we don't need to live in a climate of fear. We can't just keep sitting on our hands.

I haven't asked Zhang and Hong to come with me. I don't want to implicate them in anything. I have brought along Flame, a competent interpreter. I had thought Ray Chen was going to be my interpreter but it turns out, he's much too busy. I know Flame through Emma, who knows him through another friend.

In 2009, a friend of Emma's discovered that her Russian husband was recruiting young women for the porn industry in southeast China. He was picked up by Beijing cops outside of a Wumart, a local grocery store chain, and put straight into detention. When he needed someone to bail him out the next day, he called his wife, who then called Emma.

She had no idea what to do and so she called me. I said I'd help them find an interpreter and I reached out to an expat friend, who gave me Flame's name.

Flame worked for Emma's friend and did an excellent job. Now I need Flame. I don't know his actual Chinese name but I do know he's a talented and friendly guy. His main career is as a reporter for the Discovery Channel. In his free time, he's an interpreter. We have a good rapport and I need that for where we are going.

We're meeting Gong Jin in his office, which years ago, I once worked in as a photographer for a website called Chinese-art.com. I'm coming full circle in some weird way. I'm returning to a place I know well after many years to meet with a lawyer to try and extract a Chinese contemporary artist out of jail.

Gong Jin meets Flame and me in the building's lobby at 4 p.m. He's not a bad-looking fellow, trim and well-coiffed, although he seems a bit nervous. His eyes won't meet mine and he's tripping over his words. I'm not sure if this is his usual demeanour or if Dawu's current situation is making him sweat. After some quick but necessary introductions, Gong Jin, Flame and I ride the elevator up to the law office while I make small talk. I tell the lawyer about my short time in the building and how it hasn't changed.

Gong Jin's office is windowless and small but it has room for three chairs and an L-shaped desk. I start the meeting by telling the lawyer about Dawu and what I have managed to learn about his case. I have my fingers crossed that Gong will tell me that with a few affidavits here and a few signed forms there, Dawu's ordeal will be over soon.

Yeah, right.

Gong Jin says if the authorities don't release Dawu in 12 days, after the 37.5-day period is up, they'll probably keep him for two more months. As well, since I've never been given an official reason as to why Dawu is incarcerated, the lawyer says the authorities will need that extra time to build a solid case against my husband. He's behind bars now supposedly because he punched a cop but that's not a good enough reason to hold him beyond the 37.5 days. The police need something stronger.

Oh, great.

I don't like what the lawyer is telling me but I do like the lawyer. He's still nervous but he's upfront and knowledgeable. I'm glad because I'm paying him for his expertise. We had agreed on a fee of ¥10,000 RMB, about

CAD 1,250, for the first phase. That's all I can handle right now. I have no idea what his time usually costs.

My Spidey senses begin tingling when Gong Jin gets up in the middle of our conversation and leaves the room. He is making a call in the reception area outside of his office and neither Flame nor I can hear the conversation.

I think it's a strange move. Maybe some of Chao Hongling's paranoia has rubbed off on me. I wonder what the phone call is all about. Maybe I should give Gong Jin the benefit of the doubt. Maybe he needs to confirm dinner plans with his wife. Who knows? Everything isn't always about me and Dawu.

The lawyer joins us again and I tell him that I think Dawu has been set up. Gong Jin says it's a possibility and it's his job to find out all that he can about the case. Our meeting wraps up and we schedule another talk for tomorrow. We'll map our next steps, such as having the lawyer talk to Dawu at the detention centre. Gong Jin can gather intel for me, which I'll take to the media. I've already sent out feelers to reporters but I have nothing to back up my theories. Once I have facts, I hope the press will put enough pressure on the government to release Dawu right away.

On the way out of the building, I warn Flame of how he might be negatively impacted by Dawu's case. I tell him to be on the lookout for anything unusual, like having his mail opened or being followed. He brushes it off. He's aware that the authorities are going to be interested in him because of his link to Dawu. He says he'll be careful but not to worry. Nevertheless, I need to give him the heads up of what he could possibly expect. It's my responsibility to ensure he's going into this with his eyes wide open.

Flame says he admires how strong I am. He says I've taken on so much and haven't fallen apart. Other people would have given up already.

"Why are you doing it?" he asks.

"For Hannah," I say. "She needs her father."

My cell phone is blowing up. It's being flooded with texts and missed calls. News about Dawu? No. Jane at the Beijing Color Studio, is sick and can't teach. Oh, dear. I can't do it. I can't paint. I cancel the Sunday classes and spend a few hours refunding parents their money.

With my studio work done, I meet with Gong Jin, Flame, Zhang and Hong at the lawyer's office. Zhang and Hong are here because when I went to Dawu's studio to pick up some stuff, they asked so many questions that I ended up breaking down and crying. I was not at my strongest and I told them about my plans to meet with the lawyer. They insisted they join me for my second meeting.

Today's discussions are an absolute gong show on so many levels. I wish I had shut the door on Zhang and Hong's plan to come with me. I had said that they could join me only if they agreed to just sit and listen and not get involved. They had promised to do just that but they're reneging on their oath. I'm tired and angry with them because they're making things more complicated than need be.

The last face-to-face meeting between a lawyer and Dawu ended up being a shit show disaster. I need the next meeting to go better. Nevertheless, Zhang and Hong are giving me cause — I should say, causes — for concern. They don't like Gong Jin.

One of the major issues Zhang and Hong have with Gong Jin is that he brought his cellphone into the room with us. Dawu's friends think the lawyer is letting the police listen in on our conversation. Zhang and Hong ask me to ask Gong Jin to leave his phone in his lobby.

I think they're grasping at straws. Most people bring their phones with them wherever they go, especially professionals. It's silly but I end up asking the lawyer if he minds putting his phone in the other room. He complies and we continue talking.

We've been slogging it out for over four hours, mostly going over and over things, over and over again. Zhang and Hong and I are fighting and arguing over big and little details. Flame is trying to calm us down and Gong Jin is quietly trying to filter the facts from the BS. The lawyer is probably wondering how he got involved with such clowns.

Gong Jin says if Dawu does end up going to court, he'll be tried and then I won't get to see him again until AFTER the sentencing, which could be anywhere from five to eight months.

It's been 27 days since Dawu landed in jail. I haven't seen or heard from my husband in that time but Gong Jin says he'll meet with Dawu tomorrow. The lawyer is going to need all the information Dawu can give us on his case so we can stop him from appearing in front of a judge.

I have many questions that I'd like the lawyer to ask Dawu. To start with, did he tell the police station authorities not to contact me in those first 24 hours? I've been wondering for a while why no one called me when Dawu was "arrested." Did he tell the cops not to speak to me because he thought I'd be upset? Or was it a police move to cover-up the fact that Dawu was injured? I also want to know:

1. Are there any X-rays of Dawu's injuries? If yes, I'd like to see them.

2. Why are police saying Dawu attacked an officer?

3. What does Dawu want me to do for him?

I ask Gong Jin to look at Dawu's arm for bruises, scrapes and obvious signs of injuries, although it might be too late for physical evidence that Dawu was beaten. His wounds could be healed already.

As well, I want to ask the lawyer to tell Dawu that Hannah and I are OK and that everyone is concerned about him. I also need to know if he wants me to tell his family about what's happening and to give me access to his banking information. I need to take care of his studio rent, pay his staff and get his share of the tuition fee for Hannah's schooling. We're supposed to be sharing the cost of enrolling her in Daystar Academy, the international school. I need his portion of the fee. Otherwise, I'm not sure I can afford the large lump sum on my own. School starts in about two months.

"Dawu doesn't have any money," says Zhang in the middle of my conversation with Gong Jin.

"He should," I say. "We split the proceeds from the sale of our condo and it was a pretty sound investment."

How could Dawu have spent all of that money by now? At any rate, it's another example of Zhang and Hong disagreeing and contradicting everything I say about Dawu. It's causing me added stress and interrupting the process with the lawyer, whom I'm paying.

In the elevator after the meeting, Zhang and Hong tell me they're not happy with Gong Jin.

"He's charging way too much."

"You're getting ripped off."

"He's too timid."

"He's not doing what we want."

On top of it all, they think Flame is a spy.

"We don't know him so how can we trust him?" they ask me.

"You shouldn't be using an interpreter; he might be lying to you."

Is this Zhang and Hong's way of supporting me? It's tedious and tiring. However, no matter the aggravation, I feel like they have to be here. They're Dawu's good friends, not to mention that Zhang is his trusted studio assistant. Dawu will be pissed at me if I blow off their attempts to help him.

It's been another long and involved day. I pick up Hannah from a friend's house and then we drive to the grocery store to get the ingredients for supper. At home, I pour myself a large glass of red wine. It's been that kind of weekend.

Hannah is attending a science and math camp with Jenny for the week. I wonder if my daughter can build us a time machine to take us back a couple of years. She's smart but probably doesn't have access to the parts she'll need. Oh well. I can only dream.

The girls love their summer camp and I love that I don't have to take them there. It's one less task for me. They're picked up by a driver who brings them to a school in the Shunyi District. My own Beijing Color Studio camps are happening today as Jane is healthy again. This week's theme is cartoons and she has many creative ideas that the children enjoy. I'm glad I can count on her.

I'm not counting on Zhang and Hong for anything but trouble this afternoon. They're going to meet me and the lawyer at the detention centre. I'm bringing along a new translator as Flame is unavailable. He referred me to Ming Yuan and I'm picking her up at Chaoyang Park.

I get into my car and collect Ming Yuan. She's a young professional and has sharp English skills. She's also curious and keen to help me. We chat as I drive to the detention centre. When we arrive, I park my vehicle and get out. Zhang, Hong, Tang Funai and several unfamiliar people are already there and hanging around the doors of the institution. We all walk into the centre together.

I don't know some of the faces surrounding me. They're "Wu Yuren fans" and although they've never met Dawu personally, they respect what he has done for human rights in China. The fans are also referred to as Petitioners. These are people who visit illegally detained prisoners and organize other measures of support as well as petitioning government offices on their behalf. It's possible that some of the groupies here today have been incarcerated themselves. Illegal detention isn't new in China and Dawu isn't the first, nor will he be the last, to be held without probable cause.

The funny thing is that the strangers treat me like a celebrity. They're polite and eager to be part of my group. The irony is that they're probably known to the cops and could have been followed here. The Petitioners swell my small crew into a large entourage of about 25 people. We make an impressive entrance into the detention centre, striding in with purpose and confidence.

Our puffed chests are soon deflated when Gong Jin, our gallant legal advocate, says the authorities won't let him in to talk to Dawu. He's allowed only one appointment with a lawyer and he's already had it.

"Are you joking?" I say.

It's a rhetorical question, of course.

Gong Jin tells me that the police say Dawu's allotted lawyer time is up.

Even though Chao Hongmei wasn't qualified to meet with Dawu, the visit counts. It's unbelievable and my mouth is probably hanging wide open, catching flies.

Gong Jin says the police shouldn't be obstructing him from seeing Dawu. What the guards are doing is illegal. Gong Jin excuses himself to phone a higher authority in the Chaoyang District, where the detention centre is located, to have the decision overturned. When the call is over, he has an answer.

"We have to wait."

The lawyer was told to stand by for a few days. Then maybe he'd be let in to see Dawu. Otherwise, Gong Jin has to wait until the end of Dawu's 37.5-day lock-up period to talk to him. That'll be on Thursday, July 8 — almost two weeks from now.

I ask Gong Jin the odds of the authorities just dropping the case.

"That's not going to happen now," says the lawyer. "The first 30 days are the detention period and the next seven days are when the authorities apply for the arrest and get approval to charge Dawu and take him to court. He has been held for 28 days and I don't think the police are going to drop the case. They would have already done it by today.

"It doesn't look good for your husband. I think he'll be charged soon and his case will move to trial."

"What can he be charged with when he's done nothing?" I ask.

"Fang ai gong wu – obstructing public service and attacking a police officer," says Gong Jin.

He thinks that there's something fishy going on and believes an official or officials are lying about the claim.

"It's going to be a fight to prove Dawu didn't do anything he's accused of doing," says the lawyer.

A fluorescent light overhead is blinking on and off, on and off. The pulsing is making me unsteady, lightheaded. I feel like I'm going to faint.

I close my eyes for a couple of seconds to give my brain a break from the flashing stimuli.

There's no way I'm going to drop to the floor in here. I'm not showing any ounce of weakness. I have to bide some more time. I've been doing that for 28 days. This is a waiting game and one I'm prepared to play.

一、2380 1231元整 村衣一件
二、NBKIA 手机一部
三、钥匙 一扎 ~~中有798钥匙~~
四、牛仔裤 ~~四~~ 球鞋(白) 发带头一个
以上是群好物品. 确认无误.
签名 2010.6.1

拿钥匙 去798 彭雷瑞工作室中

上拿电瓶车

彭凯琳 13811503992

The hand-written note that Dawu left the officers at the Jiuxianqiao Police Station
just before he was transferred to the Chaoyang District Detention Center.
Jun.1, 2010, 4:45 pm, Beijing.

The handwritten note Karen gave to a staff member at the Jiuxianqiao Police Station
asking them to contact her if they had any more information about Dawu.
Jun.1, 2010, 5:30 pm, Beijing.

吴: 彭凯琳
1381 150 3992

Hannah at the Chaoyang
District Detention Center,
where she waved to the guard.
Summer 2010, Beijing.

Family members and next of kin
inquiring at the information desk
at the Chaoyang District Detention
Center. Fall 2010, Beijing.

Late afternoon exterior shot of the
Chaoyang District Detention Center. Dawu
was inside one of the buildings.
Summer 2010, Beijing.

Application Request

Beijing City Public Security Chaoyang District Branch:

Now Wu Yuren is in the Chaoyang District Criminal Detention Center, we are the family of Wu Yuren. According to Chinese Law and the Treatment of Inmates, Article 28: "For those who have been detained, and in agreement with the authorizing body, they can meet and have visits with family members". We are requesting a family visit. Please let us see my husband, my daughter's father.

Applicants

.Karen Patterson

Wu Hannah

August 19, 2010

Karen helping to bury the snake, not far from the 008 International Art Community. Jan. 2011, Beijing.

One of many Application Requests to see Dawu that were translated into English from Chinese and signed by both Karen and Hannah. We were always declined. Aug. 2010, Beijing.
<

Letters and cards sent to Dawu for Christmas while he was in the Chaoyang District Detention Center. Dec. 2010 through Jan. 2011, Beijing.

Receipt from the Red Cross showing that an x-ray was performed on Dawu at the Chaoyang District Detention Center. Jun. 1, 2010, Beijing.

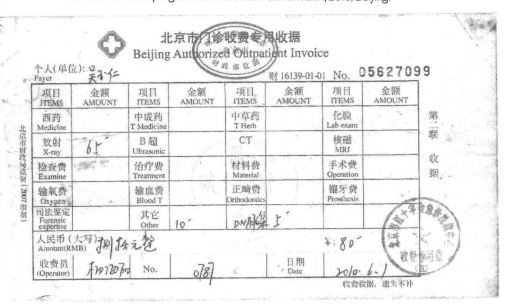

There's another bribery plot in the works. Zhang and Hong have just stopped in at the Beijing Color Studio this morning to tell me that they got a call from a guy who can get Dawu out — for the right price. This man supposedly shared a cell with Dawu and was recently released. Apparently, Dawu supplied the man with Zhang's phone number.

I'm sure it's a scam. I'm not convinced that the man Zhang and Hong are talking to can do what he's saying he can do. How can someone who only just got out himself, claim to be able to get someone else out? It sounds odd, or am I missing something in the translation?

"If you two want to pursue this," I say to Zhang and Hong, "go ahead. Keep me posted. I am not getting involved."

This is one way to keep Dawu's friends busy and one less project (so to speak) that I have to shoulder. Besides, Zhang and Hong have been annoying me lately. Even the lawyer has told me to be wary of them. (How ironic.) Gong Jin says Zhang and Hong are trying to control the situation in a very "Chinese" way. This means that they're trying to establish a hierarchy where they're at the top as the important people. They're creating drama when there shouldn't be any, as well as not listening to me, Dawu's wife.

The lawyer knows Dawu's friends don't trust him and that's part of the culture. I found that China relies heavily on interpersonal relationships. Fictive kinship is strong and because of this, Zhang and Hong have a hard time accepting Gong Jin because he isn't part of their circle. As well, they're upset with me because I went outside of said circle and chose a lawyer who works for me, Karen Patterson, and not Dawu's friends. This is why Zhang and Hong are constantly fighting with me and telling me that everyone I've hired is either no good or a spy. They are pissing me off!

Later in the morning, they call and tell me that the cost of the bribe is ¥150,000 RMB (CAD 25,000). For that princely sum, Dawu will be freed and the case against him dropped. Too good to be true? It's a lot of money and I don't have a fraction readily available. The deadline for the offer is tonight.

The pressure is on. It's tempting to call family and friends and try to raise the money in mere hours, but what if it's a ruse?

Who is this guy who thinks he can snap his fingers and get Dawu out of prison? Gosh, if only the world worked like that other than in the movies. I call Gong Jin and ask for his opinion. He says that if the cellmate can get Dawu out with the bribe, then it might be a workable solution.

Really? A lawyer is suggesting I go with graft? We are in China, though, and the backdoor often works better than the front. Nevertheless, I can't shake the feeling that Dawu's possible saviour is a swindler. Zhang offers to call Dawu's connections and ask them to pitch in financially.

Zhang and Hong raise about ¥60,000 RMB but are short ¥90,000 RMB. They've actually done a good job of bringing in some cold hard cash quickly. I still don't trust the man they want to pay off. The contact is supposedly named Qian Yuelun, an Air China employee who had been jailed for a misdemeanour. I've asked to meet him and he says no.

Meanwhile, I've been organizing interpreters to help with my phone conversations with Gong Jin. It's imperative that I don't miss a word or nuance. Other language issues are cropping up too, like the wording of official documents. I am not fluent in criminal or legal Chinese and I'm finding that my grasp of Mandarin falters whenever I'm stressed. My mind goes blank and I can't process anything. Everything might as well be in Greek. I want to be able to follow and understand EXACTLY what's being said and written. If Dawu goes to court, I will definitely need someone in the room with me to explain all the legal jargon while simultaneously interpreting what's going on.

Ming Yuan is available to interpret today and calls Gong Jin for me. The lawyer and I had talked earlier about the bribe and he had some other things to tell me but I couldn't wrap my brain around his words. Now I'll be able to know what he's saying.

Ming Yuan tells me that Gong Jin is going to apply to overturn the decision that refused him entry to see Dawu. There is a catch: we have to submit a copy of our signed lawyer-client agreement before the authorities will entertain responding to our request. No problem. Easily done.

As well, the lawyer says to expect some retaliation from the cops over hiring him. He isn't sure what's coming down the pipe but something will. I'm hoping Hannah will be left out of it all.

Gong Jin and I trade phone calls all day. Sometimes we speak through the interpreter, sometimes we talk directly to each other. In a later conversation, he tells me that the authorities governing who is allowed to visit whom in the detention centre, called to apologize.

Gong Jin has been granted access to Dawu.

"The higher-ups actually apologized?" I ask. That's incredible. I feel like the lawyer and I are making headway at last.

"I should be able to meet with your husband in 48 hours," says Gong Jin.

Amazing, amazing news! I do a little jig. I have to share what I've learned with someone so I visit the Gao Brothers at their studio. We sit on their rooftop patio, high above the streetscape of 798. We're above all the ruckus from people and vehicles fighting for space in this cramped art community. The brothers are glad to hear the lawyer is getting somewhere but add that Gong Jin is only one form of help. They say that I shouldn't sit back and assume he's going to solve all the problems. I need to do more.

The brothers have experienced the fickleness of the Chinese government and suggest I pay Ai Weiwei another visit. They also tell me to talk to Huang Rui, who has poked the communist bear with his art and advocacy work on many occasions. Huang Rui is a former Stars Art Group member as well as one of the founders of the 798 artist collective. He has been harassed by the authorities for many years. Both Huang Rui and Ai Weiwei could tell me what they think is coming next for Dawu since they've been through it already. The Gao brothers warn me to meet with the artists now, before Dawu's 37.5 days up, in case something can be done before he disappears further into the system.

It's solid advice. I have been, and still am, open to all forms of assistance. I promise the Gaos that I'll follow-up with Ai Weiwei and reach out to Huang Rui, who I'd last seen at Dawu's *RESOLUTION* art exhibition in January at the 008 International Art Community headquarters.

At the end of the evening, Zhang and Hong are still looking for ¥90,000 RMB for the ¥150,000 RMB bribe. The contact has given them an extension on the deadline and Dawu's friends are scrambling to find people who'll contribute. I won't be adding to the pot. I'm not going to be a victim of a money scam gone south.

While Zhang and Hong are working on gathering donations from various artists and others to make Dawu's bribe money, I, too, need to make money. The bills keep coming and they need to be paid even though I'm struggling to keep my head above water. I'm working at the Beijing Color Studio this end-of-June morning, putting out advertisements for painting classes and ordering canvases for those workshops. My major commitment to Dawu is distracting me from my company and it's another reason for getting him out, so I can focus on my own job.

Much of my day is spent with half of my brain thinking about my business and the other half wondering when the lawyer is going to see Dawu. My phone is my constant companion so when it rings, I snatch it up right away.

Gong Jin is on the end of the line. He says he hasn't been given access to Dawu. There will be no meeting today.

"Maybe tomorrow," the lawyer says.

Maybe. Or maybe the authorities are playing with me and tomorrow Gong Jin will be blocked again. More waiting for us.

Someone who is tired of waiting and who has decided to make another move on his own is Tang, the Troublemaker. I had thought that he understood that any sort of meddling in anything connected to Dawu was off-limits. I had asked Tang to put aside his petition for a formal review of the way the officers treated him and Dawu at the Jiuxianqiao detachment. Tang had agreed. He's moved past that and is now protesting outside of the detention centre where Dawu is being kept. Tang explains it all in a text to me. He says he was a one-person protest this morning. He went to the centre all on his own, carrying a white banner with "Let Wu Yuren Go Home!" written in big black characters.

I'm shocked by his actions. I thank him for his time and efforts but caution him that it could be dangerous for both him and Dawu.

"What were you thinking?" I ask.

Tang sort of apologizes and admits that he only wants to help. It was his idea to go to the police station in the first place and he feels guilty about getting Dawu in trouble. He also feels guilty that he was released and Dawu remains locked up.

I understand Tang feels the need to do something for Dawu but he needs to lay low, not be a loose cannon. Tang can't be firing at the government while Dawu is in jail. Tang's actions reflect on Dawu, making it look like Dawu is riling up people even from detention. I ask Tang to stop his demonstration and he promises, again, to be low key until Dawu is released.

Sometimes I wonder about these folks who take risks when they shouldn't and don't take risks when they should, or something like that. Anyway, Tang shouldn't be a problem anymore.

My phone rings and I look at the number. I don't recognize it but I answer in case the caller is connected to Dawu. The man on the other end of the line introduces himself as Wen Tao, a long-time friend of Dawu's art group. Wen Tao claims I met him in passing at the 008 New Year's party. However, from my end, our introduction was too brief to remember, as there was a lot going on that day.

Wen Tao says he wants to help Dawu. He adds that Dawu's older sister, Wu Suling, is coming from Jiangsu to see him. Uh, really? I'm startled. Dawu's family doesn't know anything about his situation. Hannah's *gugu* (aunty) and yeye, Wu Xiangshou, believe Dawu's out of the country on an art exhibition trip. I'd like to tell Dawu's sister and father that he's being detained but Zhang and Hong say it's better they are kept in the dark. Nevertheless, if they have heard the news, there's no way Suling can just waltz into the detention centre and see her brother.

I don't confirm or deny anything to Wen Tao. Besides, he could be a fraudster or a weirdo or both.

"Thanks for your call," I say.

"I really do know your husband," presses Wen Tao. "I really can help him."

I decline his offer and hang up.

Hannah and I are off to have dinner with my friend Sophie Baker. The last time Sophie and I had supper out together was the evening Dawu disappeared. How I wish I could turn back the clock.

It's Canada Day, July 1 2010, and this Canadian is celebrating by trying to figure out how the Chinese justice system works. I'm expecting Gong Jin to call me at any moment to say he has a meeting with Dawu. It has been 31 days since I've had any contact with my husband.

My best friend over the past few weeks is my phone. It's my lifeline and I don't go anywhere without it. I have it with me at the Canadian International School's Canada Day party.

Every year, the school on Liangmaqiao Road puts on a Canada Day party that's open to the public. I've taken Hannah to it in the past and that's where we are this morning. She has fun playing with other children and hopping about in the jumpy castle. It's great watching my daughter act like a kid. She misses her baba so much and I can't tell her when she'll see him again.

After the party, I call Wu Suling, Dawu's sister, to fish for what she knows about Dawu. I'm relieved that she doesn't know he's being detained but she is suspicious that she can't get a hold of him, not even through email. She tells me she thinks that I'm holding something back and this is the reason she's talking about visiting Beijing. Fortunately, I convince her that this is not the case and Dawu is overwhelmed with work at his overseas exhibit.

"I'm sure you'll find out what's going on with him soon," I say.

It's not a lie. It's just enough to keep Suling in Jiangsu. I, too, hope to find out what's going on soon.

After the call, I pick up some items for the Beijing Color Studio. I deal with some outstanding business with the Counting Sheep Boutique. In between, I take out my phone to make sure I didn't miss a message from the lawyer. I check my cell as frequently as a teenager waiting for a crush to text.

The day has stretched into late afternoon and I haven't heard from Gong Jin. I'm not sure if this is unusual since we've only started working together. I'm sure if he has news, he will contact me. A thought comes into my head, "What if he was told by the authorities to shut up and butt out?"

It would be understandable, on the one hand. Gong Jin is an upstanding citizen and a good lawyer. Working on Dawu's file may change that rank in the eyes of the Chinese authorities. Gong Jin has already challenged law officials and won – getting an opportunity to see his client.

If the lawyer is allowed to continue with Dawu's case, Gong Jin could set a precedent and be a threat to the government and its convoluted and corrupt justice system.

The communist party can't have someone calling it out for abuse of power and ignoring human rights and its own laws in the process. It could yank Gong Jin's licence and threaten him enough to make him withdraw from Dawu's case. I hope that's not what's happening.

The bribe scheme is still on the books. Zhang and Hong have yet to get the full amount — but that's their problem. While I'm thinking of getting in touch with Ai Weiwei, as the Gao Brothers suggested, he calls.

We're meeting tomorrow at 9 a.m. sharp at his studio.

48

I'm not a morning person. I like to wade into the day rather than jump feet first into it. However, bright and early, I'm off to FAKE Design, Ai Weiwei's studio. I'm heading there solo. I didn't invite Zhang and Hong to come along. I'm not bringing an interpreter either since Ai Weiwei said he'd speak to me in English.

At the studio compound, I press the buzzer to be let in. I stand there for a couple of minutes. It doesn't sound that long but when you're meeting with someone like Ai Weiwei, an important person, it's long. Did he forget about our appointment?

Ah, there he is.

He leads me to a room that's furnished with a large circular table and several chairs. A video camera is recording our meeting. We take our seats and Ai Weiwei's wife, Lu Qing, brings me tea. Before I take a sip, Ai begins heavily criticizing me for wasting time and not contacting him from the beginning of Dawu's incarceration.

Taken by surprise by Ai Weiwei's attack, I fire back that I had met with him, along with Zhang and Hong, a few weeks ago. I say that Ai had spoken only in Chinese and the conversation had been directed at Dawu's friends. I was left out of discussions.

"We saw you on June 4," I say. "On the anniversary of the 1989 Tiananmen Square Massacre." (I don't have to remind him about that. I just want to make a point.)

I also ask him why he didn't speak English to me that day. It was evident that my Chinese was not as good as his English. He huffs, annoyed that I'm challenging him. Nevertheless, it's tit for tat. You yell at me, I'm going to respond.

We clear the air and then settle down to business. Ai says I can't let Dawu become old news. It's harder to get people to react when someone is already forgotten. The artist adds that I have to keep him in the loop at all times.

The reason why I haven't been contacting Ai Weiwei is that I didn't realize he cared. I thought after that first meeting, Ai had done his part and the rest was up to me. I guess I assumed wrong.

Ai adds that I've failed to get my act together and it's too late to take advantage of the time leading up to the end of the 37.5-day period. He thinks I should have been on the authorities right away and not relented until Dawu was out. As well, Ai Weiwei knows I have done little in terms of getting the international press involved in Dawu's story.

Ai has been keeping up to date on what I've been doing and what I haven't been doing. He hasn't been talking to me but he has his sources. In his mind, I've done nothing for Dawu. That stings. I've been doing all I can.

When we talk about the root of the detention, Ai and I have different ideas of why Dawu is where he is. I say it's because he marched on Chang'an Avenue. Ai thinks it's because Dawu was the leader of the 008 and Zhengyang compensation movement. Both those reasons are related but I feel strongly that the demonstration is the real cause of Dawu's detention.

No matter what the motive was to put Dawu in prison, Ai tells me I am responsible for getting Dawu released.

"You are the only one who can help him," says Ai, looking directly into my eyes. "You need to take it on as a full-time job."

None of Dawu's friends, or even Ai himself, can help in the way that Dawu truly needs help. As I'm married to him, we have a legal relationship and it's stronger than just being a good friend. I am the key to unlocking Dawu's cell door, not Zhang and Hong. (I don't mention to Ai Weiwei that Dawu and I were in the midst of getting divorced.)

Ai is annoyed with Zhang and Hong when I tell him that they've been arguing with me. He calls them Tweedle Dee and Tweedle Dum and I laugh at his Alice in Wonderland reference. I often do feel like I've fallen through a rabbit hole and have landed in an unfamiliar and strange world. Ai tells me to cut Dawu's friends from the "team," so to speak. Tang Funai doesn't make it either. Ai says I'm to stay away from the Troublemaker. Ai Weiwei won't tolerate Tang being involved with any part of Dawu's liberation. I ask if I should keep Gong Jin and explain to Lao Ai that Gong Jin has been stalled in his quest to see Dawu.

Ai has never heard of the lawyer but I'm not surprised as they work in different circles.

"Find another lawyer," is Ai's advice. It's the only advice I'm not sure I can act on. Gong Jin and I have a signed contract and money has already changed hands.

"What else should I be doing?" I ask.

"Social media."

I need to jump on Twitter and other platforms to attract the attention of foreign journalists. I should be contacting international media as well and Ai Weiwei says he'll pass on his contacts to me. By talking to reporters, we'll shine a light on Dawu's detention and the Chinese government will do anything to turn it off.

Right then and there, he also schedules a meeting for me with an administrative assistant, Wen Tao.

Oh!

He's the guy who phoned me yesterday. Ai says Wen Tao will be a useful person to have by my side. He's a good translator, interpreter and a journalist who has worked with the Global Times in China. The Times is a pro-government newspaper but any media of any type in China is pro-government so this isn't a mark against Wen Tao.

Wen Tao sounds like someone who could legitimately help me and I had turned him away. I wonder if it was Wen Tao who tipped off Ai Weiwei about me and not the Gao Brothers?

Ai promises to support me in any way possible, including sending a team of videographers to accompany me wherever I go. All I need to do is text or call one of his two assistants, Ren Qiu and Song Ke, and tell them where I'm going. Ai also needs to know where I'm going and with whom at all times. Zero exceptions. This is not only for my own safety but according to Ai, EVERYTHING needs to be recorded in China, especially in these kinds of circumstances. He explains that the government is not above lying and manipulating words and situations. Without a recording of an event, there's no proof of what's said and done.

An hour has gone by and I have a strategy for bringing Dawu home, thanks to Lao Ai (I now feel like I can call the artist Lao Ai, an affectionate nickname). In the past 60 minutes, he has gone from insults to instructions. He has softened, satisfied that he's not wasting his time with me.

We exchange phone numbers and I leave. I'm grateful for the time Lao Ai has spent with me. He's such a busy man and in high demand. There's already a line of people waiting to meet with him. Journalists, artists, experts, curators and collectors from all over the world are vying for his attention.

I'm looking forward to getting on the right path. It's daunting, though. I'm reaching out to the world and asking people if they'll help me save my husband. Nevertheless, up until an hour ago, I've been vacillating between what to do and what not to do. I have a guide now. Ai Weiwei has given me a sword and map of what to do, when, where and with whom. I'm on my way to slay the detention dragons.

I have a long list of "to do" items from Ai Weiwei and I start ticking them off when I arrive home later that same morning. I go on Twitter and send out a tweet:

#WuYuren detained illegally! Activist Chinese Artist beaten and locked up.

I retweet Lao Ai's 140-character missive about Dawu and then search and follow reporters, media outlets, human rights groups and anyone or anything that I think will promote Dawu's case.

Public awareness is key. Ai had told me the more news we get out, the better the chances of getting Dawu out.

I'll have to track down Zhang and Hong at some point and tell them to stop what they're doing in terms of the bribe. They have yet to collect all the money anyway and Ai doesn't believe it's a viable option. I'm not dreading cutting Dawu's friends from his team. Once they're gone, we won't be working at cross-purposes anymore.

I arrange a meeting for this afternoon with Peter Foster, the journalist from *The Daily Telegraph*. We've been in touch for a while and it's about time to get the foreign media involved in Dawu's story. Peter and I have come up with some code words so we can talk without having the secret police in on our discussions. We use the term "catalogue" instead of meeting.

I've been talking to Peter about Dawu's detention for some time. He's introduced me to other journalists and today the reporter's bringing along photographer Katharina Hesse. The three of us meet at 1:30 p.m. at an unusual place for an afternoon of discussing illegal imprisonment and Chinese political tactics. We're at The Den, an expat hangout across the street from the fancy Sanlitun Shopping complex on Gongti North Road. I've been to The Den, an after-hours dance bar, many times in my single years. When you show up drunk and head upstairs for dancing, you don't really notice the state of the venue or the odour. The place is worn down and smells like stale beer and old sweat. However, there's a crowd of mostly foreigners in here now and Peter, Katharina and I don't look out of place. Perhaps that's why the reporter picked this bar.

Peter is from England and is *The Daily Telegraph's* and *The Sunday Telegraph's* correspondent in Beijing. He has been living in China for about a year and a half. Following his lead, I turn off my cellphone and remove the batteries. I think it's a weird thing to do but Peter says it's dangerous to talk about Dawu in range of an active cellphone. He tells me the Chinese authorities will eavesdrop on our conversation. It's a common strategy to get intel. I tell him about my last meeting with Chao Hongling and others when we did the same thing. He isn't surprised at all.

The reporter and I waste no time getting into everything surrounding Dawu: the present, the past and the possible future. Peter says Dawu's case is interesting and complicated. Since Peter is a British reporter working for a British newspaper, it's going to be difficult to convince his editor that a story about a Canadian woman married to a Chinese man is warranted precious inches in the paper. Peter adds that he'll write a blog post instead and this should be enough to attract the attention of other journalists — hopefully Canadians reporters among them.

The photographer, Katharina, hasn't said much since the three of us sat down. Nevertheless, she sums up Dawu's predicament in a few words.

"This does not look good for your husband."

Katharina is from Germany and has lived in China for 17 years. She knows what she's talking about. She's well-connected to the art scene in Beijing and well known for her photos of China and its people and culture. She takes my picture after our meeting is over. The backdrop is urban Beijing: the south side of Gongti North Road, The Den and the rows of 1960s apartment-style housing—stark brick buildings no taller than six storeys. It would be a cool shot under other circumstances.

My next meeting is with Wen Tao, the man I shooed away yesterday. At 6 p.m., I head to the Timezone 8 Café at 798. I do recognize him now that I see him in person. He's not a large man in height or girth. His eyes are bright and he has a face that I trust before I've even spoken to him. We certainly have never had any in-depth conversation before. That's all about to change.

We approach each other shyly. We're two people from different cultures who have been conscripted by Lao Ai into meeting each other under strange and trying circumstances. Wen Tao is soft-spoken and speaks excellent English. He talks highly about Dawu and says he's a good person and a good friend. Wan Tao admits he's putting his career in danger as he has already faced backlash from the government over the Chang'an Avenue march.

Wen Tao was recently fired from the *Global Times* for posting about the protest on the newspaper's site as well as on his own social media. I ask him if he's upset that he's been turned out of his danwei (work unit) but he says he's OK. He tells me that the media is heavily censored by the communist party and this is against his journalistic ethics.

"There must be freedom of the press," he says.

Dawu and his story are worth risking the wrath of China's regime.

Our conversation is candid. Wen Tao studied in Canada and understands Western culture. He's not trying to make excuses for China and the way the country operates.

He has some ideas on how to bend the government into letting Dawu go. One suggestion is that I write a letter to authorities that Wen Tao will translate into Chinese. Then, I should post it online.

"We have to find the balance," says Wen Tao, "between saving Dawu and offending the police and government. As well, we can't break any laws."

Yikes! I do not intend to do that, especially since I'm an expat in a foreign country where my husband is sitting in jail. Wen Tao clarifies what he means. He tells me that some of the rules in China are fluid and depend on who you are. We're up against several levels of authority and government (from the development company, to the local police, etc.) and not all of them are going to abide by the rulebook. Some people will even be above the law.

"It's going to be a challenge," says Wen Tao, "but I think that by working together, we can get Dawu out of jail."

I'm feeling optimistic, too. I ask Wen Tao about payment, as he will be my assistant. He brushes it off. His reward will be Dawu's release. We agree to meet again in a few days. Wen Tao has been the best thing to happen to me in a long time.

To move on with Ai Weiwei and Wen Tao's ideas, I have to let Zhang and Hong go. They're only hindering me and getting mixed up in silly things like the recent bribery scheme. Other causes for concern need to be addressed ASAP. Since it looks like Dawu will be staying at the detention centre much longer than I had anticipated, I have to deal with his finances.

Zhang is cordial when I arrive at Dawu's studio. We sit down and the assistant pours us tea. I ask him if he can switch gears and instead of working to get Dawu released, work on keeping his business alive. I bring up the studio rent, ¥40,000 RMB (CAD 6,7000) a year, as well as other operating costs, such as electricity. I know Dawu has the money to cover these things. He received half the proceeds from the sale of our condo and it was more than ample. Hopefully, Dawu's finances are in good order and I won't need to pay his bills.

I ask Zhang not to stand in the way when I ask Dawu, via Gong Jin, for his bank information. I'll need access to Dawu's finances to pay the lawyer and other connected expenses. I also ask Zhang for the password to Dawu's email account.

Zhang tells me in a gentle, indirect way that I have no role in Dawu's business and I should back off.

"You're right," I say. "But I think we need to be open to discussing these things. No one knows what the future will hold and I'd like Dawu to have something to come back to."

Zhang nods and pours more tea. I continue to talk and say that there is some work he can be doing while Dawu's out of commission. Zhan Yishu, the White Box Art Center curator, has some of Dawu's works from his March show. I suggest Zhang be the agent and act on behalf of Dawu to get all the pieces returned. I'll have Gong Jin approve this move when he visits Dawu.

As well, I want Dawu's family to know what's been happening with him. His father and sister are still in the dark. They should have been informed at the very beginning. Nevertheless, I had given in to the traditional Chinese way of doing things – never be the bearer of bad news.

Xiangshou and Suling aren't stupid. Ba was here in Beijing when the first detention occurred. He knows what his son has been up to. Still, we have told Dawu's family a lie to pass the time and now they deserve the truth. Zhang agrees and says the news should come from Dawu's close friends. He suggests Mao Xiangji, one of Dawu's best friends from his time at art college in Changzhou in the early 1990s.

Dawu knows many people and there are some I feel I can trust more than others. Mao Xiangji is one of those friends. He's a solid, trustworthy cool guy. He lives in Changzhou with his wife and child and whenever he comes to Beijing for a visit, I enjoy his company.

The other person Zhang believes should talk to Dawu's family is Hong. Both Mao and Hong have known Xiangshou and Suling for a long time. Giving Hong another task outside of helping me is great. Zhang will contact the friends and make the arrangements.

I've been wondering what happened to Dawu's stuff on the day he disappeared. The police should have his clothing, scooter and ID card but I think they're too scared to call me to tell me to pick it up. Zhang says he'll go to the station and see if he can collect Dawu's things.

With those points and issues out of the way, I carefully ask Zhang about the ¥150,000 RMB backdoor plot.

"Oh," says Zhang, bowing his head. "It was a scam."

I knew it! Zhang and Hong didn't know it until the man took off with the money. Dawu's friends paid up and the thief disappeared. It's sad and it sucks but I had a feeling it was all going to go sideways. Zhang and Hong would like to call the police and tell them about the swindler but how do they do that?

"Hi, police? Yeah, we'd like to report a fraudster who took all our money. We were using it to get our friend out of jail by paying a criminal to bribe a guard at the detention centre. Oh, and our friend is in there because he supposedly hit a cop."

Gong Jin isn't going to be able to see Dawu before the 37.5 days are up. I'm not sure why there was a delay but the lawyer now has scheduled Monday, July 5 as the meeting date. Meanwhile, I'm back at Ai Weiwei's studio with Wen Tao by my side. We are having a morning conference call with lawyer Liu Xiaoyan.

Liu Xiaoyan is an expert in human rights and sensitive cases in China. He's also Lao Ai's friend. The lawyer is out of the country right now and not sure he'll be able to assist us since he's tied up with other business. Oh well, it was worth a shot.

Despite Lao Ai calling Zhang and Hong Tweedle Dum and Tweedle Dee, he says I should bring them in on what's happening. They are a part of Dawu's studio and do have ears to the ground. I ask them to join us for lunch.

The meeting moves to a lovely restaurant located in a garden yard, not far from Lao Ai's studio. Zhang and Hong are here and the five of us chat about strategy. We'll stick to Gong Jin's scheduled appointment with Dawu. If the meeting goes bust, Lao Ai knows of other lawyers we can contact.

I feel much more assured that we can get Dawu out of this mess with Ai Weiwei at the helm. He's guiding me through the stormy seas of red tape, official lingo and phoneys. I'm no longer winging it on my own.

Dawu's family have yet to hear about his detention but that doesn't mean they haven't found out about it through official channels in the past couple of days. Hong is going to request Mao Xiangji go to the Changzhou police station, the station based in the province of Jiangsu where Dawu's family lives, and ask whether a letter of notice has arrived for Wu Xiangshou.

Should the police want to inform Xiangshou and Suling about what's happened to Dawu, the authorities would locate his family through his shenfenzheng (citizen identification card). Mao Xiangji needs to find out if the police in Changzhou have a record of Dawu. If they do, chances are they have already contacted the family. If they don't, then Mao is happy to let Xiangshou think Dawu is still away. It's at this point we have a difference of opinion.

I'd like Mao to tell Dawu's family the truth. Nevertheless, he must make them understand that they cannot come to Beijing. They'll only get in the way and muddle the process as they're not well connected and do not have resources or relationships in the city. I need folks who have *guanxi* (personal relationships, symbiotic relations) to make valuable connections. Not waste time. By the end of the discussion, I leave it up to Zhang, Hong and Mao to work out what to do with Dawu's family. I'm learning that I can't be in control of everything.

There is one thing I have the upper hand in: I'm a foreigner. Ai says this gives me certain advantages in China. I have better access to foreign media, embassies and it's harder for the authorities to bully me since I have the Canadian Embassy in my corner. Nevertheless, I have to be on my guard. The authorities could convince my landlord to evict me or I could be deported in an instant. They could also harass administrators at Hannah's school and have her expelled. I am trying not to think too much about the "what-ifs."

Ai suggests I start a letter-writing campaign and write to my government and governmental agencies such as the Canadian Embassy, as well as Chinese government departments like the foreign affairs office. It's a simple idea and I wish I had thought about doing it before now.

Lao Ai suggests I follow up with Tang and ask him for a detailed description of what happened in the Jiuxianqiao police station. That way, I have a good picture of what went on. My own message should contain some emotion but not be overly dramatic or vindictive. (It's a fine line since I know who to blame.) I should also hit on three points:

1. Dawu was detained and beaten.

2. No notice went out about his arrest and his detention to family or next of kin. All attempts to contact, see him and receive news about him were blocked by all official channels.

3. Not only have I been deeply upset by the situation but it is negatively affecting the life of our daughter, Hannah, who can't see her father.

Wen Tao will translate my letter and Tang's report and I'll send out the documents. The letters should be hard copies. Emails are quickly deleted. I'm to post the letters through a courier and ask each office to sign for receipt of the envelope. Thus, compiling a record of the time and date.

Before the end of our meeting, Ai mentions that there have been recent changes in the police department and there's someone new in charge. Fu Zhenghua is the director of the Beijing Municipal Public Security Bureau (police chief) and is looking to "refresh" the department's reputation. That could work in my favour. He might be more likely to do something to shine a positive light on Beijing's police detachments. Releasing Dawu would be a small public relations win for him and a big personal relations win for me.

Ai Weiwei has undoubtedly been a much-needed guiding light. I'm thankful that he took the time to meet with me this morning. Other people I connected with are also doing their part. Peter Foster posted his blog about Dawu on *The Daily Telegraph* site, making the British daily the first foreign media to write about Dawu. Finally!

Later on in the afternoon, I visited the Gao Brothers' studio in 798. Flame is along with me since Wen Tao is busy. Gao Zhen is in his gallery and I catch him up on the new path Ai Weiwei has put me on. Zhen is happy that I have a good leader but says I shouldn't put all my eggs in one basket. He suggests that I talk to other people, too, who have experienced going up against the government of the People's Republic of China. Zhen being one of them.

I chat with Zhen, who is in his early fifties, about his run-ins. He tells me that he and his brother, Qiang, paid the price for their mother's efforts to seek justice for her husband during the Cultural Revolution.

Zhen and Qiang carried on the legacy of taking China to task for the truth. In 1979, the brothers were also part of the Stars Art Group, a collection of non-professional Chinese artists who called for cultural openness. In 1989, The Stars was part of the mass demonstrations at Tiananmen Square. The event cost the brothers their freedom. Not only did the government take away their passports to prevent them from leaving China, but their performance art shows and exhibitions were constantly shut down and there were many unlawful raids on their studio.

China has a history of not just punishing one generation of a family but generations after. This is why Zhen is not only concerned about Dawu but his daughter, as well as how the case will affect future artists. Zhen knows first-hand it's not easy standing up to the authorities and says a backdoor might still swing open at any point.

"This is China," he says.

In the meantime, Zhen offers to see if any embassies will help Dawu. I'm skeptical about this route since I've already talked to the Canadian Embassy. If my own country can't help, what use is another country? Besides, Dawu isn't well-known outside of China like the Gao Brothers, Chao Hongling or

Gu Duanfan. I thank Zhen for his time, shake his hand and then give him a hug.

Huang Rui has also had his share of problems with China. Flame and I have an appointment with him at his café near the Gao Brothers' gallery. I have always liked the café as it has a great atmosphere and the most delicious fire-baked pizza. (It's rare to find kiln-baked pizza in China.) It's a beautiful place to sit, too. The upstairs overlooks the Bauhaus rooftops of 798.

Huang Rui isn't in the loop about what's been happening to Dawu. Huang Rui, in his late fifties, is taking notes and asking questions while I talk. The artist was also part of The Stars and publicly protested against government censorship. The authorities told him to leave China for five years and so Huang Rui went to France. After his period of exile, he returned to China, only to be told to leave again, indefinitely. He went to Japan and became a Japanese citizen. In the late 1990s, he returned to China to live as a visitor since China doesn't allow dual citizenship.

In 2002, Huang Rui was instrumental in setting up the 798 Art District and then defending it when developers wanted to raze the area. He has been in Dawu's shoes and the older artist's advice is worth its weight in gold. He's taking his time thinking about what to say to me. I appreciate this since the last thing I want is someone shooting random suggestions from the hip. At last, Huang Rui might be the hinge to a bonafide backdoor.

The artist says he knows a few high-ranking officials in Beijing after his years of anti-government politicking. He thinks that he can ask a certain friend, someone with whom he has good guanxi, to see if Dawu's file has reached all the way up to the city level. (The more serious the case, the higher up the chain of command it goes.) If the friend hasn't heard of Dawu, then his case is still at the local level at the Chaoyang District. (A minor incident isn't worth bothering the more important people.)

Huang Rui tells me to call him in a few days. He needs time to reach out to his contact. I thank him, shake hands and leave along with Flame. Flame has been a blessing this afternoon. Without him, there's no way I could communicate as quickly or as efficiently with my supporters.

Thanks to Flame and his excellent interpretive skills, I now have the Big Three (what I'm calling Lao Ai, the Gao Brothers and Huang Rui) working for Dawu. The older artists have been around for a long time and have had personal experiences similar to Dawu's. They are not only respected by peers (and some officials) but they have had their own run-ins with the authorities. That is key.

I collect Hannah from Qi Mei's on my way home. I'm drained but I have to keep going for my daughter. Hannah and Dawu are my two peas in a pod. Half of that pod is empty. As well, I am worried about the safety of my daughter. Who knows what could happen to her if the authorities feel cornered or lose face. They could take it out on Hannah in some way. Perhaps not tomorrow or next week but she could be severely penalized somehow in the future.

With my daughter tucked tightly into bed, I write to Diane. I ask my sister about the possibility of sending Hannah to Canada. It's better to be safe than sorry. Based on the recent emails I have received from my mom, she is crazy worried about us. It must be very upsetting for her to be so far away and not able to do anything.

Peter Foster and I are talking over coffee this morning. Although he has written a blog about Dawu, the British reporter is hoping Canadian journalists will pick up the story. He's going to contact Bill Schiller, the *Toronto Star* foreign affairs reporter, about Dawu's dilemma.

Peter will be at the detention centre with me tomorrow morning along with Zhang, Hong and Wen Tao. Gong Jin is finally seeing Dawu at 8:30 a.m. I am happy the journalist is coming along since it'll give him more to add to his story. Tonight, I'm trying not to get my hopes up, as the last meeting with Chao Hongmei went nowhere.

Around 9 p.m., Zhang and Hong drop in to see me at the Cappuccino Complex. I tell them that Huang Rui might know the man who stole their bribery money. I had mentioned the swindle to Huang Rui yesterday when we were discussing backdoors and he gave me a name. There's nothing Zhang or Hong can do with the information but they do give me some shocking news in return.

Zhang admits that $3,000 (U.S.) of the bribe money was Dawu's. I'm a little annoyed to find this out. I thought Zhang would have come to me about using Dawu's savings like this. It's a pretty big deal. Who is going to tell him about it?

I ask Zhang not to keep any more secrets from me. He promises to return the funds to Dawu and will even take the loss personally if need be. I know Zhang feels awkward and has lost face but someone needs to be accountable for Dawu's accounts. We can't use his money willy-nilly or he's not going to have anything left when he is released.

There's another potential problem that the three of us — Zhang, Hong and I — need to put a lid on. Dawu made a few enemies during his 008 and Zhengyang compensation mission. We think there are four artists who could make further trouble for him: Yu Bing, Zhang Wei, Xin Gao and He Yingpeng. Zhang Wei was the man who showed up at Dawu's studio in the spring and attacked him. Xin Gao and He Yingpeng belong to a *heishehui* (organized crime syndicate). They believe that Dawu was working on the compensation project so he could pocket every last cent. We all know that was not the truth. Dawu risked life and limb to get the money back for ALL of the residents.

Zhang, Hong and I should keep tabs on the antagonistic artists and not give them anything to hold over Dawu. I don't think they have any control over whether he stays in jail but they could certainly make life hard for me by harassing me or via other measures. I tell Zhang to keep me posted if he hears of any grumblings from the other artists.

I tell Dawu's friends about sending Hannah to Canada until all of this blows over. They think it's a good thing to do. I'm on the fence. I want to do the right thing for Hannah but logistically, it'll be a nightmare. I can't leave China at this point; it's crucial I stay here to work on Dawu's case, but I'll need to leave in order to take Hannah to Calgary. Children under the age of 12 can't go on flights alone. What happens when I try to return to Beijing? Will I be stopped from entering China? I am stuck between a rock and a hard place. Frankly, it sucks.

As it has been a long evening, Zhang and Hong are about to take their leave when they say they've read my letter online. What letter? I had only just finished a draft of a message to Fu Zhenghua, the Beijing police chief, and sent it to Wen Tao to be translated into Chinese. I didn't know he had done it already and posted it to the internet. I had thought the printed copies should go out first. Oh well. The electronic letter has been floating around Chinese group chats, Twitter and other social media platforms like Weibo (a Chinese microblogging site) for several hours. There's no going back now.

With the help of Wen Tao and Ai Weiwei, I created letters in English and had them translated into Chinese for distribution to various bodies in Beijing such as the mayor, chief of police, etc. as well as online. Letters like the following were posted on social media and went viral around China.

Wu Yuren info request letter
July 4, 2010
I am Karen Patterson, Canadian citizen, and wife of Chinese citizen, Wu Yuren. Just would like to bring to your attention a very unfortunate situation that has taken place recently, one that truly affects my life in China in a very negative way.

On May 31, 2010, my husband accompanied Mr. Tang, the owner of the Sugar Jar CD Music shop in 798, to the Jiuxianqiao Police Station to report on a criminal act of the 798 Management. Mr. Tang mentioned to WU that he had been having problems with the 798 Management, and so he decided to enlist the assistance of Wu Yuren. Being a helpful guy, my husband agreed to accompany Mr. Tang to the police station. Both Wu and Tang never returned from the police station on the night of May 31, 2010.

At the police station, it is reported that Wu Yuren was not only provoked into getting angry by the police and videotaped, but after about 3 hours, was beaten by 5 police in a solitary room, with a shirt over his head.

Wu Yuren and Tang Funai were both transferred to the detention center on Jun. 1, where Wu Yuren was placed in the criminal section, and Mr. Tang was placed in the civil section of the center. They were both given the charge of "Obstructing and Attacking a Police Officer". After arriving at the detention center, Mr. Wu requested to have an X-ray taken of his torso, as he felt injured after the beating that he received on the night of May 31.

Mr. Tang was released after 10 days, the allotted time that was stated on his detention center admission form.

However, for reasons we do not know, the time allotment on Mr. Wu's form was left blank, and hence Wu is still in criminal detention. We have no information of when he will be released, as I have not had any access to him, received any calls from the police (Chinese law states that they must notify the spouse by phone call person to person within 24 hours), nor received an official detention report. I have tried in person many times to get information but have been refused.

Last week I hired a lawyer to visit my husband, but he was also denied access to seeing my husband. Not sure if this is local policy or a further way of hiding the facts from the family and public.

I have lived in China now for close to 14 years, have married a Chinese citizen, given birth to our child, and generally enjoyed my life in China. However, I can't help but wonder how it is that five policemen can beat a Chinese citizen who is reporting a crime at a local police station? Not to mention, since May 31, I have not received any official person-to-person call, notice or information from the authorities with regards to his detention and his 'charge', including any information about the process and system of detention in China. All official channels of receiving information about my husband have been blocked. Furthermore, this event deeply affects my life in China, not to mention that of our daughter, who is almost 6 years old and misses her father. When she asks me when he will come home, I am at a loss of what to tell her.

I am asking for your help in assisting me in collecting any information about Wu Yuren and his case, including what happened at the police station on the night of May 31, why he was placed into the criminal section of the detention center, and why I have not received any information about my husband. Any assistance that you can provide is greatly appreciated.

Thank you for your time. Please contact me directly if you would like to meet to further discuss.

Sincerely, Karen Patterson

52

This is it. This is a major red-letter day: Thursday, July 8. Gong Jin has his meeting with Dawu. I'm up early and have Hannah sent off to her science camp by 7:30 a.m. She doesn't know about the meeting because she's too young to understand that even though someone is seeing her baba, it doesn't mean he's coming home after 38 days of being away.

While Hannah is off at her camp, Jane is starting the children's art workshops at the Beijing Color Studio. It will be good to have that extra income. Meanwhile, I have my usual breakfast of corn flakes topped with milk and brown sugar. I'm not nervous in the least. In fact, I'm confident that this meeting will go better than the last one.

I arrive at the Chaoyang District Detention Center around 8:25 a.m. I have to wait outside as it's too early to get in. The building is intimidating: encircled by a four-metre cement wall that's crowned with barbed wire. There's a watchtower sprouting out of the barricade that's topped off by a cheeky clump of grass — the only living thing not under a guard's watchful eye here. If I was all alone, the serious setting and the seriousness of the situation might make me anxious. I'm glad my support team has joined me.

Gong Jin, Wen Tao, Zhang, Hong and Peter Foster are waiting with me. There are many other folks milling about, waiting for the doors to open at 8:30 a.m. sharp. Spouses, parents, friends and lawyers looking for prospective clients hover at the front of the building.

Tang (can I still call him the Troublemaker if he's actually here to help?) makes a surprise appearance as does Ai Weiwei, his camera crew and a contingent of Dawu supporters. Lao Ai had told his Twitter followers about Dawu's upcoming chat with the lawyer and around 15 Ai Weiwei fans show up. In addition, there are four Petitioners here.

The Petitioners are polite and eager to help. Nevertheless, I want to make sure they're not going to hijack the cause. I tell them that Gong Jin must speak to me first after he speaks to Dawu.

All the people surrounding me now prove that Dawu is loved and has substantial backing. When the centre doors open, we all move inside. Unfortunately, Lao Ai's camera crew is told they're not allowed in the building. They'll have to wait outside.

An officer brings me some forms that I sign. The papers give Gong Jin permission to see Dawu. Then, I tell the lawyer what I want him to ask my husband. The two are scheduled to talk now for about half an hour.

I hope 30 minutes is enough time to get what I need to know.

Gong Jin seems nervous, squirrely even. He has a harder time than usual looking me in the eye. It's too late to wonder if he's in over his head. However, after the lawyer goes through the security check before heading upstairs to meet Dawu, he seems to gain strength. With every step, his back gets straighter and he holds his head higher. He's going to do well. I don't have to worry.

I look around at Dawu's supporters. They're all looking at me.

"Shall we go into the seating area?" I ask everyone.

The question takes their eyes off me while they move to the cold plastic chairs that are fastened to the floor. There's nothing fancy or inviting about this room. There are no soft surfaces. The typical institutional granite flooring is hard and the windows are tinted blue. The light that can get through is harsh. It feels like a winter's day here.

We sit and try to chat with one another. My mind can't take in the small talk and my attention constantly wanders away. I glance every few seconds at the hallway, where I hope to see Gong Jin. I'm not naive enough anymore to think Dawu will be with him.

Forty minutes later, the lawyer walks into the room. We all lunge at him, ready to hear what Dawu said. However, this dingy waiting room is not the place for a debrief. There are other people in here and it's smack dab in enemy territory. We walk outside and find Lao Ai with his camera crew at the ready to talk to Gong Jin. But the lawyer is not ready for the cameras.

Gong Jin says he won't talk until the cameras are taken away and Ai Weiwei is not included in the conversation. Lao Ai is upset and says that if the lawyer is not willing to be recorded, perhaps it means he's afraid and hasn't been truly representing his client. I'm worried there are going to be punches thrown and I do not want a fight to break out. I just want to hear about Dawu.

I don't know what to say or what to do to calm the situation. Gong Jin is my lawyer who has had contact with my husband. On the other side, Ai Weiwei has given me valuable insight and support. No matter who's right or wrong in the debate, arguing outside of the detention centre is stupid. It's a busy area. People are coming and going and vehicles are speeding by. I'd like to be able to concentrate solely on Gong Jin and not be distracted.

Someone suggests we head to the KFC outlet at the Aochan shopping centre, a mere stone's throw from where Dawu is imprisoned. We go to the fast-food restaurant and Lao Ai orders food for our group of 25 or so people.

We attract some attention from the staff and other customers but no one kicks us out. I sit on one side of the lawyer and Zhang on the other.

With several large buckets of chicken, burgers and drinks on the table, it's time to turn our attention to Gong Jin. Everyone wants to hear what has taken place inside. As soon as the lawyer begins to talk, Ai Weiwei signals for the cameras to start filming. That's when Gong Jin stops mid-sentence.

"Go away!" he tells Lao Ai. "I told you to take those cameras and go away."

Gong Jin says he had agreed to see Dawu but he hasn't agreed to be recorded. He seems nervous, fidgeting and sitting on the edge of his chair. Ai, in order to appease Gong Jin and get the information we desperately need, backs up and signals his camera operator to film from a distance. The lawyer composes himself and begins speaking … however, at a deliberately low volume. He ignores any prompts to speak up from Ai Weiwei and won't look at the man. At any rate, I'm happy to be on track. Now, where were we?

We're still in the dark when it comes to why Dawu is being held. Gong Jin says that last Friday, July 2, Dawu was officially charged with obstructing and attacking a police officer. However, Dawu claims that's a farce and he remains unclear about what put him in jail in the first place. It's not based on the graffiti written all over 798 or the fight over his stolen generator or the march. Whatever the reason, it's serious and not something we're going to figure out easily. My heart sinks into my shoes.

Dawu's being subjected to daily non-violent interrogations. It's a common tactic to get the detainee to admit guilt by hounding him for five to six hours a day. Dawu is not giving in. That gives me some sense of hope. My husband is staying strong because he has done nothing wrong.

Gong Jin says Dawu needs pocket money in order to make his stay at the centre a tiny bit better. This is the first time I hear about it. I knew he was allowed outside clothing and some petty cash but I didn't know he had to have a monthly allowance. Gong Jin says the money will give him access to food, cigarettes and soap. Dawu is asking for about ¥800 to ¥1,000 RMB a month (CAD 170) from his account.

With regards to Dawu's banking information, I hear what I don't want to hear -- Dawu wants Zhang to be in charge of handling his finances. Not me. A slow smile creeps across the studio assistant's face, as if there's a power game here and he somehow won the role of financial controller. The news hurts my feelings.

Here I am, working my ass off to get Dawu out, and all he's thinking about is that I'm trying to get my hands on his money? It's irrational and I wonder if the decision stems from being overwhelmed by his situation. I just hope that Zhang will be reasonable and take care of the spending. He's already lost some of Dawu's money because of shady backdoor dealings.

Speaking of money, Gong Jin says bailing Dawu out might be a possibility. We have to apply and the bail amount could be anywhere from ¥1,000 to ¥30,000 RMB (CAD 170 to 5,000). The lawyer will help with the application.

While being held, Dawu has heard about a lawyer who might be to represent him. He suggests I talk to Hao Jinsong. I've never heard of him and neither have Gong Jin and Ai Weiwei. It's one request I'll ignore. Lao Ai is a better connection for lawyers over Dawu, who is sitting in a jail cell. He'll have to trust me on this one.

Other requests from Dawu include retrieving his personal belongings from the Jiuxianqiao police station, such as his cell phone, money, Chinese ID card, address book, electric bike and key. As well, he wants to leave China once he is released and is asking me to organize it. Of course, I'm thinking back to those immigration papers I had prepared for him a few months ago, papers he never signed.

Finally, and the hardest to hear, Gong Jin gives us details on Dawu's health. His arm, back and shoulder are not in great shape and give him pain. He has never been given any medical attention for his injuries nor treatment or medicine. We know already that he had been airplaned at the Jiuxianqiao police station and beaten by five officers over a month ago. When I saw him on June 1, his arm was hanging limply by his side. I should ask my sister, a physiotherapist, about his injury. Diane might be able to give me some exercises to pass on to Dawu. Gong Jin can tell him how to do them the next time they meet.

Otherwise, Gong Jin says Dawu is being treated well, all things considered, and that he insists that he was never violent towards anyone and is innocent in all of this. I believe him and looking around KFC at his support group, everyone else does, too. I thank the lawyer for his work and dedication. Gong Jin says he'll be in touch about the bail application.

With the debrief over, Lao Ai takes me aside and says the lawyer is nervous and probably won't last long on the case. I guess I'll have to wait and see. I head out into the hot July afternoon and drive home.

There's a lot of information to absorb. Just when I think I'm getting to the top of the mountain, there's more hill to climb. Those pesky questions that have been hanging around for so long are still here.

What could Dawu have possibly done to deserve this? Why was he beaten so violently for something he hasn't done? All I know is that he's suffering and it could mean permanent damage to his body, mind and spirit. I wish I could hug him right now.

A Canadian journalist has picked up Dawu's story. Bill Schiller, the *Toronto Star* foreign affairs reporter, is listening to me talk about what happened to my husband. Bill knows a few details from Peter Foster, the journalist who connected us, but wants to learn more about Dawu straight from the source.

The *Toronto Star* is one of Canada's premier papers and Bill will be the first Canadian reporter in Beijing with the scoop on Dawu. We're meeting this morning at the Starbucks at the Lido Hotel. As is usual in China with expat journalists, Bill has brought along an interpreter, Mimi.

During our chat over tea, Bill says his passion is focusing on human stories and Dawu's plight fits in with this theme. I talk about how Dawu is a good father and family man even though we don't live together. I tell Bill that before Dawu was illegally detained, I had been thinking about taking him home to Canada but we never followed through with the paperwork.

Bill thinks Dawu's connection to Canada is the angle to pursue for his article. I give Bill the dates, details and anecdotes of Dawu's time in Western Canada. He visited three times, the first at the end of 2002 when he met my family and he gave two seminars on Chinese contemporary art. The second time he was in Canada was in the spring of 2004 when he taught Chinese contemporary art at the University of Saskatchewan. The third time was in 2006 when Dawu was a guest lecturer and a resident artist in the art department at the University of Calgary.

As I speak, Bill is listening intently, taking notes and asking questions. Our rapport makes me feel like I am being heard in a solid, real way. I love my friends but they can't do anything for Dawu other than lend me emotional support. Journalists have the power to bring about change.

I tell Bill about how it has been a slow and drawn-out process searching for answers, along with trying to decipher the law in China. Since I've been talking with Gong Jin, I've learned that *xingzheng* refers to civil or administrative detention. That's where Tang was placed on June 1. *Xingshi* refers to criminal detention and that was where Dawu was placed that same evening.

The Chinese justice system is not transparent but I think I have a handle on what's in store for Dawu. Since his arrest has officially been approved, he has 40 to 60 additional days of confinement tacked onto the 37.5 days. During this prosecution stage, he'll be allowed visits from lawyers but not me. Then, Dawu will go on trial.

When he goes to court, there's no doubt that he'll be convicted as close to 90 per cent of cases end that way in China. This is just how things work under a justice system that is not independent of the government. I will only be able to speak to Dawu at the end of the case, at time of sentencing, before he's hauled away for who knows how long.

After a couple of hours of talking, I invite Bill and Mimi to go to the Jiuxianqiao police station with me. An officer had called this morning to say that the detachment wanted to hand over Dawu's personal belongings to me. Bill is keen to come along and says he's prepared to dedicate today to capturing the fight to release Dawu.

We arrive outside of the Jiuxianqiao Police Station just before lunch. This is where I last saw Dawu over a month ago. My husband had been hurt, confused and worried. Zhang, Hong, Ai Weiwei, Tang and Ren Qiu (Lao Ai's main camera operator) are here too, as is Petitioner Ye Mingming. I don't know Ye Mingming personally but she was involved with the 008 and Zhengyang compensation fight. She had petitioned the government on behalf of the evicted artists many times.

Lao Ai, Bill and Mimi will wait outside while the rest of us go into the station. I walk through the doors first, followed by my entourage of sorts. It's a strength in numbers scenario where the larger the following Dawu has, the more impact it'll make on the police. It's weird to be at the detachment knowing Dawu faced so much violence in this place not too long ago. The station walls must have knowledge of what went on, but will they share it?

I remember the afternoon I saw Dawu, just before he disappeared into the maze of the police station and system. If I could have talked to him longer and not have hesitated when I saw him staring out the window, perhaps he'd be in his studio right now. However, he was cut off from me when the window was quickly slammed in my face.

I walk up to the stainless-steel counter that catches my reflection. It's not a clear image but distorted. My face ripples and bends much like my stomach is doing. I introduce myself in Mandarin to the officer behind the counter. She's wearing too much lipstick and it makes her look like a clown. In fact, she immediately goes into a comedy act by making a call and holding up her hand in front of me, indicating that she is busy. She hangs up.

I start over again. She calls someone else. At last, she tells me I have to wait by signalling to the waiting area where my entourage is quietly talking and filming. Tang is pointing to the officer photos that hang on the wall and giving a guided tour to the cameraperson of who's who and who did what on the night of Dawu's beating. I'm glad that Tang is with us today.

The officer at the counter calls for me at last. I guess she has time for me now. I tell her who I am and I'm here to collect the personal effects of Wu Yuren. She lifts up the phone and dials a number. Speaking in a somewhat muffled voice, she tells the person on the other end of the line that Peng Kailin (me) is here regarding her husband. Moments later, a high-ranking officer enters the main reception area. I recognize him as one of the men Tang was pointing out in the photos.

The cop introduces himself as Yang Yue.

"That's the one," Tang whispers to me. "He was here when Dawu was hurt."

Yang Yue invites us to follow him and we do. He is carrying a white plastic bag with Dawu's name written on it. As we stroll through a maze of corridors, I realize Yang Yue was the person who called me earlier about picking up Dawu's items.

As we walk, Tang gives the cameraperson and me a tour of the station. He shows us the rooms where he and Dawu had spent time on the evening of May 31. Tang motions down the hall and says that's where the canteen is. It's the room where Dawu was beaten around 7:30 p.m. We don't go past it but I'm sick to my stomach knowing what happened in that place a few metres away.

Remarkably, we're allowed to be filming in the detachment. We're not told to turn off the camera or to stop talking. I thought the authorities wouldn't want to give us any sort of consideration but here we are, walking and talking as if we're sightseers.

Yang Yue asks us to sit down in a small meeting chamber. It reminds me of the old school rooms I used to teach in when I was in northern China: bare white plaster walls with one third done in that institutional green colour. It's a standard paint style that you see in many buildings built in the 70s and 80s in China, especially schools, hospitals and post offices. It's a cheap and practical way of adding a pop of "colour" to an otherwise drab look.

This dreary meeting room is the same room where Dawu had been standing when I saw him. Through the opaque vinyl-covered window, I can see the outline of the tree that stands guard on the street.

Yang Yue dips into the plastic bag and begins removing items that I recognize belong to Dawu: his jeans, shirt, shoes, socks, Nokia phone, money, a blue receipt for an X-ray performed on him on June 1 by the Red Cross of China, the key to his electric bike and the note that I had left for him at the front counter. The message was dated June 1, 2010 and included my name in Chinese, my phone number and Dawu's surname. There's also a note from Dawu to me giving me instructions on where to pick up his bike parked in Chao Hongling and Gu Duanfan's driveway.

In order to claim Dawu's items, I have to sign a release form. I scribble my name on the dotted line and ask to keep the form. I don't trust the police. I'd like to have the authorized slip just in case the cops say I took Dawu's stuff unlawfully. Yang Yue does not want me to have the form. He tells me that the police have to keep it for their records. When I ask him to photocopy it for me, he says that's not going to be possible. I ask him why not and he gives me a bunch of excuses. So, I snatch the paper right out of his hand. That felt good!

Chao Hongling has never said that Dawu's bike is parked at her place. I bet the police have it. They do. I ask Yang Yue where the bike is and he says it has been picked up and is at the back of the station. This means the police have read Dawu's note to me and knew where to find the bike. Why didn't they go a step further and call my number that's also written on the paper? The petitioner, Ye Mingming, notices this, too and is spouting off to the officer about it. She tells him that I should have been contacted right away about what was happening to Dawu. She says what the officers did to me was unacceptable. Agreed! I then ask Yang Yue to explain to me why the authorities never informed me about Dawu's detention.

"I don't really know what to say," says Yang Yue, sitting down slowly in a chair. There's sweat dripping off his forehead and he slumps into a corner. I'm standing over him and I feel large and powerful in the position. I could strike him or beat him if I wanted. Why not? He is part of the organization that disabled Dawu's life. This man cowering in front of me is part of a corrupt and evil system that lies and attacks its own people.

I bring up the attack on Dawu but Yang has no answers. He says he is not sure about what happened. Averting any eye contact with me, the cop tells me that he doesn't know of any assault at the detachment. He doesn't think any of his officers would do such a thing. However, Tang remembers Yang Yue from that night.

I ask Yang Yue if he was on duty that evening. He responds by sucking his teeth and then says he doesn't remember.

"It was a long time ago."

It was just over a month ago, not long at all, but he's hiding something. That we do know. I push him harder in response to his lame answers. I ask him to check with the front desk to see if he was on duty. Yang Yue looks at me with wide eyes but stays silent.

"*GO TO THE FRONT DESK AND CHECK!*" I yell in his face in Chinese.

He remains rooted to his chair.

I'm taking more risks inside the detachment because there's a Canadian journalist outside the station. I don't think the police know Bill is waiting for me but if something does happen to me here, I won't disappear.

I change tactics and point to the doorway, silently yet forcefully ordering Yang Yue out. Nevertheless, the grown man acts like a little kid afraid to leave the room and scrunches down in his chair.

"Is this meeting over?" he asks in a high-pitched voice.

"No," I say firmly. I'm only getting started.

Yang Yue is refusing to answer any of my questions. When I ask again, why Dawu was assaulted on May 31, the police officer squirms in his chair. Just then, I see another cop walk by the open door. Tang tells me the officer was also at the station that night.

"He was probably the one who ordered the beating," says Tang. "That was Xiu Dawen."

Xiu Dawen is one of the top police chiefs in the detachment, ranking slightly above Yang Yue. I've seen Xiu Dawen's name recently. On the way into the police station, I had spotted a notice board detailing who was on duty and when. Luckily, May 31 was still up. Xiu Dawen's name, along with his photo, was listed as the duty officer for that evening. The duty manager oversees everything. He must have known about Dawu.

I'm putting the pieces together but instead of making me feel like I'm on to something, I'm getting angrier. The authorities keep adding lies to their cover-up and making me go in circles. I tell myself to calm down. The cops have the information I need. I know this. They know I know but they're going to make me pay for it. I have to do this above board.

I back away from Yang and take a pause. I ask him politely if I could have a photocopy of the release form. He sighs, stands up and asks me to follow him. Yang Yue escorts me upstairs to a photocopy machine and stands beside me as I make one copy. I now have concrete evidence that Dawu was in this police station. I'll show the form to the lawyer the next time we meet.

Back in the meeting room, I'm talking with my entourage when I get another glimpse of Xiu Dawen. He pokes his head in the door, sees us and bolts.

"Xiu Dawen!" I call after him. "Xiu Dawen!"

He doesn't acknowledge he heard me so I dart into the hallway and shout at him as he's trotting away.

"Xiu Dawen, why didn't you contact me after the night of May 31?"

He turns around.

"It had nothing to do with me," he says while flapping a dismissive hand at me. He then disappears into a room. I'm furious and my face is beet red from the exertion of keeping a thousand bad words from exploding out of my mouth. No one in this country is going to take responsibility for my husband's pain and suffering. No one!

The members of my entourage shake their heads when I come back into the meeting room. Yang Yue is as pale as the building's white plaster walls. He tells us that we can report Dawu's beating and the detention to the district police bureau's complaint section. I'd like to laugh. What a silly suggestion. Like it'll do anything. Nevertheless, I write down the bureau's phone number: 8595-3500. I will be lodging a severe gripe.

My group decides it's time to break for lunch. Lao Ai has long since left the station and his camera operator, Ren Qiu, also leaves since he has other things to do today. I thank him for coming and ask him to also thank Lao Ai. We agree to get in touch later on.

Outside, I catch up with Bill Schiller and Mimi, who have been patiently waiting for me. I wonder how Mimi feels about the situation. Does she ever think about her government's actions against its own people? How does Mimi interpret what the authorities say and pass their words along, honestly and openly, to the foreign press?

Mimi, Bill, Tang, Zhang, Hong, Ye Mingming and I go to lunch at a food court in a local shopping complex nearby. Over a bowl of noodles, Tang tells us that Xiu Dawen and Yang Yue were both on duty that night of May 31. He clearly remembers them. They would have to have known that Dawu was beaten — either because they did, or another officer told them about it, or they heard Dawu crying out. The station is small and Dawu would have been screaming in pain. There's no way the officers didn't hear him.

Although I don't want to return to the detachment, I think it's best that we pick up Dawu's electric bike. I don't want to leave it there and have it mangled by a vindictive cop. Bill and Mimi won't be coming with us. The reporter has to return to his bureau to write up the story. He says his article will be published in the next day or so. I thank him profusely.

Zhang, Hong and I go back to the police station right after lunch. It's awkward and embarrassing walking through the doors again. Not to mention, I'm worried that someone might confront me over this morning's verbal fireworks. Anyway, I want Dawu's bike in my possession. This way, the police have nothing of Dawu's. (Except for Dawu.)

Zhang asks the receptionist at the front counter for the bike. She calls an officer who leads us out the back door, the same door Dawu was whisked through in June, and grabs the bike for us. It has been sitting outside in the inner courtyard for over a month. The rain has pelted it and the sun has burned its rays into it. The bike is rusty and dusty.

Hong suggests we leave it at the police station as evidence. Zhang and I ask Hong to explain what he means by "evidence." He says that he's looking out for Dawu's best interests and by leaving the bike, it shows that Dawu had been here. I point out that we already have all the evidence we need. We have the X-ray receipt, Dawu's phone (possibly with texts and photos), notes and a copy of the release form that I signed. What other evidence do we need?

Hong is adamant that the electric bike needs to remain at the detachment. I can't help but fight with him over his thinking. We're yelling and swearing at each other while Zhang is mute on the matter. Hong and I are standing in the middle of the station parking lot, arguing loudly. Several cops come out to watch us and smirk and laugh at our heated discussion. Jeez-us fuck! We look like absolute idiots. Total nincompoops! It's bad enough to be struggling to get answers about Dawu; it's unnecessary to have to fight with Hong over this bike inside the police compound. Urgh, too much going on.

Here I've been trying to come across as serious and composed to the police and in one move, I look like a fool. I'm screaming over a fucking electric bike that the owner can't even ride right now, or possibly ever. I want to hit a button and be immediately transported somewhere other than this parking lot. I've lost face and credibility big time.

The bike remains parked at the detachment. For now.

I'm tired and embarrassed and want to go home. In the car, I go over some notes in my head. What is happening with the complaint Tang brought against the police? What about the statement he wrote based on his own experiences? Do we need to follow up on it? As well, I've been receiving emails from family and friends aboard since Dawu's been put in jail. Do I need to be concerned that the authorities are tracking my computer correspondence? Should Gong Jin be involved in the next phase of Dawu's defence? If yes, what will Lao Ai say our next steps are?

54

Tomorrow would have been the day that Dawu got out of detention if he hadn't been formally charged a few days ago. The end of the 37.5 days is up but the nightmare is not over. It's a strange feeling not knowing what the future holds. It's like I'm drifting through outer space: there's nothing to see, nothing to hear, nothing to hang on to, nothing to stop me from floating far, far, far away.

Hannah hasn't given up on her baba. She asks for him daily and her stuffies are still going to jail. All I can do is tell her over and over again that I'm working on bringing her father home. What does that mean to a child?

One thing I can do is clean house, so to speak. Yesterday's ordeal made me realize things have to change. I need a working team, not a bunch of circus clowns. I call a meeting to be held at Dawu's 798 studio. I want to address the drama and dynamics of the team. I'm sick of fighting with Hong. His good intentions are more like harmful manipulations. My mom calls folks like Hong do-gooders. They cause more stress "helping" instead of solving the problem. When Dawu was first in trouble, Hong and Zhang were all I had. The team has grown and it's not only about Dawu's friends anymore. There are a hundred different moving parts and a bigger picture.

There are also many hangers-on who want to be involved in Dawu's case but are useless. These people include those who read Twitter posts or other social media and are curious about what's going on. They've been showing up at our meetings and for our visits to the detention centre. Their intentions are to support Dawu but they ask me or Zhang or Gong Jin so many questions that they cloud the real issues. They also get details muddled and post false information online, causing confusion and crossed wires.

I need to surround myself with people who can help, not groupies who post their captures on social media for their own gain. Some groupies have been posing for selfies in front of the detention centre where Dawu is being kept. That's uncalled for. I need a sleek and slick team that can deliver results.

It's interesting. With all my jobs and business dealings and ventures, I had never focused on being a manager. I just hired out of intuition and the right fit. I realize now that I have to be proficient at picking people right for the "job" and weeding out those who don't cut it. My measure of success is clear: getting Dawu out before any further harm is done to his body, mind and spirit. Now, who can help me with that?

I have an idea in my head of who should be on my consolidated team. At the meeting, I make no bones about who made the cut … and who didn't. I ask Zhang to stay on the team. He actually can't be taken off the list since Dawu made him his banker and financial controller. As well, Zhang will remain as the studio manager in Dawu's absence.

Wen Tao is a valuable asset. He gets my nod. Wen Tao has many assets, including being a translator, social media guru and my trusty assistant.

Ai Weiwei is our team lead. He has the name and star power to make the government sit up and listen. He has agreed to keep guiding me.

Ren Qiu is our camera operator. His job is to record the fight for justice.

I tell Hong to go home to Nanjing. He and Mao Xiangji are supposed to visit Dawu's family to fill them in on his recent incarceration. That can be Hong's task until we require his assistance again. Otherwise, we don't need him in Beijing.

I say to Hong that I'm grateful for his help and I know he's been a strong supporter of Dawu's ever since he was his teacher in Changzhou in the 90s. But the team is slimming down and, unfortunately, Hong is not needed. He hangs his head and leaves. No doubt, he's annoyed at me but it's for the best. Sure, I probably made him lose face but he was constantly fighting with me. Not the best. It feels like I've fired someone, and I kind of have. It wasn't fun or easy but it was necessary.

Another person I have to let go is Gong Jin. He's not at the meeting and I'll call him later. The more the new team chats about Gong Jin, the more we agree that we need a lawyer with teeth: someone who isn't nervous and will go on the attack against the government. We can't be dicking around. We have wasted enough time with Chao Hongmei and it looks like Gong Jin isn't up for taking on the authorities. He hasn't been proactive and is scared of being filmed talking about Dawu. Lao Ai thinks it's best to consult with the lawyer he suggested, Liu Xiaoyan.

Liu Xiaoyan was busy the last time we talked and he is still busy. The lawyer doesn't have time to have face-to-face meetings with me but he can dispense advice over the phone or email. As for Gong Jin, I'll pay him what he's owed and move on. I'm sure he will be relieved. I also won't need Flame's services anymore, because I have Wen Tao to translate and interpret for me. Tang Funai will stay on the team but will warm the bench. We won't need him daily.

We will need his valuable intel on what led up to Dawu being taken into detention, as well as information about the cops who are possibly involved. He'll be a good witness if the time comes.

We will survive as a group only if we keep our tempers in check. I think I'll be fine now, as I won't be aggravated by Hong. He was the instigator during the moments I lost it. Yesterday's fight between him and me at the police station was a total disaster in that regard. We can't let something like that happen again if we want to be taken seriously and somewhat professionally. Cops can sense weakness and will exploit our group dynamics to pit us against each other. We must present a united front.

I also have to make sure I take care of me by getting enough sleep, talking things out with friends and trying to maintain a somewhat normal life. I can't afford to let my emotions bubble over and splatter on the floor in front of everyone.

After the team renovations have been made, we tackle writing our grievance to the district police bureau. Yang Yue had told us we could send one to its complaint section. We compile a list, starting with the fact that the police didn't use proper procedures when Dawu was in their custody. The cops never contacted me despite having two pieces of paper with my phone number on it.

As well, we request that the district office investigate the following:
- the May 31 beating of Wu Yuren
- why Karen couldn't meet with Wu Yuren while at the police station on June 1
- why the lawyer wasn't allowed to see Dawu on July 5
- why no one at the police station responded to Chen Jun (the man who was attacked at the 008 compound) and other 008 protesters when they asked, repeatedly, for a reason for Wu Yuren's detention
- why Dawu was never shown his X-ray or the results

During the meeting, another journalist calls me. Peter Simpson works for the South China Morning Post as a freelancer and is the ex-husband of my good friend Debbie Mason. Their young son, Frank, is friends with Hannah. I know Peter personally but not well. He has heard my story from Debbie and wants to do a VOA (Voice of America) radio interview with me. Perhaps he could come to the *ducha* (complaint bureau) when I hand in the grievance? We set up a time to meet.

There's more good news. Bill Schiller's article was published in the Toronto Star in Canada today. The headlines reads, "Husband of Canadian woman beaten, held 36 days." The story includes Dawu's time in the Canadian West as well as details about Hannah and I. It's important to draw empathy from Canadians. Hopefully, some might feel like taking action and ask both the Canadian and Chinese governments to do something for Dawu. At the very least, Canadians will see what China is doing to its citizens. I email the link to my sister, other family and friends like Gord Hoffman.

I'm in contact with a myriad of people in North America, including my good friend Gord, who returned to the U.S. several years ago. He's the guy I took to the exhibit where I first met Dawu in 2001. That seems ages and ages ago. Gord taught Dawu some funny rapper slang like "Mac Daddy" and "Bitch, please!" My husband uses the phrases when he's joking around. I wonder if he's keeping his sense of humour or if the long days of internment have drained him of any levity.

I'm frustrated and sad. It's Thursday, July 8 and the 37.5 days are up. Dawu has not been released. Of course, I knew this was going to happen but it doesn't make the day any easier. My team is working hard and there's nothing else they can do to make time move faster or make the authorities realize they've made a gargantuan error in judgment. The media is starting to pay attention and Dawu's story is being heard. What if all of this doesn't work? What else can I do?

If Dawu hadn't been officially charged several days ago, he would have been free today. Hannah would have her baba back. However, there has been no word from the Chinese authorities regarding dropping or throwing out Dawu's case.

Tomorrow, I have three big meetings. Lao Ai and I will talk in the morning. Then in the afternoon, I have an official appointment with the Canadian Embassy. The next meeting has nothing to do with Dawu at all: it's about the sale of the Counting Sheep Boutique.

***

My new streamlined "Get Dawu Out" team is ready to be tested on Friday, July 9. We gather at Ai Weiwei's to discuss next steps. Lao Ai gives me some feedback on my letter that's going out to officials. He says I need to rewrite it to make it concise, instead of rehashing all that has already happened. The authorities know we know Dawu was beaten. What I should do in the letter is make a stronger call to the government, asking for an investigation into the cover-up of the assault. As well, I should ask why Dawu hasn't received proper medical treatment. I should also add that the media's interest in Dawu's story is growing and this will damage the reputation of the police in Beijing. That should wake the authorities.

It turns out that Liu Xiaoyan, the lawyer Lao Ai put me in touch with, won't even be able to consult with me over the phone. The attorney is loaded with other work. Ai Weiwei has another person in mind for the job. He names Li Fangping, a proven human rights lawyer who is not afraid to sink his teeth into the establishment. He recently represented Zhao Lianhai, a man seeking justice for children who were harmed by tainted dairy products in 2008. That year, six babies died and 300,000 infants got sick after several

Chinese companies added melamine, a chemical used to make industrial products such as glue, to infant formula. There was a cover-up and when the matter finally became public, China put pressure on lawyers to dissuade them from taking the affected families' cases.

Zhao's son was one of the children who fell ill because of the contaminated milk. Zhao formed a support group for those affected by the scandal and was arrested and detained in 2009. The father went on trial for inciting social disorder and was sentenced to two and a half years in prison.

Li Fangping has also been involved in defending Tan Zuoren. Tan is a civil rights advocate who was charged with subversion after asking the government to investigate the deaths of thousands of schoolchildren during the Sichuan earthquake. Many of the schools in the area collapsed during the disaster, while other buildings were still standing. Lao Ai tried to testify at Tan's trial but was detained by police. Ai was also involved in exposing the corruption that led to the shoddy construction of the schools.

Li Fangping can't meet us in person today but I speak to him over the phone in Lao Ai's office. The lawyer says he'll work on Dawu's file until he's sentenced. Sentencing is the last step before he's released or sent to prison.

Since Li Fangping will now be assisting the team in applying for Dawu's bail, I have to dissolve my contract with Gong Jin. I phone him and say that I want to go with a lawyer who has more experience with human rights, as this might prove to be a very sticky case. He agrees and is relieved, saying he wasn't comfortable in the role. Gong Jin also waives the remaining ¥4,000 RMB (CAD 667) that is owed to him.

"Put that money towards the new lawyers," says Gong Jin.

It's a win-win for both of us and a good way to get out of something that was potentially awkward. He did good work and I feel bad I had to let him go, but I'm confident that Li Fangping will be stronger where we need it the most.

It's 2 p.m. when Wen Tao, Ren Qiu and I go to the Canadian Embassy for a meeting. The other day, I had received a call from Darren Becker, the deputy head of mission, on behalf of Canadian Ambassador David Mulroney. The Canadian government wanted information on my current situation. The agenda today is a fact-finding mission and I'm scheduled to speak with Darren, Jack Oliver, who I've talked to several times already, and Victoria Bodlington, an embassy political counsellor.

Outside of the embassy gate, there's a long line of people waiting to go through security. Wen Tao and I pass through easily as we both have proper documentation. I'm Canadian and Wen Tao is a permanent resident.

Ren Qiu is Chinese and the guard isn't letting him past the front door. They exchange words and I get the feeling that the camera operator should stand down or else we could all be removed from the premises.

I ask Ren Qiu to wait for me here.

"We can get footage another time," I say.

It's not worth getting kicked out of my own embassy over a few minutes of filming people talking. Ren Qiu accepts, probably because he lost face when he quarrelled with the guard in front of all these people and didn't win. I can tell, though, that he is disappointed he won't get any shots.

My meeting is being held in the embassy bar and is rather out of the way. There's not much employee foot traffic in this part of the building. When I worked at the Australian Embassy, the bar would be the last place we would take someone. Maybe Canadian officials have done this is on purpose. Maybe they don't want nosy staff, both Canadians and Chinese, to see me until the officials know more about who I am and what's going on. Fair enough.

After joking about getting a drink at the embassy bar, we get down to business. At the table are Darren, Jack, Victoria, Wen Tao and me. Canadian Ambassador David Mulroney won't be joining us but the personnel present are well-qualified to talk to me.

Jack is a consular process expert and explains to me how Canada can potentially help Canadians who are detained. For example, if a Canadian is busted for drugs in China, then consular services are provided to him or her. Jack could visit the accused and ensure the prisoner is being treated fairly, among other things. However, we're not dealing with a one hundred per cent consular case. I'm Canadian but I'm not in jail.

My Chinese husband is not Canadian nor does he have permanent residency or even a visa application in the system. This is an important line when dealing with consular issues: the embassy can't help those who are not its citizens. It will, however, help me and my Canadian daughter, because we are definitely affected by Dawu's situation. Nevertheless, there will be problems with how this looks to China.

The Chinese authorities will see it as Canada overstepping its boundaries and putting a foot where it doesn't belong – right smack dab in China's business. It's not going to be good for Chinese and Canadian relations. Dawu isn't a citizen of Canada, he's a citizen of China and therefore, Canada should not be meddling in China's domestic affairs.

Canadian embassy staff and I discuss the possibility of the existence of a video recording from the night of Dawu's beating on May 31. All Beijing police stations record video surveillance — it's been the law for the past few years. The staff suggests that Li Fangping finds the Jiuxianqiao detachment recording, along with any related documentation, and possibly view what's on it.

Darren agrees to ask the Chinese Ministry of Foreign Affairs to provide me with an official statement of what had happened at the police station and why Dawu has been a detainee for a month and a half. He tells me to be patient as this might take some time. He adds that I'm doing very well by not falling apart, considering my current situation. We sort of laugh at the remark. I explain that I can't let myself go. Dawu's release is based solely on my efforts. No one else will fight as hard for him. As well, I have to be strong to support my daughter.

I tell the staff that I am concerned about the safety of Hannah and me in Beijing. I don't have hard evidence that I'm being watched by guoan but instinctively, I know I am. I had thought about sending Hannah to Calgary to live with my sister but it has turned out to be too complicated. My daughter is too young to travel alone and I can't leave China. Darren, like my Chinese supporters, suggests that I be vigilant at all times.

The embassy personnel say they can pass on my letters to Chinese and Canadian authorities as well as confirm facts when asked by Canadian and foreign media. They add that they'll contact members of Parliament (MPs) in Canada on my behalf. I bring up the possibility of Dawu moving to Canada but they say he can't apply from prison. I'll have to wait until he's out.

Victoria says the ambassador, David Mulroney, has specifically assigned her to be my liaison. She and I will meet once a week for updates. Victoria speaks good Mandarin and has been concerned about me ever since she heard about my plight from Jack several weeks ago. It's reassuring that my country stands behind me.

Before Wen Tao and I leave, I profusely thank Darren, Jack and Victoria. I appreciate that the ambassador has taken notice of Dawu's case and is concerned enough to have his staff meet with me. Jack says that David is that kind of man, interested in these sorts of human rights matters. I'm grateful Dawu is getting a high level of attention and hope it'll be what is needed to liberate him.

Later that afternoon, I join Lily Lim at Comptoirs de France, a high-end bakery about a 10-minute drive from my home. We're hashing out some details over the sale of the Counting Sheep Boutique. Our business partners are busy and so it's just the two of us.

The sun is shining and it's a warm summer day. I'm still buzzing (no, not from a drink) from the meeting at the Canadian Embassy and I give Lily the details. She's gobsmacked and her jaw drops open over what has happened.

She says it's amazing that I'm going through all of this while selling my shop. I tell her it's a necessity — this way, I'll be able to focus completely on getting Dawu out. On that note, we centre our attention on the business at hand.

In the evening, the beautiful weather turns nasty. Clouds cover the stars and the rain begins. It pours so heavily that even through my closed window, I can hear the raindrops smash themselves, hard, into the pavement.

The *New York Times* and *The New Yorker*, major international news publications — not to mention signposts for what's going on globally — have published pieces on Dawu. The *NYT* (*New York Times*) article came out a few days ago, Thursday, July 8, and reporter Edward Wong had interviewed me over the phone for it. His story is called "Chinese Artist Who Led Protest Has Been Jailed, His Wife Says." One of my quotes is how arcane I find the Chinese legal system.

The New Yorker piece hit the shelves on Monday, July 12. Staff writer Evan Osnos had met Dawu in March after his protest march, so he has a bit of a personal connection. Osnos' story is great for exposure but the headline is a cause for concern. The column is titled "Little Ai."

While the piece does point out that the Chinese government has made some progress in terms of its rule of law, Dawu's legal woes prove it still has a way to go in a justice system troubled by unfair trials, corrupt judges and more. However, the column describes Dawu's new nickname as being one coined by those who are linking his activism with Ai Weiwei's activism. While somewhat true, comparing Dawu to Lao Ai in a world forum could be problematic.

The "Little Ai" headline instantly associates Dawu and Ai. Dawu had been a part of one of Lao Ai's exhibitions in Germany in June 2008 but otherwise, they have never worked directly on art or activism projects together. Ai Weiwei's family history gives him some protection when it comes to criticizing the government. He is still harassed and watched by government officials but because of his modicum of built-in immunity, he probably won't disappear. Unlike Dawu.

Ai is already a known dissident. Anyone associated with him might be automatically seen as one, too. Thus, by connecting Lao Ai to Dawu, my husband is tarred with the same brush. Anyone in authority in China who reads Osnos' piece will have more ammunition to go after Dawu. However, from an outside's perspective, it's clear that both artists have similar aspirations: to influence change in China. It's also the reason why Lao Ai knows how to help Dawu.

My phone is ringing off the hook at all hours. Reporters from around the world are calling me, wanting quotes and updates on Dawu. I try my best to answer their questions. Being interviewed is part of my daily routine now. Like Ai Weiwei said, Dawu can't afford to fade from the front page.

My friend Gord Hoffman thinks I should consider writing my own article, expressing my opinions on what's happening to Dawu and me. It could tip the public opinion scales towards Dawu and put more public pressure on the Chinese government. I'm not sure I have the fortitude to put my thoughts into a formal written piece. I don't even have the energy to pick up a fork, let alone pick at the computer keys.

Gord is a commercial lawyer in the U.S. and has some connections with human rights representatives there. He says his friend Evan Sharpe with Human Rights In China (HRIC) is going to bring Dawu to the attention of the head of the organization. HRIC is a non-governmental organization (NGO) promoting fundamental rights and freedoms in China, among other social advocacy work. As well, the NGO highlights human rights abuses in the country.

HRIC was founded in 1989 after the Tiananmen Square massacre and has offices in Hong Kong and New York, as the organization is banned in mainland China. Gord thinks HRIC could bring awareness about Dawu's situation and force the Chinese government to let him go.

Gord also suggests several people who might be able to help me with Dawu's case. That's a relief as I feel like I'm in a knowledge vacuum. My internet is monitored, Chinese law is not open and transparent and I'm not getting legal advice from the Canadian Embassy. One name Gord puts forward is Jerome Cohen, a leading human rights lawyer in New York City.

Eva Pils, a German lawyer based in Hong Kong, is another person who could aide in my quest for answers. She's a formidable academic who teaches Chinese law at the Chinese University of Hong Kong. She's an expert in human rights and knows Li Fangping, Dawu's lawyer, professionally and personally.

Gord, an excellent problem solver, says I should start a letter-writing campaign to the prime minister of Canada, Stephen Harper. It could create some buzz. Gord also tells me to ask my friends anywhere and everywhere outside of China to write to the Canadian and Chinese governments. As well, he suggests friends abroad hold protests outside of Chinese embassies or consulates to raise global awareness.

My network of allies is expanding but I have to watch who I talk to. I don't want a media circus. I need to balance the media coverage Dawu is getting with legal consultation and representation. Fake news is always a possibility, especially in China, and I have to ensure that the reporters I'm talking to pass muster. Of the many journalists who are contacting me, I only trust international reporters. I do not talk to journalists who are directed by the state media here in China.

ALL newspapers, TV channels and any sort of mass media or communications in China are owned and monitored by the Chinese government. It controls foreign media. International journalists operate in China under strict rules and management and Chinese reporters are highly censored and often don't report on matters considered human rights abuses by any other country.

Ai Weiwei and Wen Tao are worried a Chinese government-sanctioned reporter will interview me and get details to skew in the foreign press, putting Dawu at risk. We have to trace each reporter's credibility to make sure she or he isn't backed by the Chinese authorities. To do that, we conduct full-scale internet searches on journalists. Wen Tao, who is a journalist, asks around about each reporter.

Meanwhile, I've mailed my letters to government officials in Beijing via EMS, an express post company. I've also gone to the ducha with journalist Peter Simpson to hand in the complaint about the Jiuxianqiao Police Station. Nothing to report there, thankfully. I showed up and handed in the claim. Ren Qiu filmed the non-event and then Peter did a VOA (Voice of America) radio interview with me. It went on air in the U.S. within a week.

I'm in weekly contact with Victoria Bodlington at the Canadian Embassy. She has contacted the Canadian federal minister of foreign affairs, Lawrence Cannon, about Dawu. I'm hopeful the minister can get the Chinese government to move towards dismissing Dawu's case. These types of high-level, minister-to-minister discussions are beyond my scope but not Victoria's.

I'm meeting with yet another lawyer at his downtown Beijing office. Yan Jianguo is a criminal and human rights lawyer who knows Ai Weiwei and Gord. Lao Ai thinks Yan might have a window into why Dawu has been illegally detained. The lawyer doesn't have any insight into the case but he gives me some tips. He says we should post Dawu's story on a national police website as they've started a blog to appear more transparent, among other things. As well, Yan says there are too many departments involved in Dawu's case and we can use it to our advantage. There's the police station in the community of Jiuxiaoqiao, where the so-called crime was committed. Then, there's the city district where the police station is located, Chaoyang District. Then there's the city, Beijing and territory Beijing sits in (Beijing is like Washington D.C., U.S. and is its own national territory).

We're dealing with many and various hierarchical levels of government and it's all very complicated. Yan suggests that we lodge a complaint at the district level at the Chaoyang Fenju, a branch office in the Chaoyang District.

When I mention getting a receipt for an X-ray — but no X-ray report, Yan's eyes light up.

"This is a serious piece of evidence," he says. "Dawu never got the results and you, as his wife, should have had the right to see or hear what the X-ray found. It's strange and suspicious."

At the end of our meeting, I have some possible leads. Nothing that will break Dawu out immediately, though.

Gord, the wonderful man he is, has managed to speak to Jerome (Jerry) Cohen for me. A top human rights lawyer, Jerry knows his stuff and tells me, via Gord, to retain a second lawyer for Dawu. The name he gives me is Yan Rouhu, another human rights lawyer who could be part of Dawu's co-counsel team. As well, I need to get my hands on any papers that could be useful for when the case goes to trial. The X-ray receipt, for instance, proves that Dawu was injured. So, if he was injured, why wasn't he treated? I should also push the authorities to let me see my husband, all the while continuing to talk to the media about Dawu. Keeping him top of mind is vital to his cause. People must be reminded that an innocent man is behind bars.

Most Chinese people in China don't have access to world newspapers. They're generally not available and aren't translated into Chinese. As well, the Chinese media aren't interested in what's happening to Dawu. This means that Wu Xiangshou still isn't in the know. Hong and Mao Xiangji have told Suling over dinner but have yet to tell Ba personally about Dawu's detention.

Dawu's sister is keeping the news to herself but she's been calling me constantly, asking if she can visit Beijing to help. I tell her that there's not really much that she can do here. In truth, she'd only be in the way.

I feel terrible about Ba being in the dark. Before Dawu and I split, it was Ba who kept us up to date on the special days in the Chinese calendar. He read the *Zhōngguó nóngmín niánjiàn*, the Chinese Farmers' Almanac, every day and knew the exact time to get married or move into a new home. He's a fountain of knowledge and a great resource. I miss not being able to ask him which date is the most auspicious when trying to goad the detention guards into letting me talk to Dawu.

During Dawu's previous meeting with Gong Jin, my husband had told him that he was able to follow the 2010 FIFA World Cup soccer from the cells. This was because some of the guards helped the detainees by bringing in contraband newspapers for them to read. I'm glad Dawu's being shown some kindness. The tournament is winding down and I wonder if Dawu knows who's in the finals.

Hannah has been creating drawings and art pieces for her dad almost daily. I've been collecting her work in a box. Perhaps one day, she can show her creations to her baba in person. Hannah's stuffies still go to jail sometimes but she is otherwise a healthy and happy five-year-old. I keep my anger and frustration to myself, pushing it further and further down in my soul. Besides, I'm not sure how to explain lawyer and embassy meetings to my daughter.

Whenever I go out in Beijing, many people stop and ask me to update them on what's happening with Dawu. Folks are curious and, I hope, concerned about my husband and me. I'm talking to Dana, my counsellor, but I don't see her regularly. I just don't have the time. My whole life revolves around the detention centre and Dawu.

I'm receiving loads of support from expat friends as well as friends in Canada and around the world. A friend of my dad's in Canada, Rosemary Baxter, is helping me draft a template for a letter to Canadian politicians by Dawu's allies, such as the office of Prime Minister Stephen Harper, Canadian Minister of Foreign Affairs Lawrence Cannon and a Calgary MP Lee Richardson. Rosemary and her husband John are not ones to shy away from voicing concern over a cause, regardless of whether it's local, provincial, national, or in Dawu's case, international. The gloves are coming off.

Rosemary's wording is concise and she creates the perfect template for me. It's complete with addresses and names and all I have to do is send it to my contacts for distribution. Many CC me in their emails and I'm pleased the letter campaign is catching on in a big way.

During all of this, Mike Kuo has been a good friend. He has been helping around my studio with errands and little chores. It's his birthday near the end of July so as a thank you, I treat him to a performance by the U.S. singer Usher. After the concert, we meet up with Badr and some others to watch the last game of the World Cup. It's Spain versus Netherlands and Spain wins it, 1-0. I'm out until about 6 a.m. sharing laughs, singing my heart out at karaoke and having some drinks. It's a fun night but at the end of it, I return to the Cappuccino Complex with the same problems. Nothing much has changed and tomorrow I'll be in the same Kafkaesque scenario all over again.

I've been wearing the same clothes for about two months now. Capris, a black cotton top and flip-flops make up my wardrobe. You want me to do my hair and put on make-up? I'm just trying to get out the door.

I'm not about pretty right now. I'm about getting Dawu out of jail.

One thing that does lighten my load is the sale of the Counting Sheep Boutique. Nina and I finally sell it to Lily and Natalie, who have given us a tidy sum each. It isn't dollar for dollar but I'm glad that the business is continuing. Not only that, I'll retain my friendships.

Signing the contract is a bittersweet moment for me. I've learned a lot and met some amazing friends and clients through the company. However, both Nina and I feel that Lily and Natalie are perfectly suited to take over the boutique. Nina is returning to Europe; as for me, well, I've got my eyes on the prize here in Beijing.

I sit down with Li Fangping and my team, including Zhang, Wen Tao and Lao Ai, on the afternoon of Monday, July 19. The lawyer is comfortable being filmed and I take this as a good sign that he's not going to be skittish when push comes to shove in the legal arena.

Li Fangping's strategy is to begin by challenging the courts on the lawyer visit limit. It was illegal. Dawu should have been allowed four visits during his 37.5 days of detention. The lawyer will ask for access to the X-ray and order that a doctor visit Dawu for an examination — and treatment, if need be. Li Fangping asserts that I should apply to see Dawu and bring Hannah with me. I have a legitimate reason to see my husband and my rights are in question here.

I like Li Fanging. He says he's a champion of openness and I believe him. He tells my team that there will be no secrets and we must be honest at all times given that we've publicized Dawu's claims of innocence. The public will be watching us and the more transparent we can be, the more we can mobilize public attention to put pressure on officials to drop the case.

Li Fangping thinks Dawu's trial date will be most likely set within the next three months. He says the court will probably be open for anyone to attend but the government has a sneaky way of preventing supporters from getting seats at the hearing. For example, the trial could be scheduled to be heard in a room with only four chairs, two of which are taken up by court police.

The lawyer adds that the authorities claim that a closed source has given them evidence that Dawu obstructed justice. The allegations are on recordings that are being retained by the police. Li Fangping will try and get access to them. Meanwhile, he won't shy away from giving interviews to the foreign press. He's all about shining publicity on Dawu. He also has no problem being filmed by Lao Ai's team. This lawyer is not afraid of being seen or heard by anyone. He's fearless.

I am afraid to discuss the cost of Li Fangping's services and I'm nervous it's going to be expensive. The man is a prominent human rights lawyer and lays his life on this line for his clients. When I broach the subject, Li Fangping says payment will be around ¥12,000 RMB (CAD 6,000). What a relief! We sign the contract.

All of this legalese would have made my head spin if it was in English, but we're speaking Mandarin. Nevertheless, Li Fangping has given me the impression that he's a bull in a china shop. He's going to do what he needs to do and he's not afraid to break some things while doing it.

Eva Pils, another human rights expert, holds Li Fangping in high regard, too. I have lunch with her on Sunday, July 25 while she's in Beijing from Hong Kong. We talk about Dawu and the possibility of an open trial. Eva says that they're technically called "open" but are, in fact, closed. The Chinese authorities could fill courtroom seats with friends and family of the prosecution. As well, embassies and foreigners have to apply to attend a trial and rarely receive permission.

"Do not count on Canadian Embassy representatives being in the courtroom," Eva says, "or the international media."

She warns me to be vigilant about my surroundings, who I talk to in person and my email and other correspondence. I've heard it before and know that the secret police are watching my every move. They know where I live and I'm sure they are following me wherever I go. It's not as if the guoan have to be secret.

I've become involved in an issue that connects to Dawu in a major way. He has always been upset over the fact that China prefers development over its people. A few weeks ago, the Beijing Cultural Heritage Protection Center approached me to do a painting project with children to provide awareness of the destruction of *hutongs*, courtyard alleyways and houses, in the city. The centre is raising awareness about the need to preserve older architecture and homes in Beijing. Hutongs are being razed and people are losing their centuries-old houses so that shiny steel luxury highrises and shopping malls can replace them.

I fill the Beijing Color Studio with kids and Jane takes charge of the project. The children paint a clay model hutong gate that'll be auctioned off at a fundraiser. I think about the irony of how I'm participating in an interesting and important preservation movement, one that aligns with Dawu's beliefs and activism. I can't imagine what it must be like to be a hutong owner and have the government come in and smash your home down, with little or no compensation.

Yes, Dawu did the right thing by holding the prospective developers of the 008 and Zhengyang collectives responsible for destroying peoples' properties and livelihoods. His mission came at a cost and no one should have to endure what he's going through. No one.

At the fundraiser, I meet Guo Jian, a Chinese artist who participated in the Tiananmen Square events. Guo Jian has been living in Australia for the last few years and recently returned to Beijing. We talk about the rapid urbanization of China and Dawu's struggles. We are filmed by Shannon Van Sant, a documentary filmmaker working on the same topic, and Roseann Lake, with BLUE TV.

Guo Jian and I sit in the sun, drinking refreshments and eating nibbles while recounting our experiences for the two journalists. I tell them that before Dawu was shoved into a cell, he spent all his resources working on getting compensation for the people of 008 and Zhengyang. He had quit his art to champion the collectives. It took all of his time and energy. Now it's taking all of my time and energy while I champion him.

Dawu has been in pain for the past couple of months. Li Fangping has been in to see him at the detention centre and he can't move his arm past his shoulder. My husband hasn't received any medical attention or treatment from the guards. What makes matters worse for Dawu, is that he sleeps with 25 men on a flat bed made to hold 10 people. This means he's forced to lay on his bad side half the night, further aggravating the injury he received during the May 31 police beating.

Li Fangping visited Dawu on Monday, July 26 and told him he'd apply for access to the X-ray. Dawu asked that the lawyer keep a low profile. My husband said the police told him that since his case is "small," it's better not to blow the "little things," like a sore shoulder, out of proportion. Ha! That's the exact opposite of our plan of action.

My team believes that the authorities told Dawu to tone things down because they're feeling the heat from a department somewhere above them. We think this means that our efforts at international attention are working.

Dawu adds to our knowledge pot by saying before the police officers assaulted him, they repeatedly slapped him across the face and taunted him.

"Who is hitting you now?" they'd asked. "What evidence will you use against us, big guy?" It appears that the cops already knew their plan for Dawu even before they beat him.

Dawu believes that there's a video recording of him being dragged from one room to the cafeteria, where he was attacked. Our move is to get that footage. Our strongest indication now that proves Dawu was beaten is the receipt of the X-ray and our witness, Tang Funai. However, the judge will have to agree to call Tang to the stand. I've already been warned by the lawyer that a judge could simply ignore our witness.

Meanwhile, the officer who claims Dawu inflicted damage to his finger could be brought forward at trial. As well, the entire staff on duty at that time could be called. This wouldn't be good for Dawu's case. The cops have at least three months to construct and align their stories.

When it comes to the trial, we know it'll be sometime at the end of October and in the same district where the event took place, Chaoyang. We're hoping to have a judge from outside the area preside over the hearing. He or she might be less biased than a local judge, who could go easier on colleagues.

Corruption knows no boundaries, though.

One way to influence who the judge is going to be, is to make city hall take an interest in Dawu's trial. We'll do that by raising his profile on the international stage. We need more media coverage.

Li Fangping assures me that Dawu's in high spirits and mentally strong despite everything. He feels encouraged after learning that so many people, organizations and groups around the world are reaching out to help him. I'm happy with Lawyer Li and the outcome of Monday's meeting. There's a lot of work to do in the next three months. Dawu and I are fortunate to have all this support and belief in his innocence. Ai Weiwei sums it up in a beautifully accurate description when he's interviewed by Canadian Globe and Mail newspaper reporter Mark MacKinnon.

"Wu Yuren is one of those cases where some stupid police at a very low level made a very stupid mistake, and now they're going to sentence Wu Yuren just to justify this decision."

— July 26, 2010 "For jailed artist's family, Chinese justice is little more than revenge" Mark MacKinnon, *Globe and Mail.*

Li Fangping rocks. He's a couple of years younger than I am and reminds me of a children's book character: a mouse named Geronimo Stilton. The well-dressed rodent is thin and has an overbite, much like the lawyer. Lawyer Li is well-dressed, too.

The lawyer says that about 90 per cent of charges in China move towards sentencing. This means it's likely that Dawu will go to prison. When he's convicted, he'll probably receive a sentence of one year. The time will be accumulative and not added on to the months he's already spent behind bars. For example, if Dawu is sentenced to 12 months of prison after serving four months in detention, then he'll only serve eight more months. Li Fangping also says Dawu will probably serve his time in a work prison in Tianjin, a city southeast of Beijing about a 90-minute train or taxi ride away from the Cappuccino Complex. This is the first time I've heard of the prison. Li Fangping thinks that early release is the best scenario but failing that, then prison is better than detention as I'll be able to see Dawu.

More foreign reporters are asking for Dawu's story. Wendy Wong with Radio Free Hong Kong interviews me and my reporter friend Debbie Mason sets up a CBC (Canadian Broadcasting Corporation) call for me. As well, I'm writing almost daily on a blog I've created called *WYR's Incarceration: Seeking Truth from Fiction.* I'm tired of telling and retelling the same information every time a journalist contacts me. On a blog, it's all out there for the world to read.

I'm hearing from people all over the place, who have had similar experiences to Dawu's in China. Many of the stories sound the same. Someone is kidnapped by the police and locked up without access to family or legal counsel. It's a backwards justice system made worse by the fact that officers don't want any *mafan* (trouble) so they are eager to pass detainees on to the next step to be someone else's problem.

Thanks to a very good friend of mine who lives in Hong Kong, Dawu's name is on prayer lists. Maxine and I met in Beijing in the early 2000s when we were English examiners at the British Council. We had a lot of fun together and meet up on occasions in Hong Kong after she moved there to teach English. Maxine has told her church what's happening to my husband. The Anglican ministers at the St John's Cathedral, including Andrew Chan, have added Dawu along with Hannah and me to the Prayer Requests section of the church's weekly program. The ministers have tried to get permission for detention visits by Beijing Anglican leaders but unfortunately, the centre won't let anyone see or contact Dawu.

My letter-writing campaign is ongoing. Each message is in the same format: I introduce myself, explain Dawu's situation and then ask for immediate action to have him released. I finish off the letter by saying that the international media and China observers are watching the Chinese government closely concerning Wu Yuren. Not to mention, our five-year-old daughter is wondering when she will be able to see her daddy again. Fingers crossed this plea moves someone in high authority to do something worthwhile. It's a long shot.

I've hand-delivered around 15 letters to government officials and I'm not receiving any responses. It's disheartening but as I've said, expected. Li Fangping has advised me against sending letters to any government department or agency based in, or related to, Chaoyang. He thinks it's a waste of effort as they'll be least likely to cooperate.

My liaison at the Canadian Embassy, Victoria, has arranged a meeting with the ambassador for me. I'm introduced to David Mulroney on Friday, July 30 and he instantly puts me at ease with his graciousness and friendly demeanour. I run my fingers through my hair, suddenly regretting my decision to forgo make-up and a nice outfit. Oh well, too late now.

Our talk at the embassy is informal and Victoria terms it "officially unofficial." It is not a public affair. Over tea, David and I discuss the lead-up to Dawu's beating and his illegal detention. I weave his art and activism into the conversation. The ambassador and I talk about human rights and freedom of expression in China and move on to what he can do for my husband.

David says the letters from my supporters to Canadian federal representatives have ended up on his desk. Family and friends have been writing and emailing Canadian Prime Minister Stephen Harper about Dawu. The PM's office is "acknowledging receipt" of the letters and writes:

"Please be assured that your comments have been carefully reviewed. I have taken the liberty of forwarding your message to the Honourable Lawrence Cannon, Minister of Foreign Affairs, for his information and consideration."

The letters have been sent on to David and it's the big reason he noticed the issue in the first place and decided to act. He admits Dawu's situation is an unusual affair and that makes it compelling in various ways. David offers to take my letter to the Chinese Ministry of Foreign Affairs in Beijing. It could spur China to acknowledge the situation and offer a reason as to why Dawu is behind bars.

At the end of our lovely tea, David gives me the phone number to his direct line and says he'll plan to have Victoria attend Dawu's hearings … if China will let the Canadian Embassy through the door. I really do feel that Canada is listening to me. With China, I'm screaming into an abyss.

I thank David for his time and we agree to keep in touch. I'm sent home with a box of delicious mini fruit and chocolate tarts that were served with the tea. Hannah will love the treats.

A couple of days later, Victoria emails me with an important update. Finally, on Monday, Aug. 2, I know why Dawu was arrested. Someone at the Chinese Ministry of Foreign Affairs had called Victoria and explained Dawu's situation. She was told that on May 31, 2010, after a dispute with the 798 management company, Dawu and Tang Funai retaliated by spray painting abusive language on the walls of the management company as well as on the walls of the small police detachment on site at 798. Of course, local police from the Chaoyang District's Jiuxianqiao Station went to investigate, but Dawu and Tang would not cooperate with them and insulted, threatened and bullied the officers.

Dawu cursed, pulled and grabbed at an officer videotaping the scene for evidence. As a result, Dawu inflicted an injury to the right hand of the cop. Because of this, under clause 277 of China's criminal law, the local public security bureau made a criminal detention of Dawu, who was suspected of the crime of endangering public affairs. A request to arrest him was made on Friday, June 25. A week later, on Friday, July 2, the Beijing municipality Chaoyang District Procuratorate approved the arrest.

The Canadian government has managed an official breakthrough for me. At last, I have a formal response from the Chinese authorities, even if it's all BS. It's not true. The cop hurt his finger while attacking Dawu, not the other way around. The police are switching up the details and turning the blame back on to Dawu. By this point in my dealings with the Chinese government, I know it protects its own. The justice system is rigged.

The next Monday, Aug. 6, Li Fangping has another visit with Dawu. Wen Tao and I also are at the detention centre but there are no cameras or detention groupies accompanying us as we escort the lawyer into the jail. We pass a lineup of family and friends waiting outside the high metal gates of the centre. Every time the fence slowly rolls open to let a vehicle in or out, people peer into the courtyard, hoping for a glimpse of their loved one. However, all they usually see are walls. The detainees are never near the exit. For some people, though, this is enough. It's better than nothing at all.

To me, this speaks volumes of how little information is given to families. We're grasping at anything, since we've been told nothing. I'm not the only wife left in limbo. We are dealing with a state that despises human rights. Dawu is proof of that.

During my debrief with Li Fangping, I find out that my husband's arm remains injured and untreated. Li Fangping says Dawu told him that the inmates are required to sit on a bench for five or more hours a day with their backs straight. They're not to move a muscle.

"Why are they being forced to do that?" I ask.

"Control," says the lawyer.

As well, Dawu has been moved from Room 107 to Room 411. Apparently, this signifies that his case has moved to the prosecution stage. (Numbers beginning with 7, 8 or 9 mean that the case is in the court/trial stage.) This brings him closer to trial.

Daily, Dawu is asked to confess to assaulting the officer. My husband is being told that if he owns up to what he did, his sentence will be lighter. Li Fangping says that's a common tactic used by the authorities to trick detainees into a confession. Dawu refuses to say he's guilty of anything they throw at him.

While in detention, Dawu is imagining the type of life he wants to build after he gets out. He is well aware that 90 per cent of cases like his will receive some sort of time in prison. He says if he has MORE than six months left to serve, he will leave China after being released. If he serves LESS than six months, he'll consider remaining in China.

He has a list of questions for me, beginning with the personal art project that I was building for Canada. He's wondering if the initiative is still in the works. It is not. John Franklin called me one recent warm and dry August morning. I was at my studio when he gave me the sad news. He couldn't proceed with my contemporary and avant-garde project because China had pulled out of his project. At least I don't have to worry about whether Dawu will be participating. Nobody is.

Dawu has told the lawyer that he wants me to say thanks to Chao Hongling, Gu Duanfan and other artists for their support and assistance. Dawu also wants to know how his father and sister are doing. I feel guilty that I forgot to tell the lawyer to pass on to Dawu that his sister knows about his situation. In other family matter, Dawu asks that Zhang give me money for Hannah.

Hannah is curious about the Chaoyang District Detention Center. She wants to visit the place where her father is living. On the evening of Monday, Aug. 9, I think it's time to show her. Hannah is happy and content after a fun playdate with a friend who lives not far from the jail. I drive my daughter to the centre and park out front. We get out of the car and walk by the dull grey administration office. Behind it and a six-metre tall barbed wire fence, is a two-storey yellow cement building. I assume this is where Dawu is spending most of his time. The tiny windows in the block are lit up and Dawu must behind one of them. I've heard that the lights never go out. They burn 24 hours a day.

Hannah is excited to see where her dad has been staying but she's confused about why we can't go into his home.

"I just want to see him for a couple of minutes," she says.

I give her my standard answer.

"Mom is working hard so we can see your daddy soon."

We pass by some guards and I say hello. The officers tell me that they know Hannah is Dawu's daughter, they can see the resemblance. They think she's a cute little girl.

"We'll tell Wu Yuren that his family was here," says one of the men.

I take some photos of Hannah in front of the jail's high fence. She waves at the guard in a tower, but of course, he doesn't return the little girl's gesture. My reaction to seeing my daughter here brings up many emotions. Anger, frustration, resentment, sympathy, pity, embarrassment, disappointment, sorrow, sadness – they all combine in the pit of my stomach, fermenting into a poison. Most days, I'm good at keeping the venomous froth down.

People are constantly telling me that I'm being so strong. But what would it be like to actually NOT be strong? Say, to fall apart? I'm not sure what that would be like because I have always been "strong."

I've run my own businesses in China, gave birth to and am now raising my daughter without the help of my family – all these things culminate in being able to shoulder the world. But being strong is tiring. I would like someone to be strong for ME. Maybe this is just what being a woman is all about. Women are the pillars holding up the family when everything is crashing down around them. My mother is the pillar of my family. My sister and I have learned from her to be the pillars of our own families. We will not let our families be crushed.

Later in the month, Hannah and I both go to the Chaoyang District Detention Center to see about applying to see Dawu. I'm told by the guards that since my husband's case has officially moved to the prosecution stage, a family visit is out of the question.

"Can you show me the exact law where it says me and my daughter are not allowed to see Dawu?" I ask.

The officer's reply is nervous giggles.

I've been compiling papers, articles and anything that will help me make sense of the Chinese justice system since this ordeal started. I take out my book of collected legal documents and show them to the officer.

"I've seen something different," I say, pointing to a line of text. "Here it clearly states the opposite of what you're trying to get me to believe."

The guard has backup, though. Another detainee's lawyer has been patiently waiting behind me and tells me I'm wrong.

"You will NEVER be able to visit someone inside," he says. "Forget about it."

Oh, OK. I guess my version of the law is out of date. Whatever. Just another day of frustration. I take Hannah by the hand and we leave. I fight to keep my tears from spilling over and onto my daughter.

More disappointment is in store for my family. I have to take Hannah out of Daystar Academy. Dawu's legal fees combined with him being out of work and me having to step back from the Beijing Color Studio, has left the prestigious school out of reach at the moment. The school has agreed to refund Hannah's fall tuition. The administration usually does not return payments but it understands the predicament I'm in.

I've enrolled Hannah in Grade 1 at the Ritan School, where she'll start in a few weeks. The school isn't far from our home and it has an international section. It's cheaper, too, at only ¥8,000 RMB (CAD 1,300) each semester.

Ritan is the best I can do until I know more about what's happening with her baba. I had to reveal Dawu's situation to the administration, as I had to give them Qi Mei's name as one of Hannah's guardians. Since Hannah is registered as a Chinese student under a Chinese passport, the school needs a Chinese parent on the paperwork. Since Dawu can't sign anything from detention, I've asked Qi Mei for the favour. Thankfully, Hannah's former ayi is fine with it and we go to a notary office to make the guardianship official.

I'm told by Victoria that I've made a terrible mistake with that move. The Chinese state could take Hannah from me at any moment. I fix the error as soon as I can.

I'm trying to make up for the fact that I have to send Hannah to a less-esteemed school by planning a spectacular sixth birthday party for her. I have secured a cooking class for her and her friends at the Hilton Hotel. The children will be dressed in white chef hats and coats and will be cooking different items. The day is close to the Mid-Autumn Festival, a traditional holiday in China associated with the harvest and the full moon. This is when families gather to look at the moon as well as eat moon cakes – round cakes with a sweet filling. It's my favourite time of year, especially in Beijing, because the weather is often perfect (not too warm, not too cold) and the leaves are turning golden yellow and ruby red. However, a couple of days before Hannah's party, the cops decide to visit me, dimming my slightly brightened mood.

On Tuesday, Aug. 24, the police come to my home. Even though it's a polite visit, I'm glad Hannah is at school. I know the officers are at my door because I can see them when they buzz my apartment. The Cappuccino Complex is set up with a video camera at the front entrance of the building. I let the cops in and they poke around my home and ask me a few questions – nothing aggressive. After about 15 minutes, they leave.

The police hadn't been threatening but their visit scares the crap out of me. I don't know what they wanted and I forgot to ask if they had a search warrant. Perhaps they simply wanted to confirm that I still lived here. I don't know.

Victoria has some news for me. I meet her at the Starbucks not far from the embassy. It's our weekly update and catch-up meeting. She mentions that Lawrence Cannon, the Canadian foreign affairs minister, is coming to China in October, soon after an important Canada-China conference on Oct. 13. Oct. 13, 2010, is a milestone for the two countries: it's the 40th anniversary of Canada and China establishing formal diplomatic relations. It's sort of a big deal. The relationship began in the 19th century when Canadian missionaries worked with local communities in China to build schools and medical clinics. The anniversary is an opportunity for Canada to remind the PRC of the importance of maintaining a good rapport.

Victoria and/or the ambassador, David Mulroney, will ask the minister to raise Dawu's case with his Beijing counterpart. It's a good idea and Minister Cannon should have already received letters from me and my supporters explaining Dawu's detention. Victoria adds that three other ministers are visiting China in the next few weeks. Any political figure from Canada that has access to political figures in China is worth contacting, so I'll send letters to the industry, transport and health ministers. The embassy will also inform them about Dawu on my behalf.

I'm energized by the news and I post about Cannon's upcoming visit to China on Twitter. It's not long after my tweet that I get a call from Victoria. As soon as I hear the fire in her voice, I know she's angry.

"ANY and ALL contact with the embassy is to be confidential," she says. "It should definitely NOT be on social media."

I've broken our agreement. I'm so, so, so sorry I reneged on my promise to keep my dealings with the embassy off the record. It wasn't something I had done on purpose. I was excited and not thinking about the repercussions, only about the future. I feel horrible that I didn't keep my word. I immediately delete the post. Fuck. I need to slow down. Focus.

At least a children's birthday party isn't wrought with (much) drama. It's sad that Dawu can't be here but I know he'll be thinking about his daughter. Being Hannah's mother for the past six years has been glorious and she's such a great kid. The cooking party is a hit with my daughter and her eight friends and they all had so much fun. Hopefully, this is what Hannah will remember in the years to come instead of the bad stuff.

A non-profit organization that helps at-risk detainees in China is taking an interest in Dawu. The Dui Hua Foundation is based in the U.S. and its executive director, John Kamm, has asked to be kept up to date on Dawu's nightmare. John also highly respects Li Fangping.

Lawyer Li has been, and continues to be, a solid source of support for me. He sends me emails under a pseudonym and one message outlines the law according to the United Nations' Standard Minimum Rules for the Treatment of Prisoners. Wen Tao translates the resolution in Mandarin for me so I can add it to my letter directed to Chinese government officials.

92. An untried prisoner shall be allowed to inform immediately his family of his detention and shall be given all reasonable facilities for communicating with his family and friends and for receiving visits from them, subject only to restrictions and supervision as are necessary in the interests of the administration of justice and of the security and good order of the institution.

Standard Minimum Rules for the Treatment of Prisoners

Adopted by the First United Nations Congress on the Prevention of Crime and the Treatment of Offenders, held at Geneva in 1955, and approved by the Economic and Social Council by its resolutions 663 C (XXIV) of 31 July 1957 and 2076 (LXII) of 13 May 1977 Page 13

According to the words above, China is not upholding the law in its treatment of Dawu. However, there are some people who agree with what China is doing to him. On Sunday, Sept. 5, I'm at the Sino Swiss Hotel for a swim along with Hannah, Jenny and Emma. The hotel has one of the nicest pools in the city and best of all, you don't have to be a hotel guest to use it. You can pay the entrance fee and swim all day long and buy beer and snacks poolside. I've been coming here every summer while I've been living in Beijing and it's a joy.

Hannah and Jenny are happily splashing in the water when an acquaintance strolls over to me. The woman is German and married to a Chinese artist who knows Dawu well. I think the woman is going to say hello but she launches into a rant about Dawu and how she agrees with the authorities' decision to put him in jail and that Dawu must have been stupid to do what he did back in the spring.

"By marching on Chang'an Avenue he was only making his own problems," says the woman.

"Why was he wasting his time looking for compensation?" she asks, rhetorically of course. "He should have just moved out of the compound and moved on."

I'm shocked. I wasn't expecting this response. I'm sure my mouth is gaping wide open as the expat — and ex-friend — goes on to say that her husband was once in trouble but he was smart and learned his lesson. "He will never dare to speak out against the government again," she says.

I try to explain that Dawu didn't plan to end up behind bars but the woman won't hear anything except that Dawu's an imbecile. I'm hurt and angry at her words. How is it that she doesn't have a modicum of sympathy for me or at least Hannah, who is swimming nearby? I leave the hotel pool with waves of outrage crashing in my head.

One of my concerned friends and a client, Liora Mandel, asks if I'd like SCIO (Scientific Consciousness Interface Operations System) therapy done on Dawu. SCIO is basically energy readings done via a biofeedback device.

Liora's friend, Allison, can do it remotely. She's like a medium and doesn't need to connect with Dawu face-to-face.

"Might as well try it," I say, and give Allison permission to read Dawu. Allison sends me the results afterwards. The findings report that Dawu has recent face, head, neck and upper body trauma. He also tested high for radio-active substances. Emotionally, he seems stable but he did test high in "guilt" and "reflection." I take this to mean Dawu's upset about causing his family grief and is thinking about what he has done or should have done.

In terms of therapy, Allison focused her technological healing on mending Dawu's nerves, tissues and bones of his upper body. She set the biofeedback device to run all night on a program to give Dawu spinal pain relief. I hope it works and takes away some of his suffering.

I've been talking to my counsellor, Dana, a few times. She encourages me to play my favourite music, eat right, exercise and meditate. As well, I've been doing yoga, seeing my friends and managing to keep a hand on my studio business. I'm doing everything to try and stay grounded. Nevertheless, at the end of the day, everything remains up in the air.

I haven't forgotten about Zhang Wei. He's the artist who made trouble for Dawu and accused him of taking the lion's share of the 008 and Zhengyang collectives' compensation. It was Zhang Wei who barged into Dawu's studio in March and pretty much caused Dawu's dad to have a stroke and end up in hospital. It was also Zhang Wei who tried to sue Dawu for the settlement money. I've been keeping this Zhang Wei clown on my radar and if I'm ever in the same room as him, I'll let him have it. Well, it looks like I'm going to get my chance.

The UCCA Center for Contemporary Art (UCCA) is holding an exhibition and the opening is tonight, Sunday, Sept. 25. Guess who is showing his work at the institution? Zhang Wei. I spot his name on the list of exhibitors.

I know there are a few Zhang Weis in the art community, so I call around to confirm that this Zhang Wei is indeed THE Zhang Wei, who was spreading terrible lies about Dawu. Ma Ling says she's certain that the UCCA exhibitor is one and the same, as do some other artist friends of mine.

This will be interesting.

There are many people at the UCCA this afternoon. It's a huge space and filled with interesting works from some of China's best artists. I think I'll be able to find Zhang Wei easily. I've seen him before and I know he's bald and in his late forties, about five years older than me. I'm going to teach this prick a lesson or two. Fuck you for trying to sue Dawu, who is behind bars and never took any of your money.

I tour the center and find Dawu's nemesis' work. Then, I find Zhang Wei. He's talking to a group of artists.

"Perfect," I think to myself. "I'll have witnesses."

Zhang Wei sounds smug and I'm annoyed that he's here with his art while Dawu's rotting in a cell. When I hear a convenient break in his conversation, I make my move.

"Zhang Wei," I say to him.

He turns towards me, eyebrows raised as if expecting a question. Oh yes, he's going to get a doozy of a question.

"Hey, Zhang Wei, do you know who I am?" I say in Mandarin. "I am Wu Yuren's wife and he is presently behind bars. I can't believe you were going to sue him."

Zhang Wei's face morphs into one of shock. His eyes open wide and so does his mouth. He stands there looking at me as if I'm a ghost. Good. I've scared him.

"Oh, wow," says Zhang Wei. "I had heard about Wu Yuren. I have the utmost regard for him and I feel sorry for him and you but what are you talking about me suing him?"

"Don't you dare deny it," I say, almost choking on my anger. "You attacked my husband last March and it caused a lot of pain and suffering. Dawu would never take more money than what he was owed."

Zhang Wei is now shifting from side-to-side and hasn't lost the surprised expression. He's uncomfortable and embarrassed as an audience is gathering around us.

"I didn't attack Wu Yuren," he says. "I have no idea what you are talking about."

"Yes you do, liar! I can confirm you're the man who was at Dawu's studio. I have your phone number. I've talked to you before. But hey, if you're not the guy, then your phone isn't going to ring when I call you."

I start searching for Zhang's number in my cell's contact list and the artist takes the pause to address the crowd.

"I don't know what is going on here," he says. "Look, Wu Yuren's wife is accusing me of something I didn't do. I have no idea what she is getting at."

I finally find the number I'm looking for and press "dial." I have Zhang Wei's ass now!

Silence.

Followed by more silence.

And more silence.

I check my phone to make sure the call hasn't been disconnected. No, it's ringing…somewhere.

"Hello?" says a man on the other end of the phone.

I quickly hang up before everything in my body turns to rock. I can't move. I'm so mortified I've transformed into a statue.

"There you go!" bellows Zhang Wei. "It wasn't me. Don't you know that there are many Zhang Wei's in the art scene?"

His voice shatters the stone that I've been cast in. I'm horrified and embarrassed and so is everyone around me. Some folks look away while others laugh and snicker. If I could transform myself into a fly and fly away, I would.

I have clearly fucked up and have the wrong guy. The wrong Zhang Wei. I mumble an apology.

Before I walk away, humiliated, Zhang Wei tells me he cares about Dawu.

"I wish you luck in getting Wu Yuren out of prison," he says.

I fucking hate my life. I make a beeline for the door and exit out of the UCCA Center and into my car. I need to go home. I'm overwhelmed and not thinking straight. I thought I had the whole detention thing handled but the past few minutes are a real indication that I'm in over my head.

The next day I sit down with Dana and tell her what had happened with Zhang Wei. She says that mistakes are made in the heat of being overwhelmed. She offers kind words and a hug.

Later that evening, I attend my Beijing TaiTais Book Club. We're at a friend's house in Shunyi. Our host has many lovely antiques, art and little things that distract me from having to focus on the horrible parts of my life right now. The ladies ask me about the developments in Dawu's case and I tell them everything ... except for the Zhang Wei incident. That's way too shameful.

My book club buddies are always supportive but I think they're also curious to know how I managed to marry a man who ended up in jail. Many of the women in the group married husbands whom I would call "normal." You know, men who have good careers, are solid financial providers for the family, good fathers who would NEVER get themselves into the situation that Dawu is in. I, too, often wonder how I got here. What did I see in Dawu when I married him? He was fun and a good guy but what else was there? He definitely wasn't a provider economically. He kept weird hours. His values were radically different from most other Chinese people. Why did I marry him?

***

Around 6 p.m. on Monday, Sept. 27, I get a call from an agent with the *Gonganju*, the Public Security Bureau (PSB). The PSB deals with a wide range of things in China, including expats. The bureau is involved in visa processing, documentation and registering foreigners. The PSB isn't the secret police but they do share intel. The agent on the phone says the bureau wants to "have a chat about your husband's situation." I'm wary about the appointment as the man insists that I come alone. Good thing the meeting location is not in a back alley or some teashop, I might not be here tomorrow. However, we're meeting at the bureau in the Chaoyang District.

No one wants a meeting with the PSB. What if I get kicked out of China? At any rate, despite being told to come solo, Lawyer Li is going to accompany me to the office.

At the bureau, Li Fangping is told to wait outside. Inside, I have seven male uniformed agents and an interpreter all to myself. I think they're trying to intimidate me but I'm calm and cool. They've asked me here so the PSB could respond to the six letters that I've sent to city officials. What I hear next throws me for a loop.

As far as I know officially, Dawu had been jailed because of the spray painting at the 798 district that devolved into a fight with police outside the Jiuxianqiao Police Station. The PSB, though, say something altogether different. According to these men, Dawu is being charged with obstructing public security because of three incidents that took place INSIDE the Jiuxianqiao Police Station on the evening of May 31. His charge is NOT related to any of his actions at the 798 Art District.

The agents state that they have strong evidence to support that Dawu verbally threatened a police officer inside the Jiuxianqiao detachment. The men also say that Dawu beat a cop and, while my husband was pummelling the officer, Dawu rudely snatched another officer's video camera away while he was filming the scene. The PSB is categorically denying it was Dawu who was assaulted by an officer.

I'm not going to react to the lies. There's nothing I can do to change the "evidence" today but I will bring up some pointed questions. When I ask the agents if Dawu could be seen by medical staff, they say he's already been treated. The police have a record of an emergency doctor doing an examination on Dawu once he was transferred to the detention centre. The physician didn't observe any injuries and since Dawu didn't mention to the doctor that he had been beaten, then there was no beating.

Hmm, strange logic.

"Can I see that examination report?" I ask.

"Not until the trial," an agent says.

As well, apparently, Dawu has signed many documents that state that he wasn't assaulted by police and that he agrees with everything the cops are reporting about his arrest.

"Can I see those signed documents?" I ask.

"Not until the trial," an agent says.

"Can I see the video of Dawu grabbing the camera?" I ask.

"Not until the trial," an agent says.

"OK, boys, so when is the trial?" I ask.

"Sorry, we don't know. You'll have to get your lawyer to ask at the investigation bureau. We do not have the authority to tell you."

Of course you don't.

What a farce. Although from this chat I do understand why Tang Funai only received 10 days in civil detention and then was released – because he wasn't assaulted. Dawu had been hurt and it's proof of an altercation.

***

In early October, I receive an email from Corinna-Barbara Francis of Amnesty International with the title *"URGENT ACTION CHINESE ARTIST BEATEN BY POLICE."* Amnesty International is a human rights-focused NGO based in the U.K., and it's asking for urgent action on behalf of Dawu. The organization is calling on the Chinese authorities "to immediately initiate an investigation into allegations that Wu Yuren was beaten in detention." (Oct. 1, 2010) The global movement wants supporters to write to the Chinese government to ensure Dawu isn't being tortured and has access to his family, lawyers and medical attention.

It's thanks to my very first close friend in Beijing, Patti Wang, that Amnesty is on board. Her friend, Sammy Liang, works for the NGO in Hong Kong and Patti contacted him about Dawu. Another acquaintance has contacted me about Dawu. I met Shannon Van Sant, a documentary filmmaker, at the hutong destruction fundraiser. Shannon is wondering if there's any footage or photos of Dawu's February march on Chang'an Avenue.

Shannon is making a documentary about artists, including Ai Weiwei and the Gao Brothers, who have had their studios demolished. She wants to include Dawu's story in the doc and asks if she can film me going to court. I think it's a good idea but I'm not sure when the trial will take place. I tell her I'll let her know when I have a date.

In my home country, 40 years of Canada-China diplomatic relations are marked by a national conference in Ottawa from Oct. 13 to 14, 2010. Lawrence Cannon, the Canadian foreign affairs minister, is in Beijing soon after, on Friday, Oct. 22. Minister Cannon meets with his counterpart in Beijing, Yang Jiechi, the Chinese foreign minister. The Canadian politician talks about Dawu, as well as Liu Xiaobo and others who are detained in China.

Victoria tells me that the Canadian minister raised the issue of Dawu during a walk with Yang Jiechi through one of the gardens at the Canadian Embassy. She says that while the pair was strolling on the grounds and had reached a cherry blossom tree, Minister Cannon brought up Dawu.

"How do you know this?" I ask.

"On these high-level visits and talks, items to be raised are carefully scheduled," says Victoria.

Canadian Citizenship, Immigration and Multiculturalism Minister Jason Kenney had passed through Beijing on official business in September.

Before the minister's visit, another Canadian politician had suggested I seek out Kenney.

Bob Rae, the Liberal Party of Canada foreign affairs critic, had heard about Dawu through friends of mine living in Ontario. However, Victoria warned against Kenney saying anything about my husband to anyone in China. She suggested that some people in the Chinese government didn't like Kenney and so wouldn't listen to him, as they didn't respect him.

Meanwhile, in Canada, Lan Lijun, the ambassador of the People's Republic of China to Canada, isn't responding to interview requests from Canadian national media about Dawu. A Chinese embassy staffer states that it's understood that Dawu abused and attacked a policeman during an investigation.

"We wish the public could understand that China is a country under the rule of law. Our judicial system will deal with this case in the light of the law." Wednesday, Oct. 20, 2010.

The Beijing Color Studio is zipping along, despite the fact that I'm running on full cylinders elsewhere. Jane is doing a great job keeping the studio afloat. At least I don't have to worry about my business. Alas, I have to worry about staying in the country.

I have to find Dawu's shenfenzheng, his personal identification card, and extend his zanzhuzheng, his temporary residence permit to stay in Beijing. Otherwise, he won't be allowed to live in the city when he leaves detention. The zanzhuzheng is a document that gives him resident status in Beijing and it runs out on Dec. 30, 2010. My visa is connected to Dawu's zanzhuzheng and so without his extension, I'm not allowed to be a resident of China, despite being legally married to him since 2003.

I have no idea where the shenfenzheng is. Perhaps Zhang will know? I'll ask the studio assistant the next time he phones. Zhang, along with Hong and Lao Ai, call and text me regularly for updates. Lao Ai is on Twitter and I follow him. My team has coalesced over the past few weeks and we work well together. There will always be bickering but we're not constantly at odds.

While at the detention centre dropping off Dawu's monthly inmate allowance (about ¥1,000 RMB or CAD 160), I met someone who has just, as of this morning, shared a cell with Dawu. The former inmate heard me give my name to a clerk and asked if I was Wu Yuren's wife.

"Yes," I say.

"I've just spent the past three weeks with your husband," says the man. "I was released today and I'm picking up my remaining allowance. Wu Yuren talks about you and your daughter all the time."

I'm floored and then regain my composure. It's an opportunity to learn what is REALLY up with Dawu on the inside.

Mr. Cao, Dawu's former cellmate, says my husband has been spending much of his time drawing. While the detainees are sitting quietly on the wooden bench for five hours a day, Dawu imagines what he's going to sketch. Later, he puts his thoughts on paper since he's managed to convince a guard to supply him with the necessary artist's tools.

Dawu has done fine portraits of all his cellmates and the guards. I'm glad to hear he's using his brain, time and talents and not wasting away. In fact, he hadn't been actually drawing much in the past eight years so it's good he's getting back into it. He's very talented.

Mr. Cao also tells me that there is a detention centre inmate pecking order – Dawu is at the top. The hierarchy is a way of distinguishing who is who and who does what in terms of housekeeping in order to keep the peace. The former inmate has good memories of cleaning the floor with Dawu. They were on their hands and knees, wiping the cement floor when Dawu said the back and forth motion was like painting a big canvas. Mr. Cao laughs at the recollection and says Dawu was really fun to be with. He adds that Dawu misses Hannah terribly.

Dawu has a good relationship with all the guards and other staff and I'm not surprised. Dawu makes friends quickly. I am surprised when I find out that Dawu is no longer the lean man I knew before he went into detention. Mr. Cao laughs when I ask if my husband is still skinny.

"He's fat!" says Mr. Cao. "We get three meals a day and no exercise so we all have big bellies."

The former inmate doesn't remember if Dawu's arm hurts but they've only known each other for about a month. My husband's health seems to be fine, but everyone in the centre has some kind of nasty skin rash. That's communal living for you and not having the ability to wash yourself, clothing and sheets regularly.

I had thought that being behind bars would curtail Dawu's smoking habit but it sounds like that's not going to happen. He used to smoke one to one and a half packs of cigarettes a day. In prison, he's puffing away two packs a day. Inmates can't buy their own smokes; they're "acquired," so Dawu must have a dependable cigarette source inside.

Mr. Cao says Dawu knows about Liu Xiaobo's honour and is pleased. A couple of weeks ago, on Wednesday, Oct. 8, the creator of the 08 Charter was awarded the Nobel Peace Prize for what the Nobel Committee called "his long and non-violent struggle for fundamental human rights in China." Mr. Cao says Dawu read about the prize through a Chinese newspaper approved for the centre. No doubt, the pro-Chinese Communist Party media had a different perspective from Dawu's, as China is fiercely opposed to Liu Xiaobo and what he stands for: political reform.

For Dawu, Liu Xiaobo is an impetus of change. The prolific writer and academic in his mid-fifties lived through the horrors of the Cultural Revolution and the massacres of Tiananmen Square. Liu Xiaobo saw the need for change and wasn't afraid to ask the Chinese government for it.

For Dawu, signing the 08 Charter, Liu Xiaobo's petition calling for immediate government reforms in China, gave him a chance to participate in his country's political future. He had hoped the document would make a difference and the rights that many nations take for granted, such as freedom of speech, might be realized. Instead, the Chinese government used Liu Xiaobo as a warning to other critics. Chinese authorities arrested Liu Xiaobo and charged him with inciting subversion of state power. After a sham trial, Liu Xiaobo was sentenced to 11 years in prison and two years of deprivation of political rights. Dawu is making sure the Nobel Peace Prize winner is not being forgotten.

My husband is using his prison time to educate other inmates about Liu Xiaobo and the need for political reform in China. Mr. Cao says Dawu has a captive audience of impressionable young men who have nothing better to do than to listen and learn. In fact, Mr. Cao seems to be so impressed with Dawu that he's almost sad to have left the cell and the camaraderie they shared.

I'm happy I've heard all of this. It's a snapshot from the inside, something I have not been able to get. Before Mr. Cao heads out the detention door, I get his number in case I want more information. It is somewhat peculiar that Mr. Cao is alone on his release date. He does call his wife on my phone but no one answers. I ask if he wants a ride or needs bus fare but he claims he's fine.

When I share my Mr. Cao encounter with Chinese friends, they wonder if he was a plant, a government informant. I think back over our chat and dissect every comment and question. I come to the conclusion that Mr. Cao is genuine and who he says he is. For one, I don't visit the detention centre on a regular basis. Thus, I don't have a pattern so he couldn't have known when I was going to turn up at the jail. As well, Mr. Cao showed me his signed and stamped release papers and I saw him physically retrieve his cash from the clerk. Our meeting wasn't arranged.

A trial date is being arranged. On Tuesday, Nov. 2, Li Fangping and I are at the Chaoyang District Courthouse. (I used to live 40 metres away from here.) We're supposed to meet a Ms. Wang at 9:30 a.m. to talk pre-trial.

Ms. Wang is not to be found. When I phone her to ask where she is, she says she's at a different courthouse, Wenyuhe Criminal Courthouse, out in buttfuck nowhere. (It's actually around the corner from Dawu's first art studio at the 008 International Art Community. How ironic.)

Once at Wenyuhe, I'm not allowed to join the meetings. Only Lawyer Li and the judge can be in the room. The judge refuses to meet with foreigners and it's her prerogative to exclude me. I sit for over an hour in the waiting room beside the metal detector machine. Fun. Not.

Li Fangping emerges from the pre-trial discussions with a court date: Wednesday, Nov. 17, at 9:30 a.m. The case will be heard in this courthouse (as apparently many criminal cases are tried out in the boonies) and Dawu will be tried by a panel of judges. He's refusing to accept the charges against him and the lawyer says that's OK. Dawu's claim to be innocent has been consistent. Only one witness to the trial (as in trial watcher, not defence witness) will be allowed into the courtroom along with Li Fangping. That witness will be me since I'm Dawu's wife. However, because I'm a foreigner, I'll have to apply to the court for access.

Lawyer Li says I probably can't take an interpreter into the proceedings with me but I will ask. If they won't let me go in, then a friend, maybe Lao Ai or one of Dawu's family members, can go in my place. The court will be open and all Chinese are welcome. Dawu's supporters do need to bring their Chinese ID cards. Foreigners have to apply to be in the room.

Yet another "official" version of why Dawu is being charged with obstructing and attacking a police officer came out in the pretrial. Authorities said Dawu injured a cop by grabbing a video camera out of his hands. The officer's finger was hurt. There was no mention of Dawu beating anyone.

The injured officer is finally revealed and it's Xiu Dawen, the guy who was a jerk to me at the Jiuxianqiao detachment. He didn't look hurt when I saw him in July.

The lawyer will pass all this information on to Dawu tomorrow at the detention centre. Fingers crossed I get to attend his trial with an interpreter.

I feel like I've been living in my vehicle these past few months. I've been driving all around Beijing going from appointments and detention visits, to Hannah's playdates and school. I keep playing the same tunes and the songs have become my theme music. The following 20 songs are the soundtrack of my life at the moment.

1. *Crazy Train* - Ozzy Osbourne
2. *Free* - The Lighthouse Family
3. *Breaking the Law* - Judas Priest
4. *I Fought the Law* - The Clash
5. *This is It* - Michael Jackson
6. *Disarm* - The Smashing Pumpkins
7. *Folsom Prison Blues* - Johnny Cash
8. *Times They are a-Changing* - Bob Dylan
9. *Huck's Tune* - Bob Dylan
10. *Bad Reputation* - Joan Jett
11. *We are the Champions* - Queen
12. *Mother* - Pink Floyd
13. *Rebel without a Pause* - Public Enemy
14. *Subcity* - Tracy Chapman
15. *Hurricane* - Bob Dylan
16. *I Know it's Over* - The Smiths
17. *If I Should Fall From Grace with God* - The Pogues
18. *Sunny Side of the Street* - The Pogues
19. *Black Boys on Mopeds* - Sinead O'Connor
20. *Paranoid* - Ozzy Osbourne

I play my soundtrack many times during the lead-up to Dawu's trial. I have face-to-face discussions with Victoria and Ai Weiwei and the rest of my team. I visit Zhang to get the money needed for all the fees coming up. I have to pay the court, lawyers and application costs and so far, I've spent close to ¥15, 000 RMB (CAD 2,500). I apply to be at the trial, send press releases out to the media, meet with Canadian and international television and newspaper reporters. I also text all of Dawu's Chinese friends to ask them to be at his hearing.

Not everything is going as I've planned. Officials at the court dodge my calls and I have yet to hear if I can attend my husband's trial. Li Fangping can't get access to important evidence. He had been told by the district court that not only would he be able to view the video evidence against Dawu, he would also be able to make copies to have at the proceedings. However, after Lawyer Li received the electronic files, all but one were corrupted. The one that did open, only showed Dawu standing at the front gate of the Jiuxianqiao Police Station. Li Fangping hasn't been allowed access to the uncorrupted footage. I dearly hope it's not a harbinger of what's to come.

My close expat friends aren't going to be at Dawu's trial. When I let them know that they have to apply to attend court, they change their minds and decide not to come. They fear the authorities will remove them from the country if they are seen supporting Dawu. I'm taken aback and try to explain to them that if the authorities are going to grab anyone and chuck them out of China, it is going to be me — not friends of mine. Still, they won't be there. I am annoyed but move on.

Ai Weiwei says he'll be at Dawu's trial. Cases like my husband's are common all across China and Lao Ai is working on several documentaries showing the rampant human rights abuses around the country. Even though Ai is afforded some protection from the government, he's been a victim of police brutality too, and was beaten in 2009 after being an advocate for environmentalist, writer and activist Tan Zuoren. Tan was arrested for "subverting state power" in connection with the investigation into the deaths during the Sichuan earthquake. When Lao Ai attempted to testify at his friend's trial, the artist was roughed up so badly that he had to be flown to Munich, Germany to be treated for a cerebral hemorrhage.

Lao Ai and our team strategize on how to muster the media as well as arrange for camera operators to film the events outside of the courthouse on trial day. The documentary filmmaker, Shannon Van Sant, is coming to my home tomorrow morning to take footage of Hannah and me preparing for the proceedings. I'm not sure at this point if Hannah will be coming with me to the courthouse but I'll explain to her what's happening to her father.

Dawu's father is now fully aware his son is in jail. Suling told Wu Xiangshou about it. I'm glad Ba knows about Dawu and I'm glad I didn't have to tell him. I didn't want to be the one to break Ba's heart.

I get calls from Dawu's father and sister regularly. They're apprised of the upcoming trial. Xiangshou and Suling are far away in Jiangsu province and feel helpless. Ba offers to take Hannah while I'm sorting things out. I appreciate it and I'm grateful for the family support but I say no. I'm her mother and I'd like her to stay with me.

On the morning of Wednesday, Nov. 17, 2010, trial day, I have yet to receive word that I can attend the proceedings. Li Fangping texts me and says I'll probably have to sit it out. I do not react well to the news and let off a stream of harsh words in my head.

"FUCK! OFF! I hate this shitty country. I can't believe this. Go to hell all of you. My husband deserves my support. What the fuck are you scared of? URGH!!!"

I say these things silently because Shannon and her cameraman are at my home recording Hannah and I getting ready for court. Since 7:30 a.m., we've been filmed having breakfast and chatting about the upcoming day. It's weird being watched while I put on my make-up (this day requires I try and look my best) and do Hannah's hair, but Shannon wants the pre-trial footage to be real and not faked. She even films the ayi taking Hannah to school.

I decided that it's best for Hannah if she doesn't go to the courthouse. She doesn't completely understand what a trial is and so I don't think she should come along with me. Besides, I'm not allowed into the courtroom and it will be a long wait for me, let alone a six-year-old hoping to see her dad.

Legal clerks at the Wenyuhe Criminal Courthouse had told me the doors open at 9:30 a.m. sharp and not a minute sooner. I'm planning to get there half an hour early so I can speak to Dawu's supporters and the media outside before the trial. However, as Murphy's Law would have it, I get lost while driving to the courthouse.

I miss a turn because I'm talking to Shannon so I keep speeding down the highway, past where I need to be. My attention span is all over the place. It's not only because I'm nervous but because I'm also being interviewed. (Note to self: Karen, you cannot drive and talk about human rights at the same time!) When I finally get my vehicle headed in the right direction, I've lost 15 minutes. I'm going to be late.

A nervous Lawyer Li calls me on my cell while I'm driving.

"Where are you?" he asks hurriedly. "You're supposed to be in the courtroom."

China's letting me into the trial. Yay! But not with an interpreter. Boooo.

Arriving outside Wenyuhe at 9:29, I see a healthy throng of supporters: friends, artists, colleagues, journalists, camera operators, petitioners, detention groupies and common folk from the area. There must be at least 200 people who have showed up for Dawu. My heart swells. I recognize many of the faces in the crowd, including Honghong. I give him a quick hug and then I turn to the supporters, yell to everyone, "Let's hope for a fair trial!"

Uniformed cops have cordoned off the area. I'm late so I duck under the police tape, run the few metres to the courthouse at full speed and sprint up several steps into the jam-packed lobby.

I push my way through the crowd to a holding room used for security checks. I have to turn in my cell phone, car keys and handbag, which are all put in a locker. I'm given the key and told not to lose it. (The key or my mind?)

I'm trying to keep my heart out of my throat — or throat out of my heart, whichever it is — while being led up three flights of stairs to Courtroom #16. I'm overwhelmed with emotion and adrenalin and I've had no time to prepare for seeing Dawu for the first time since June 1, 2010, over four months ago. What's he going to look like, be like, act like?

Courtroom #16 is a basic, medium-sized room. It's not fancy and there's a huge People's Republic of China emblem on the wall, looming above the judges' heads. China's red and gold badge is found all over the country but today, the symbol comprised of wheat sheaves, stars and the outline of the famous Tiananmen Gate reminds me how much power the People's Republic of China holds over Dawu.

Underneath the emblem sits the presiding judge, judicial official, court secretary and another People's judge. The prosecution team (two men and one woman) sit on the left side of the judges. Li Fangping and his second chair, Lian Qilei, are on the right side, directly across from the opposing counsel. Dawu sits in a big black chair in the middle of it all. He isn't in shackles or handcuffs but the chair has a wooden lap bar to restrain him. As well, an enormous cop sits on Dawu's immediate right, ready to flatten my husband if he decides to respond physically to the proceedings.

Me? I sit almost directly behind Dawu, in the fourth seat of a five-seater bench. On my left is a cop and on my right are three young adults in their late teens or early 20s. They look out of place and I assume they're the children of the judges or the prosecution team. The young people are here to take up valuable courtroom real estate. Victoria is not here. Her request to attend the trial was denied.

I'm pleasantly surprised when Dawu looks over at me and smiles. He does not appear to be a defeated criminal. His bearing is proud and he gives off an air of confidence. He's dressed in standard-issue Chaoyang District Criminal Detention Center garb: a grey padded two-piece outfit. Underneath the prison clothing, he has on a black polo shirt with white buttons. On his feet is a pair of black taiqi shoes (black shoes made of cotton), the kind that every Chinese male retiree wears when he hangs out with friends or shadow boxes in the park. I had imagined Dawu with white hair, believing the stress of jail had aged him but there's no hair to see. It has been closely cropped. Dawu is clean-shaven and his face, like Mr. Cao had told me, is rounder than usual.

The court begins and Dawu's asked to give his testimony. I'm proud of the way he is conducting himself. He speaks politely and has considered what and how he would give his testament today. At one point, the lead judge asks Dawu to speak up.

"Your wife looks like she's straining to hear you," she says.

I am having trouble hearing Dawu. I've been shifting in my chair while trying to listen to my husband, who is facing the judge, not me. As well, I've learned many new words over the past few months but there are still some legal phrases in Mandarin that have me guessing at the context. The lead judge, a middle-aged woman, often glances at me during the trial. Her face stays blank and I can't read if she's sympathetic or sizing me up as a traitor's wife.

The three officers from the Jiuxianqiao Police Station are next to testify. Xiu Dawen, Yang Yue, and one other man are all witnesses of the prosecution. The cops don't look as powerful today since they're in civilian clothing. The officers are called to the front one at a time and take a seat on a soft padded chair within arm's reach of Dawu. Each cop tells his side of the story, which I know is mostly lies. I bet they've been rehearsing what they're going to say over and over again. One theme is central – Dawu attacked them.

The officers speak pragmatically. There's no edge to their voices or venom dripping off their words. Xiu Dawen holds up his finger to show it was hurt. The cops are cross-examined by both Li Fangping and Lian Qilei and the presiding judge and judicial official ask questions for clarity. Dawu is given the opportunity to respond to what he has just heard. He asks each of the three men a simple question,

"Did you hit me?"

They all blatantly lie in his face, in court, by denying they laid a finger on him.

Dawu handles the officers' testaments and responses with a kind of calmness and maturity that I can't really explain. I'm proud of him for keeping his cool and not being defensive.

Next up is our witness, Tang Funai. He's nervous — jumpy almost. I understand. The formality of court, along with the seriousness of the trial, is overwhelming. Plus, it was Tang who got Dawu into this mess.

Tang testifies to what happened on that May night and how he believes that Dawu must have been beaten. Tang says based on the screams and sounds he heard coming from Dawu in the cafeteria, he was being assaulted.

Tang is then cross-examined by the prosecution and asked questions by the judges. Dawu isn't allowed to talk to him.

All four witnesses are then taken outside of the courtroom to wait while the video evidence is shown. Lawyer Li had tried to get access to the "damning" footage but from what I see here, it's a joke. The recording simply shows a 2.5-minute segment of Dawu, Tang and Yang Yue, among others, arguing and moving around inside the police station. You can hear Dawu yelling out the cops' ID numbers and saying how they've taken his cellphone without a warrant. Dawu then asks someone not to move or touch him. My husband doesn't punch nor hit nor grab a camera. At one point during the earlier testimonies, the officers had all stated that Dawu had walked on his own accord into the corridor. But in the video, you can see a hand pushing his back, urging him forward into the hallway.

One witness is brought back into the courtroom. It's Xiu Dawen, who was the evening shift's duty officer at the Jiuxianqiao detachment on May 31. He's also one of the cops who beat Dawu. Xiu Dawen is shown the video and a judicial officer gets out of his chair and pauses it several times, asking Xiu Dawen to explain or confirm details.

The footage is flimsy and wouldn't hold up in almost any other court in the world. But this is China. Li Fangping certainly has trouble with the video. He thinks it's been tampered with and there are jump cuts (manipulation where the transition between two shots appears to "jump" in time or location). He asks the prosecution about it and one of the opposing side's lawyers says he isn't convinced it's been altered. However, Li Fangping argues that there are segments of footage missing from the beginning. The tape has been edited to show the clips of Dawu shouting and upset, not the parts where he was hit and verbally abused, the part that started it all.

Jeez. The trial hinges on this footage. It's supposed to be THE evidence that the authorities have on Dawu. There's nothing here to show that Dawu hurt an officer. There's also nothing here to vindicate my husband. What the video should do is expose this case as being shoddy from the start.

Every now and again, I catch words and cheers from the folks outside the courtroom. They're singing and chanting "WU YUREN!" It lifts my spirits inside the courtroom — and Dawu's too, I'm sure.

During the morning session break, I finally get a chance to see him. Dawu is waiting, under guard, for the trial to resume in a room down the hallway, by the washrooms. I pretend to need the toilet and walk past where he's being held.

"Hi," I say, popping my head into his room. "How are you?"

"I'm fine," says Dawu.

"That's enough!" says the guard.

At least I had that moment, brief as it was.

The trial reconvenes and I sit through a couple of hours of lawyers talking and witnesses lying. There's no sign of Dawu's X-ray taken in June at the detention centre but Xiu Dawen shows the court his "injured" finger. He holds up the bandaged appendage and tells the story of how Dawu punched him.

After the second recess, proceedings are winding down. The lead judge turns to Li Fangping and asks him what he wants.

"I want to see the original tape in its entirety," says Lawyer Li without missing a beat.

The judge looks at the prosecution team and asks them to consider his request. Then, four hours after the trial began, it's adjourned. A date for continuation hasn't been chosen yet but Li Fangping is told it'll be a least a week before court reconvenes. Dawu is the first to be whisked out of the courtroom by guards. I leave with Lawyer Li and when we exit the courthouse, I immediately raise my arms to supporters in a sign of victory. Dawu isn't free but he is most definitely innocent. I've believed it in my heart and his blamelessness has been made abundantly clear in court.

Outside, police are carrying large signs directing journalists to an area the cops have designated for interviews. Li Fangping and I walk a few metres together until we hit the cordoned-off area where we can visit with supporters and speak to media. During this walk, a walk that seemed to go on forever, Li and I have a chance to get our stories straight before we hit the crowd. We will talk about the video and show a united front on what has just transpired.

I hit the scrum to talk to reporters from the Associated Press, *South China Morning Post*, BBC, *New York Times*, National Public Radio (NPR) and members of the Canadian press: CTV (CTV Television Network), Global TV, *Globe and Mail* and many others. Of course, I see no journalists from Chinese or state-run media outlets.

I had been warned by political and media-savvy friends a couple of days ago to focus on the positives that came out of today's proceedings and not to badmouth the government. I tell reporters that the video recording was seriously edited and had jump cuts. I don't say anything against the judges or the prosecution team or the cops who testified against my husband. As I'm finishing my last interview, a prison van carrying Dawu pulls out from behind the courthouse.

Almost everyone around me starts chanting his name and cheering for him. I'm relieved to see Victoria outside the courthouse and she gives me a hug. Others who came today include Ai Weiwei, the Gao Brothers, Zhang, Hong and Gu Duanfan, among a sea of others. Social media is abuzz, too, with news about Dawu's trial.

Shannon and I go for lunch after I'm done with my media interviews. We talk about the video recording and other evidence that doesn't add up to Dawu being shut away for months. Seeing his friends, supporters and the foreign media outside the courthouse has put me in a great mood but it doesn't last. I'm feeling melancholy and blah now. There's more court to come and I'm wondering if I can sustain my energy into next week's proceedings.

I say goodbye to Shannon and get in my car and drive and drive and drive. I play my theme music while I decompress. I don't have a destination in mind. My vehicle is my safe place. I am all alone and don't have to interact with anyone. After a couple of hours of aimlessly wandering, I'm ready to go home.

Hannah wants to know what happened at the trial and I tell her what would make sense to a six-year-old. I explain that her baba was surrounded by many people and there were long hours of talking. I say her dad looks good and he even has a big belly. That makes her laugh.

I call Ba and Suling and tell them everything. Like me, they're incensed about the bogus video but happy to hear about the people chanting Dawu's name.

The following day, I meet with Lawyer Li for a debrief. It's just the two of us and he speaks plainly. He says court went well and he is glad the judge took the request for the original video recordings seriously. The footage introduced at court begins with Dawu shouting something like, "I will fight till the death." The lawyer would like to know WHAT provoked his client to utter such a sentence. However, Li Fangping is doubtful that he'll get to see the original videos.

Besides the tampered footage, Li Fangping highlights the fact that there were major differences between the testimonies of Dawu and the three police witnesses. The lawyer believes that the judge and prosecution both noticed these inconsistencies and that influenced the decision to adjourn the trial and schedule a second session for a later date.

When I ask Lawyer Li about how Dawu's trial was different compared to similar criminal trials in China, the lawyer says Dawu's hearing set a precedent.

"The police sent their own officers to appear in court as witnesses," he says. "That's highly unusual."

The lawyer tells me that a number of initiatives have pushed Dawu's case to the top level of importance. My continuing letter-writing campaigns addressed to the Canadian and Chinese governments, along with Amnesty International's letter-writing campaign, is focusing international media attention on Dawu. As well, the possibility that I, a foreigner, was attending the trial helped raise Dawu's profile. Most trials in China are off-limits to expats but because I'm Dawu's wife, I had a right to be there. I was getting to peek behind the curtain.

There's the odd mention on Twitter and Facebook from a few expats about Dawu having a retrial to take place sometime in the upcoming week. This is the first I've heard of a retrial. Li Fangping tells me that retrial is the wrong terminology. Since the video is an important piece of evidence and the defence found problems with it, court is adjourned until the original footage is located and he views it. Dawu is being tried by a panel of judges, not a jury, so proceedings will continue. There won't be a new trial.

The court will give Li Fangping three days notice in advance of the next session date. The trial will return to Wenyuhe. Lawyer Li says the case will probably end with Dawu serving some time, perhaps a year.

What? That goes against all reason! He's innocent.

"It has to be that way," explains Li Fangping, "otherwise, it'll be too much of a shock to the Chinese legal system to simply acquit Dawu or give him a gentle sentence. The judges won't be able to make such a reformed decision."

Ai Weiwei is interested in the video recordings, too. I catch up with the artist a few days later. He tells me he gave an explosive interview in English to several international outlets on Dawu and the situation of human rights abuses in China while the trial was taking place. The Chinese government doesn't give people proper access to the justice system and it angers and frustrates not only Lao Ai but many in Chinese society who see and experience the massive corruption and widespread injustice across the country.

Waiting for the trial to reconvene is tedious. I thought I was used to the "hurry up and wait" regime but it turns out I'm not. Almost two weeks have passed since Dawu's first court appearance and we don't have another date scheduled. Time is dragging on. I have a terrible migraine and I'm surprised that I haven't been having them every day since June.

Meanwhile, I'm keeping in contact with journalists, NGOs, Victoria and other advocates for Dawu. I'm also hoping to have a conversation with a high-profile reporter from Australia, Jason Gorman.

I've sent Gorman an email and a text about Dawu. The reporter eventually calls me towards the end of November.

"You've got 30 seconds to prove to me that you are worth my time to speak to you further regarding your husband," he shoots at me. "I have done many stories on human rights and yours is no different. Begin now."

I should tell him to fuck off but I don't in case he's a link to helping Dawu. I tell Gorman about Dawu's disappearance and detention but I guess I don't impress the reporter and we are done after about 45 seconds of me talking. I never hear from him again. What a dick.

Jerry Cohen, John Kamm and Eva Pils have done all that they can for me. They must get several requests a week for help, as there are thousands of cases like Dawu's across China. The regime violates human rights every day, from the repression of ethnic minorities, to controls on religious freedom, to illegal detention. The list goes on and dates back several decades. There hasn't ever been a proper investigation into the events of Tiananmen Square in 1989. As I'm well aware, anyone who dares speak up is shut up quickly and sometimes disappears, all under the guise of "the law."

While I'm attending the Western Academy of Beijing's yearly bazaar, friends and acquaintances are telling me to leave the country after Dawu gets out. It's something I've been thinking about for a while. I'm at the annual event to promote my Beijing Color Studio. The academy is a top (and expensive) international private school only open to expat passport holders. Several times throughout the year, the school hosts a sale and invites small businesses and entrepreneurs to sell their wares and services. I participate every year, with my first bazaar being under my NU2YU Baby Shop banner, followed by the Counting Sheep Boutique and now, my studio. I have a table where I talk about workshops and day camps. It's a good way to connect with past, present and future clients and to network and build connections in the expat community.

Jane comes with me and we explain to prospective customers what we do. I'd like to only talk shop but my personal life keeps interrupting. Some folks have heard about Dawu's trial and I receive many, many questions. Most people are sympathetic and suggest I leave China once Dawu is released. I've played with the idea of moving back to Canada a few times and yet, I remained in China.

On Monday, Nov. 29, 44 children are painting and having fun in my studio, which is great to see. The Beijing Color Studio was asked to do the workshop by Dini Lipskar. Dini runs the Ganeinu International School, a Jewish school. Dini and her husband Rabbi Shimon are well respected leaders in Beijing's Jewish community. Dini organizes an annual fundraiser and this year, the idea is to have the kids create artwork that'll be sold to bring in money for the new synagogue.

Jane and I are running the show and I'm pleased the event is going well. I'm also pleased that Dini says she'll put my family's name in for prayers. I'm glad I've met her and impressed with how much she does for the community. How she has time for anything and anyone else amazes me considering she has so much going on — and on top of it all, five kids!

During some much-needed downtime in my studio the next evening, I get a strange call on my personal mobile phone. No name or number pops up on the screen.

"Ping's lawyer needs to make contact with him inside the detention centre immediately," says a rough voice.

Ping is a nickname that only immediate family use for Dawu. When I press the man on the other end to explain what he's asking me to do, he quickly says he'll call me back in a few moments.

The phone rings again several minutes later. The man repeats his urgent message about Ping needing to see his lawyer ASAP. Again, the caller will not reveal his name nor location.

It's dark outside and I'm all alone in my studio. A horrible thought starts to creep its way into my mind. Could the caller be sitting in an unmarked police car outside and be waiting to grab me? Has my time come? Have I rocked the boat too much and now I'm going to be carted away? Fuck.

Trembling, I call Li Fangping. The lawyer is taken aback by my news but says I'll be fine. Dawu will be, too. Since it's almost 6 p.m., visiting hours at the detention centre are over. Rushing there would be a waste of time and energy. Lawyer Li says he'll arrange to visit Dawu soon. I just hope everything is OK.

I ask my conscience if I should go early tomorrow morning to check on my husband. My brain tells me no, that the caller's requesting Li Fangping and not someone who drops off money and socks for Dawu.

I didn't recognize the anonymous caller's voice but I did hear people talking loudly in the background, as if the man was in an office. Is the secret police or someone from the Chinese government screwing with my head? I'm frightened and feel like I'm back in the early days of Dawu's detention, when I didn't know who to trust.

The next evening, the caller phones me again. I think he's calling from a roadside payphone this time, because I hear the rattling of traffic in the background.

"Ah, do you remember me?" he asks. "I called you last night about something."

How could I forget?

"You must send Ping's lawyer to see him in the detention centre."

It's the same message. When I press for more details, the caller passes the buck.

"I'm just the middleman for someone on the inside," he says and hangs up.

I take it Li Fangping hasn't been to see Dawu. I call the lawyer right away and he says he was too busy to go to the centre. Hold on! What if this is an emergency? Why else would I get two calls in a row? I'm freaking out and again, I question if I should go to the centre. But someone could be setting a trap for me. If I leave now to see Dawu, I could be grabbed and shoved into the trunk of a vehicle. Never to be found. The idea of disappearing frightens me into staying put. I have a sleepless night, and in the morning, I receive a text message from Li Fangping. He has an appointment at the detention centre for Monday, Dec. 6 — a few days away. Perhaps now that he has confirmed a meeting with Dawu, the calls will stop.

I'd better get a move on and find Dawu's shenfenzheng and extend his zanzhuzheng so I can extend my own visa. Luckily, Zhang finds the ID card for me (it was among Dawu's personal items) but I have to apply for Dawu to get his zanzhuzheng extended or else I'll be kicked out of the country at the end of the month, the end of 2010.

While I'm at the district office applying for new permits, I have to play the "Dawu" game. The cop behind the desk recognizes me immediately.

"So, has he come back yet?" he asks.

"Who? You mean Wu Yuren? He's in Beijing and so busy that I thought I'd help him out by applying for his extension."

The man chuckles.

"Wu Yuren needs to apply in person. Where is he? I think he's at the criminal detention centre."

"Yes," I say, "but that does mean he's still living in Beijing and eligible for the extension."

The man smirks before pointing out the window to some apartments in the distance.

"Your husband is not living in one of those."

I then ask if there's a policy that bars inmates in detention centres from getting extensions. The officer says that he's not sure but there's no way HE is going to grant anything for Wu Yuren. When I push back, the man then agrees to call my local police bureau as it gives extensions and renewals on government-issued documents. Urgh. Some days, it's hard to complete even banal tasks in China.

While I'm driving to meet Emma at the Bookworm Café, I receive a third call from the anonymous man. He's polite but firm when asking why the lawyer hasn't seen Ping yet.

"Li Fangping will be there on Monday," I say. "By the way, how is Dawu doing?"

"I don't know those details," says the man. "I'm only the caller."

"If you can, would you let those on the inside know that there hasn't been another court date set?"

"Yes," says the man before getting off the phone.

I SEE YOU SEE ME

How I feel these days by Karen Patterson

Before
Not long ago
We saw each other
Laughing, chatting, bragging, connecting
A sense of normalcy

Then
You heard the news, read the story, felt the vine
Her life, a wreck
Like an upside-down cake
You are sorry for her, almost embarrassed

Now
We meet, perhaps on the street
I see you see me
Not sure what to say, not sure how to act
Awkward silences engulf us

I see you
I talk to you? I run from you, turn away?
But I want a hug, need to be held, tell me everything is ok
Don't get it, I hope you never do
But wait, it's me, not a freak

You see me
Turn, walk away, avoidance
Mouth opens, nothing comes out, gape
Silence through the eyes. contact
God, I don't envy her

Truly
It
Couldn't have happened
To a nicer
Person

But it did
I don't blame you
After all, It's his fault
He is the crime
Victim

Ruinous
Relationship changes
Marriage
Betwixt and Between
A chasm now exists

Child
Most important
Parental responsibility?
Tears, fears
Baba, I miss you.

61

It turns out the official room reserved for counsel at the detention centre is out of order. It's being renovated and so Li Fangping can't see Dawu on Monday, Dec. 6, 2010. What a fine time for the centre to spruce up its offices. The missed visit doesn't go unnoticed by my anonymous friend. He telephones that evening.

"The lawyer didn't visit," he says.

"We tried to see Dawu," I say. "It was impossible."

"Get the lawyer in to see Ping right away!"

Tomorrow, dude. Chill, and quit phoning me.

My fears about being taken by the secret police have somewhat subsided. I don't think the caller is from the government or guoan anymore because the more I think about it, the more I realize they don't need a ruse in order to get me or Li Fangping out of our homes. The police know where I live and could walk in and take me from my apartment at any time. No one would bat an eye.

The detention centre's office renos are completed the following day and Lawyer Li spends over an hour and a half with Dawu. I wait in the lobby with Wen Tao, Ren Qiu and Tang Funai.

After the meeting ends, Li Fangping says my husband wants the government to hurry up and reconvene the trial in the next few days. I know that won't be happening. The Chinese government is too wrapped up in putting out fires regarding Liu Xiaobo. He's supposed to receive his Nobel Peace Prize at a ceremony in Oslo, Norway, soon. The government authorities are working overtime to remove any and all evidence of this event from the internet.

Liu Xiaobo is scheduled to be handed the Nobel gold medal, a diploma and prize money at a gala in a couple of days. However, he's in prison in China and there's no one who can go to Norway in his stead. His wife, Liu Xia, is under house arrest and his three brothers aren't able to attend either. There's a travel ban for Chinese dissidents, activists, artists, journalists and other supporters. China won't allow anyone from the mainland to be at the Nobel ceremony.

On Friday, Dec. 10, a lone chair is placed in Oslo's city hall. Neither Liu Xiaobo nor any of his family is present at the event, and the chair symbolizes their absence. It's the first time in more than 74 years that a recipient hasn't been able to receive the prize in person. The gala is being televised internationally and I'm watching it, alone, in my studio. It's important to me as someone whose husband is being illegally detained and being denied freedom of speech. It's also important because I'd like to describe the ceremony to Dawu one day. He looks up to Liu Xiaobo and feels like he's a part of fighting for reform in China. So much so, it's imprisoned him, too.

The government must be losing face over Liu Xiaobo. A "criminal's" criticism is influencing the whole world. It's powerful.

Maybe Dawu would know about the ceremony today. It's unlikely he'll hear any of the details while locked up. He has been in jail for more than five months and it looks like he'll be in there for Christmas and the start of 2011.

***

My team is discussing the possibility of the authorities and Dawu reaching a deal. We're secretly hoping that there won't be another day in court. Dawu could be "released" based on some sort of agreement or conditions, such as he doesn't go to the media with his story.

Dawu's anonymous phone caller makes another call to me and thanks me for sending Li Fangping to Ping. The man on the other end of the line asks if I can meet him. I'm wary but if we meet in a public place, I should be fine. I pick the lobby of a five-star hotel, the Kempinksi Hotel, for the rendezvous.

I've been to the Kempinksi Hotel for various reasons over the years. I've met clients, had meetings and gone to networking events there. It's not far from 798 and is run mostly by expats. It'll be full of people at 6 p.m., when I arrange to meet the caller.

"Don't tell anyone," he advises, "and come alone."

I accept his terms and drive to the hotel. I park close to the main door, which is well-lit. I walk into the lobby and sit down. I'm clutching my phone hidden in my jacket. I have no idea who I'm meeting and I have to trust that he's not going to kidnap me. Needless to say, I am scared. It is very cloak and dagger-ish.

I've been watching the main hotel entrance when I see a wee Chinese man creeping around the doorway outside. He's wearing a dirty brown, rough down jacket. He sees me and waves me over. Is this my evening caller? I was expecting more of a ski-masked, thug kind of guy, not this little man.

I go over to him and he comes through the door and extends his hand. "I'm Mr. Song," he says.

I shake his hand and we move over to some benches facing the hotel's well-staffed service desks. Mr. Song reaches into his jacket and pulls out two handmade envelopes, not guns or detonators. I am relieved. I sense that the man is not the joking type but he's not here to harm me.

"You can't tell anyone about what I'm going to give you," he says.

He hands me the envelopes and asks me to promise that if I take them, I must destroy them immediately. I agree and see the envelopes have my name written on them in both Chinese and English, along with my phone number.

Oh my god! I think I recognize Dawu's handwriting.

I open the first envelope and see it contains a painting of Santa. The second envelope has some other Chinese ink and brush painting and some line drawings of inmates sitting on hard benches. Each inmate is wearing identical clothing and has the number 4-11 on their backs.

"Who sent these to me?" I ask Mr. Song.

"I can't tell you."

In a blink of an eye, the man shuffles out the door and scampers away. I'm left with another mystery. I do know that I've been given some contraband, something I shouldn't have outside the detention center.

At home, I let Hannah see the Santa picture and then I take the envelopes and put them away. Did Dawu send the drawings to us so we'd have something for Christmas? It's not like I can ask him.

The holidays are almost upon us and I don't have Dawu's zanzhuzheng extended or a visa for me. I've written to officials, including the PSB (Public Safety Bureau). I also visit the PSB office and get the runaround. Of course! What's new? However, at last, an agent says he can arrange for both documents to be completed around Dec. 20.

Li Fangping suggests we do a holiday postcard campaign and have Dawu's supporters address notes directly to him at the detention centre. It'll keep Dawu top of mind during the Christmas season and let the guards and officials know that his family, friends and acquaintances are thinking of him. According to the lawyer, this is a common campaign around this time of year.

Dawu also needs warmer clothing for the winter. It gets down to -10 C in Beijing in the cold months and the cells can be chilly. I buy some items at the Sunny Gold Street Market, one of the many markets where you can purchase cheap clothing or shoes or things for the home. It's not top-quality stuff but it's priced reasonably. For Dawu, I get a set of cotton long underwear and a cozy woollen grey vest "made" by the American label Tommy Hilfiger. (It was a knock-off.)

Later in the morning, I drive to the detention centre to drop off the goods. (Clothing and money drop-offs are Monday to Friday, 8:30 a.m. to 11:30 a.m.). I arrive at the centre and notice there's no lineup. Great! My favourite guard, Mr. Li, is at the front desk. Our relationship has evolved into a sort of casual familiarity over the past few months. It had started off on the wrong foot during my first visit to the detention centre. This was when Mr. Li told me Dawu was going to be executed. Now the guard is polite and happy to see me. He makes coming here bearable.

I nod at Mr. Li and he nods back. Today, his job is checking, repackaging and distributing the clothing coming in for the inmates. Prisoners are not allowed to have items with snaps, buttons, zippers, strings, tags or labels. (An inmate could choke on a button or someone could use a zipper to slit someone's throat or wrist.) I had chosen Dawu's new clothing carefully and they're nothing but seams and material.

Mr. Li points at Dawu's vest and shakes his head. "I can't accept this."

"Why not?" I ask. "What's wrong with it?"

"It's wool," he says. "It's not unreasonable that some desperate inmate will go to the trouble of unravelling the entire vest and then use the yarn to create a noose and hang himself with it."

Oh.

***

Dawu's zanzhuzheng and my visa are supposed to be in the works for Monday, Dec. 20. I get the usual hassle from the clerks at the bureau.

"You should have filled out this other paperwork first."

"You should have gone to that office before us."

"You can't do this from here."

Grrr! Nothing goes from A to B. If I can't get a visa by the end of the month, I'll have to sell my Beijing Color Studio. I do not want to do that but I can't run it from Canada, and Jane can't afford to buy out the ¥50,000 RMB cash (CAD 8,333) lease. I have no choice but to advertise the studio on Beijing Café, an online expat buy-and-sell network.

I get some bites and meet some candidates. I'm sad talking to prospective buyers about how fun and prosperous the business is. Fuck. This. Sucks.

I've been trying very hard over the past few months to keep my temper in check. I've lost my cool more than I'd like to admit. I do it again at the Jiangtai Police Station while trying to secure my visa.

Yet again, officers won't give me any information or help me figure out what I need to do. I explode in Chinese and English in the main waiting room of the detachment and rant and rave about the lack of fundamental human rights in China. I even manage to weave Liu Xiaobo and his Nobel Peace Prize into my heated speech. I had thought that most of the audience in the station were uneducated bumpkins who wouldn't know what I'm talking about. However, when I look around the lobby, I realize there are other expats, people who speak English, in here with me. Oops. If I could shrink to 1 centimetre in height and leave undetected, I would. Alas, I can't and I'm stuck looking like a ranting loser foreigner, the worst kind of expat.

It's not a proud moment. My fire is doused and I run out of there. I made a fool out of myself but I'm frustrated, desperate and I panicked. However, it's no excuse for dropping some F-bombs. It certainly did nothing for my dignity.

We're going into the holidays with no trial date. This is my first Christmas without Dawu since we started dating in 2002. Christmas isn't a big deal in China but it is for my family. Regulations at the detention centre make it impossible for me to give Dawu anything over and above his monthly prison allowance and some clothing. However, he is receiving a ton of holiday cards from all over the world, thanks to Li Fangping's card campaign.

On the morning of Saturday, Dec. 25, Hannah and I open stockings and gifts. At around 2 p.m., we head to Victoria's for a gift exchange and dinner. A few weeks ago, she told me that the ambassador was worried about Hannah and me and suggested Victoria and her husband, Wang Fang, take us in for Christmas.

Wang Fang is a Chinese artist like Dawu so there's some synergy — not to mention, Victoria and I spend a lot of time together and she becomes a good friend. Victoria and her husband don't have any children but Ray Chen and his partner join us with their son so Hannah isn't the only child at supper. We all share a lovely dinner and I feel a little less lonely.

Later that evening, I drop Hannah off at home with the ayi and I go to a friend of a friend's home. Krish cooks a huge and delicious Indian dinner that we eat around 10 p.m. There's much talk about Dawu and how brave I am and questions about what's next for me. I do know that if I get my visa, I'm taking Hannah on vacation next month. I'm saying "fuck it" to waiting around for the trial to continue. Hannah and I are going to Thailand. I deserve a break.

Finally, on Monday, Dec. 27, my visa is extended. It's thanks to Lawyer Li. He had stepped in and personally asked officers at my local police station to assist me. I can breathe easier knowing I'm not going to be kicked out of China and I can take my tropical trip. On the final day of 2010, Hannah and I, along with Emma and Jenny, gather for lunch at our favourite restaurant, Element Fresh. Being with great friends is a good way to end the year. While we are there, we run into Ai Weiwei. It's apparently his favourite hangout, too. He says hi to us and then gives me a hug and a hongbao (a special red envelope usually filled with money and given to children at Chinese New Year). I try to give the hongbao back but the artist refuses, saying that it is the least he can do and it must be hard for me at this time of year without Dawu. I thank Lao Ai as he heads out the door.

I open the envelope after he leaves and it is ¥800 RMB (CAD 135). Wow, that was sure nice of Ai Weiwei. He didn't have to do that. I'll be in touch with him as soon as I learn the next court date. Hopefully, everything will be completed by Chinese New Year at the beginning of February 2011. Many things have changed since last year.

Last February was the march on Chang'an Avenue. The protest has never been mentioned in any of Dawu's official charges or at his trial but there has always been the suspicion that it's the root of his present situation. At that time, too, I was ramping up business at my Beijing Color Studio. Now I'm thinking I won't even be in business this upcoming February. Renewing my visa for 2011 had been down to the wire and I hadn't pulled down any of my ads looking for prospective buyers for my studio. However, I've found someone who is interested in it.

I receive a call from Gino, an Italian photographer in Beijing, who wants to take over my space for the end of January. That's soon. We discuss the cost of the studio and other details and I find out that he doesn't want most of my equipment -- he has his own. He will take on Mike, the studio cat, though. I have only a couple of weeks to empty out the Beijing Color Studio.

I tell my staff about the impending deal and while they're disappointed, they understand. Jane, Kai and Belinda will all find other work easily as they're talented professionals. The studio was a good base for Jane to build a solid clientele and expand on separate projects. I sell my lights and booms to another fellow expat who has an established photo studio in Beijing.

I'm upset with my decision to close my business but it's giving me some much-needed flexibility. If I have to leave China, I can. I've been thinking of returning to Canada. Life is easier there. Just getting a new visa here took hours of not only my time but Li Fangping's too. I can't expect him to intervene whenever I run into red tape (aka being stigmatized because of Dawu).

It's the beginning of 2011 and there is still no trial date set. Li Fang-ping has met with Dawu and there is some troubling news. My husband is suffering from intense headaches that make it difficult for him to get up in the morning. He was given some basic painkillers one time and the pills did not work. Dawu has asked for a CT scan (computed tomography scan) but so far, hasn't been seen by a physician. My team, including Tang Funai and Song Ke, another one of Lao Ai's camera operators, write letters to the centre's authorities asking for medical treatment for Dawu. We think he's getting headaches because of the beating he received last May.

Detention centre officials have also stopped giving Dawu his holiday cards. I'm not sure why. He's not allowed to have a small photo of Hannah either. Li Fangping brought a postage stamp-sized picture of Hannah, decked out in her soccer gear, to hand over to her father. The lawyer showed Dawu the photo through the glass separating them but the guards wouldn't give Dawu the picture of his daughter.

Dawu does let me in on a secret. He was the one who sent the drawings to me before Christmas. He had Mr. Song smuggle them out of the jail. Now one of the art pieces makes total sense. One drawing was of fried fatty pork, watermelon, pears, chocolate, bread and cucumbers. It's all the food items that Dawu has been craving while in jail! Maybe he'll have a chance to enjoy a good meal soon. I can't wait to tell Hannah the news.

I've been talking to reporters and checking in with supporters, NGOs and, as always, the Canadian Embassy almost every day. Hannah and I go on some outings and I take her skating on Houhai Lake with her friends. The lake is in the middle of Old Beijing and it's pretty with pagodas, bridges and weeping willows along the banks. As well, I hold a garage sale to sell off the remaining furniture, fixings, art supplies, and much more from the studio. I want to get this all gone by the time Hannah and I leave for Thailand. I also host a "last hurrah" studio party one evening for all my friends and clients. It's the last chance for them to paint and enjoy the lovely space that was once the Beijing Color Studio.

I'm officially unemployed. To pay my bills, I use money from the 2009 sale of my condo as well as proceeds from selling the Counting Sheep Boutique. Also, I should have some work coming up soon as a destination service consultant with a friend's business.

In the middle of January, Li Fangping is told he can go to the Wenyuhe Courthouse to review the original version of the video evidence in Dawu's trial. Fingers crossed we have access to the whole footage and not only the edited segments.

We arrive at the courthouse in the afternoon on Monday, Jan. 17. Lawyer Li is allowed past the lobby but not me. I'm expecting to wait in the foyer for a while so I settle in with my phone. I barely have time to send a text message when the lawyer comes bouncing out into the lobby with his characteristic big smile and some papers in hand.

"Why are you out already?" I ask.

"There is NO tape!" says Li Fangping. "It doesn't exist anymore!"

I'm at a loss for words. I'm stunned that the video footage that supposedly would put Dawu away for years and years has mysteriously vanished.

"What's going on?" I finally ask the lawyer when I start driving towards Beijing.

"I have papers stating that the Jiuxianqiao Police Station replaced its old video cameras with brand new ones back in July 2010. Despite the fact that police policies call for video camera footage to be held for six months, specifically for court case requests like ours, somehow, the tapes are gone."

"Gone?"

"Yes, gone! The footage we saw at court, such as the tape where Dawu was supposedly threatening cops, was the original. It has disappeared along with the old cameras. There is no other footage available."

Because there is no other footage.

That weak excuse of losing the tapes took the police station and the government TWO MONTHS to create. Really, guys and gals, you should have done better than this, seriously. Anyway, Li Fangping believes we'll be told about a court date soon. Chinese New Year is approaching and he thinks the trial will conveniently reconvene when many people, including him, me, journalists and other Dawu advocates, won't be in Beijing.

Lawyer Li is going to be visiting his family in the countryside during the holiday and I'll be in Thailand. Great timing, China! Many Chinese and expats leave Beijing for several weeks around the Chinese New Year. Chinese living in the big city often travel to their hometowns to join family for celebrations. Many expats go on vacation — and they might as well, since their Chinese counterparts are away.

***

Meili, Honghong's wife, calls to ask if I have time to join them for lunch tomorrow. I do and the three of us meet at a Chinese restaurant in the Lido Hotel the next day. I am curious about their intentions, as a lunch date is out of the ordinary for them.

Meili and Honghong are happy to see me. They ask how everything is going and then get straight to the point. They feel that I have done all that I can for Dawu and that I should leave China for good. They suggest that after my trip to Thailand, I pack up my things in Beijing and leave. They believe Dawu will be fine without Hannah and I and will settle into life quickly after he's released from jail. They tell me that they can take it from here, along with other friends of Dawu's. I'm free to go.

I tell them while I understand their concerns, I am the only one who can help Dawu. I'm his wife and next of kin. Nevertheless, Meili and Honghong say they'll work out a plan.

"Raise Hannah in Canada," Honghong says.

I reply that I'll think about things. There is still a lot to do such as the upcoming court case and getting my own business in order.

As I'm closing down my business and moving my equipment out of the Beijing Color Studio, Li Fangping calls with news of Dawu's trial.

"We have a date," says the lawyer. "Friday, Jan. 28, at 9:30 a.m. at the Wenyuhe Courthouse."

Urgh, that's the exact date and time that I'll be flying to Thailand with Hannah. Murphy's Law at its finest. Li Fangping and I think the authorities knew when I was leaving and thought I wouldn't have the balls to change my flight. It turns out to be easy to change. Li Fangping, on the other hand, can't change his plans and asks another lawyer, Liu Liao, to take over at the upcoming proceedings.

A week before Dawu's trial, I drive to the 008 International Artist Community. This is Ground Zero. I don't know why I end up here. I had been running an errand in the area and found myself in the wreckage of what was once a thriving and vibrant art complex.

Dawu had his studio in the C block of the community and although it's completely deserted, the section is still standing. It hasn't been hit by the wrecking ball like the other blocks. Those areas are now flat and bare and there's not even any rubble left to show that there had been workspaces and homes here.

On my way to 008, I passed by the Zhengyang Art Community. It too, has also almost been demolished. A roadway runs straight through what was once the compound. The wide lane will make building easier for the developers. Huge trucks bringing in huge loads for construction now have ample room to manoeuvre.

***

I have to apply again to attend the next stage of Dawu's trial. I also request that an interpreter be allowed in the courtroom with me. A representative of the Canadian Embassy also applies to be in the room during the hearing, too.

My application is successful but without an interpreter. The Canadian Embassy's application is denied. Of course!

***

I do not put a lot of stock in superstition. However, I will do almost anything at this point to keep Dawu from spending more time behind bars. He has been in detention long enough. Perhaps the righting of a wrong will change his luck.

The snake that Dawu drowned to use as a model for a piece of art in 2009 has been striking some controversy in detention. Dawu had kept the reptile in a clear jar in his studio. It was in a corner of the room until a couple of months ago, right up until Dawu's first trial in November.

Dawu is living with about 25 men in a single room and sharing a single toilet. Needless to say, they're somewhat comfortable with each other and trade all kinds of stories. One morning in late October 2010, Dawu was chatting with a cellmate. The man said he had a horrible and vivid dream the night before. When Dawu asked what the dream was about, the man told him he had seen a great snake die.

In China, a snake is a symbol of honour, good luck, great harvest and reproduction. Dawu's cellmate didn't know what his dream meant to him — but to Dawu, it meant revenge. He had caused the death of a snake and now it was making him pay the price for killing it. It had been wrong of Dawu to assume that the snake's life was his to take. It was basic animal rights abuse.

Like the snake had been trapped in the jar, Dawu was trapped in detention. While the snake had been drowned, Dawu was also being suffocated. The snake and Dawu were entwined and its fate would be Dawu's as well.

I've learned that in China, there's a tradition of righting wrongs called *yuan*. This is the belief that wrongs suffered by any individual person must be addressed and righted. OK, so maybe the snake wasn't a person but it had a right to life. Dawu believed that his cellmate's dream was the serpent drawing attention to this. Dawu needed to right the wrong.

How could Dawu atone for his sins to the serpent? He could give it a decent burial for a start. During a meeting with Li Fangping, Dawu gave instructions for me, Zhang and Hong to remove the snake from his 798 studio and bury it.

Hong was in town when the three of us carefully moved the snake from the studio to Zhang's Jeep. We drove out to an open field not far from Dawu's studio, found a quiet spot and then Hong and I started digging with shovels borrowed from Dawu's neighbouring compound.

After a half hour of scooping out hardened dirt, we had made a hole deep enough for the big snake. Next, we had to get the serpent out of the glass jar filled with alcohol. Zhang picked up the vessel and dropped it, smashing it into pieces. Fluid gushed out and was immediately soaked into the dry ground. Amid the glass shards, laid the coiled snake. It was my job to don gloves and pick up the scaly corpse. Although I knew it was dead, it was still freaky to grasp the heavy snake and carry it over to the hole. I kept imaging that she might snap into writhing action and rip my head off. It was an angry spirit.

I heaved the snake into the hole and Zhang and Hong covered it with dirt the best they could. We stamped on the grave with our boots and wished the snake a good journey to wherever dead serpents slither in the afterlife. Perhaps it would release Dawu from its grip.

The snake hadn't forgiven Dawu by the time his first trial rolled around. Maybe by now, it thinks Dawu has had enough time to think about what he did. Maybe in the second trial we'll see a reversal of karma. I have nothing to lose so why not cross my fingers and knock on wood and hope Dawu flies the coop.

I've been sending out requests asking journalists to be at the trial. Lao Ai and his camera people will be there. The friends and supporters who are still in the city will come to the courthouse. There might not be as many as in November and this is exactly why the government decided to hold the trial around Chinese New Year – less attention.

The evening before Dawu's trial, I pack for Thailand. I've managed to change our flight so Hannah and I leave at night instead of first thing tomorrow morning. My plan is to go to the courthouse without Hannah and watch the trial. When it's over, I'll have a debrief with the new lawyer and Wen Tao and then pick up my daughter and head to the airport for our flight at 6:30 p.m. Never a dull moment here! I am so looking forward to this vacation.

The next morning, Friday, Jan. 28, I don't make a wrong turn during my drive to the boonies and I arrive at the Wenyuhe Courthouse by 9 a.m. There's a large crowd again of about 150 people. It's great to see the support for Dawu and hear people chanting his name. The police presence today is stronger than the first trial. I notice more officers around the building.

I talk with the international media gathered outside before I go into the courthouse. While glancing around at the crowd, I don't see Lao Ai but I see the familiar faces of Zhang and Hong, among many others.

A good friend of mine whom I had met in Beijing, Zoe Watson, is organizing a rally in Australia. It's coinciding with Dawu's trial and Zoe will be at the Chinese Consulate in Toorak, Victoria, around the same time Dawu will be in the courtroom. I'm happy for the show of solidarity several thousands of kilometres away.

At 9:30 a.m., Dawu is back on trial. He looks OK but not as good as he did in November. I don't think he has had any treatment for the headaches he's been experiencing and it shows. He looks rough, tired. He nods to me while walking to his chair. After Dawu is seated, he turns and looks at me but a judge and the white-gloved cop sitting next to him reprimand him with short barks. He slowly turns away from me.

I'm sitting next to three young Chinese women who look to be in their late teens or early 20s. They're obviously plants, filling seats that could have been used by Dawu's friends. On the other side of me is a male cop. He is here to make sure I don't do anything out of line.

Li Fangping can't make it today so an alternate lawyer, Liu Liao, is representing Dawu. The lead prosecutor offers the report on the video evidence that Li Fangping had shown me. The document states that the original footage from the Jiuxianqiao Police Station no longer exists because of either camera replacements or videos being recorded over. Nevertheless, the woman claims what the court saw and heard in November is enough to convict Dawu with interfering with public service with violence. He must be re-educated to change his violent behaviour.

During closing arguments, the lead prosecutor says she can promise that the evidence they have on Dawu is reliable. The prosecution stands behind its claim that he obstructed and attacked a police officer.

When the judge asks for my husband's response, he says he stands by his claims. He tells the court that there's no concrete evidence against him. Everything has been faked.

"I have no confidence in the system."

Dawu is told by the judge to keep his comments to himself.

"The court doesn't want to hear that kind of talk," says the judge.

Today's proceedings are brief, just over an hour. I'm out of the courtroom a little after 10:30 a.m. There was neither a verdict today nor any date for sentencing given. At the debrief at a restaurant nearby, Liu Liao speculates that Dawu will be found guilty and sentenced to 12 months. Since he has already served eight months, he'll have four more months to spend in prison. The lawyer thinks the sentencing hearing will be held around Feb. 20, right when I return from holidays with Hannah.

I feel crappy and angry about the trial. It was a waste of time. If Dawu's verdict and sentence were already picked out of thin air, then why make him return to court? However, four months in prison is better than a year. It's obvious to me now that this trial business has been all a show, just to give the impression that the justice system is doing its job. It's just going through the motions, not genuine.

I'm disappointed by all the lies and fantasies concocted by the prosecution and the cops. They've made a total sham out of the trial. The legal system is corrupt and the police are unscrupulous and untrustworthy. The whole thing has been a gross miscarriage of justice. I have no respect and zero trust for the Chinese authorities. This gives me plenty of reasons for leaving the country and never coming back.

I hear from Lao Ai via a text. He wasn't at the courthouse because he had been put under house arrest for the day. Secret police arrived at his home this morning and told him that he wasn't leaving his compound. He had no choice but to stay. Nevertheless, he went on social media and tweeted about China's terrible human rights record.

It's such a relief to get on the airplane and zone out. Hannah and I are leaving for almost a month of vacation. On our way to Thailand, we stop in Hong Kong. We see friends who live in the city. Poppy and her husband are originally from the U.K. and they have two lovely daughters a bit older than Hannah.

Hannah and I take in Disneyland and it is awesome. We spend 10 hours there and go on as many rides as we can. We even buy Mickey Mouse hats with ears and have our names stitched onto the back. Of course, Hannah is wondering why her baba isn't with us.

I do feel guilty about having fun with my daughter while Dawu remains in his cell. Nevertheless, there's nothing I can do right now to get him released and there's nothing he can do about it either. It's a lose-lose situation. I might as well get away and hang out with Hannah. She needs a mom who is happy — not constantly angry, frustrated and tired.

In Thailand, we go swimming, read books and I unplug. It's important that I don't engage with social media or my blog during this time. I need to unwind and decompress. I want Hannah to be a child here and not have to worry about people asking about her father or staring at her when we go out. Despite the break from Beijing life, my daughter is noticeably clingy in Thailand. Dawu's detention has left its mark on her.

She is dealing with an underlying fear of being left behind or abandoned. Whenever we're walking, she's vigilant about traffic.

"Mom," she says. "I don't want you to get hit by a car. How would I get back to Beijing if Baba is in jail?"

Hannah brought a small notebook on the trip and every day she draws pictures of what she does, sees and eats so she can show Dawu when we're all together again. It's heartwarming to see her committed to including him in our trip vis-a-vis her little book. Not a day goes by that Hannah doesn't mention her dad.

During the three-and-a-half-week trip, there has been no news about a date for Dawu's sentencing. I'm reluctant to leave Thailand on Sunday, Feb. 20, and that's a first for me. I have never balked at coming "home." It doesn't help that the film I watch on the flight from Bangkok to Beijing is based on the true story of a man who was wrongly convicted in the U.S. The movie, *Convicted*, makes me think of Dawu, as well as how my struggle to clear his name also has all the ingredients for a good film.

I have undergone something of an evolution during Dawu's detention. I went from someone who had shut her eyes to what has been going on in China to someone whose eyes are wide open. Human rights are non-existent in this country and it has taken Dawu's illegal detention to shake me awake. I'm wide awake now.

In early January, Allyson Klayman, a U.S. independent filmmaker, released the trailer for her documentary on Ai Weiwei. The film was called *Ai Weiwei: Never Sorry* and focused on his activism and artistic work. Lao Ai sticks up for all of China. When he hears of injustice in his country, he mobilizes a crew of people to make a documentary such as a film about the Sichuan earthquake. Ai Weiwei once told me that Dawu's case was the very tip of an enormous iceberg. I know that all too well now.

Dawu's march on Chang'an Avenue was included in the trailer for Klayman's documentary. I was excited Dawu's issue was in the film. However, there is so much going on in China that a million documentaries and a million books couldn't begin to highlight all the human rights abuses here. Some of us, including me for 15 years, chose to bury our heads in the sand for a long time and ignore what was happening. At the start of Dawu's troubles, when I told expat friends what was going on, I had the impression that they didn't believe me. It did sound ludicrous.

"My husband is locked away and can't see his family or a lawyer because he asked to be compensated after the government allowed his studio to be ripped down."

Through my fight for Dawu, people are coming out of the woodwork with atrocities they've been facing. Many people have found themselves face-to-face with the government after daring to confront the Chinese machine. Dawu's situation was NOT a one-off — it's systemic to the entire nation.

While I was in Thailand with Hannah in January and February of 2011, the Arab Spring was heating up. There were anti-government uprisings in the Middle East and North Africa. People in those countries were calling for regimes to be replaced by more pro-democratic leaders, amid a wider struggle for human rights. I remember watching the uprising from my fancy hotel room and thinking about what would happen if the movement came to China.

I surprised myself by actually being glad that Dawu was behind bars because this was just up his alley. He would have been front and centre of any demonstrations in Beijing, ending up back where I am trying to free him from.

Once home in Beijing, I heard about the Jasmine Revolution that was taking shape in the city and across the country. The Chinese government had tried to block news of what was happening in Egypt and Tunisia but since VPN technology was improving, Chinese from various backgrounds were jumping the firewall. They were motivated by Arab Spring and organized protests under the banner of the Jasmine Revolution.

I wasn't sure what this revolution would look like but I was very interested in seeing it with my own eyes. I thought about Dawu and wondered if he had access to news about the protests. Probably not, as he was limited to local papers and they'd never cover this sort of news.

Another recent story catches my eye. It's about a barefoot lawyer, Chen Guangcheng, who has just released a video of himself under house arrest in Shandong province. I try to do some research online about him and find some bits and pieces.

Chen has been blind since he was a young child due to an illness. He learned to read braille and went to study massage therapy as many blind citizens do in China, as they aren't encouraged to seek other professions. However, Chen took an interest in the stories of injustice he heard around him and got hold of some law texts written in braille. He became what some in China call a barefoot lawyer, someone who has some basic knowledge of the justice system and can help those who don't have any knowledge of the system or don't have money to connect with a real lawyer.

Barefoot lawyers are becoming common in rural China where not many people have access to services, much money or high levels of education. Chen was involved with bringing the issue of forced family planning to the attention of the international media, which of course, embarrassed the Chinese authorities. That was the last case he worked on before he was hauled off to prison for four years for "damaging property and organizing a mob to disturb traffic." Obviously, a trumped-up charge.

Chen was recently been released from prison, although he remains under house arrest in his hometown of Dongshigu. Li Fangping was part of Chen's legal team and when the lawyer tried to visit his client, he was harassed and beaten several times by police. Chen and his wife are also repeatedly beaten and harassed. They were able to film and release a video of Chen talking about his situation because they hid a charger and a cheap phone in a wall.

In Chen's footage, he talks about the Chinese government cracking down on ordinary people, not just human rights activists and lawyers: regular folks who are trying to defend and understand their own rights. The regular citizens are being beaten, threatened and intimidated into silence. One typical issue is being overcharged regarding taxes. Most people feel like they can't say anything about paying the local government more than they should. This is what is happening every day in China. I can't ignore it anymore.

I feel stuck. China is my country, my home for close to 15 years, and I love it. But it does not love its people. My husband is an example of that.

On an art forum website that I follow, I see that Liu Bolin, one of Dawu's contemporary art colleagues, has done a work that's a silent protest of forced eviction. Liu Bolin's studio was demolished in 2005. It's risky to speak out against the Chinese government via your artwork like this. The government is always watching and it will take you and your studio away if it sees any anti-government slant in your art. However, Liu Bolin has a work-around. His series of pictures, Hiding in the City, is on display in a gallery in New York City. The artist has painted his body in order to blend in with selected backgrounds, almost making himself invisible.

On Sunday, Feb. 27, 2011, I attend a Jasmine Revolution rally in downtown Beijing. I'm disgusted by all the human rights shit going on in China and the growing pro-democracy movement here is one way to protest against the government.

Many of China's activists have identified freedom, democracy, human rights and human dignity as "universal values and a core base of Charter 08." However, the government sees these universal values as interference from Western nations, not conditions tangible for Chinese citizens. Authoritarian governments and dictatorships rule by complete control. Thus, the Communist Party of China doesn't allow its people freedoms that the Western world does. Freedom of speech, expression, religion – all fundamental human rights, do not exist in China.

The Chinese government blames the West for interfering and giving Chinese citizens ideas such as freedom of speech. China has a very practiced and successful propaganda program geared towards the masses. Through years of brainwashing, many people agree with whatever the party says. The internet causes the Chinese government major concern because people with VPNs are figuring out the truth online and seeing what is happening abroad.

The Jasmine Revolution is spreading across China because the Chinese people are tired of being ground down by the authorities. There have been soaring inflation rates over the past several years, corruption in all levels of government, a widening income gap between rich and poor and social inequality. It all adds up to people who have no say when it comes to power. The protesters don't want to overthrow the government, only improve conditions. People are disgruntled, such as workers who are laid off and not guaranteed job security (also known as "the iron rice bowl") or citizens who are forced out of their homes because of "development." The folks coming to the Jasmine Revolution protest are calling for an end to one-party rule, as well as government transparency and accountability.

I park my car and walk alone towards the demonstration about a block away on Wangfujing Street, a pedestrian street, and close to the first McDonald's restaurant in China. The protestors chose a symbolic place to ask for political and economic reforms. McDonald's represents the West. The fast-food chain is heavily in demand in China and usually people's first experience of anything Western in China.

This is the first protest that I've ever attended in China and there are thousands of people of all ages and all walks of life here, from high school students, to middle aged workers, to journalists. Wangfujing Street is a top tourist site in Beijing and many foreigners will be caught in the demonstration today, much to the embarrassment and horror of their Chinese guides. The government will be losing face.

Thanks to social media, the Jasmine Revolution is taking place in several main centres around China. I heard about today's protest through Facebook and Twitter. As Liu Xiaobo once said, *The Internet is God's present to China.*

(Index on Censorship blog, Nov. 1, 2006).

Wen Tao, Ai Weiwei and other activists also made sure I knew what was going on today. I want the entire country to wake up and come join me on Wangfujing Street. I want to tell them to remove the fear and barriers and start shouting for change. I believe that while most Chinese don't and won't dare to wear their heart on their sleeves, inside — inside their hearts — they do feel empathy and compassion for folks like Liu Xiaobo, Dawu, etc. If the ordinary Chinese people could unshackle themselves from the fear built up by years of propaganda, then they might be able to see clearly. Then it will be the government officials, the cops and the guoan who have something to fear.

I don't see anyone I know amongst the protesters. Online, organizers of the Jasmine Revolution had urged people to walk while chanting, "We want food! We want work! We want housing! We want fairness!" Some people are shouting the slogan as well as carrying jasmine or other white flowers. In Chinese culture, white flowers are mostly used for funerals. Using white flowers today sends a strong message to the government.

During the protest, I witness a foreign journalist being pushed and shoved by police officers. Regular shoppers are being mixed in with the demonstrators, too. One such person is the U.S. Ambassador to China, Jon Huntsman Jr. He's caught up in the crowd.

I stick around for about an hour before the cops start clearing us off the streets. I see some folks being arrested and hauled away. I wonder if any will end up with Dawu in his cell.

Driving home and reflecting on the day, I think I was part of the largest demonstration in China since Tiananmen Square in 1989. The government is obsessed with putting out any flames of dissension and it did a good job today. However, embers are still burning across the country.

The lack of rights and freedoms in China is stark when held up against Canada. Another example is when an officer from the local Jiangtai Police Station pays me an unexpected visit at home. The cop, Zhang Xindong, has a small body cam attached to the lapel of his uniform. I had just showered and changed into my PJs. I'm not dressed to receive guests. Lovely. Hannah is spending the night at a friend's so she's not at home for the "social call."

Mr. Zhang Xindong wants to know what I do every day. As well, he wants to confirm if Dawu still has his 798 studio. I nod, yes. Mr. Zhang Xindong is surprised to hear that Dawu hasn't been sentenced yet.

"All in due time," the cop says with a smirk.

There's no official reason for the visit. I think Mr. Zhang Xindong came to see if I'm still living where I claim I do. It was also a power move. The police want to show me, again, that they can find me at any time.

Encounters like this make me want to leave China right away. I've had to temper my flight-or-fight response and I've been working on two plans: one to stay and one to go. If Dawu is going to be in prison for a while, I'll stay in China and find a permanent job. I've already applied for a position with an international school and I've been doing some networking with the Viva Beijing Women's Professional Network.

It's a strange feeling not being busy with the Beijing Color Studio. I've been doing some training again with Shelley Warner's Asia Pacific Access. I'll be working with expats relocating to Beijing and Chinese families returning to Beijing after spending years abroad with multinational corporations. I can't wait to start.

If I leave China, I'll go back to school. I've been continuing with my application for my Masters of Arts degree in Intercultural and International

Communications at Royal Roads University. Who knows what will happen in the upcoming months but the possibility of studying for a degree is an exciting one. It gives me something to look forward to, rather than focusing on the limbo I've been in while waiting for Dawu's verdict or sentencing. It's agony.

Hannah keeps asking about her baba and I keep saying the same thing.

"I'm working on getting your father out of jail."

It seems to placate her for a few hours.

Dawu knows all about the Jasmine Revolution. Li Fangping tells me Dawu heard about it through the prison guards. He's glad that people are getting out and protesting and wishes he could stand with them. The crackdown after the Jasmine Revolution has been brutal and the authorities are targeting known activists, pro-democracy advocates, dissidents, Chinese journalists and lawyers who have worked on any and all human rights cases. It makes me feel sad and scared. I'm angry, too, at the authorities. For me, China has gone from being my home, to being a prison. I may not be behind bars like my husband but I'm certainly not allowed any kind of political freedom.

Lawyer Li fears that he'll be targeted for his human rights work. The lawyer hasn't been active in the Jasmine Revolution but that doesn't mean he's off the hook. I feel for him and am worried that he could be grabbed anywhere and put into prison at any time.

Li Fangping has worked for the Ruifeng Law Firm in Beijing for more than 12 years. He's known as an outspoken critic of the Chinese courts, the Chinese Communist Party and is not willing to bow to political pressure. As a result, he's often hassled and followed by the police and authorities.

Before the Tiananmen Square massacre's 20-year milestone in 2009, Li Fangping couldn't make a move without the police. He had absolutely no freedom. Police physically escorted him around Beijing the second he left his home. It was a politically-sensitive time and other defence lawyers were facing the same challenges.

A week before Dawu's first appearance in court in November 2010, Li Fangping was under a one-day house arrest to stop him from going to a legal conference in Beijing. A day before Dawu's court date, Nov. 17, Li Fangping was harassed by the police after the lawyer checked in with a previous client fighting the tainted milk scandal.

Three days before Liu Xiaobo's Nobel Peace Prize ceremony in Oslo, Li Fangping was taken to the airport on Dec. 7, 2010, and flown to the far southeastern province of Fujian. The lawyer was kept there under police "protection" for several days.

Authorities have tightened security since the Jasmine Revolution and Li Fangping is not taking any chances. He sends lawyer Liu Liao to meet with my husband at the detention centre on Monday, Feb. 28. I had hoped to have some news about Dawu's verdict to deliver but there has only been silence from the courts.

Liu Liao guesstimates that Dawu's sentencing will come after the "big'" government meetings early next month. The high-level talks are the National People's Congress (NPC) and the Chinese People's Political Consultative Conference (CPPCC) national meeting. The NPC is the highest organ of state power and the national legislative body for the People's Republic of China. The CPPCC is another political legislative advisory body.

The delegates meet once a year in the spring to go over major issues, pass laws, etc. While they're in discussions, everything comes to a standstill in the country. I won't be expecting a verdict or a sentence in the next couple of weeks.

Meanwhile, Dawu remains in detention and since he's not working, he's beginning to feel the pinch on his bank account. He's thinking about passing on his studio space to someone else so he doesn't have to keep paying for it. I'm trying to find a new tenant for his two-storey, nicely renovated space, which rents for approximately ¥3,000 RMB (CAD 500) a month. I've had to tell Zhang that he won't have a job or a place to live soon but he understands. He knows that the longer Dawu remains locked up, the more money he is losing.

I'm becoming obsessed with people who have similar stories to Dawu's. On Friday, Mar. 4, I read a story online by the *China Digital Times*, a news aggregator website based in California, about the tragedy of Zhao Wei. Zhao was a college student murdered by Chinese railway authorities a couple of months ago, in January 2011.

The article has been purposely ignored by most Chinese news outlets. It's a shocking and disgusting story. Zhao, a 23-year-old, fourth-year student at Hebei University of Technology, boarded the 1301 train from Tianjin bound for Inner Mongolia on Saturday, Jan. 22. He sat in Car 12. A classmate and companion sat in Car 11.

According to Zhao's classmate, Zhao was taunted by a train attendant over the issue of a seat change. Zhao complained about the matter to the train conductor. Later that night, Zhao traded seats with someone in Car 11 so that he could sit next to his classmate. He told the classmate it seemed he had somehow gotten on the train conductor's bad side.

At around 3 a.m., the railway police came and led Zhao away from Car 11. Zhao's parents received a call around 8 a.m. and were told that Zhao had jumped from a building at the Daqing Railway Station and was being treated in a hospital. Unable to get clear confirmation about where their son had been taken, the parents went directly to the Daqing Railway Station, where police told them their son had already died.

Zhao's parents asked to see the police photographs that were taken after the alleged jump but the authorities said there were none. The parents also asked to see video surveillance footage from the scene and were told that the station was not equipped with video surveillance, which apparently wasn't true.

When family members were finally allowed to view Zhao's body, they found wounds that apparently could not be explained by a jump from a building. All attempts by the Zhao family to petition various government offices in various jurisdictions for further investigation failed.

Zhao's case is eerily similar to Dawu's. In both, there has been:
- a lack of factual information presented to family
- obvious cover-up by authorities
- denial of beatings/injuries
- a lack of surveillance camera evidence or a willingness to show it

It makes me so sad that this shit is happening ALL THE TIME here and NO ONE cares. Many Westerners don't care about what is happening in China unless it happens to them. Many Chinese don't care because they either don't believe their government is wicked or they are scared of getting involved. People are blind in many ways to what is happening below the surface of China.

The NPC and CPPCC meetings are finished, yet there's no word on Dawu's pending verdict and sentence. The Chinese government has just sentenced a man who was criticizing the Communist Party via a blog. The man got 10 years in prison for subversion. Dawu is lucky he doesn't have the word "subversion" mentioned in his charge. That one word adds many years of imprisonment.

It has been almost two months since Dawu's last court appearance on Jan. 28. Hannah is getting impatient and wants to see her father. She asks for him nearly every hour and writes little sentences and draws lovely little pictures for her baba. She'll give them to her father when he's released ... whenever that is!

On the bright side, Dawu's time in prison is adding up. If he's sentenced to 12 months, then he only has three more months to spend behind bars.

It's a positive way of looking at things.

At the end of March, I attend a book club event at the home of one of our members in the gated community of River Garden in Shunyi. Sally has a lovely home and the TaiTais have a great evening with good food, wine and conversation. Everyone remains concerned about Dawu but not one of these women has been part of the crowd outside of the Wenyuhe Court-house to support Dawu during either of his court dates. I guess the reality is too shocking for them but I can't make it any easier or downplay it. It's my re-ality every day. Some expats also fear reprisals from the Chinese government.

If the shoe was on the other foot prior to my present experience, I doubt I would be at the courthouse protesting the detention of one of my expat friends' husbands. When I look at it this way, I can't really blame the women for not knowing much about what I'm going through. Perhaps their husbands would be uncomfortable with them attending the courthouse. I'll never know and I'm too scared to ask them directly. Despite my conflicting feelings, the book club is a good community for me.

***

I catch sight of a post on the *China Digital Times* saying Lao Ai is possibly moving to Germany. We haven't been in touch as much in the past couple of weeks so this is a surprise to me. Sort of. I know the artist-activist feels discouraged in China. He has been held under house arrest, beaten and the authorities are only cracking down harder in attempts to quell the Jasmine Revolution. It sucks. I wonder what Dawu's career will look like when he's back in Chinese society.

I wish I could take Hannah and leave China this instant. But Dawu needs my help. I am going to leave once he's out of prison. My sister Diane has given me the name of an online career coach based in Calgary. We've been working together on a plan for me.

China was once the rosy apple of my eye. The shine has gone off it. It's hard for me to live here and forget what's happening all around me. It's not just the one-off events like the Jasmine Revolution but all the systemic human rights abuses being covered up by a façade of economic miracles. It's wrong. I need to get out, but I will wait for Dawu to get out first.

I've been searching online for jobs and homes in Calgary and Van-couver. I sometimes wonder what would have happened had I gone through with my plan to leave China back in the fall of 2009. I was so, so close to leaving. I had packed up the house, booked my flights and even had a go-ing-away party ... only to change my mind. Was it worth it?

I won't fully know the cost of that decision until Dawu's out. The emotional upheaval has taken a toll on Hannah and me. Hannah is scared and worried about her dad. I'm scared and worried about all of us. I feel that I've given up my beloved studio because of Dawu. I've stopped going to art exhibitions. I feel embarrassed to be out socially. I dread people talking to me, knowing they'll ask about my husband. I never have any good news to share. To top it all off, I don't trust China anymore.

I don't think I'll back out again if I decide to return to Canada. China is a hellhole. I've seen what this country truly thinks of its people. I am starting to hate China. How can I live here with a conscience and raise my lovely daughter? Forget it! But urgh, I'm stuck here for now because of Dawu.

I'd like to sell my car and wouldn't you know it, Beijing has just introduced a bizarre vehicle buying/selling/registering system. I can't sell to just anyone. I have to sell to someone who has a Beijing licence plate. For someone to get a car, they have to submit their name into a draw for a Beijing licence plate. Only 20,000 plates a month are issued and around 200,000 people are competing for them. That limits my buyers. Limiting my buyers even more is the fact that most people want new vehicles, not used. I've been talking with friends and it sounds like many expats are now having problems selling their automobiles.

***

Dawu's family checks in with me every week. Zhang and Hong talk to them, too. It's easier for Ba and Suling to speak to Dawu's friends as they can chat in the same dialect of Chinese. Chao Hongling, Gu Duanfan and others have also been calling me but our conversations are less frequent after the second hearing.

Hindsight is 20/20. In the quiet of March, I've been thinking about Dawu and me. I've been thinking about his march on Chang'an Avenue, about his various outbursts of anger towards me and about our relationship. Dawu had been the leader of the 008 and Zhengyang artists and he took his job very seriously. The compounds were part of the rapid urbanization of China that the government was sanctioning – at a cost to its people. Dawu was not going to close his eyes and pretend nothing was happening. He was standing up for his people and he expected me to be by his side.

I might have been, if I hadn't had to pay all the bills and look after Hannah. Actually, if Dawu had come right out and asked me to help him then, I probably would have. Instead, he pushed me away. I let him.

I think back to the last conversation I had with Mrs. Fan, my counsellor in 2007, about Dawu not wanting to meet her to work on marriage and relationships issues. She had said that Dawu wouldn't talk to her and she figured it was possibly due to the abuse and violence that was born out of the Cultural Revolution and had been passed on to the next generations. I can't help but think about his *IMPERIAL CRIMINALS* photo works and giving himself the stamp of "political criminal." It's all starting to come together.

I do admit that I had stopped listening to him. He had said and done some hurtful things. At some point, I had to stop caring. Dawu didn't want me to go to Australia and I went anyway. He had organized the march while I was on vacation with his daughter. That was the turning point. If I had been in Beijing then, I probably would not have let him march. He needed me to hash out a solution at the time. But I was gone in more ways than one.

I am here for Dawu now. I have stayed in China with his daughter and one day at a time, I've been chipping away at the Chinese government. It's like the old Chinese proverb, "An ant may well destroy a whole dam."

63

I t's Sunday morning, Apr. 3. I'm puttering around my home, about to wake Hannah, when my cellphone rings. It's a number I don't recognize. Another anonymous middleman?

"*Wei?*" I say. (Hello in Mandarin.)

Silence.

"Wei?" I repeat.

"Hi."

"Dawu?"

"Yes, it's me. I only have a couple of seconds to tell you that I'm getting released."

Holy cow! I'm talking to Dawu! I have a thousand questions for him but he only has one for me.

"Can you pick me up near Huairou?"

"Yes! When?"

"Later this afternoon, around 4.

"This afternoon?"

"I'll phone later with an exact time and place. Oh, and don't bring any media or tell anyone about this."

He hangs up.

My mind fills with theories and suspicions. Is Dawu really coming home? Today? Is he really out of detention? Is it a coincidence that we're meeting in Huairou? I'm supposed to travel there today around 4 p.m. to visit Debbie at her country home. Did the guoan already know this because they've been listening in on my calls?

I quickly wake up Hannah. I don't tell her about her baba in case plans fall through or this is a hoax. Hannah and I are supposed to meet Debbie at her cottage. First, we have to get Debbie's son Frank.

Frank is around Hannah's age and they are friends. Frank's father is journalist Peter Simpson and when he drops his child off to me, he asks about Dawu and how the second trial went. I'm dying to tell Peter that I'm going to see Dawu soon but my lips are sealed. Dawu told me to keep quiet about his release and I have to do what he asks.

I'd like to tell my family, Dawu's family and all our friends about the new development. Zhang, Hong, Chao Hongling and Gu Duanfan deserve to hear the news as does Li Fangping and Ai Weiwei. Nevertheless, I don't trust the system.

I want to make sure Dawu shows up at 4 p.m. and is allowed to leave with me.

I'm still waiting for Dawu's call in the afternoon when I start driving towards Huairou. Out on the highway, I'm excited and trying not to speed too much. My mobile phone rings and I pick it up. It's Tania Branigan, a journalist with *The Guardian*, a U.K. newspaper. Tania has written articles on Dawu prior to his detention and during his incarceration. Maybe she's calling me now because she knows about my husband's release?

I pull over at the side of the road to speak with her.

"Have you heard the news?" she asks.

"Yes! I'm on my way to pick Dawu up."

"Oh, that's not what I'm talking about. This morning Ai Weiwei's offices and studio were raided. Ai and Wen Tao have disappeared."

"What?"

My head and heart flood with worry. Tania fills me in with what she knows. Lao Ai was taken by the authorities at the Beijing airport and Wen Tao was picked up somewhere else in the city. It's horrible news amidst, hopefully, good news. It's as if China has a revolving detention door for critics and activists — when one gets out, another one goes in.

Since I had let my guard slip with Tania, I tell her I'm on my way to fetch Dawu. She wishes me a big huge hug of luck and says goodbye.

I'm back on the highway again and about 20 minutes later, my phone rings. This time it is Dawu. I pull off to the shoulder and start jabbering on about Ai Weiwei being in trouble.

"He's been taken by the police," I say. "Can you believe it?"

"Shhh," says Dawu. "I don't want to know."

How can Dawu not care about his fellow artist-activist? The man who was the impetus for getting him out of prison?

The phone goes dead.

Oh, oh. I hope nothing is going sideways.

When Dawu calls back a little later, he blurts out that Hannah and I should meet him at the roundabout in Huairou. The traffic circle is just off the highway and I know where it is. It's about 3:30 p.m. and we're already heading that way.

What is Dawu going to look like?

What am I going to say to him? Does he know how much his family and friends missed him? Wow, this is too much. I put Coldplay's *Life In Technicolor ii* song on and blast it. Hannah and Frank are shouting at me to turn the music down. I don't care. I like the tune and it's pushing away the bad thoughts flying around my head.

I try not to think that I'm being played — that this is some sort of scam. I'm a bit wigged out since I have Debbie and Peter's son in the car with me. If something does go south, Frank will be going down with Hannah and me. I have to trust my gut that everything is going to work out.

I'm familiar with Huairou, having driven out here on numerous occasions for visits to my friends' country homes. The roundabout is wide, with green space in the middle and lots of room to park. I slowly drive around the traffic circle. I don't really know what I'm supposed to be looking for but I'm sure that Dawu will find me. He knows my car, my little white-as-snow Honda Fit.

I pull to the side of the roundabout and park. I'm fully off the road so other vehicles can pass. I also make sure that there's enough room in front of me and behind me so I can speed away if need be. I put on my sunglasses so I can observe people without them knowing that I'm spying on them. Hannah and Frank are in the back seat, happily playing with toys. It's a good time to tell them what's going on.

I don't want Hannah to be shocked when Dawu appears at the car, as if out of thin air. She hasn't seen her father for about 10 months so this is going to be a big deal. Her face is all smiles when she finds out she's going to see her dad soon, very soon.

"Now?" she asks.

"I hope so!" I say.

Frank isn't too concerned about what's happening. I don't think he knows why Hannah's dad hasn't been around recently. Meanwhile, Hannah and I are on full alert, intently watching out the windows for any sign of Dawu.

"When will he be here?" asks Hannah after only waiting a few minutes.

"Shortly," I say and give her and Frank some sweet snacks. It's a good way to keep them both occupied for a few moments.

Twenty minutes later, the standard vehicle commonly used by the Chinese government, guoan and others, rolls up behind me. There are no markings on the black Audi with tinted windows. It must be carrying Dawu. There's no hiding the fact that the car is an official vehicle.

I take a deep breath and emerge from my Honda. I'd rather be outside my vehicle, not sitting in it like the proverbial sitting duck. I leave the kids in the back of the car but they quickly remove their seatbelts and turn around to watch the scene unfolding in front of them.

A secret police officer wearing a bulletproof vest over his plain clothing gets out from the driver's side of the Audi. Oh, crap. Should I be wearing a bulletproof vest, too? Guns are totally illegal in China so who's going to shoot the cop? Another cop? What's about to happen here? (Who needs Netflix when you live in China?)

"Are you Peng Kailin?" asks the officer.

I nod. That's when I see Dawu climbing out of the backseat of the car. When he stands up straight, I notice he's dressed to impress. He's wearing a nice three-piece grey-blue suit complete with brown leather loafers. He has a fresh haircut and looks like a businessman. Well, there's a first time for everything. Nevertheless, this is not how I had expected this to go down.

I've been imagining Dawu's release for the past several months. I've been envisioning Dawu and I walking out the front door of the detention centre to cheers and throngs of reporters jostling for an interview. It was how Gerry Conlon, one of Guildford Four, left prison in the U.K. in 1989. *In the Name of the Father*, a film based on the Guildford Four, is one of Dawu's favourite films and I wanted his release to resemble the movie. Sigh. If I couldn't have that, maybe Dawu would have a Nelson Mandela-esque release. Mandela had spent 27 years behind bars in South Africa and, on Feb. 11, 1990, was freed. Mandela and wife Winnie raised their fists in the air in front of a crowd upon his liberation from Victor Verster prison.

The moment unfolding in front of me now is the opposite of what I've been dreaming about. It's just like meeting a Chinese friend on the side of the road. Exactly how the government wants it. One hundred per cent normal. Low-key. Banal.

The authorities want Dawu to look and act like nothing has happened. It's almost as if I'm picking him up after he spent a couple of hours at an offsite business meeting. I was driving to Huairou anyway, I might as well swing by and fetch Dawu so he's home in time for supper.

Dawu walks towards me and then embraces me. The hug feels like I'm coming home. He is in my arms and I can touch him. He's not a figment of my imagination. He's not a ghost.

My husband introduces me to the driver, who teases Dawu about not trying to get back into jail now that he's seen me. The joke adds some comic relief and breaks the ice. We all laugh.

Everything is going to be fine. It's safe enough that I go to my car to retrieve Hannah. I tell Frank to stay put and that we'll be back in a moment or so.

Hannah and her baba hug and there are huge glorious smiles on both of them. I still can't believe that this moment is happening. What the fuck? Dawu has just been released!

He looks good, although his face is pudgy and pale. OK, so maybe he has a few more grey hairs. Dawu envelops all three of us in a bear hug. The driver is polite and stands to the side, giving us our time. He offers to take photos of us and we have some pictures snapped of our reunited family. It's a surreal moment.

Debbie will be wondering where we are so I call her. I tell her we're on our way to her home after a special delay.

"You'll understand why when we get to the country house," I say.

"Is Dawu coming here with you?"

"Yes! He's free."

Debbie says she is going to prepare a tasty dinner for all of us. We'll have a welcome home feast for Dawu. In the car, I keep looking at my husband. He keeps looking at me and Hannah. I have a million things to tell him and many questions. I focus on this moment and work backwards.

"So, how did you end up here," I ask, "and why aren't you wearing prison-issue clothes?" I ask.

Dawu says he was forcibly removed from his room last night around 1 a.m. He was in his underwear and put straight into a van. He wasn't told why or where he was going. He was then driven to a "hotel" at an undisclosed location on the edge of Huairou.

Apparently, the guoan have these "black" hotels throughout China where they keep higher-profile inmates and detainees. The authorities don't want to open the front door to the detention centre and release a prisoner who could drum up attention. That would mean losing face for the nation. The hotel keeps everything under wraps and on the down-low. This morning, Dawu was taken clothes shopping but had to borrow a pair of shoes from one of the guards at the hotel. My husband was also taken for a haircut to spruce him up.

Dawu has something to say to me right off the bat. He criticizes me (in a fun sort of way, not mean) for going on about Ai Weiwei's arrest. Dawu was freaking out during our conversation as he was surrounded by guards, secret police and other authorities who could hear what I was saying. During his time in detention, Dawu had to prove he was NOT connected to Lao Ai and here I was, yakking up a storm all about the artist-activist.

Dawu, Hannah and I spend the next 24 hours with Debbie and Frank. I take my first free moment with Dawu to examine his shoulder and assess it as much as I can, since I'm not a physiotherapist.

He has reduced mobility: he can't do a full windmill with his arm, and says he's still in a lot of pain. When he's not using the limb, it dangles at an odd angle from his shoulder. No doubt, Dawu also has some deep emotional and mental scars, ones I can't see yet.

At Debbie's home, Dawu shares some stories about detention but really, we just hang out together. There'll be time for an intense Q & A in the days ahead. For now, it's all about family time. Hannah and Dawu are inseparable. She sleeps between us, hugging her dad, who has finally come home.

The three of us head to the Cappuccino Complex the next afternoon. There's no fanfare, no big party and certainly no apology or compensation waiting for us from the Chinese authorities. I'm worried the secret police might come for him at any second, but Dawu is confident that he's free. He says he has been released on parole and is under house arrest.

There is not going to be a sentencing. Dawu has been released on house arrest because the authorities don't have enough on him to keep him in prison. But they can keep him contained for a year and watch him. He's under supervision by the court and has to phone his parole officers weekly. Dawu also has to disassociate himself from Ai Weiwei and can't leave the country. He doesn't have a studio anymore, so he has to live with me.

Plunk.

Dawu is back in my life. Right in the thick of it. He never did disappear from my thoughts, though, and the core feeling of being a family remains. It's remarkable. The focus in the early days of Dawu's release is to have Hannah and her baba reconnect and rebuild. For Dawu and I, it's to figure out what happened to him, why and by whose actions. There's a lot that I still don't know. Dawu has some of the answers but the Chinese government has most of them. It will never let us see the complete picture.

Dawu phones Xiangshou and Suling and tells them he's home. I send out a news release on my blog. I add that Dawu won't be giving interviews. His release terms bar him from talking to journalists and contacting the media. I speak to a few reporters about Dawu. I also email Victoria at the Canadian Embassy and she passes on my happy news to David Mulroney. I let my team know what's happening but there are two important people missing from my crew: Ai Weiwei and Wen Tao.

I find out more details about Lao Ai's arrest. He was at the Beijing airport on Sunday, Apr. 3 and about to board a flight to Hong Kong when he was taken into custody. Authorities also raided his studio and snatched computers, hard drives, CDs and notebooks. Wen Tao, Ai's good friend and fearless assistant, also disappeared on the same day from the Caochangdi area of Beijing.

Wen Tao had accompanied me almost everywhere and was by my side at many meetings. He offered advice and, most importantly, was my interpreter. I'm sad to hear that he's facing an unknown future. There has been no news about where he is being held.

The Chinese government is taking a hard line against those speaking out against it. That's why I'm confused about Dawu's release. Why was he let out now when the authorities are increasing the pressure on activists? Nonetheless, the police never had a concrete case against Dawu despite how hard they tried to create evidence. They had video footage that didn't add up to much of anything except some shouting and shoving. Meanwhile, Dawu had mountains of evidence that he was innocent and hadn't attacked a police officer.

Dawu thinks his release is partly due to me being a foreigner. Chinese officials realized that Dawu's Canadian wife was not going to stop coming after them. Not only did I get the international press on Dawu's side, I had the Canadian government, agents from the Canadian Embassy, Amnesty International and other human rights NGOs gunning for China. It was all too much for the government. It backed down and freed Dawu. Saying that, I do believe the timing was NOT coincidental. I think that setting Dawu free while, at the same time, detaining Lao Ai, was on purpose.

Li Fangping is a big reason Dawu is home. The lawyer never let me or the team down even though he could have easily bailed when things got too hard. He's happy to hear Dawu is with me when I give the lawyer the good news over the phone. However, the fate of our friends, Ai Weiwei and Wen Tao, is weighing heavily on his mind. Li Fangping could be next to face reprisal. The Chinese government is gathering those who have engaged in political reform and continue to do so, like the lawyer, and is trying to muzzle them.

As the week goes on, news of my husband's liberation is making the rounds. Ai Weiwei's detention and Dawu's release spread like wildfire in the artists' community. Friends like Zhang, Hong, Chao Hongling, Gu Duanfan, the Gao Brothers and Ma Ling visit Dawu. I'm sure that the police know who's coming and going from my apartment. Dawu told me to be prepared for being under surveillance because of his house arrest. The authorities are monitoring my place and have probably bugged my phone, too.

Everyone is happy to see Dawu and he's happy to see them. He is tired, though. He hasn't slept well in months and he needs his rest. Socializing exhausts him.

He has gone from sitting on a wooden bench or being interrogated for six hours a day for 10 months with restricted sunlight and no physical activity, to being surrounded by family and friends.

Shortly after his release, Dawu is given a huge box of Christmas cards and letters, ones that had been kept from him while he was incarcerated. A brave guard thought Dawu should have them now. It's a nice gesture but one that doesn't erase terrible memories of detention.

Dawu loves spending time with Hannah. Before tucking his daughter into bed, Dawu talks to her about why some good people can be mistakenly detained by authorities. She's trying SO HARD to understand how and why her baba disappeared from her life for close to a year. Afterwards, in the quiet of the evening, I bring Dawu the box of artworks that Hannah had been creating for him. He cries when he sees the huge collection and starts going through the lovely drawings and projects that Hannah made for him.

Ai Weiwei and Wen Tao have been missing for more than a week. Dawu is surprised Lao Ai is spending so much time in detention, especially since he pushed the Chinese government for years and hadn't received major blowback. I've been blogging a bit about Ai and Wen Tao and asking my supporters to write to the Chinese government and demand to know where my two friends are being held.

As well, I approach Victoria about Wen Tao since he has permanent residency status in Canada. It turns out that the embassy can't find him either. This is about all I can do. Anything else might risk Dawu's house arrest and put him back in jail.

My focus is getting Dawu back to normal. I make sure he's eating well and sleeping well. I take him to have his arm examined by medical professionals. Since Dawu didn't receive treatment on his injury right away, there's not much that can be done now. His limb will always have reduced mobility. His terrible headaches subside after he was released and then go away for good.

I take Dawu for a traditional Chinese bad energy release therapy, known as *guasha*. It involves firmly rubbing a smooth blade made from a cow horn on an infected site of the body. The practice causes a red rash to appear and it's through the rash that bad energy is removed. Dawu's back is given the guasha treatment and turns a deep red instantly and lasts for many days. His bad energy is gone.

Emotionally and mentally, I think Dawu is fighting with some demons. How could he not? He was under daily interrogations with the police pressuring him to admit his mistakes. Thank goodness, Dawu wasn't tortured. But living in detention was not easy. He was bored, couldn't sleep, had no privacy, had no exercise and was watched 24/7. He couldn't move without asking permission. Dawu seethes with anger and bitterness whenever he talks about the Chinese government. He hates what it is and what it stands for: oppression.

Despite being under house arrest, Dawu isn't stuck at home and he starts taking Hannah to and from school. This is a nice change from the past year or so, when I regularly dropped Hannah off. I'd have to stop a few metres away from the front entrance of her school gate because Hannah didn't want her classmates to see that her mom wasn't Chinese. My daughter was teased and bullied for not being 100 per cent Chinese. It was horrible. Dawu loves his time with Hannah and they're inseparable.

Dawu doesn't know what the future holds. He doesn't know what impact his house arrest will have on his career. He hates the local authorities and the government even more. Lately, he has been spending time alone and reflecting on what's happened and what's to come. It's no use trying to get him to talk to Dana, my counsellor. Dawu's not interested in therapy, no matter the benefits it could reap. Meanwhile, I listen to his stories and he listens to mine. I tell him about burying the snake and how it felt like a scene from a murder. Dawu's relieved that the serpent had a proper burial. He believes he righted a wrong.

Dawu thinks it's a weird coincidence that I met Mr. Cao. It was fate that he was getting out of detention when he noticed me. Dawu clears up some of the mystery around Mr. Song, my anonymous caller. He was an intermediary from an internal network of detention guards and inmates. Mr. Song had never been inside but had connections. Dawu and I laugh about how scared I was after receiving the first few calls. It all seems comical now that Dawu is sitting beside me.

I do have something to confess to Dawu. It wasn't my finest moment but I tell him about when I confronted Zhang Wei, the wrong Zhang Wei, at the UCCA Center for Contemporary Art.

"I did say I was sorry," I add.

Dawu immediately picks up his phone and calls Zhang Wei to apologize. The artist is glad to hear that Dawu has been released and laughs about the mistaken identity. The two have a good chat.

Dawu has been allowed by the state to visit his family in Jiangsu province. I'm wary of letting him go but it's a sanctioned trip. I have to trust that he'll be fine.

Dawu is away for about 10 days at the end of April. He sees his dad, sister and nephew and has a good time in his hometown. With Dawu gone, I'm left with thoughts of what I should do now. I've spent the past 10 months working every single day on his release. I ate, slept and thought about his detention continuously. I never had an end date so I never had a concrete "moving on" plan.

Now that my job is done, I can do what I want. I have a couple of routes I want to follow and I'm free to follow them, I guess? What is my future? Does it connect with Dawu's plans? No. We're husband and wife in name only.

While Dawu was detained, people had told me to leave China. Now that he's out, people are telling me to stay in China. They say that I've worked so hard to get my husband back and so I should remain by his side. However, I thought I had already made up my mind to leave and to move away from the craziness here. The power politics of China aren't about to stop just because Dawu is home. Dawu, on the other hand, is supportive of Hannah and me leaving. He, of course, can't leave because he's under house arrest.

On Friday, April 29, Li Fangping is kidnapped after leaving the Yirenpeng Center, where he's a legal advisor. No one knows where he is. I'm worried for him and hope he's not suffering.

A little less than a week later, Li Fangping is released. He had been interrogated for 30 hours and was handcuffed to a chair to sleep. The human rights lawyer has been working tirelessly and courageously for the betterment of his country and the government is punishing him for it.

Li Fangping is a beacon of hope for those who are being crushed by the government. When Dawu's tenacious and brave lawyer was detained, my hope for China turned to dust. It will not admit its human rights abuses and it has the people in its arsenal to fight any dissension. Some Chinese folks agree with the government and believe that critics must pay the price for speaking out. I heard it from a couple people, one of whom I call a close friend. Strangers are also making my life harder.

The other day, I walked to my car parked in my designated spot. To my dismay, someone had slashed my tires. I called the ST Auto Club (roadside assistance) and when a mechanic showed up, he asked me who I thought ruined my tires. The man said he knew they were damaged intentionally because of the lack of damage to the rubber. I have no clue, absolutely no clue, who did it but it must have something to do with Dawu. Was the slasher sending a message? Would Hannah be targeted next? What could happen to her? That was all I needed to move on and away from Beijing.

In the middle of May, Dawu and I have a long talk. He has a tough decision to make. He has to weigh how China is treating his family with being alone when his family leaves for Canada. There's no easy answer and in the end, Dawu agrees that Hannah and I must go.

Dawu is concerned that I'll be blacklisted in China forever and that the authorities will always be following Hannah and me. Just because he's been released, doesn't mean the game has ended. He's just starting another round. Also, we don't want to raise Hannah in a paranoid environment.

I'm worried about leaving Dawu behind. He's under house arrest for at least a year but he promises to behave and not speak out against the government. He can work on his art to keep him busy. My fingers are crossed that his artwork won't anger the authorities.

Dawu's moving, too. On Friday, June 10, we meet with the property owner of my Cappuccino Complex unit. She wants to talk to us in person, not over the phone. The landlord says she's been receiving calls from the local police station since Dawu was first detained. The cops have been pressuring her to kick Hannah and me to the curb. The woman is fierce, though, and says she wouldn't give in to their demands. How could she leave a mother and a daughter homeless? Nevertheless, the police are making it harder and harder for her to ignore their orders. She has no choice now but to ask us to leave.

The landlord adds that she has been waging a battle behind the scenes on our behalf. She says that she has proclaimed Dawu innocent all along. Dawu and I are impressed by her words and understand why we have to look for another place. Dawu finds one near 798 to live and work and will move in after Hannah and I are gone.

We're packed and ready to leave China by early July 2011. Dawu is giving almost everything in the house to us. A dining room table and two benches he designed and had custom made are coming across the ocean with his daughter and me. He wants Hannah to have ALL of the furniture, including our lovely antiques, to be part of Hannah's inheritance.

Before I move, I say goodbye to Ai Weiwei. He was released to house arrest in Beijing on Wednesday, June 22. Dawu and I pay him a quick visit, giving both of us the chance to thank him for everything and to see him healthy and alive. Wen Tao remains missing and Li Fangping is keeping a low profile.

I have dinners and farewells with my friends, including the TaiTais. Victoria, Ray Chen, Dawu and I have a final supper at a nice Chinese restaurant across the street from the Canadian Embassy. It's great that Victoria can finally meet Dawu. I ask her to send my many thanks to David Mulroney.

It's Bastille Day when Hannah and I leave China for Canada. Thursday, July 14 is France's national holiday, marking the day in late 1700s when revolutionaries stormed the Bastille, a fortress. I don't feel much like a revolutionary today. I feel like I'm making a narrow escape.

After the initial excitement of Dawu's release, we had grown apart again. We decide to make the split permanent but will hold off on getting a divorce until he's safely out of house arrest. The past few months have been strange. It was as if we had one more chance to come together as a couple. However, our time as husband and wife is over. We do make great parents.

One quiet night before I left for Canada, Dawu asked me if I could have done more for him. I pretended not to hear the question. Later, however, I sat him down in front of the computer and asked him to search our names. There were so many hits that he was glued to the screen for three whole days. When he finally pulled himself away from the internet, a kind of unspoken respect formed between us. It was then that he realized what I was capable of doing and what I did for him.

I had once thought China would be my home forever. But dreams realign themselves. Hannah and I move to Calgary, the city where I was raised but a place that my daughter has only visited a handful of times. My family is overjoyed to see us, especially my mom, who was always worried about me living in China.

Hannah and I rent the main floor of a bungalow in the Shaganappi area of southwest Calgary and she attends Alexander Ferguson School, a local arts-based curriculum school. She loves meeting her new teachers and her classmates become her friends. No one teases her about her non-Chinese mom.

I start my Masters of Arts in intercultural and international communications but end up putting it aside. I go back into destination services consulting as well as obtain my real estate licence in 2015. There are some days when I wish I still live in China but those days are getting farther and farther apart, particularly with the recent developments there.

Dawu is under house arrest now until April 12, 2012. The government has also banned him from exhibiting in local art shows in China. Dawu has many friends who make sure he's healthy and not floundering after everything he went through.

I don't regret leaving Dawu behind. We are better friends than ever before. He's doing what he does best and living his life on his terms. Although Dawu's pursuit of justice cost us both dearly, I'd never turn my back on him. Hannah has her baba. I have a friend and Dawu has his freedom.

"Successively, the battlefield, the prison, I have all gone through;
and these have not deprived me yet of my pure, music-like virtue."
Translation from Chinese into English of the calligraphy work
Dawu created in secret while behind bars Dec. 2010.
The poem was originally written by Ming Dynasty scholar, philosopher, political
theorist and soldier Huang Zongxi (1610-1695 AD)

"Owning our story can be hard but not nearly as difficult as spending
our lives running from it. Embracing our vulnerabilities is risky but
not nearly as dangerous as giving up on love and belonging and joy—
the experiences that make us the most vulnerable.
Only when we are brave enough to explore the darkness
will we discover the infinite power of our light."
Dr Brené Brown, Ph.D, LMSW (University of Houston, Houston, Texas U.S.) is a
badass professor, lecturer, author,
TEDX Talk speaker and podcast host

With the help of some sympathetic guards, Dawu was able to get a hold of drawing and painting materials while behind bars. Calligraphy and other artworks made by Dawu were secretly passed to Karen on the outside through a convoluted network of middlemen. Dec. 2010, Beijing.

Sketch drawing by Dawu showing the inside of his cell. Inmates sat on benches without backs for 5-6 hours per day, not allowed to speak or interact with each other.
Dec. 2010, Beijing.

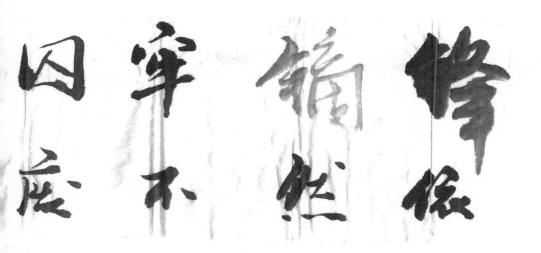

Christmas and New Year 2010
greetings for Hannah painted
by Dawu behind bars.
Dec. 2010, Beijing.

Favourite food stuffs painted by Dawu. Dec. 2010, Beijing.

Dawu reunites with Karen and Hannah at the roundabout in Huairou,
a small city about an hour north of Beijing. Apr. 3, 2011, Huairou City.

Hannah and Dawu embrace on the day of his release. They hadn't seen each
other for over 10 months. Apr. 3, 2011, a village just outside of Huairou City.

Hannah and Dawu on the streets of Manhattan, taken the same day the three of us visited the Statue of Liberty. May 2015, NYC, U.S.

EPILOGUE

Hannah and I returned to China at the end of 2012 so that Dawu and I could officially get divorced. It was time for us to move on. I was happy when the government removed his exhibition ban in 2014. What a relief.

Dawu remarried and moved with his wife and their son from China to the U.S. in September 2016. Dawu couldn't live an ordinary life after being branded as a troublemaking artist-activist and the label was affecting his family. Their home was regularly visited and approached by the cops despite Dawu being "free." He was monitored and harassed by the authorities and he was tired of it. He was worried the stigma of being a criminal would fall onto his son. He didn't want his child living in China, a land that had been polluted, including the human heart. So, they left for New York City (NYC).

The Big Apple is overflowing with good galleries and art foundations. It's also a culturally rich area in a democratically-controlled country. Dawu has a valid green card as a legal permanent resident and works on his art. He exhibits in the States and overseas while raising his son and enjoying his new life. Hannah spends time every year with her baba and brother in New York. It's the perfect place for her as she loves singing, acting, dancing and, of course, seeing shows on Broadway!

***

In 2012, after I had completed my first year of my Masters of Arts online program at Royal Roads University, I thought that it was the right time to start writing my book about my ordeal of getting Dawu out of detention. I began reviewing correspondence and documents that I had collected. I was working away in my kitchen when, all of a sudden, I didn't know if I was in Calgary or Beijing. My mind was flip-flopping and it scared me.

I stopped writing.

I also become even more of a news junkie back in Canada. I listened to stories about China, the poor way Canada's Indigenous people were treated as well as following murder investigations in my city. Every story got me riled up and angry. I didn't know how to channel or deal with all these swirling and terrible emotions.

On a trip to a conference with FIGT (Families in Global Transition, a support and resource organization for families and individuals living and working overseas), I had a breakdown. It was 2013 and the meeting was in Washington, D.C. On my way to the U.S. capital that October, I passed through Toronto. I had some time in the city and I learned that there was an

Ai Weiwei retrospective exhibition, titled *ACCORDING TO WHAT?*, being hosted at the Art Gallery of Ontario (AGO).

I was excited about the prospect of see Lao Ai's works outside of China. I first went to the AGO gift shop to buy a catalogue from the show and saw heavy plastic replicas of *hexie* (river crabs) being sold as part of Ai Weiwei's merchandise. (The term hexie in Chinese characters has a similar meaning/sound as harmonization, a common term used in Chinese government propaganda.) I picked up a river crab and brought it to the cashier. While in line, I heard a woman ask the cashier if the money from the sale of the river crabs went to Lao Ai or the Chinese government. The woman said she did not want to support the authoritarian regime but she would support Ai. I jumped in and said, "I agree, and from what I know of Ai Weiwei, he would never allow the government to make money off him."

I really didn't know if that was true but I felt it was and no sooner had I said those words, then a crowd of people, eager to know more about Ai Weiwei, surrounded me. They asked me about Lao Ai's life and what he was like in person and I tried to answer them. Then I scurried out of the gift shop and into the exhibit.

I had seen many of Ai's works already in China. It was awesome to see them in Canada. While looking at the artwork, I was remembering things about my time in China, even before Dawu was detained. I was not sure exactly what triggered me but all of a sudden, I felt weak and I burst into tears and just cried for close to 45 minutes. Finally, I gathered my thoughts, took a deep breath and left the venue.

It wasn't until I sought therapy at the Calgary Counselling Centre with a counsellor who had travelled through China that I began to realize I was suffering from post-traumatic stress disorder (PTSD). I had never experienced PTSD before and thought it was something that only soldiers went through. I didn't think PTSD applied to me.

PTSD is a mental health condition that can develop following a traumatic event. People experience flashbacks, nightmares and be under severe stress. I experienced flashbacks and anxiety, not to mention I was constantly thinking about Dawu's sudden disappearance as well as my fight with authorities and the things I went through. It all took a toll on me and I hadn't realized it.

PTSD not only left me confused and in an emotional mess, but I felt the need to support others going through traumatic events. When a young man, a friend of a friend, was brutally swarmed and beaten to death outside of a Calgary nightclub in November 2013, I watched all the news reports.

I didn't know this young man but I felt I needed to support his family and follow his story. At any cost. I even attended one of the hearings for the accused. It was interesting to see the inside of a Canadian courthouse but I had no reason to be there. I've even gone to funerals for other people who have been caught up in terrible situations. I went to support others when I should have been supporting my own mental health.

With counselling, I started to open up and look at my experiences during Dawu's detention. I had rarely cried during that year. I had been so strong and put up a front with everyone. What I failed to realize was that it all came at a cost. I had shoved my own feelings, frustrations and emotions aside. I was an onion and in Canada, I could start to peel back the layers. With each layer, the tears flowed. I could focus on looking after myself but it would take time and support, something that I could easily access in Canada.

There is no magic cure for PTSD and today, I can still be triggered by thoughts of Dawu being in prison. As well, even though I listen to the news daily, I don't get involved like I used to. I need to keep that distance or else it can overtake my daily life.

I was in a vehicle collision in February 2018 and I found that the PTSD from the crash built on the PTSD that was lingering from my last year or so in China. It makes driving a bit more anxiety-inducing, as many feelings and memories come back as a result. Part of processing my thoughts is writing this book. It is as much of getting the story out as it is about processing the traumatic ordeal for me. Other things that have helped are the passage of time and talking about it to friends and professionals. Also, understanding what triggers PTSD has helped me to look after myself better, not be so raw, but to take care of me for me. PTSD is real and should be taken seriously.

A trip to Athens, Greece in the summer of 2019 has re-awakened my passion for photography. Dawu had mentioned my name to an American/Greek curator, Vasia Deliyianni, in the early spring and I was invited to be a part of her international exhibit, *ART: KEY TO CONFLICT RESOLUTION*. The work that was accepted was a digital image that I made in 2005 in Beijing. *BACKGROUND* was made up of 36 portraits of migrant workers. I chose to photograph their backs instead of their faces to preserve their dignity. Migrant workers are at the bottom of society in China. People see through them, as opposed to seeing them for their talents, skills, hard work or contribution to the community.

I've learned the hard way that China can't be trusted with upholding human rights or the rule of law. However, there are people who have worked on bringing the stark truth to the world. Ai Weiwei, the Gao Brothers, Wen Tao, Li Fangping, Zhang and Hong and many, many others.

Lao Ai is living and working in Germany with his family. I'm in touch with him through social media.

I never got a chance to see Wen Tao in person again after I left China. He wasn't released until mid-summer 2011 and I had moved already. Wen Tao had been detained in a secret location, along with many more of Lao Ai's Chinese employees. I keep tabs via social media on my incredible interpreter and translator who is living, working and raising his family in Beijing.

Li Fangping remains in Beijing as an attorney. The Gao Brothers are living and working in both Beijing and NYC. I've lost touch with Zhang and Hong over the years.

I had softened my views on Tang Funai but Dawu has a theory that makes me harden towards the Troublemaker again. Dawu believes that Tang set him up. The cops wanted Dawu in custody and to do that, they sent Tang with some choice bait to lure Dawu to the station. The authorities knew Dawu couldn't let a wrong go. He would step up and help Tang.

We have no proof that was what happened. Dawu thinks Tang was desperate for cash and desperate enough to be a tool of the police. Needless to say, Dawu does not keep in contact with him.

U.S. documentary filmmaker Shannon Van Sant went on to win Amnesty International's Award for Best Human Right's documentary in 2012. Her project, *Ai Weiwei and Artists Protest in China*, included Dawu's struggle and detention and also features Ai Weiwei and the Gao Brothers, among others. I cry every time I watch the documentary.

Chen Guangcheng, the Barefoot Lawyer, immigrated to the U.S. He escaped house arrest in China in the spring of 2011. He wrote a memoir, *The Barefoot Lawyer*, that was published in 2015.

In the summer of 2017, Liu Xiaobo died due to multiple organ failure. He died while still in custody serving his 11-year sentence in China. The authorities had repeatedly denied his release under medical parole. Many who knew or followed the 61-year-old Xiaobo were devastated by his death. The human rights warrior's death made China look brutal and inhumane. Scratch the surface ever so slightly and China is a dangerous place for too many to be.

I don't expect people to understand my opinions about China. If you've been there as a tourist or lived there for a short time, it is a beautiful country. However, I've met the beast lurking in the shadows and I can't stay silent.

IN MY OWN WORDS –
A PLEA TO READERS

I have a duty to tell my story and add to the collective voice calling out for change in China. Dawu's ordeal was not, and is not, an isolated event. It is part of a growing problem in China, one where the government not only denies freedom and democracy but exercises a blatant disregard for human rights.

A transformation in me was forming on how I viewed China. For she was now more than just "China," she was really in my mind now made up of two wholes. The first whole was pretty much the Chinese people, stretching top to bottom, east to west, regardless of what they did or didn't do for work. Most were kind and good natured, working towards survival, depending on their circumstances. Of course, I have my fondest memories with these folks, and I would include my ex-husband and many, many others in this group, to be sure.

The second part of China, the one that I had fought with over the past 1.5 years or so of my being in China, was the regime - ruthless, autocratic, authoritarian party state that exists above the crowd, above the fray, but carries influence into everyone's lives in China - at all levels. The regime makes decisions with regard for keeping themselves in power, not that they will be voted out, but keeping the party alive. It took me a while to sort out that I could, in fact, both love and dislike China, in a healthy, reasonable way. Maybe I wouldn't return to live in China but I would accept that she had these two sides and deal with my feelings about them accordingly. Sometimes it must sound like I hate China but nothing could be farther from the truth. In fact, I love China - her culture, food, language, history, art, people; I just think that the government can do much better.

We can do better as humans. Human rights in China are not improving. Over the past decade, since Dawu was beaten and illegally incarcerated, we are reminded on an almost daily basis of the abuses and injustices in China. Two Canadians are illegally detained in China today. Michael Kovrig and Michael Spavor were living and working separately in China when they were arbitrarily detained on Monday, Dec. 10, 2018. The arrests were seen as a direct retaliation by the Chinese government for the arrest of Meng Wenzhou, the chief financial officer of Huawei, a Chinese telecoms technology company. Ten days before Kovrig and Spavor were taken, Canadian authorities executing a U.S. extradition warrant arrested Meng at Vancouver International Airport.

Kovrig, a former diplomat working as a conflict mitigation consultant, and Spavor, a consultant who arranged business travel to North Korea, are being held in isolation while facing espionage charges. No trial dates have been set. In the meantime, Meng is staying at her Vancouver mansion and enjoying all the legal rights and freedoms that Canada has to offer while fighting extradition to the U.S. to face criminal charges, including conspiracy, bank fraud and many others.

Robert Schellenberg is yet another example of how China's authoritarian regime reigns supreme. Weeks after Meng Wenzhou's arrest, Schellenberg was sentenced to death after a 15-year jail sentence for drug trafficking in China was overturned. The authorities claim that in 2014, Schellenberg tied to smuggle methamphetamine from Dalian, in northern China, to Australia, using plastic pellets hidden in tires. Schellenberg said he was being framed by criminals. During the retrial, some of his statements were mistranslated. From media accounts, his sentence has not yet been carried out..

Just as Canadians face serious trouble in China, many Chinese citizens will experience the inhumane treatment and violation of their human rights by their own government. The minority Turkic ethnic group made up of Uighurs, Kazakhs, Kyrgyz, Hui and others, are persecuted by China. Many of the mostly-Muslim minorities live in the autonomous Xinjiang region in northwest China, where they have a language and culture vastly different from the Han Chinese. China's grasp is tightening in the area and the people are being oppressed.

The government is trying to erase the minority population by killing their culture, religion and ethnicity. Reminiscent of the Mao era, they are forced into "re-education" programs in camps where they are indoctrinated with communist ideology as well as other assimilation tactics. Members of the ethnic groups are arbitrarily arrested, detained and under constant electronic surveillance and monitoring.

Hong Kong is another autonomous area where the Chinese regime is clamping down. When the British handed Hong Kong back to China in 1997, it was expected to remain independent from China for at least 50 years. Nevertheless, China has crept into the special administrative region, taking over the Hong Kong government bit by bit.

Since the summer of 2019, thousands of Hong Kong residents, activists, students and workers have been fighting the Chinese communist government's fugitive offenders amendment bill. The extradition law works by fast-tracking anyone who is before the courts in Hong Kong, to a trial in Beijing.

This law is being seen as an aggressive effort by China to target people it doesn't like and sentence them under its corrupt and unjust justice system. Protestors with the Anti-Extradition Law Amendment Bill (Anti-ELAB) movement are being thrown into jail left, right and centre.

In January 2020, the global head of Human Rights Watch, an international NGO in New York City that carries out research and advocacy on human rights, was barred from entering Hong Kong. Kenneth Roth was supposed to attend an event to launch a yearly report on worldwide human rights. One could see how this might happen if Roth was entering Beijing, but Hong Kong? It's a setback and a sign of worse things to come.

It wasn't the citizens to blame for the decisions that their government made, it was the regime side of China making those decision. Common folks have no say. They can't vote out the communist party, like we can in democratic countries. So, for instance, when the Chinese government prevented the news about COVID-19 getting out or squashing the doctors and medical staff from saying anything, it wasn't the people doing that, it was the mechanism of the regime. It is also why it isn't reasonable to refer to COVID-19 as the "Chinese Virus" as some world leaders would say. A better label would be the Chinese Communist Party or CCP Virus.

We can't seem to turn on the evening news or the radio without some horrific story about China. She is always in the news these days, for better and for worse, and is making the writing of this plea that much more challenging … sigh. Stop doing what you are doing, China.

Please, no more detentions, clamp down on protests, culture elimination camps or viruses.

STOP!

Sadly, human rights abuses continue in China, amidst the backdrop of a 'Xi Jinping Thought' style of government that holds zero-tolerance for ANY form of dissent. It is not enough to say that China will deal with it, it is her problem or wow, look how many citizens she has lifted out of poverty. Impressive, yes, but not the point. That kind of thinking has not worked in the past and shows no signs of working in the present or into the future.

We must not be bullied by China's threats of economic retaliation or eye for eye style sandbox politics, let alone the regime's insistence that *what happens within our borders is solely our concern.*

No. Wrong.

We as a global community must create a system that makes China stand down from such abusive behaviours. We can no longer sit on the sidelines, waiting for her government to take responsibility, to be accountable. We must be the agents of change from our own corners of the world. We can't forget that sanctions helped to topple apartheid in South Africa not too long ago, giving us all some hope. We wanted a global village and addressing human rights abuses is one of the many responsibilities of that village. Together, we can make a difference. I know because I've seen it.

How can you help?

- Donate to various human rights organizations around the world, and/or participate in their letter writing campaigns.
- Letter write to your local/provincial/state/national head of state - letters do work!
- Thank you for reading *Taking On China*. Please suggest this book to your friends, family and/or book club members and share it, talk about it, debate it.
- Be informed, ask the hard questions.
- If you are overseas for more than a few weeks, always register your presence with your embassy. They can't help you if they don't know where you are.

ACKNOWLEDGMENTS

This book has taken me close to eight years to finish, not a quick write by any stretch of the imagination. In the fall of 2018, I heard about the arrest and detention of Meng Wenzhou and realized then that my story needed to, once and for all, be told. Feelings of "I am too late" rapidly disappeared as I realized that my audience might be even more captive and that this sort of stuff that I was going to be writing about vis-à-vis our story, was still going on. It didn't end when Dawu or I left China, if anything, resumed, ramped up. At this time, too, I had reached out to many publishers with what I had thought was a well-put-together story package but to no avail. I received countless letters saying the same thing, "Great story, a story that needs to be told … but not with us. So, sorry."

I set about looking for help this time, as I found that I could only do so much on my own, kind of like learning a language, you can only do so much without a class or language partner, etc. Well, this was me in terms of writing my own story. I had come across a woman at a trade fair in the fall of 2012 who did exactly what I was looking for; she helped "normal" folk put their memoirs into book form. She introduced me to a few of her clients and I decided that she was who I needed on my "team" to finish this project. Regardless of how the end product would be received.

Part of the process of writing any book or memoir like this is to unpack and walk through the details in order to process one's feelings. This is precisely what I needed to do, as I was still somewhat triggered by certain aspects of the whole experience. Thank you and much admiration goes to Lea Storry, of Our Family Lines, for helping ME to write MY own story. Thank you!

Journalists around the world are the torchbearers for ourselves and/or our communities, regardless of what we may be facing, regardless of what predicament we may find ourselves in. They bravely dig deep to abstract the essence of the story and then share. In my story, I have nothing short of respect and gratitude for the many brave journalists in (and out of) China who decide to pick up a human rights story and share the flame. Special thanks to Barry Acton (Global TV), journalists and program hosts at the Canadian Broadcasting Corporation/CBC (notably The Current and Cross Country Check-Up), Tania Branigan (*The Guardian*), Michael Bristow (BBC World-Service), Richard Cuthbertson (*Calgary Herald*), Gillian Findley (CBC), Peter Foster (*The Daily Telegraph*), Katherine Hesse (freelance photographer extraordinaire), Andrew Jacobs (*The New York Times*), Jas Johal (Global TV), Lucy Kearney (Associated Press), Roseann Lake (Blue Ocean

Network TV), Louisa Lim (National Public Radio/NPR), Mark MacKinnon (*The Globe and Mail*), Fabiano Maisonnave (Folha De S. Paulo), Isolda Morillo (freelance journalist in Beijing, China), Evan Osnos (*The New Yorker*), Bill Schiller (*Toronto Star*), Peter Simpson (*South China Morning Post/SCMP* and VOA), Gillian Steward (*Toronto Star*), Wen Tommy Tao (freelance journalist in China), Shannon Van Sant (freelance documentary film maker), Eric Volmers (*Calgary Herald*), Edward Wong (*The New York Times*), Wendy Wong (Radio Free Hong Kong) and many, many others who listened to my dilemma and hoisted it up on to the internet, keeping us in the news. Thank you!

Guidance for how to navigate the murky waters of human rights abuse cases in China (as there is definitely no handbook or brochure!) was greatly assisted by the following brave, gracious and generous people: Jerome A. Cohen (Paul, Weiss, Rifkind, Wharton & Garrison LLP, New York City, U.S.), Corinna-Barbara Francis and Sammy Liang (East Asia Team, Amnesty International), the staff at HRIC, John Kamm (Duihua Foundation, San Francisco, U.S.), Li Fangping (Ruifang Law Firm, Beijing, China) and Dr. Eva Pils (associate professor at The Chinese University of Hong Kong Faculty of Law; presently professor of law at the Dickson Poon School of Law at King's College, London, U.K.). Wu Yuren and I are eternally grateful for your wisdom, support and guidance, knowing that he may not have been freed without your help. Thanks be to you.

I'd like to include a large thank you to the staff of the Canadian Embassy in Beijing, during the time of 2010 to 2011, for assisting me with my ordeal, helping in the best and only way possible. I am eternally grateful to Ambassador David Mulroney, who took up my case and genuinely listened. Thank you!

I'm forever thankful to the office and members of Stephen Harper's government for acknowledging letters and inquiries about Wu's situation, forwarding the letters and emails on to the desk of the ambassador in Beijing and for raising Wu Yuren's case during high-level talks with Chinese government officials. Your diplomacy was en pointe.

An enormous THANKS to my team at the time of getting Wu Yuren out of jail, especially Ai Weiwei, who provided solid advice, found me a kick-ass lawyer and got me in front of the foreign journalists and press. Like in a relay, he passed the baton to all those who he felt could help. Which they did. Gord Hoffman, for solid support, guidance and taking phone calls at weird hours. Wen Tommy Tao - so grateful to have met you and had you on my team, the best assistant anyone could have. Ray Chen and the many interpreters who helped out along the way. Thank you!!

To all my friends, family, colleagues, clients and associates who supported me through the thick and thin, too numerous to list, but you know who you are. You were all instrumental in hearing, helping and hoping alongside me while I put memories to paper. And to the folks who had a similar tale to tell but chose not to have their situation mentioned or alluded to in my book, I respect and appreciate your decision and I thank you for feeling you could say no. We still live in troubling times and one can sometimes never be too safe. Thanks, everyone, too, for answering my seemingly odd and random questions. You helped fill the gaps when my memory failed me over the past 10 years - thank you!!

Several readers who took the time and focus to read the manuscript over and make comments prior to printing, thank you, as I am very grateful for your help and support: Sophie Baker, Rebecca Melenka and several others. A big shout out to Jason Sweet of Jason Sweet Ad | Design | Photo for the front and back cover artwork and map. Made the book that much more special! Thank you.

Thank you to Wu Yuren, Dawu, who has been supportive of my book-writing project from the very beginning but especially now that he is living in New York City. He has been on the other side of texting or Facebook messenger, answering my many, many questions over the past year. Without you, well, this story would be none to tell. Thanks a huge bunch!!

China Digital Times, an online news agency, was instrumental to me. It let me go back in time and find facts and articles to fill in the background on the political, economic and social context of China leading up to, during and after Dawu's detention. Thank you for keeping the real news from China flowing.

Diane Gatterdam, an activist of a very special kind, living and working in New York City, supported me online during Dawu's detention and during our first in-person meeting at Eli Klein's gallery in 2015 for Wu's exhibit, handed me a crisp new copy of Chen Guangcheng's book. It was a sign that I, too, should be writing my story. Thank you for putting it where it needed to be. Thanks also to Rosemary Baxter for her letter writing campaign.

My loving, supportive and awesome sister, Diane, who not only kept track of all the emails from me over the years but was able to produce records of blogs I had written. This made putting my book together so much easier. Thank you for all of your love and unconditional support. My dad and step-mom, Gordon and Michal Patterson, and my aunt and uncle, Ike and

Diana Lanier, were the first in our families to go to China (1980s). Thank you for inspiring me to take that first step to engaging China. I love you all.

I can't forget about my mom, may she be resting in peace up in heaven and where she is probably thrilled to see this project completed. She would be happy to know that Dawu is safe and that I was able to move through the drama of China and come out the other end with a book. This one is for you, mom, love you!

Again, a very special thank you to my daughter who has not only had to hear me talk about this book but has witnessed me being shut away in the basement for the past year (and prior, too), writing, editing, thinking and talking about that time in China. Thank you, Hannah, for your endless and tireless support of me and for me while I took this journey under the same roof as you and our Chihuahua, Lucy Puppet. This is for you two, too. Loads of love to you both.

SELECTED READINGS ON CHINA

Being passionate about reading and China resulted in a growing library in my house and an interest in collecting the written word on China. These are books that I have read before or during the time of writing my book and are not all about human rights. I don't think I will ever stop reading about her, as China continues to intrigue me. These reads were all entertaining, important, enjoyable, informative and/or useful in their own right for me between 1994 to 2020.

Novels/Fiction

Gao Xingjian - *Soul Mountain*

Lisa See - *Snow Flower and the Secret Fan*

Ma Jian - *The Noodle Maker*

Ma Jian - *Red Dust: A Path Through China*

Marjorie Flack - *The Story of Ping*

Nell Freudenberger - *The Dissident*

Wang Shuo - *Please Don't Call Me Human*

Yu Hua - *Brothers*

Memoir/Scar Literature/Non-fiction/Autobiography/Biography

Aisin Gioro Pu Yi - *From Emperor to Citizen: The Autobiography of Aisin Gioro Puyi*

Anchee Min - *Red Azalea*

Chen Guangcheng - *The Barefoot Lawyer: A Blind Man's Fight for Justice and Freedom in China*

Chen Guidi and Wu Chuntao - *Will the Boat Sink the Water? The Life of China's Peasants*

Denise Chong - *Egg on Mao: The Story of an Ordinary Man Who Defaced An Icon and Unmasked A Dictatorship*

Edgar Snow - *Red Star over China*

Fuchsia Dunlop - *Shark's Fin & Sichuan Pepper: A Sweet-Sour Memoir of Eating in China*

George Wang & Betty Barr - *Shanghai Boy, Shanghai Girl:*
Lives in Parallel

Jan Wong - *Red China Blues:*
My Long March from Mao to Now

Jung Chang - *Wild Swans:*
Three Daughters of China

Li Cunxin - *Mao's Last Dancer*

Li Yiyun - *A Thousand Year's of Good Prayers: Stories*

Li Zhensheng - *Red Color News Solider:*
A Chinese Photographer's Odyssey Through the Cultural Revolution

Li Zhisui - *The Private Life of Chairman Mao:*
The Memoirs of Mao's Personal Physician

Lijia Zhang - *Socialism Is Great:*
A Worker's Memoir of the New China

Mara Moustafine - *Secrets and Spies: The Harbin Files*

Michael Bristow - *China in Drag:*
Travels with a Cross-Dresser

Michael David Kwan - *Things that Must Not Be Forgotten:*
A Childhood in Wartime China

Michael Levy - *Kosher Chinese:*
Living, Teaching, and Eating with China's Other Billion

Nien Cheng - *Life and Death in Shanghai*

Peter Hessler - *River Town: Two Years on the Yangtze*

Rachel DeWoskin - *Foreign Babes in Beijing:*
Behind the Scenes of a New China

Rosemary Mahoney - *The Early Arrival of Dreams:*
A Year in China

Sidney Rittenberg and Amanda Bennett - *The Man Who Stayed Behind*

Sidney Shapiro - *An American in China:*
Thirty Years in the People's Republic

Simon Winchester - *The River at the Center of the World:*
A Journey up the Yangtze and Back in Chinese Time

T.K. Chuster - *Sex Rice and Rock'n'Roll:*
Quintessential Chinese Street Language and Subculture Companion Volume One

Wang Chunqing - *You May as Well Sing, Brother*

Wei Jingsheng - *The Courage to Stand Alone:*
Letters from Prison and Other Writings

Xinran - *The Good Women of China:*
Hidden Voices

Yu Jie - *Steel Gate to Freedom: The life of Liu Xiaobo*

Political/Historical/Socio-Economic Reference
Chris Patten - *East and West*

Daniel Burstein and Arne de Keijzer - *Big Dragon - The Future of China: What it Means for*
Business, the Economy and the Global Order

David Mulroney, Middle Power - *Middle Kingdom:*
What Canadians Need to Know about China in the 21st Century

Eva Pils - *Human Rights in China:*
A Social Practice in the Shadow of Authoritarianism

Evan Osnos - *Age of Ambition:*
Chasing Fortune, Truth and Faith in the New China

Harrison E. Salisbury - *The New Emperors:*
China in the Era of Mao and Deng

Jonathan Manthorpe - *Claws of the Panda:*
Beijing's Campaign of Influence and Intimidation in Canada

Julia Lovell - *Maoism: A Global History*

Leslie T. Chang - *Factory Girls:*
From Village to City in a Changing China

Lloyd E. Eastman - *Family, Field and Ancestors:*
Constancy and Change in China's Social and Economic History 1550-1949

Louisa Lim - *The People's Republic of Amnesia: Tiananmen Revisited*

Nicolas Kristof and Cheryl Wudunn - *China Wakes:*
The Struggle for the Soul of a Rising Power

Philip Pan - *Out of Mao's Shadow:*
The Struggle for the Soul of New China

Stella Dong - *Shanghai: The Rise and Fall of a Decadent City*

Business Etiquette in China/How to Do Business in China/Etc.

Frank T. Gallo - *Business Leadership in China:*
How To Blend Best Western Practices with Chinese Wisdom

Laurence Brahm - *The Art of the Deal in China:*
A Practical Guide to Business Etiquette and the 36 Martial Arts Strategies Employed by
Chinese Businessmen and Officials in China

Mayfair Mei-Hui Yang - *Gifts, Favors and Banquets:*
The Art of Social Relationships in China

Scott D. Seligman - *Chinese Business Etiquette:*
A Guide to Protocol, Manners, and Culture in The People's Republic of China

Stanley Chao - *Selling to China:*
A Guide for Small and Medium Sized Businesses

Chinese Contemporary/Avant-garde Art/Tea Culture
Huang Rui (editor) - *Beijing 798:*
Reflections on Art, Architecture and Society in China

John Clark - *Chinese Art at the End of the Millennium*

Kit Chow and Ione Kramer - *All the Tea in China*

Liu Tong - *Chinese Tea: A Cultural History and Drinking Guide*

Martina Köppel-Yang - *Semiotic Warfare: The Chinese Avant-Garde 1979-1989*

Popcorn, translated by Liu Jun - *Chinese Stuff: Essentially Chinese*

Wu Hung - *Chinese Art at the Crossroads:*
Between Past and Future, Between East and West

AUTHOR BIOGRAPHY

Karen Patterson lives in Calgary, Canada, with her daughter and dog. She is a dedicated full-time real estate agent, who also assists expats moving to Calgary to settle in and find schools for their kids as a freelance Destination Service Consultant. As if that isn't enough, Karen enjoys providing culture awareness training as a cross-cultural trainer. Travelling, walking, reading, attending theatre, dance and opera performances and art exhibitions rounds out her time when not working. Dining with friends help keep her happy and balanced. This is her first book.

(Left to right) Hannah, Karen and Lucy Puppet. Apr. 2020, Calgary, Canada.

family lines
stories for generations

ourfamilylines.ca